Property & Casualty PATHFINDER

COMMEMORATIVE EDITION

William H. Cummings M.B.A.

PATHFINDER PUBLISHERS

3500 DePauw Blvd. Suite 1111 Indianapolis, IN 46268 (317) 872-1100

email: info@PathFinderEdu.com visit our website: www.PathFinderEdu.com

SPECIAL THANKS TO SPECIAL PEOPLE

A text as comprehensive and detailed as the PATHFINDER Property and Casualty text could not be written without the help of many talented and caring individuals.

For their technical help and insurance expertise we thank the late H. P. "Pete" Hudson, Gregg Huey, Randy Montgomery, John Stanley, and Bill Morrison.

Thanks to Jen and Will Doss for their graphic arts, page layout, and attention to detail; and to Phil Apsey for his humor and creative style. And a special thanks to Mary Ellen Cummings, whose inspiration drove the process of developing a new look for PATHFINDER'S special Commemorative Edition.

Pathfinder Corporation
3500 DePauw Boulevard, Suite 1111
Indianapolis, IN 46268

TABLE OF CONTENTS

FOREWORD

The dictionary defines a *Pathfinder* as, "One who discovers a way, especially one who explores untraveled regions to mark out a new route." We chose the name PATHFINDER for this text for you, the student. The PATHFINDER will chart a course for your journey into a challenging and exciting new frontier – a career as a Property and Casualty insurance professional.

The PATHFINDER has been carefully constructed to make your first steps into this new frontier the right ones! It is designed to eliminate the most annoying problem in basic insurance training – frustration . . . frustration for new Agents, managers, and trainers. The source of this frustration is easy to identify. During the next few months you will be expected to learn a tremendous amount of information that is often technical, occasionally confusing and, in the beginning, totally foreign to you. This task in itself is a challenge. It can become unbearable if your study material is written at a level that only experienced Agents can comprehend. Students can become disheartened, and managers can resent the amount of time required to "translate" illogically constructed manuals filled with ill-defined jargon.

Relax! The PATHFINDER eliminates all of these frustrations. It employs hundreds of illustrations and examples that you can relate to your everyday life. It is written with the assumption that you know nothing about insurance, and insurance terms are defined before they are used. The PATHFINDER reduces complex insurance concepts to a level that is easy to grasp, and then builds upon your growing knowledge and confidence. If you do not have a doctorate in business administration, finance or economics – relax. If insurance is new to you, the PATHFINDER was written with you in mind! The authors of the PATHFINDER are professional insurance trainers who have prepared tens of thousands of new Agents like you to take state licensing examinations.

As you thumb through the PATHFINDER, you will discover many unique features, such as a section devoted to improving your test taking skills, and a unique combination Glossary-Index which provides a quick, easy-to-use tool for finding specific information . . . eliminating an endless safari through the pages. And the PATHFINDER offers something else you will appreciate – a sense of humor. It is written in a crisp conversational manner that will take the weariness out of your journey. The PATHFINDER actually makes studying fun.

The PATHFINDER's usefulness will not end when you earn your license. As your career develops, the PATHFINDER will remain an invaluable reference, and the cornerstone of your future insurance training and development. The clear, precise examples that will help you pass your exam will be just as helpful in communicating complex insurance concepts to your clients – and that will put dollars in your pockets.

Sit back. Relax, and allow the PATHFINDER to show you the way. Welcome to the world of Property and Casualty insurance.

The PATHFINDER

Trails to Your Success

Illustrations aren't just window dressing. They provide hooks where you can "hang" facts. Does something affect the customer or the company? Is there coverage or not? The illustrations provide a quick visual reference and make organization easier.

Glossary not only defines important terms, but gives a quick reference to where they are used in the text.

Notes columns line every page. These columns are for two kinds of notes — first, those we've written you — key points outlined for easy reference. Second, space for those you write yourself.

Sample test is found in Part 5. To be licensed, you must not only know the material but be able to transfer that knowledge to a testing situation. Towards that end, you'll find a part of the text that is **NEVER** passed over by successful students . . .

Tips on test-taking, and taking this test in particular. Pathfinder has been in the business for over three decades, and we pass on to you what we've learned about taking tests. Remember, not only do you need to **know**— you must **show** what you know.

Pathfinder Gives You The Keys

KEY ideas are contained in the NOTES and ILLUSTRATIONS They can give a framework for your thoughts.

ENRICH your understanding of technical terms with the plain language GLOSSARY & easy to use INDEX.

SKILLS — Develop your test-taking skills with the SAMPLE TEST and TEST-TAKING TIPS.

INTRODUCTION TO CHARACTERS

Two of the most powerful teaching devices that can be used in a text are pictures and examples. An illustration is a particularly succinct method, as an artist can often express very complex ideas with a few strokes of the pen. Examples, on the other hand, are often counterproductive if a completely new example is used to portray each important point. For this reason, we have created some imaginary characters that we use repeatedly in our examples and our illustrations. After you have worked with these characters for a time, they will become a type of symbolic shorthand for you as they always represent the same viewpoints. This process allows us to use many more examples to aid your learning process than space might otherwise permit.

This text uses two primary symbols. Joe Insured, on the left, represents the insuring public. The role of the insurance company is played by Mr. Policy.

A third important symbol is "the Other Guy" whom Joe has injured.

Both Joe and Mr. Policy are journeymen actors and can play many characters, and assume various personalities as represented by their numerous costumes.

Eat at Joe's

Like the average client, Joe has a job (he is a restaurant owner) and a family – a typical family. Meet his wife, Jolene, and their three children: Joe College, Betty Jo, and Little Joe.

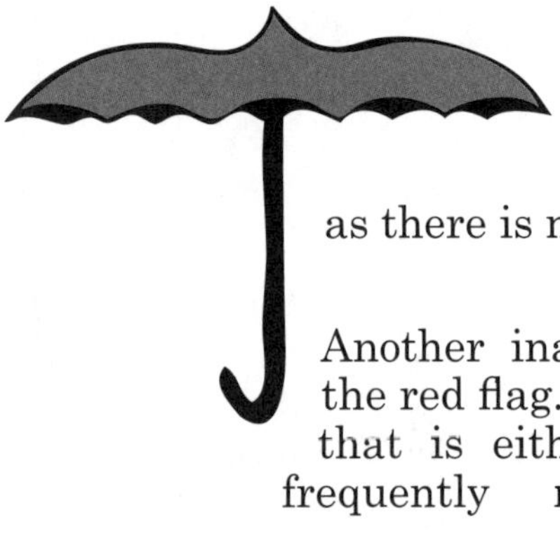

A less human symbol that often appears is the umbrella. When it is shown to be up and open, coverage exists. If it is folded, spindled or mutilated, Joe is out of luck as there is no coverage.

Another inanimate, but important, symbol is the red flag. This is used to emphasize a point that is either critical to your understanding, or frequently misunderstood, or both.

As used, these symbols provide a mental "hook" upon which your mind can hang the new ideas and concepts which will be introduced.

How Insurance Was Invented
or Is Lloyd's of London Stealing Zeus' Thunder?

There was a time very, very long ago when the gods often left their homes on Mt. Olympus to walk among men, learn their ways, and help them solve their problems.

It was after one of these forays that Zeus returned to Olympus, his brow etched with worry. For days the heavens were wrapped in the gloom of dark clouds, for nothing could rouse the king of the gods from his black mood. All of Olympus was abuzz with worry. What could be done? Surely something must be done to wrest their master from this state. It fell to Apollo, Zeus' favorite, to approach the king . . .

"Sire, what is troubling you, for surely none of us has caused you such displeasure?"

"Ah, no, my son, not you – it's man."

"Man," the godly chorus affirmed. "Ever since he was spawned, there has been nothing but trouble . . ."

"No," Zeus muttered, shaking his head, **"not this time. This time it is not man's fault, for the world I have created for him is full of risk and peril. A man can work and prosper all his life, only to lose all with a single stroke of misfortune."**

"Ah . . ." the gods now understood. Zeus was angry with himself, for it was he, who created the world that man now called his own, and it was he who created the risks and perils which robbed man of the fruits of his labors.

“But what can be done?” they asked among themselves, for surely no one would dare suggest that Zeus undo his own handiwork.

Finally Athena, wisest of the goddesses, stepped forward. “Father, may I suggest a contest?”

“A contest?”

“Yes, Sire, for surely one of us on Olympus should be able to invent a tool that will make man equal to the world’s perils.”

“Bully,” shouted Zeus in his best Teddy Roosevelt imitation. **“Grand idea! But we must be careful, for to give man too much would destroy his will to work. Mercury! Heralds! Spread the word to all on Olympus . . . a contest, honors and glory for he who gives man a fighting chance.”**

Quickly, word of the quest spread through the heavens. All were eager to participate, for all knew the value of Zeus’ friendship and respect.

Soon the day for judging the entries was at hand. All of the gods and goddesses, the important and the unimportant, gathered near the throne of Zeus to see who would win . . . who would give man his chance.

First to show his entry was Vulcan, armorer of the gods. His answer was a sword . . . keen of blade, massive in size, yet so perfectly balanced that a child could wield it without strain.

All were impressed. Zeus, however, was not.

“Fine as your blade is, oh Vulcan, can it stop fire? – for I have seen man lose all by fire.”

The bearded god grew silent and hung his head. “No, Sire, it cannot fight the blast of fire.”

“Then you have failed, my friend.”

And so it was . . . one after another . . . the gods failed. If their tool could conquer the wind, it was of no use against the hail. If it was able to offer protection from the lightning, it could not stop the wind, and so on and so on. Finally, all of the major gods had displayed their answers to man’s dilemma, only to have Zeus point out the weakness in each.

“Is there no one with an answer?” lamented the heavenly king.

All looked around for an answer. None was sounded. Finally, a small voice piped out from the very rear of the throne. “Sire, I have the tool which will give man a chance.”

“Who said that? Come forward!”

Like the waves on the shore, the crowd parted, and before Zeus stood a minor god . . . one so minor that in fact none knew his name.

“And what is your answer, small one?”

“This,” the stranger replied, producing a scroll of paper.

Laughingly, the divine audience jeered at the newcomer – but Zeus did not laugh. **“You do not amuse us,”** thundered the master of Olympus as he prepared to hurl a lightning bolt.

“Wait!”, cried Athena, “hear him out. Perhaps he can succeed where strength and magic have failed.”

“Yes, Sire, my magic comes only from logic, and my strength only from numbers.”

“Very well, explain.”

“First, Sire, man loses all to the perils of the world because he faces them alone. Sire, do all men suffer the fate that has so disturbed you?”

“No, only a very few lose all, but there are many that lose a great deal.”

“And some that lose nothing, Sire?”

“Yes, there are those who lose nothing, but . . .”

“Suppose, Sire, that groups of men would join together and that each member of these groups would pay a little of what they own to a pool, and that out of this pool would come the wealth to make whole the losses of any one member . . .”

“Hmmm, wise, small one, but what if one man faced greater risk of loss than another? – say a farmer as opposed to a teacher. A farmer has property to measure his wealth, while the teacher has ideas, which are difficult to destroy.”

“Well, Sire, we would group only like risks together. Thus, all would be equal among the members of each group.”

“Don’t some men lead riskier lives than others?”

“Yes, Sire, but with experience we could predict which type of man is more likely to suffer a loss, and have him pay more into the pool.”

“But how would we know what a man’s risks truly are?”

“Sire, we would have many men to deal with. Although some would surely surprise us with greater losses, there would be others who would be just as surprising with fewer losses. We could accurately predict the picture among all men in a group by using this Law of Large Numbers.”

“But how do we assign man to the proper group?”

“Sire, we have men make statements to us on something called an application – and these statements, which I humbly have named Representations, would give us an accurate picture of each man’s risk.

“But what if man did something purposely to cause his own loss? Surely then your plan would fail.”

“Ah, your majesty. I, too, have considered this. We would announce to each man that there would be certain risks, like the one that concerns you, for which we could not offer protection – these, Sire, I call Exclusions.”

“Interesting, stranger. Pray continue.”

“With variations, Sire, my plan could protect all that man owns – his animals, his crops, his house – even, Sire, his health – and, may I be so bold, his life.” The stranger noticed a dark look form on the imperial brow. “No, Sire, man would not become immortal, but he could guarantee that his family would not suffer financially if he were to travel across the River Styx before his time.”

Zeus pulled himself to his feet, **“Stranger,”** he trumpeted. **“Come forward. You have done well. What do you call this plan of yours?”**

"Sire, I call it Insurance – and this piece of paper I hold in my hand is the most important part of the plan – for it contains the promises the group makes to each man."

"The most important part, you say. Then from now on, all shall know this paper by your name. What is your name, young god?"

"Policius, Sire."

"Good, then I proclaim that all shall call these papers, 'Insurance Policies' for all time."

So you see that long before those crusty British sea captains met in the dark of the London coffeehouse named Lloyd's, Zeus, with a little help, gave man the gift of insurance on those lofty slopes of Mt. Olympus

Part I
INSURANCE BASICS

Notes

1

KEY TERMS & CONCEPTS

1 As you begin your study of Property and Casualty insurance, it is important for you to build a working vocabulary of insurance terminology. In this chapter, you will be introduced to the key terms and concepts that serve as a foundation for the balance of this text. Since these are words you will encounter over and over throughout this text, it is not necessary for you to spend hours memorizing definitions. Simply attempt to gain a basic understanding of their meaning and let the many applications which follow reinforce your understanding. On the other hand, as you work through this chapter, you must be careful to recognize the subtle (and not so subtle) differences that distinguish how these words are used in insurance as distinguished from their everyday usage.

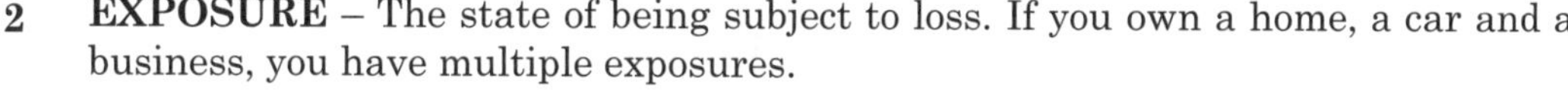

2 **EXPOSURE** – The state of being subject to loss. If you own a home, a car and a business, you have multiple exposures.

3 **RISK** – Chance of loss; uncertainty of loss; probability that a loss will occur. For example, what is the probability (risk) that a building will burn down or that the crop will be destroyed by hail? Individuals may transfer their risk (or a portion of it) to an insurance company.

chance of loss

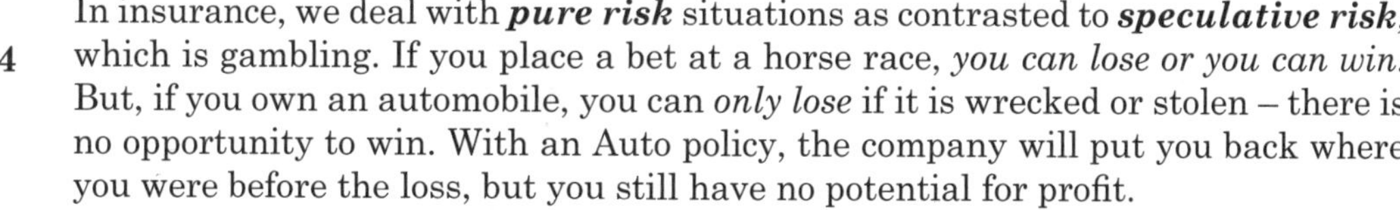

4 In insurance, we deal with ***pure risk*** situations as contrasted to ***speculative risk,*** which is gambling. If you place a bet at a horse race, *you can lose or you can win.* But, if you own an automobile, you can *only lose* if it is wrecked or stolen – there is no opportunity to win. With an Auto policy, the company will put you back where you were before the loss, but you still have no potential for profit.

5 As you can readily see, if you own anything or do anything you have a risk exposure. If you have a house, it might burn. If you have a front walk, somebody might slip and be injured.

6 There are several ways you can deal with risk. You might **avoid** a major risk exposure by not putting a swimming pool in your backyard. You could **reduce** risk by shoveling your walk during the winter. You could **retain** some risk by choosing a deductible when purchasing auto insurance. You can **transfer** most risks to an insurance company, and, as you will see, you are then **sharing** risk with all of the other Insureds of that company that also fit your risk profile.

Notes

1 **LOSS** – A **financial** hurt; the basis for a claim under an insurance policy; the amount for which the insurance company becomes liable to pay the Insured in the event of the Insured's financial harm. If there is no financial hurt, there is no loss. And, the amount of the insurable loss will not exceed the financial hurt. Insurance companies are not inclined to underwrite *sentimental value.* Joe's gold ring worth $1,000 is insured for $1,000. He cannot insure it for $2,000 because his grandfather gave it to him.

dollar value of the hurt

2 There are two types of losses: direct and indirect. A **direct loss** is the actual destruction of the insured property itself. An example of a direct loss would be the Insured's car being crushed by a meteor. An **indirect (or consequential) loss** is any other form of financial hurt that occurs as the result of a direct loss. Indirect losses result from the **loss of use** of the insured property. An example of an indirect loss would be the Insured's renting a replacement automobile after the meteor destroyed his car.

the stuff itself

loss of use

3 Notice that we are using the words differently than you might use them in normal conversation. In insurance, even a *chain of events* kind of loss can be a direct loss. If someone runs a stop sign, skids on the ice, and then smashes into a tree, which then topples through Joe's roof, the damage to Joe's house is direct. If Joe must move into a motel until his roof is repaired, his additional expenses would be considered an indirect loss. Please recognize that indirect losses are losses to your pocketbook and can only occur when there is first a direct loss.

4 The theory of insurance deals with the transfer of risk among members of society. The basic concept is not that difficult. Many insurance historians trace the basic concept of insurance back many centuries to the Chinese. In a principally agrarian society, Chinese farmers were faced with the problem of getting their crops to market. Most of them simply loaded their crops on a boat and used the rivers as transportation. Occasionally though, a boat would overturn and an entire harvest would be lost. The farmers began to transfer this risk to other farmers in a brilliant, yet simple, way. Ten farmers from one area would get together at harvest and load the boats by putting one-tenth of every farmer's crop on each boat. If a boat sunk, each farmer lost a little, but no one lost everything.

Notes

This concept of sharing risk is the basis of all insurance products.
1 A modern-day policyowner trades a small known loss (premium) for the insurance company's promise to pay for a large, unknown loss should it occur. All of the policyowners lose a little, but no one has to take the risk of losing everything.

2 A slightly more traditional definition would say that **insurance is a device that provides for the transfer of individual risk to a company.** In turn, the company will, for consideration, assume losses suffered by the Insured up to a predetermined limit. This is done by contracts in which an insurance company agrees, for consideration (premium and statements on the application), to indemnify or *make whole* the Insured in the event of specified losses from specified perils.

you. . .

3 **PROPERTY** – ***Stuff;*** belongings, possessions, assets; anything that you can acquire and own is property. Though *intellectual property,* like an idea, patent, or copyright is possible, most property is tangible – things you can see, feel, or touch. For example, your house, your furniture, your car, your dog, and your boat are your property. Property insurance is a contract to pay for damage or loss to your property caused by perils such as fire, lightning, or wind, as specified in the policy.

STUFF

4 Property insurance can be written on a **specific** or on a **blanket** basis. A Boatowner's policy might specify that it covers a *14 foot Tracker with a 100 horsepower Mercury outboard engine.* A Commercial Property policy might cover *all of the Business Personal Property of the Acme Furniture Company.* The blanket approach is very useful if the insured property might be located at any of several locations. If insured on a **blanket basis**, Acme would not have to be concerned if they had $1 million of furniture in the store and $1 million in the warehouse or if they had $1.5 million in the store and $500,000 in the warehouse.

property

5 **TWO PARTY CONTRACT** – A contract of insurance in which there are only two parties or persons involved: the **Insured** and the **insurance company**. **All property contracts are two party contracts** as the agreement only concerns two parties. If a loss occurs, the relationship between the company and the Insured becomes an adversarial relationship (tug-of-war): the Insured wants the most s/he can collect and the company wants to settle the claim equitably but not overpay.

6 **CASUALTY** – (Also known as **liability**.) As a member of society, you are granted certain rights, but with each of those rights come certain duties. For example, you have the right to drive your automobile but you have a corresponding duty to use care in the operation of your automobile so that you do not injure other people (called Bodily Injury or BI) or damage their property (called Property Damage or PD). Casualty insurance is designed to pay for damage you might do to someone else or their property.

...The Other Guy

7 **THIRD PARTY CONTRACT** – A contract of insurance involving three parties: the insurance company, the Insured and an **unknown third party**. **All casualty (liability) contracts are third party contracts.** They are designed to protect the Insured(s) against lawsuits by an injured third party for BI and PD caused by a negligent Insured.

casualty

Notes

1 **PERSONAL LINES vs. COMMERCIAL LINES** – Insurance can be written to meet the needs of individuals or businesses. Personal lines include the property and casualty coverages that protect an individual or a family, such as Homeowners and Automobile. The Commercial lines include coverages designed for businesses, such as the Commercial Property policy, the Commercial General Liability policy and the Businessowners policy. The distinction between Commercial Lines and Personal Lines is now almost more important than the distinction between property insurance and casualty insurance, as many policies contain both property **and** casualty insurance. The distinction between Personal Lines and Commercial Lines is now so important that this book is now subdivided into those two major sections.

Home . . . the office

INSURABLE INTEREST – In property insurance, insurable interest is any
2 **financial interest** a person has in the property at the time of the loss. You have an insurable interest in property when its damage or destruction would result in your direct financial loss.

what have you got to lose

The amount of insurance that you can purchase on property
3 is theoretically limited to the amount of your insurable interest in that property. For example, if you only own $78,000 worth of contents in a rented building, then you are limited to insuring just the contents for up to $78,000. You cannot insure the building because you have no insurable interest in it. However, it is not necessary to own something to have insurable interest. A TV repair shop has insurable interest in a television in which they have invested time and materials until such time as the bill is paid. A business that leases a building has an insurable interest in betterments and improvements it makes to that building until the end of the lease.

It is also possible to purchase property insurance based upon the
4 assumption that you will have insurable interest in the near future. For example, if you purchase a house with a closing scheduled for September 20th, you could buy the necessary Homeowners policy a week or so prior to closing. However, since benefits are only paid if you have insurable interest **at the time of the loss**, a fire on September 18th would not pay you a dime – even though you own a policy.

INDEMNIFY – To make an Insured **financially whole**; to restore an Insured
5 who suffers a loss to his original financial condition . . . but **not** to make him better off than he was before the loss occurred; to compensate for what has been damaged or destroyed.

One of the fundamental principles of insurance is that the policyowner is not
6 supposed to profit from a loss. By only agreeing to **indemnify** in the event of a loss, the insurance company removes the incentive for intentional losses.

make whole not rich

LIMIT OF LIABILITY – Despite the name, both Property and Casualty contracts
7 have a limit of liability that establishes the degree to which a company will indemnify following a loss. In Property insurance, suppose that I have insured my $150,000 house for $100,000. Further assume that I suffer a $20,000 loss. The limit is $100,000, the loss is $20,000. I will collect $20,000. The Rule of Three L's says that I will collect the **Lower of the Loss or the Limit**. Alternatively, if I suffer a total loss of my home ($150,000), I will collect only $100,000. In this case, the limit is lower than the loss.

Rule of 3 L's

Lower of the Loss or the Limit

Notes

In a Casualty contract, the Limit of Liability dictates how much the company will
1 pay on your behalf in the event you injure someone else or their property. Of huge importance in liability insurance is the idea of **occurrence limits** and **aggregate limits**. Personal lines liability policies typically have only an occurrence limit; *we will pay up to $100,000 for any occurrence for which you are the negligent party.* For another occurrence the following day, there is another $100,000 and so on. This is an example of **restoration** or **nonreduction** of limits. On the other hand, Commercial liability policies normally have an aggregate limit as well, which limits the total for all occurrences within the policy period.

2 **EXCLUSIONS** – Losses that the policy specifically states are not covered by the contract. Exclusions typically fall into one of three categories:

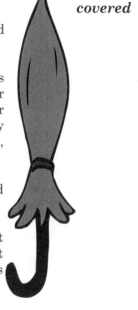

things not covered

3 **CATASTROPHIC LOSSES** – such as war, nuclear catastrophes, floods and earthquakes.

LOSSES THAT ARE BETTER COVERED ELSEWHERE – Homeowners
4 policies, for example, exclude automobile losses because they are better covered under an Automobile policy and vice versa. Also, there are a number of very common exclusions for losses that are better covered by specialty policies, such as Equipment Breakdown, Business Income, Flood, Aircraft, Workers Compensation and Marine.

PREDICTABLE LOSSES – such as deterioration, wear and tear, rust, and
5 mechanical breakdown. A loss must be **fortuitous** to be covered, which means it must be unexpected and unforeseen – something that happens by chance. For example, your automobile insurance policy won't pay for a new set of tires when your old ones wear out because those are predictable losses. It would pay for the same tires destroyed in a wreck because that is a fortuitous (accidental) loss.

INHERENT VICE – Though most exclusions are self-explanatory (e.g. flood,
6 war, mechanical breakdown), the words *inherent vice* are a little unfamiliar to most. Inherent vice is a property loss resulting from a latent defect natural to the property itself. For example, an auto will eventually rust – it's the nature of iron. This loss is characterized as inherent vice and is excluded by most property contracts.

PRO RATA – in proportion; share; ratio. The term *pro rata* is used frequently
7 in property insurance such as in Pro Rata Refund, Pro Rata Coverage, and Pro Rata Liability clauses. It also shows up in liability insurance if multiple companies are involved in the same claim. Notice that pro rata does not mean equally. Suppose that you and I share a pizza. If I eat 80% of it and you eat 20%, splitting the $10 tab pro rata dictates that I pay $8 while you pay $2. Sharing equally would cause us both to pay $5. Only in the fluke circumstance where we each ate the same amount of pizza could we split the bill both proportionately and equally.

PIZZA = PAYMENT

PRO RATA

LIBERALIZATION CLAUSE – This clause simply states that if the insurance
8 company, during your policy period, improves the terms or benefits of new policies of the same form to new Insureds for the same price, then your policy will automatically have the same improved rights and benefits as the improved policies. For example, if you owned a Commercial Property Policy and if new policies had additional coverages for the same price, then your policy would be interpreted as also having the new benefits.

I have to admit it's getting better... - the Beatles

Notes

ASSIGNMENT – In property and casualty, assignment is the legal transfer
1 of ownership of an insurance policy from the current policyowner to a new policyowner. An assignment must be agreed to in writing by the old policyowner, the new policyowner and the insurance company. The Commercial Property Policy refers to assignment as *Transfer of Your Rights and Duties Under This Policy.*

CANCELLATION/NONRENEWAL – Cancellation is the termination of coverage
2 during the policy period. Nonrenewal, however, is termination at the end of the policy period.

3 **REFUND OF UNEARNED PREMIUM** – By this point, it should be obvious that a policy can be cancelled midterm in two ways:

- Joe can always cancel his own policy.
- Within statutory guidelines, Joe's company can cancel the contract.

4 In either instance, Joe will be due a refund of premium for the time that coverage was paid for but not provided.

However, in most states and with most **Commercial policies**, the question of
5 who cancels whom has a major bearing on the amount of the refund. To illustrate, let's assume that Joe owns a commercial building for which he pays a six month premium of $1,000. If the company cancels Joe at the end of three months, he is due a pro rata refund of $500. If Joe cancels the policy after three months (assume he sold the building), then most jurisdictions allow the company to pay Joe's refund on a short rate basis – he might receive $450. The amount the company can penalize Joe is subject to state regulation but is normally around 10%.

Commercial Lines

Company cancels
– pro rata
Joe cancels
– short rate
Personal Lines
– pro rata

The rationale for the short rate refund is fairly straightforward. The costs of
6 issuing an insurance policy are *front-end loaded.* It is in the beginning of the policy period that the company costs of commissions, inspections, and issuing the policy are paid. If Joe cancels midterm, the company might well lose money on the policy through no fault of its own – hence the short rate refund.

Memory Device: If the company cancels Joe's Commercial policy, they are the
7 **pros** in the transaction, and he gets a **pro rata refund**. If Joe cancels the company, he gets *short-changed* – a short rate refund.

CERTIFICATE OF INSURANCE -
8 Frequently in the business world contracts require one party to show the other party that they, in fact, have the insurance required by the agreement. The party requesting proof of insurance keeps the certificate and becomes the certificate holder. If the insurance shown on the certificate is cancelled, the insurance company must endeavor to notify the certificate holder of the cancellation.

ENDORSEMENT – A written modification
9 or addition to a policy, usually accomplished by adding additional pieces of paper (called endorsements) to the policy. The purpose of an endorsement is to modify the original agreement to fit the needs of one specific policyowner. Today, the terms *endorsement* and *rider* are used interchangeably.

1 **NAMED INSURED** – In a personal lines contract, the Named Insured(s) have the rights and duties under the policy. While other persons may be afforded coverage under the contract, the Named Insureds maintain the contractual rights.

more than you think

2 **FIRST NAMED INSURED** – The Commercial Package Policy makes a further distinction between Named Insured(s) and the **First** Named Insured. The First Named Insured is the **first entity listed** on the Declarations under the Named Insured category. This First Named Insured is the entity who has the right to cancel the policy, the right to change the policy, the duty to pay the premium, and is the individual who will be notified should the insurance company wish to cancel the policy.

3 **ACCIDENT** – A **sudden, unforeseen and unintended event** that happens at a **known place** and a **known time**. For example, a car rounds the bend, slides on the ice and hits a telephone pole. The driver did not foresee the ice being on the road and did not intend to slide on the ice. The event happened at a known place and a known time. Also called a **fortuitous** event.

single event

happens by chance

4 **OCCURRENCE** – An accident but also including **continuous and repeated exposure** to injurious conditions that result in bodily injury or property damage. The definition of *Occurrence* is much broader than the definition of *Accident* because an occurrence includes not only sudden and swift losses, but also **losses that occur over time**. For example, the Occurrence definition would include coverage for the following kinds of losses: injury to skin as the result of the repeated use of a skin lotion; crops that are damaged by fumes escaping continuously from a manufacturing plant; paint damage to a home caused by repeated exposure to chemicals from trucks going to and from a construction site, and the injury caused by breathing asbestos particles over a long period of time. Accidental losses would be covered by a policy written on an Occurrence basis but not vice versa.

all accidents are occurrences... not all occurrences are accidents

Conclusion

1 By this time your head is probably swimming with all the definitions you've been exposed to in Chapter 1. Don't worry, you'll see all the things you learned here used in context in later chapters. Let's do a quick review of some of the more important terms before moving on.

2 If you have anything, or do anything, you have **exposures**. If you have a car it might be stolen. If you drive the car, you might hurt someone. This chance of loss is known as **risk**. Insurance is a **pure risk** situation as you can only lose. **Speculative risk** offers the chance of gain or loss and is simply gambling.

3 A **loss** is a financial hurt, not a sentimental hurt. If your house burns, that is a **direct loss**. If you have to spend extra money to live in a motel while you rebuild, that is an **indirect loss**.

4 **Property** is stuff and insured under a **Two Party contract**. **Casualty** policies are **Third Party** contracts and pay for damage you do to the Other Guy. You buy insurance; you must have or expect to have a financial interest in the subject of the insurance. **Insurable interest** must exist at the time of loss if you are to collect under the policy.

5 The **Rule of three L's** says that we will pay the **lower of the loss or the limit**. Personal Lines policies have only **occurrence limits**. The policy limit applies to each separate occurrence. Commercial policies also have an **aggregate limit** which describes the total dollars available in any policy year despite the number of occurrences.

6 **Exclusions** spell out what the policy does not cover. Exclusions are typically **catastrophic losses**, losses **better covered elsewhere**, or **predictable losses** (like **inherent vice**).

7 If you want to **assign** your policy, you'll need company permission. If a company honors its policy with you this year but does not want you next year, that's **nonrenewal**. If they terminate your coverage mid-term, that's **cancellation**.

8 The ranking Insured in a Personal Lines policy is the **Named Insured**; in a Commercial contract it is the **First Named Insured**.

9 **Accidents** happen at a given time; **occurrences** can happen at a specific time or over a period of time. A train wreck is both an accident and an occurrence. Black lung disease is an occurrence but not an accident.

10 There are over 40 definitions in this chapter. We've hit just a few here that will give you a basic foothold on how property and casualty coverage works.

The Chapter 1 Quiz is combined with the Chapter 2 Quiz, and can be found at the end of Chapter 2 on page 2-23.

CONTRACT LAW AND UNDERWRITING

2

1 In layman's terms we say that Property and Casualty Agents sell insurance policies. In legal terms, we might say that the Agent is aiding in the establishment of a legal contract between the company and the Insured. For this reason, it is important for you as a prospective Agent to have a solid understanding of the basics of contract law. In fact, as a Property and Casualty Agent, it is even more important for you than it is for a Life and Health Agent. As a Property and Casualty Agent, you are typically given the authority by the company you represent to *bind coverage.* That is the power to start the contract and obligate the company prior to the company receiving any money or even having the opportunity to study the application.

2 Obviously, with this power you've been handed a two-edged sword. You have a great tool to help your clients and the perfect weapon to commit professional suicide. A good knowledge of the fundamentals of contract law will go a long way in assuring that you use your power beneficially.

3 From personal experience, most of us know one party to the contract because the *Policyowner R Us.* But before we look at how a contract is formed, many of us need to know just a little more about the other party to the contract – the insurance company.

Notes

TYPES OF COMPANIES

1 There are several ways of classifying companies within the insurance industry today. One method is by examining the corporate structure of the company.

Lloyd's of London

2 Probably the most startling fact about Lloyd's is that it is not an insurance company and does not issue policies. It merely provides a vehicle for associations of individuals to write insurance. The roots of this historically rich organization began in 17th century England when merchants gathered at the coffeehouses to do business and exchange ideas.

3 As you are aware, England has limited natural resources, and her growth depended in large measure on commerce that could be developed through shipping and trade. Her success in trade was due in part to the willingness of wealthy individuals to insure the ships and cargoes involved. An informal system slowly evolved in which the person seeking insurance would post a proposal in a coffeehouse, stating the amount of insurance required along with the details of the risk involved, such as the ship's condition, name of the captain, nature of the cargo and the ship's destination. Those willing to assume a portion of the risk would write their name under the proposal and hence became known as underwriters.

4 The most enterprising of the coffeehouse proprietors was Ed Lloyd of Tower Street. He began making information available concerning weather conditions, ships, tides and captains. He even published a newspaper containing such data. While he was never directly involved in the business of underwriting, the most renowned insurance organization in the world still bears his name.

5 Today Lloyd's functions much as it did originally. However, substantial financial requirements are now placed upon the underwriters who are organized into syndicates (associations) controlled by managing Agents. Usually several of the over 250 Lloyd's syndicates are involved in underwriting a single risk. While the primary function of Lloyd's is to provide property and casualty coverage for normal exposures, it is most famous for underwriting highly unusual, one-of-a-kind risks.

6 Lloyd's most important contribution to our industry today is probably its ability to reinsure insurance companies around the world, thus spreading the risk and providing additional insuring capacity. In the same way an individual can transfer risk to an insurance company, that company may transfer some of its risk to still another insurance company. This process is called ***reinsurance***. There are two types of reinsurance:

- **Facultative** - where reinsurance is negotiated on a policy by policy basis.
- **Treaty** - a blanket agreement in which company B automatically reinsures 25% of all policies written by company A.

Stock Companies

1 A stock company is a corporation that is organized to conduct the business of insurance and is actually owned by its stockholders or shareholders. Shares of stock are sold to the stockholders to provide the capital (money) that the corporation needs in order to get started. This capital sustains the corporation until it makes enough money to operate from current income. Since the stockholders own the company, they are entitled to share in the company profits, which are paid to them as a dividend - a return on their capital investment. On the other hand, individuals who have purchased insurance from the company, called policyowners, do not participate in company profits and never receive dividends as they have no capital investment in the company.

For the benefit of the stockholders . . . they own it

2 In short, a stock company may be characterized by the fact that:

- It is operated for the ultimate benefit of the stockholders.
- A portion of the earnings is paid to stockholders as dividends.
- The board of directors of the company is elected by the stockholders.
- **It does not pay dividends to its policyowners.** The policyowners do not participate in company profits, and, therefore, these companies are referred to as *non-participating* companies. As you will see in the next section under mutual companies, there is another type of dividend called a "policy dividend." For the moment, remember that stock companies do not pay policy dividends.

Mutual Companies

3 The most important legal difference between a mutual company and a stock company is that a mutual has no stockholders and exists, therefore, for the benefit of the policyowners. Because it has no stockholders, a mutual must be started in a different manner. The first step for a new mutual company is to find a required number of individuals willing to purchase a minimum amount of insurance from the company. Since most people would be reluctant to apply for insurance from a company that could only be formed if enough applications are taken in advance, it is almost impossible to start a mutual today. Most mutuals are now formed by mutualizing an existing stock company. Many of the huge mutuals with which you are now familiar - Prudential, Metropolitan and Equitable of New York - were formed in this manner.

For the benefit of the policyholders . . . no one really owns it

4 Today's mutuals are technically classified as mutual legal reserve companies, which means that they meet the same capital requirements that are placed on stock companies. Most states do require mutuals to incorporate, and the policyowners control the corporation by voting for the board of directors that operates the company.

Notes

1 While the biggest legal difference between a mutual and a stock is that a mutual has no stockholders, the most visible difference is that **the mutual company pays policy dividends to policyowners** and the stock does not. It is important to note that these policy dividends are not a return on investment in the sense of the dividends paid by stock companies to stockholders. In the truest sense, policy dividends are *a return of premium overcharge.* In setting premium rates, a company makes many assumptions regarding mortality (death), anticipated earnings and expenses. Although **a policy dividend is never guaranteed**, generally company projections are quite conservative, the company does better than anticipated, and a dividend is paid. While some money must be held as surplus in the event of adverse experience in the future, the excess surplus is returned to the policyowner as a **dividend - a return of unneeded premium**. Because the policyowners participate in the profits of a mutual company, the mutual company is often called a *participating company.*

Dividends to policyowners

Dividends not guaranteed

2 A mutual company, then, may be distinguished from a stock company by the following:

- It is operated for the ultimate benefit of the policyowners. It has no stockholders.
- It generally pays *policy dividends.* Since the policyowners do participate in the profits of the company, it is called a *participating company.*
- There is no capital stock, so no stockholder dividends are paid.
- As there are no stockholders, the policyowners elect the board of directors of the company.

Reciprocals

3 From the viewpoint of the policyowner, a **reciprocal insurance exchange** operates like a mutual company. The biggest difference is structural. A reciprocal is an **unincorporated** entity managed by an **attorney-in-fact** generally offering homeowners or auto insurance to the public. Each Insured member is known as a **subscriber** and agrees to share in the other subscriber's insured losses as they agree to share in his. It is from this *reciprocal promise* that the name is derived.

combo

4 In most jurisdictions, these not-for-profit organizations are regulated just like mutuals and must belong to the Insurance Guaranty Associations of the states in which they do business.

Notes

Fraternals

Clubs that offer insurance

1 In the late 1800's and early 1900's, waves of European immigrants began to land on the shores of this country. While they came for many reasons, they were welcomed as necessary labor in the factories of America, which were operating at full capacity throughout the period known as the Industrial Revolution.

2 These new city dwellers naturally grouped together in accordance with their ethnic and religious backgrounds and often formed fraternal societies to maintain their national heritage. Such religious and social fraternities began to provide small amounts of insurance, generally burial insurance, for their members.

3 They grew rapidly until the turn of the century. They have since declined in importance, although some very large fraternals still exist today, including the Aid Association for Lutherans, Independent Order of Foresters, Lutheran Brotherhood, Woodmen of the World, Knights of Columbus and Modern Woodmen of America.

4 Fraternals are not normally incorporated under state insurance laws as are insurance companies, and they are usually subject to slightly different regulations than stock or mutual companies. They do, however, closely parallel mutual companies in their organization and operation. The biggest difference is that you must join the fraternity in order to buy fraternal insurance.

Self Insurers

Retain risk

5 Self insurance can appear in many forms from the very informal to the highly structured. Technically, a person who has no health insurance, for example, is self insured. If Joe Insured calculates that his family would need $500,000 in the event of his death, he might buy only $250,000 in coverage if he already has $250,000 in the bank. He is self insuring for $250,000.

6 Most of us self insure in automobile insurance by selecting a deductible. When our car is worth less than the gas in the tank, we drop collision damage to our own car.

7 Many large companies self insure their property and casualty exposures. Rather than paying an insurance company, they set aside about the same amount they would have paid in premium and pay claims out of this fund. They then buy **stop loss** coverage from a traditional company to cover losses which go beyond a specified limit.

Risk Retention Groups

Group self insurance

8 Risk retention groups generally address commercial liability exposures and simply take self insurance to another level. Suppose our buddy Joe Insured owns a restaurant where he serves liquor. If he cannot buy Liquor Liability coverage, he might decide to self insure. If he joins a risk retention group comprised of all the other bar owners in his state they have the Law of Large Numbers working on their behalf. They collect their own premiums and pay their own losses.

9 Risk retention groups are generally not subject to the same regulations as an insurance company and normally do not belong to the state Insurance Guaranty Association.

Notes

Government Insurers

1 In terms of dollar volume and number of policyowners, the federal government is by far the biggest insurance company on the face of the earth. Social Security and Medicare alone involve just about every U.S. citizen. In addition, programs are available for military personnel (Servicemen's Group Life) and their dependents. (Tricare).

Uncle Sam

2 The federal government also provides or subsidizes insurance for some catastrophic perils like flood. State government is involved in providing insurance for those who cannot buy through normal channels in the areas of medical expense, homeowners and automobile insurance. State government also plays an important role in Worker's Compensation insurance in most states.

OTHER WAYS OF CLASSIFYING COMPANIES ‡

3 While consumers are most likely to classify companies by structure - Stock or Mutual or Fraternal - there are several other important ways to classify companies.

BY ORIGIN (WHERE?)

4 In order for an insurance company to be granted a charter in a particular state it must have sufficient resources on hand to pay claims. The company anticipates that eventually enough policies will be sold to allow the Law of Large Numbers to work properly.

5 Some states have exceedingly high requirements and others substantially lower. Therefore, knowing the state in which a company was formed (chartered) could tell you a lot about the financial resources of a company.

6 A company chartered in Illinois, for example, would be considered an Illinois **domestic company**. If a company is chartered in another state, territorial possession or Washington D.C., it would be considered, in Illinois, a **foreign company**. Therefore, a company chartered in California would be a foreign company within the state of Illinois. A company chartered in another country would be viewed as an **alien company**.

***Here* = Domestic**

***Not here, but in U.S.* = Foreign**

***Outside U.S.* = Alien**

7 Almost always, a company's home office is in the state in which it was formed - it is said to be *domiciled* there. Therefore, if we assume that we all live and work in Florida, a company domiciled in New York would be considered foreign. A company domiciled in Canada would be an alien company.

‡ *This symbol indicates material important in Thomson Prometric test states.*

Notes

BY AUTHORITY

1 A company is automatically granted the right to do business in its state of origin. If that company wants to do business in other states, it must apply to those states for approval as an **authorized (or admitted)** company. For example, a company domiciled in Indiana and authorized to do business in Kentucky, Ohio and Illinois is only an authorized (or admitted) company in those states. In any other state the same company would be an **unauthorized (or nonadmitted)** company.

Admitted = Authorized

Nonadmitted = Unauthorized

2 Requiring a company to be authorized before doing business in a given state gives that state's residents the assurance that their own state officials have approved the financial soundness, the method of operation and the policies sold by almost any company soliciting their business in that state.

3 The *almost* applies to a situation that rarely occurs on the life and health side of the business but transpires with some frequency in property and casualty insurance. It is possible to buy insurance from an unauthorized insurer in what is known as a **surplus lines transaction**.

4 Here's how it works. Suppose you are an Ohio resident and need an insurance policy unavailable from any Ohio authorized company.

5 If the coverage you need is available, say, from a Texas company unauthorized in Ohio, you do not have to fly to Dallas to purchase it. You could buy what you need through an Ohio-based Surplus Lines Agent. Typically, states grant this additional license only to individuals who are already Resident Agents in good standing and place some additional administrative requirements upon them.

BY FINANCIAL SOUNDNESS

6 One important task you have as an Agent is to make sure you are insuring your clients with policies from companies that are financially sound. This due diligence effort is particularly important if you are an independent Agent representing, say, 20 companies.

7 There are several independent rating services that assess the financial strength of insurance companies based upon that company's claims experience, investment earnings, level of reserves, management and other factors. The dollars set aside to pay claims are held in the insurance company's **General Reserve**. The A.M. Best Company, Moody's Investors Service, Standard and Poor's Insurance Rating services are some of the better known rating organizations. One of the easiest ways to determine the financial soundness (or unsoundness) of an insurance company is to check them against the ratings they are given by one of these services.

General Reserve: money to pay claims

8 For example, a superior company on the A.M. Best scale gets an A+. A grade of C or C- is considered marginal. A rating of D, E or F is below (or way below) minimum standards.

Notes

INSURANCE CONTRACT FORMATION

1 **CONTRACTS** – Insurance policies are legal contracts. A contract is simply an agreement between two or more parties. A contract has certain required elements.

2 **Rules of Contract Construction** - *The prime directive* for the creation of any agreement is the **Doctrine of Utmost Good Faith**. In short, no agreement, whether or not there is a written contract, will work unless the parties want it to work. Both rely on the good faith of the other.

Mutual reliance or. . .

"never enter into a contract with anyone who you need a contract with"
- My dad

3 When determining just what an insurance contract will provide, the courts will look to the **reasonable expectations** of the parties. For instance, the courts would not look favorably upon a liability insurance contract that was sold to a gas station and contained a provision excluding any injury involving petroleum products. Such a contract would not meet the reasonable expectations of the Insured.

4 Normally, the terms of an insurance policy are defined in one of two ways:

- Definitions found in the policy
- Everyday and ordinary meaning, for those words not defined in the policy

5 Insurance policies are unlike most contracts in that the parties do not bargain for terms. Insurance policies are by their very nature standardized documents. The Insured is offered the policy on a take it or leave it basis. Because of this, any part of the contract which is **ambiguous**, unclear, or subject to more than one meaning, will always be interpreted in favor of the Insured and against the company. We call such contracts **Contracts of Adhesion**.

6 Memory Hint: Adhesion. . . the company wrote it, now they are *stuck* with it.

7 Here is an example of how **adhesion** works. A property policy excludes damage caused by earth movement. The exclusion itself then lists several examples of earth movement, all of which are natural occurrences. The Insured's building is damaged by movement of the earth *which was caused by a man-made occurrence, blasting.* At least one court has found that by listing several examples of earth movement, all of which were caused by Mother Nature, that the term as it appeared in the policy was ambiguous, and that coverage for the damage should be found in this particular case.

we're stuck with it

8 It should also be apparent that this concept flows directly from the **Doctrine of Reasonable Expectations**. Many courts have also held that statements outside the policy itself, e.g. sales materials and even the statements of Agents are sufficient to create an ambiguity, and thus invoke the rule of Adhesion.

Notes

REQUIRED ELEMENTS OF A CONTRACT

1 **OFFER** – One party must make an offer to the other party. In Property and Casualty insurance the company normally makes the offer by issuing a policy.

2 **ACCEPTANCE** – The second party must accept the first party's exact offer. The Insured normally accepts the offer by paying the premium. The combination of an offer and an acceptance is called an **agreement**.

3 **CONSIDERATION** – Consideration can be broadly defined as **something of value**. The parties to the contract must exchange consideration. Consideration in a property and casualty contract consists of the following: the Insured gives the company the premium for the policy and the statements made in the application for insurance; the insurance company gives the Insured the promises contained in the policy.

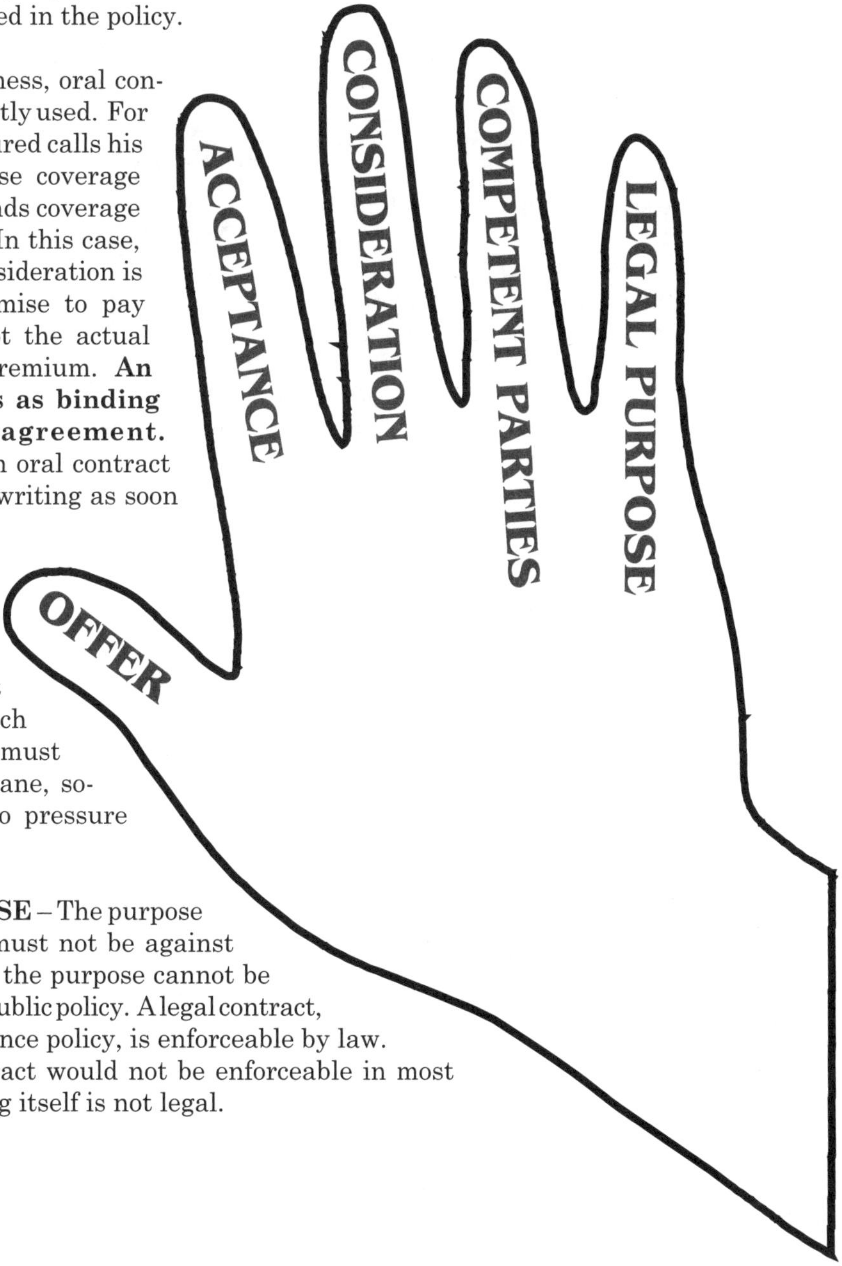

4 In the P&C business, oral contracts are frequently used. For example, the Insured calls his Agent to purchase coverage and the Agent binds coverage over the phone. In this case, the Insured's consideration is actually the promise to pay the premium, not the actual payment of the premium. **An oral contract is as binding as a written agreement.** However, such an oral contract should be put in writing as soon as possible.

5 **COMPETENT PARTIES** – The parties to the contract must be competent, which means that they must be of legal age, sane, sober and under no pressure or duress.

6 **LEGAL PURPOSE** – The purpose for the contract must not be against the law. That is, the purpose cannot be illegal or against public policy. A legal contract, such as an insurance policy, is enforceable by law. A gambling contract would not be enforceable in most states as gambling itself is not legal.

Notes

OTHER CONCERNS ABOUT CONTRACTS

1 **TRUTH** – The concern is how to define *truth*. The next five terms relate to the accuracy of the statements made by the proposed Insured when applying for a policy or when filing a Proof of Loss. As you will learn, there are varying degrees of the truth required when purchasing insurance.

2 **WARRANTY** – With regards to an application for insurance, a warranty is a statement held to be the **absolute literal truth**. A breach of warranty is sufficient to render the policy void, whether the matter warranted is material (relevant) or not, or whether it contributed to the loss. In a Property policy, the Named Insured may have to warrant the existence of certain conditions that will diminish the risk of a loss, such as that there will be an operational burglar alarm or sprinkler system. If any warranted condition is not met by the Insured, there is no coverage. Warranties are still used in certain situations, such as Ocean Marine policies, Director's and Officer's Liability polices and in case of fraud.

It won't Float
Warranty must be true

3 **REPRESENTATION** – Requiring an applicant to warrant his statements is considered to be far too strict in many forms of P&C insurance. The public is, in many instances, simply unable to make statements which are absolutely literally true. As a result, a more liberal approach is taken in most P&C contracts in that the statements made by the applicant are taken as representations, not warranties. A representation is a statement which is **true to the best of the applicant's knowledge and belief**. Under most policies, except in cases of fraud, all we expect from our applicants is to tell us what they, in good faith, believe to be the truth.

Representations true to the best of my knowledge and belief

4 **MISREPRESENTATION** – A misrepresentation is a false statement (**a lie**) on an application or a Proof of Loss statement. If the misrepresentation concerns a **material fact**, then the policy can be voided. A fact is material if the insurance company would not have issued the policy for the same price if it had known the truth. For example, an applicant for a policy states that her office building is constructed of steel and concrete, when in reality it's made of straw. She also states that the building is brown when it is actually pink. These statements are both misrepresentations but only one of them *is* material to the risk. The insurance company would not have rejected the application on the basis of the color of the building. However, the fact that the building is constructed of straw, not steel and concrete, is material.

Notes

1 **CONCEALMENT** – **hiding the truth** or **telling a partial truth**. Concealment is the failure of the applicant/Insured to disclose to the insurance company a **material fact** on an application or on a proof of loss. The applicant/Insured has the duty to reveal all material information. Failure to do so may void the contract. The Doctrine of Utmost Good Faith requires the proposed Insured to tell the truth, *the whole truth,* and nothing but the truth.

hiding the truth

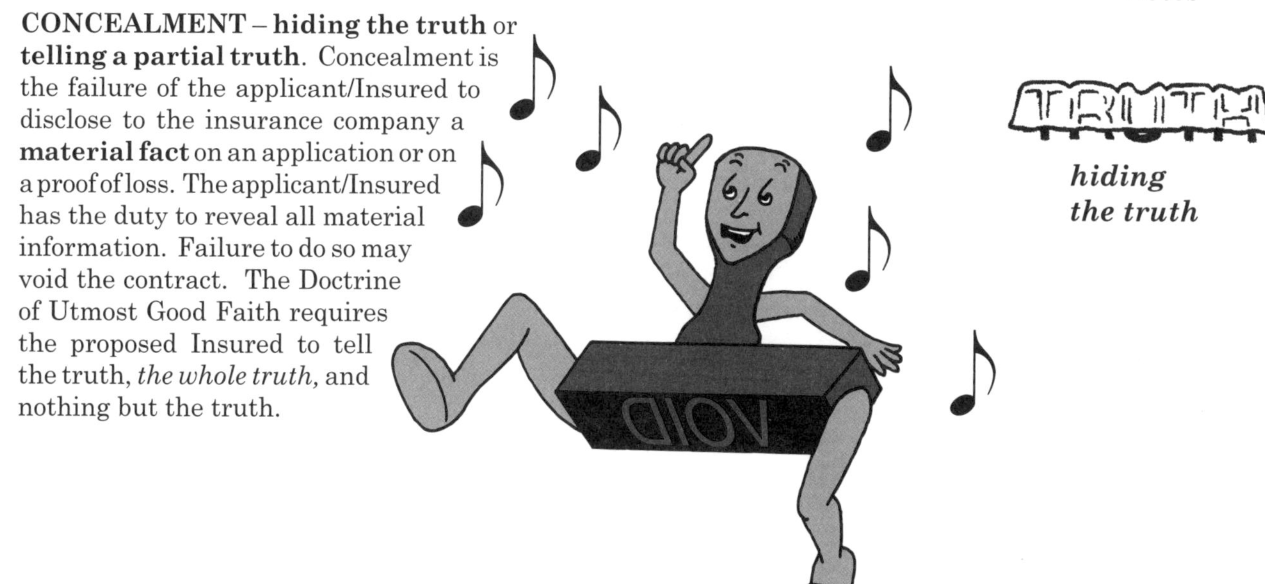

THE MATERIAL AND INTENTIONAL TWO-STEP

2 **FRAUD** – Fraud is an intentional act of deception or cheating in order to financially benefit yourself at the expense of another. An example of fraud would be an Insured claiming a loss that never occurred in order to collect. Fraud will release the insurance company from its obligation to pay the claim. Fraud may be perpetrated by an Insured, an insurance company or an Agent.

the result of a lie

3 **FIDUCIARY** – A fiduciary is an individual who has a responsibility for the financial affairs of another. As an insurance Agent, you have a fiduciary responsibility to your clients for the safekeeping of their premiums and a limited responsibility for their financial affairs. You are, therefore, forbidden from using your policyowners' money for your own purposes.

holding somebody else's money

4 **WAIVER** – A waiver is the intentional and voluntary relinquishment of a legal right. For example, when buying Auto insurance, Joe might be offered a coverage called Uninsured Motorists. If he declines the coverage, he might do so by signing a *waiver.* Joe is knowingly giving up the right to pursue Uninsured Motorists' claims with the company.

5 Another example concerns the completion of an application for insurance. Suppose that Joe does not answer all of the questions on the application, but the company issues the policy anyway. The company is said to have **waived its rights** to receive an answer to those questions.

6 **ESTOPPEL** – Estoppel is little more than the legal consequences of a waiver. Under this doctrine, one party to a contract may be estopped (stopped) by his past words or actions from asserting a right granted him in the contract.

7 In the above example, the company had waived their right to receive answers to certain questions on the app. If they tried to cancel the contract or deny a claim on this basis, they would be estopped from doing so.

Notes

1 **BINDER** – Many types of P&C coverages are *oral contracts* – applied for and activated orally. In these situations, the Agent must have the authority to bind the insurance company to the risk before a policy is issued. The process involves the use of a binder, which may be either oral or written. In either case, a binder provides the Insured with **immediate temporary protection**. If the binder is verbal, it should be followed by a written binder as soon as possible.

2 A binder may also be used to modify existing coverage. If Joe has coverage for one auto, he may simply call his Agent when he purchases a second car to have the new car added to his existing policy. In either case, a binder is an **interim agreement** that provides coverage until the actual policy or endorsement is issued. A binder, however, does not guarantee that a policy will, in fact, be issued. The company, as a result of its research and investigation, may decide not to issue the policy. If the company decides not to issue the policy, then it may either cancel the binder in order to discontinue the coverage or it may just let the binder expire. Therefore, binders in most jurisdictions have three possible expiration dates:

- If the policy is issued, the binder expires **at issuance of the policy**. The policy's effective date is backdated to match the origination date of the binder.
- If the insurance company declines to issue the policy and no formal cancellation is given, then the binder remains in effect until its **expiration date**. Binders are normally issued for a limited period of time, such as 30 or 60 days.
- If the insurance company declines to issue the policy and sends out a formal cancellation of the binder, then the binder expires on **the day after receipt of the notice of cancellation**.

Know This

3 **COUNTERSIGNATURE** – Many states have laws requiring that newly issued policies sold by a nonresident Agent be countersigned (signed a second time) by a licensed *resident* Agent of that state before delivery to the policyowner.

DISTINCT CHARACTERISTICS OF AN INSURANCE CONTRACT

4 **PERSONAL CONTRACT** – Property and Casualty contracts are personal in nature. Most people assume that the policies insure the property, but actually, they do not. They insure a person's **insurable interest** in the property. Since P&C contracts are personal in nature, they are not assignable to another without the prior written consent of the insurance company.

5 **CONDITIONAL** – Insurance policies are conditional in nature because certain future conditions or acts must occur before any claims can be paid. For example, the Insured must pay the required premiums, suffer a loss, notify the company of the loss and provide adequate proof to support the claim. The company will verify the accuracy of the claim before paying it. Conditional statements are **"If. . ., then. . ."** in nature. "If there is a loss, then the company is obligated to pay."

6 **UNILATERAL** – Insurance contracts are unilateral in nature because **only one party, the insurance company, makes any legally enforceable promises**. The policyowner promises nothing, not even to pay the premiums. If Joe Insured fails to pay the premium, the policy will simply lapse.

Notes

1 **ALEATORY** – Aleatory contracts are contracts in which both parties realize that one party may obtain far greater value than the other party under the agreement, and in which payment depends upon fortuitous (unforeseen and unexpected) future events. There is an element of chance involved. For instance, Joe might pay $1,000 a year for 50 years for Homeowners insurance and never suffers a loss. His neighbor, Joe Kool, had paid only one year's premium when his house burned to the ground and his company paid $156,000 on the claim. The Law of Large Numbers tells us that insurance will never come out even for each individual - it works out as predicted only for the group.

2 **ADHESION** - As we have pointed out, insurance contracts are contracts of adhesion - the company wrote it; they're stuck with it.

3 **PARTS OF A POLICY** – P&C insurance policies are made up of four sections: (Remember the acronym **DICE**.)

4 D **Declarations** – The Declarations Sheet is usually the first page of any policy and contains the following basic information: the Named Insured(s) and the property which is to be protected, its description, the policy period and the premium. This is the **"Who, What, When, Where and How Much"** section – the fill-in-the-blanks section.

"W's" - like limits

5 I **Insuring Agreement / Coverages** – The Insuring Clause / Coverages section contains the insurance company's promises. It is the "heart" of the contract. It establishes the obligation of the company to provide the insurance coverages as stated in the policy.

promises

6 C **Conditions** – The Conditions section of the policy spells out the procedures that enable the parties to function effectively under the contract. They establish the rules of conduct between the parties of the contract, such as: how to report a loss, appraisal provisions, time and manner of paying a loss, subrogation, cancellation, assignment rights and definitions of terms. The policy Conditions are the bulk of the policy.

ground rules

7 E **Exclusions** – These are the perils or types of losses that are not covered, such as intentional acts, losses due to war or catastrophic losses. The Exclusions are particularly important in "All Risk" policies.

no's

Notes

UNDERWRITING ‡

1 Underwriting is the process of selecting, classifying, pricing and insuring a risk. Once a group with a similar risk level is identified, the next step in estimating premium cost is to estimate the cost of claims for that group.

2 While it is impossible to predict if Joe Insured's house will ever suffer a loss, the probability of loss for a large group of Joes with similar houses in similar neighborhoods with similar fire departments at similar distances is **very predictable**. This device, known as the **Law of Large Numbers**, is at the heart of all insurance underwriting.

3 **INSURABLE RISK ELEMENTS** – Not all risks are insurable. Those that are share the following characteristics:

- There must be a large number of homogeneous (similar) risks for the **Law of Large Numbers** to work.
- **Uncertainty** is insurable where intentional losses are typically excluded.
- The loss must be **economically significant to the applicant**. You would not insure a disposable lighter because it is economically insignificant. You could not insure a stranger's house; his house would be economically significant to his family, but not to you.
- Losses must be **measurable in dollars**. Each Insured must contribute premium in accordance with the amount of risk that he or she wishes to transfer.
- **Catastrophic losses** that impact many Insureds simultaneously are excluded in most forms of insurance. If the Martians declare war and invade your neighborhood, your house and car would not be covered.

4 **SOURCES OF UNDERWRITING INFO** – The underwriting process is 100% dependent upon valid information. With it, good underwriting decisions are made; without it, underwriting becomes a nightmare. In most cases, the majority of the important information will be obtained through one of the following sources:

- the application itself
- physical inspections
- consumer credit reports

5 While the first two sources require little explanation, there are several important concerns about consumer credit reports. The credit report is helpful to underwriters as it gives information concerning the applicant's finances, background and reputation.

6 However, the insurance company must adhere to the requirements of the **Fair Credit Reporting Act** while collecting this and any other consumer report. Specifically, the Act requires that the applicant must be **notified in writing** that an investigative report is being ordered. The applicant has the right to question the validity and source of any information retained on file. If the validity of the info is questioned by the consumer, the credit reporting agency must reinvestigate the case. Not only must any inaccurate info in the file itself be corrected, but also any reports transmitted in the last six months containing the error must be retransmitted with the correction.

Federal Law

Advice and Consent

Notes

Right to question 7 years

1 The Act provides many additional rights to the consumer regarding credit information, but the central intent of the law is to give consumers the right to review their credit report and have any incorrect data reviewed and corrected. The Act, furthermore, limits the retention of credit data to **seven years** except for bankruptcy, which can be retained for **ten years**.

The Agent is the company's eyes and ears

2 **FIELD UNDERWRITING** – While the amount of work an Agent must do before submitting an application to his/her company varies from company to company, the Agent is often an important additional source of information. Your responsibilities will certainly include helping the proposed Insured to accurately complete the application. You may also be required to conduct a drive-by or initial inspection of the property. You could be required to photograph the proposed risk or summarize your impression of the exposure involved.

3 Obviously, it is to your benefit to take your field underwriting responsibilities seriously. If you consistently submit unacceptable risks to your company, you waste everyone's time and seriously jeopardize your relationship between you and your clients and between you and your company.

RATING CONCEPTS ‡

4 Insurance premiums are computed by the use of insurance rates. A **rate** is the price for each unit of exposure. For instance, a **rate of $2.00** per square foot would necessitate a premium of $2,000 for a 1,000 square foot premise. A good rating system should generate premiums that reasonably cover the anticipated losses, pay the expenses, allow a reasonable underwriting profit and allow the company to remain competitive. Both competition in the marketplace and regulatory authorities tend to encourage sound rating approaches as the insurance laws of most states prohibit rates that are **excessive**, **inadequate** or **unfairly discriminatory**.

5 While this text is not designed to teach you how to rate an exposure, you should be familiar with the various rating approaches in use in today's marketplace.

A "fire resistant structure" is defined as "concrete and masonry which will resist fire for at least two hours."

6 **Class rates** apply to all members of a large group of rather homogeneous exposures. If listed in a rating manual, the rates are known as **manual rates.** The advantage here is simplicity and the disadvantage is the lack of flexibility. Rarely, if ever, would all of the exposure units be truly homogeneous. Therefore, some risks are being undercharged and others overcharged to create the simplicity of average or **class rates**.

7 **Individual rates** are utilized when there are not enough similar exposures to mathematically justify a class rate. Here, an underwriter might start with a class rate and then modify it by lowering it for positive factors like brick construction and raising it for negative factors like a poorly rated fire department. At the end, we have a rate that is unique to one Insured. This approach is perfectly legal as long as the modifications are consistently applied from one Insured to the next.

8 **Merit rates** are again a modification of class rates based upon the likelihood of losses. Under **schedule rating,** additions or reductions are applied to reflect specific characteristics of the risk - like the use of sprinklers. With **experience rating**, additions or reductions are made to reflect the actual loss experience of the risk in previous years. With **retrospective rating**, the premium for a specific year is adjusted for losses in the same policy year.

9 **Judgment rates** are rates based exclusively or (more likely) partially on the judgment of the underwriter.

Notes

RATE FILINGS

1 In most states the rates charged by insurance companies must be filed with the Department of Insurance. Some states are **prior approval** states, which require that the rate plan be approved before use in that state. Others are **file and use** states which only require that the rates be filed before they are used. Certainly, if the rates are ever **disapproved**, companies may not continue their use.

2 **Rating Bureaus** save Property and Casualty companies millions of dollars in the rate-making and filing process. Even a small P&C company might offer several hundred products to the public in 10 different states. If each company took on the responsibility of creating and filing rating plans for all of its policies in all jurisdictions in which it does business, the costs would be prohibitive.

3 A Rating Bureau calculates rates for specific types of insurance and files them with the states within their jurisdiction. Many rating bureaus also write the policies and endorsements for which the rates were developed. Companies who subscribe to a particular rating bureau may use the rates and state filings of their bureau. They are then only responsible for filing any **deviations** they make to the policy to differentiate their product.

4 By far, the largest rating bureau in the country is the Insurance Services Office (ISO), which makes rates and prepares policies for most property and casualty product lines. The *standard* policies referred to in this text are ISO contracts.

ASSESSING UNDERWRITING ACCURACY

5 Though much of the insurance business is about predicting the future, all we really have to go on is a clear understanding of the past. **Loss and expense ratio** data is used to decide about account renewal, the continuation of agency contracts and whether or not to tighten underwriting standards for a particular product line.

6 Loss and expense ratios can be calculated for a specific account (Ford Motor Company), a line of insurance (personal auto), an agency (the Walker Agency) or an entire company. A **loss ratio** is calculated by dividing the losses for a particular period (say, $400,000) by the total premium received for the same period (say, $1 million). $400,000 ÷ $1 million = 40%. If expenses for the same period were $500,000, then the **expense ratio** is $500,000 ÷ $1 million, or 50%. The **loss and expense ratio** would be $900,000 ÷ $1 million, or 90%. For the company involved, these figures would show an **underwriting profit** of 10%.

INSURANCE DISTRIBUTION SYSTEMS

7 Within the Property and Casualty insurance arena there are four basic ways in which our products are distributed to the public:

- Exclusive Agencies
- Direct Writers
- Direct Response Companies
- Independent Agencies

8 In an **exclusive** or **captive agency** arrangement, the insurance company contracts with an agency (an independent business) to market insurance exclusively for that one company.

1 **Direct writers** are exclusive Agents or employees of the one company that they represent.

2 Companies who utilize **direct response** marketing do not use agencies in the traditional sense. They advertise for customer inquiries, and insurance is then sold by telemarketers who hold whatever licenses are required.

3 **Independent agencies** sell the policies of numerous insurance companies with whom the agency has contracted on a nonexclusive basis.

POWERS OF AGENCY

4 Any of the basic distribution systems of the insurance industry fit nicely under the general laws of agency. The insurance company is the **principal** and it appoints legal representatives - **Agents** - to act in its place. As the Agent, you must clearly understand your powers, duties and responsibilities to avoid confusion, delay and loss to your company, your customers or to yourself.

Principal = Company

Agent = You

5 **THE AGENT** - As an Agent, you are the legal representative of your insurance company. Your legal obligation is to serve your company. However, you are morally obligated to serve the interest of your clients as well. As an Agent, you solicit insurance business on behalf of your insurance company. Your words or acts are binding on the company, because legally you are the company in that you have been authorized to act on its behalf and are subject to certain rules.

- A **captive Agent** has signed an agency contract with a company which demands that the Agent represent that one company exclusively.
- An **independent Agent** has contracted with multiple companies whose agency agreements do not demand exclusivity.

6 NOTE: The laws in some states refer to Agents as *producers* or *intermediaries.* In this text, we will refer to anyone who sells insurance as an Agent.

7 **AGENCY AGREEMENT OR AGENCY CONTRACT** - You and your company will enter into a contract, called an agency agreement, which will tell you specifically what you can and cannot do, and how you will be compensated. For example, the agreement might state that you can bind coverage for personal lines policies, but that you cannot bind coverage for commercial lines policies. Your relationship with your company will be framed by this agreement, so study it carefully.

8 **AN AGENT CAN EXTEND THE COMPANY'S LIABILITY** - Your actions as an Agent may extend the company's liability if you act outside the authority specifically granted to you in the agency agreement. Your words and actions are the company's. If you say or do something beyond the scope of your authority, the company is bound by your actions. For example, if you exceed your authority to bind coverage, your company will be bound by your actions.

9 **AGENT'S KNOWLEDGE** - Your knowledge as an Agent is deemed to be the knowledge of the company because legally you are the company. Therefore, be certain to pass along all of the relevant information given to you by your clients.

10 **SOLICITORS** - Some states license an individual as a solicitor who contracts with an Agent to represent that Agent's product line to the public. Normally, a solicitor is not empowered to obligate the company in any way.

Notes

1 **BROKERS** - The term "broker" is one of the most misused and misunderstood terms in the insurance industry. You will hear broker used in many different ways such as, "He brokered the business to another Agent," or "She is a licensed broker." In each example, the word "broker" has a different meaning. While, in time, you should learn all the different ways that the term can be used in insurance jargon, first learn the legal definition of a broker.

2 You know that, **as an Agent, you are the legal representative of the company**. On the other hand, if you are an insurance broker, your legal responsibility is just the opposite. **As a broker, you are the legal representative of the client.** A broker determines the client's needs and then seeks to find the best product offered on the market by the numerous insurance companies that provide such products. As a broker, your legal obligation is to your client, not to the companies providing the products.

3 As an Agent you have an agency agreement with the company that you represent. Legally, you can represent more than one company, but for each company that you represent, you will have a separate agency agreement. On the other hand, as a broker, *you would not have an agency agreement* with any company. There is a significant legal difference. As a broker, your words and actions are not legally binding on the company.

4 Because of the confusing terms and the difficulty in establishing legal responsibility, there is currently a trend in most states to no longer issue brokers licenses.

5 **AGENT AUTHORITY** - As we have discussed, your authority as an Agent is specifically stated in your Agency Agreement. As we have mentioned, your actions outside this agreement can extend your company's liability. As an Agent, you have three types of power or authority. They are Expressed, Implied and Apparent.

- **Express Authority** - Express Authority is *specifically granted* to you in your Agency Agreement, such as the power to bind coverage. You must strive to operate within the scope of your Express Authority.

- **Implied Authority** - The Agency Agreement cannot cover every last detail of your duties. Implied Authority covers the powers that are not specifically given to you in your Agency Agreement, but *they are the powers that you can imply or assume that you must have* in order to do your job. For example, physical inspections are a necessary prerequisite to many property and casualty policies. Therefore, you can imply that you have the authority to schedule physical inspections.

- **Apparent Authority** - The two types of authority discussed above concern the relationship between you and your company. Apparent Authority concerns the relationship between you, *your customers,* and your company. As long as you act within your contractual powers (your Agency Agreement), you will have no problem. But, if you should say or do something you are not authorized to do, and the public could logically assume that an insurance Agent might have such powers, then your company will be bound by your actions. Even though you did not have the authority to bind coverage on a commercial risk, your company could be liable for the risk because your word is the company's word. The company would, however, have a valid cause of action against you. You can avoid these problems by operating within the scope of your Agency Agreement.

Conclusion

1 This chapter revolves around you, the Agent. In it, you learned about the kind of company organization for which you work. We examined the policies you offer from the viewpoint of contract law, and you were given a brief introduction to underwriting. Finally, you were shown what powers you have and don't have as an Agent.

Types of Companies

- **Lloyds Associations** – Individuals grouped in syndicates acting as companies. The individuals comprising the syndicates are personally liable for losses.
- **Stock Company** – Run for the benefit of stockholders, no dividend to policyowners.
- **Mutual Company** – No stockholders, run for the benefit of policyowners, can pay a policy dividend to policyowners.
- **Reciprocal** – Operates like a mutual, managed by an attorney-in-fact.
- **Fraternals** – Operates like a mutual, but you must join the club to buy the policy.
- **Risk Retention Groups** – Self insurance on a group basis.

Classifying Companies

By Origin
- **Domestic...** formed in this state
- **Foreign...** formed in another state
- **Alien...** formed in another country

By Authority
- **Authorized or Admitted...** approved to do business in this state
- **Unauthorized or Nonadmitted...** not approved to do business in this state. . . but the policies can be sold in this state under certain conditions by a **Surplus Lines** Agent

By Financial Soundness
- A+... Good
- F... Awful

Contract Law

2 To form a legal contract there must be an **offer** and an **acceptance**. There must be an exchange of **consideration**. A proposed Insured's consideration is payment of the premium and the statements made in the application. The company's consideration is the promises contained in the policy. The contract must be formed between **legally competent parties** and it must serve a **legal purpose**.

Notes

1 Statements in the application that must be the absolute truth are **warranties**. Statements that must be true to the best of your knowledge are **representations**. A **misrepresentation** is a lie, and a **concealment** is the failure to disclose the whole truth.

2 A **binder** is used to provide immediate, temporary protection. It may be written or oral. There is no guarantee that a policy will be written simply because a binder was issued.

3 Insurance contracts are **personal** in nature; we are insuring your **interest in the property**, not the property itself. These contracts are **conditional** – if a loss occurs, then we will pay. Insurance policies are **unilateral**. . . only one entity makes an enforceable promise – the company. They are also **aleatory**; there is not, necessarily, an equal exchange of value. And, insurance policies are **contracts of adhesion** . . . the company wrote it, they're stuck with it.

4 The four parts of the policy include: the **Declarations**, the **Insuring Clause**, the **Conditions**, and the **Exclusions**.

5 **Underwriting** is the process of selecting and classifying risk. **Rating** is the process of pricing an acceptable risk.

6 An **Agent** is the legal representative of the company. The Agent's authority, which is spelled out in the **Agency Agreement**, is called **Express Authority**. Powers not spelled out in the agreement but presumed therein are called **Implied Authority**. The authority the public believes an Agent possesses is known as **Apparent Authority**. A **broker** is the legal representative of the client. A **solicitor** is the legal representative of an Agent. Since brokers and solicitors are not legal representatives of the company, they could not legally bind the company.

Notes

RISK MANAGEMENT ‡

1 In recent years, it has become fashionable to apply the term Risk Management to what was once called Insurance Management. In many circles, this is only a matter of semantics. However, the trend is for agencies to become true Risk Managers for their clients.

2 True Risk Management is not simply obtaining the broadest and least expensive coverage for the premium dollar. Risk Management seeks to protect the assets and income of the household or business it is serving. Insurance is viewed simply as one of many approaches for minimizing risks that the client faces.

3 The Risk Management process involves four specific steps:

- Identification and evaluation of the risks
- Consideration of alternatives to manage these risks
- Choosing the best alternative and implementing
- Evaluating and reviewing

4 In most households and in most businesses, many risks are obvious while others are easily overlooked. Therefore, most Risk Managers use some systematic approach in the task of risk identifications. Commonly used tools could include physical inspection, questionnaires, checklists and analysis of financial statements.

5 In evaluating the risks uncovered, there must be some measurement of the potential severity of the loss as well as the likelihood that the loss might occur. Many Risk Managers then place the risks identified into one of three piles:

- Those that would bankrupt the household or the business
- Those that would require substantial borrowing to avoid bankruptcy
- Those whose losses could be offset with existing income or assets.

6 The alternatives for addressing the subject risks boil down to four - avoidance, reduction, retention and transfer. However, the specific form that each of those devices can assume vary greatly. A homeowner might **avoid risk** by choosing not to own a pit bull or a trampoline. A business might **reduce risk** with a sprinkler system or a burglar alarm. **Risk transfer** could involve insurance or the subcontracting of certain operations. In making a decision, the Risk Manager must evaluate the benefits and the costs of each alternative.

7 Once the decision is made and implemented, monitoring the Risk Management program is absolutely critical. Invariably, risks will be overlooked or mistakes will be made in conducting the program. Careful monitoring may identify these problems before they become too costly. Furthermore, change is inevitable. New concerns arise and old ones diminish. Resources may grow or shrink, and new policies or new technology may immerge. Risk Management is a dynamic process not a static one.

Notes

Insurance Agent's Errors and Omissions Loss Prevention ‡

One of an insurance agency's biggest exposure to loss is the potential lawsuit that
1 could result from an Agent's error or omission. An Agent owes a duty to perform as a professional insurance Agent to both their customer and their principal, the insurer. Customers of an insurance Agent expect the Agent to give proper risk management/insurance advice to the customer. The customer also expects the Agent to follow the customer's instructions, place the customer's order for policies, endorsements, and provide other services promised by the Agent. The Agent's principal, the insurer, also has expectations of the Agent. The insurer expects the Agent to be the eyes and the ears of the insurer. The Agent has a duty to provide the insurer with complete, honest, non-biased information about the risks that the Agent has placed with the insurer.

Sadly, there are many situations where an Agent fails to meet their duty owed to
2 their customer and to their principal, the insurer. Agents can breach the duty owed to their customers in many ways. Some of the major areas of customer and insurer errors and omissions claims exposure are misrepresentations; delays in processing coverage; cancellations errors; agency agreement violations; policy change errors; and inadequate coverage claims. When an agency is named in an errors and omissions lawsuit, it is likely that the agency personnel involved in the transaction will also be named in the suit.

There are many positive steps that an agency can take to eliminate 90% of their
3 errors and omissions claims exposure. Every agency should have **policies and procedures** in place for every type of transaction handled by the agency. These **policies and procedures** should be **communicated to everyone** in the operation. And **everyone** in the operations should follow the **same policies and procedures.** Probably the single most important step that an agency can take is to get everyone in the habit of **documenting all transactions, conversations, requests . . . bottom line - DOCUMENT, DOCUMENT, DOCUMENT!** Many times an Agent does everything the right way but fails to write it down. With no evidence, other than the Agent's memory, the E&O claim is almost a sure loser for the Agent.

An agency that has established policies and procedures in place that are followed
4 by everyone in the operation has gone a long way to control error and omissions losses. Even the best run agency cannot totally eliminate the potential errors and omissions claims exposure and so a good risk management tool is to purchase Insurance Agent's Errors and Omission coverage.

CHAPTERS 1 & 2
KEY TERMS & CONTRACT LAW

1. Which of the following statements about insurable interest is NOT true?

   (A) The seller of a home still has insurable interest in the home for up to 30 days after the deed has been transferred.
   (B) A lending institution has an insurable interest in any properties on which it holds mortgages.
   (C) A repairman has insurable interest in the equipment he has serviced until the repair bill has been paid.
   (D) A tenant has an insurable interest in any improvements he's made to a building he rents.

2. The purpose of insurance is to accomplish which of the following?

   (A) Eliminate risk.
   (B) Mitigate risk.
   (C) Avoid risk.
   (D) Transfer risk.

3. An insurance contract in which the applicant cannot bargain for terms, rates or benefits, and whose language is drafted completely by the insurance company is referred to as a(n)

   (A) Unilateral contract.
   (B) Contract of Adhesion.
   (C) Aleatory contract.
   (D) Executory contract.

4. To be binding, a contract between two parties must include all of the following EXCEPT a(n)

   (A) Consideration.
   (B) Legal purpose.
   (C) Written instrument.
   (D) Offer and acceptance.

CHAPTERS 1&2 • KEY TERMS & CONTRACT LAW QUIZ

5. A customer requests immediate coverage on a boat she just purchased. The Producer gives the customer an oral binder over the phone. Coverage commences

   (A) when the policy is delivered to the customer.
   (B) when the written binder is received by the customer.
   (C) when the initial premium is received by the Producer.
   (D) at the end of the initial conversation.

6. The principle under which the purchaser of insurance must be in a position to lose something of value is called

   (A) Indemnification.
   (B) Consideration.
   (C) Subrogation.
   (D) Insurable interest.

7. All of the following statements about concealment are true EXCEPT that

   (A) Concealment is the failure to disclose a material fact.
   (B) Concealment is an intentional misstatement on an application.
   (C) Concealment must be intentional to affect the policy.
   (D) Concealment can be grounds for voiding the policy contract.

8. A binder is

   (A) The same as a policy.
   (B) A written document.
   (C) A substitute for an insurance policy.
   (D) An interim agreement between the parties.

9. The Fair Credit Reporting Act requires that

   (A) The applicant cannot be advised of the name and address of the reporting agency.
   (B) The insurance company, if requested, must provide the Federal Trade Commission with a list of applicants rejected during the previous calendar year and the reasons for such actions.
   (C) No outside reporting agencies may be used to collect confidential information.
   (D) The applicant for insurance must be advised that a consumer report may be requested.

10. The insurer's promises to the insured would be found in/on the

    (A) Declarations page.
    (B) Provisions section.
    (C) Insuring clause.
    (D) Conditions section.

11. Which of the following is the insurance company's consideration in a property and casualty contract?

    (A) The oral or written binder.
    (B) The policy itself.
    (C) The promises contained in the policy.
    (D) The payment of a claim under the policy.

Questions 12 - 14 refer to the following terms. You may use a term once, more than once, or not at all.

(A) Representation
(B) Warranty
(C) Misrepresentation
(D) Concealment

12. Jack Davis applies for insurance coverage on his factory. Most of the statements Jack makes on the application are considered to be a

    (A) (B) (C) (D)

13. Jack also tells the Producer that he has a sprinkler system in the factory and affirms that it is always operable. Jack's statement is a

    (A) (B) (C) (D)

14. Although Jack responds truthfully to all questions asked by the Producer over the telephone, he does not inform the Producer that the factory next door is on fire. If Jack presented a fire claim on his factory later that same day, the company would probably deny the claim on the basis of Jack's

    (A) (B) (C) (D)

CHAPTERS 1&2 • KEY TERMS & CONTRACT LAW QUIZ

15. A written binder may terminate on all of the following dates EXCEPT

    (A) Its expiration date.
    (B) The policy issue date.
    (C) The policy application date.
    (D) The day after notification is received that the company has cancelled the binder.

16. Which of the following statements is true about the principle of indemnity?

    (A) It encourages the insured to purchase policies with face values larger than the value of the protected property.
    (B) It states that the insured should not profit from a loss.
    (C) It relieves the insurance company from paying for property losses caused by the insured.
    (D) It gives the insured the right to collect the full replacement cost for every property loss.

17. All of the following are true concerning a Stock Company EXCEPT

    (A) It is owned by policyowners.
    (B) It is owned by shareholders.
    (C) It pays dividends to stockholders.
    (D) It is a non-participating company.

18. The dollar limits for a specific coverage are found in the

    (A) Policy conditions.
    (B) Declarations.
    (C) Provisions section.
    (D) Insurance company's rate manual.

19. Which of the following is a synonym for "indirect loss"?

    (A) Consequential loss
    (B) Total loss
    (C) Partial loss
    (D) Secondary loss

END

QUIZ ANSWERS & EXPLANATIONS ON NEXT PAGE

CHAPTERS 1 & 2
KEY TERMS & CONTRACT LAW
QUIZ ANSWER KEY

1. A. Insurable interest is defined as a financial interest. There would be no insurable interest in property which has been transferred. Remember that insurable interest is a broader concept than ownership, and includes a lien interest (B&C) or a use interest (D).

2. D. Insurance does not eliminate or lessen (mitigate) risk, it spreads the risk around (transfers).

3. B. Because the insured is handed the policy (contract) on a take it or leave it basis, all ambiguities are decided against the company, and in favor of the insured.
   NOTE: Adhesion - one author. Unilateral - one promissor.

4. C. Oral agreements are as binding as written ones (within certain limitations). The other answers are three of the five essential elements of a contract.

5. D. The coverage begins as soon as the negotiations are complete (the end of the conversation). NOTE: It is good practice, however not mandatory, to follow up with a written binder.

6. D. Insurable interest is the insured's financial interest in the covered property; indemnification is making the insured whole after a loss occurs.

7. B. Concealment is the intentional failure to disclose a material fact, which can affect coverage. An intentional misstatement of a fact on the application is a misrepresentation (which must also be material to affect coverage).

8. D. A binder, whether written or oral, is an agreement which acts as a bridge to effect coverage prior to the issuance of a policy. NOTE: The binder does not replace the need for the policy, nor does it mean that the company must issue the policy.

9. D. Not only must the applicant be notified that a credit report will be sought, but the applicant must also give permission to obtain the report. These reports are always obtained through outside agencies, and the agency is identified so that the inaccuracies can be challenged.

CHAPTERS 1&2
KEY TERMS & CONTRACT LAW QUIZ ANSWER KEY

10. C. The Insuring Clause is the heart of every policy; it contains the company's promises (consideration).

11. C. The Company's promises are the value, which are exchanged for the premium and the statements on the application, and are found in the Insuring Clause.

12. A. The standard of truth required for most statements on the application is a subjective one, "true to the best knowledge and belief of the applicant."

13. B. Statements on the application regarding alarms and sprinkler systems are an exception to the basic rule and require the absolute truth.

14. D. The intentional failure to disclose a material (important) fact is concealment.

15. C. The very purpose of the binder is to act a "bridge" during the application process.

16. B. The principle of indemnity states the policy will not pay more than the actual amount of the loss, in other words the purpose of insurance is to "make whole not rich." NOTE: Indemnity does not always mean replacement cost, which is only one of many methods of valuation.

17. A. Stock companies are owned and run for the benefit of the stockholders. Policyholders do not participate in the success of a stock company.

18. B. All information that applies to a particular policy, insured, or risk is found in the declarations.

19. A. A "direct" loss is damage to the property itself. An "indirect" loss is the "loss of use" that is the consequence of the "direct" loss.

BASICS OF TWO PARTY COVERAGE

3

PROPERTY ROOTS

At one time in the long history of the human species it was really true that if you
1 wanted something done, you did it yourself. If you wanted to eat, you hunted or planted crops. If you wanted shelter, you found a cave or built a cabin. Modern civilization began when some amongst us developed *excess capacity*. For instance, suppose I was a truly fantastic farmer with an abundance of land. Year after year I could regularly produce more food than my family could consume. Now, further suppose that you can't even grow dandelions, but you are a great salesman. Between the talents of us both we could create the seventeenth century version of a Farmer's Market. In so doing, you have been relieved of the responsibility of growing food to feed your family.

One immediate result of our
2 alliance is that you no longer need to live on a farm. In fact, it is to your advantage to put your seventeenth century Kroger's in the middle of the biggest population you can find – a city or town populated by other non-farmers like yourself. Even in a country as young as the United States, major cities like New York, Boston and Philadelphia had begun to grow exponentially by the early 1700's. However, the growth of the cities magnified the effects of problems like fire. When we were all farmers, a fire at my house did not affect you. But if we are both Philadelphia merchants with our businesses next door to one another, my fire could definitely jeopardize your business or your home and your future.

"... but, there's no evidence that Mrs. O'Leary named you as a beneficiary."

FIRE INSURANCE COMPANIES

1 While most of us learned in elementary school that Ben Franklin established several fire departments in the 1730's, we were not taught that in 1752 he also helped to found one of the first fire insurance companies in North America. People bought fire insurance (as Property insurance was called in those days) for one of two reasons:

- They wanted to buy
- They had to buy

2 The first reason is self-evident. If Joe's great-great-great grandfather owned a thriving restaurant in the 1750's, his entire livelihood was probably tied up in that business. If he was in the middle of a big city, surrounded by several hundred thousand people in wooden structures lit by candlelight and heated by fireplaces, he would not have to be a rocket scientist to realize that his business and his home are at risk. The fact that the local fire department is a bucket brigade augmented by a horse-drawn fire truck only helps to further dramatize the risk.

3 However, there are always a few hardheads who don't recognize that they need to insure their property but are placed in situations where they must do so. If great grandpa Joe wanted to expand his restaurant or buy a new house, he might seek money from an investor or a bank. And even in the 1700's, he would have been no more successful at borrowing money on uninsured property then you and I would be today. In many respects the growth of commerce and industry that has led to the standard of living that we enjoy today can be attributed to the mechanism of insurance. Providing capital for expansion is already a risky business. The additional risk of fire rendering the borrower unable to repay his debt could easily nullify the entire transaction. Without fire insurance, the growth of modern civilization could have been slowed to a snail's pace.

PROPERTY RULED THE ROOST

4 While today's purchasers of either commercial lines or personal lines insurance may well be focused on the Casualty coverages, for at least 200 years Property insurance was the major interest of most buyers... and fire was the principal peril of most Property policies. For the first 100 years, most Property companies were small, local arrangements much like the one Ben Franklin started, and the policy issued by one company bore little resemblance to those issued by any other. This changed dramatically following the near disastrous New York City Fire of 1835. Though not as well known by most Americans as the Great Chicago Fire (mostly because the New York fire lacked Ms. O'Leary, the cow, the lantern and the song), the New York fire had a much greater impact on the Property insurance business. What we learned is fairly obvious in retrospect. If a community is insured through one company, and if that company only insures one community, both the company and the community are in deep soot if half the town burns to the ground. For the insurance mechanism to work properly, the risks of any one company must be spread over many cities and towns, and the collective risk of any one community must be spread throughout hundreds of companies.

Notes

CALLING FOR STANDARDIZATION

1 By the 1850's, it was not unusual for dozens of fire insurance companies to be selling policies in one community. As a result, Great Grandpa Joe could be insured by Flamethrower Mutual one year and by Firecracker State the next. Since the two policies probably did not at all resemble one another, a great deal of pressure was placed on property carriers by the public, the courts and even the more thoughtful corners of the industry itself to standardize the Property Insurance Contract.

2 A rather famous court case (Delancy v. Rockingham Farmers Mutual) in 1873 was the straw that broke the camel's back. In examining what must have been a real gem of a policy, the court had this to say:

3 > *This compound (meaning the policy), if read by an ordinary man, would be an inexplicable riddle, a mere flood of darkness and confusion...should some extremely eccentric person attempt to examine the involved and intricate net in which he was to be entangled, he would find that it is printed in such small type and in lines so long and so crowded as to make the perusal of the document physically difficult, painful and possibly injurious.*

4 There were several early attempts at standardization. The State of Massachusetts proposed a standard policy form in 1873 and this was followed by the State of New York in 1887 and again in 1918. While the early twentieth century policies did not contain the night and day differences of their predecessors, it was not until the New York Standard Fire Policy of 1943 was approved for use in practically all jurisdictions that we found a policy that met with the approval of most consumers, companies and state regulating agencies.

THE STANDARD FIRE POLICY (SFP)

5 Since 1943, the 165 contract lines of the Standard Fire Policy have governed the Property (and to an extent) the Casualty coverages contained in policies issued in this country. While the conditions of the modern Businessowner's Policy or the modern Homeowners Policy may be more generous, the basic, guiding principles of these policies regarding concealment, exclusions, written endorsements, requirements in the event of a loss, appraisal, subrogation, and much, much more all stem from the Standard Fire Policy.

... gee whiz, it only took us a century and a half

6 Until the mid 1980's, the influence of the Standard Fire Policy was obvious. Most states required that the Standard Fire Policy be a part of every policy that contained property insurance – which was almost every contract. If a policyowner was so inclined, he or she could peel back all the pages of the contract and find, at the bottom of the stack, a Standard Fire Policy.

Notes

1 In one sense the Standard Fire Policy was a fantastically flexible contract. It could be used to insure almost any property in which you had the necessary insurable interest. You could use this contract to insure a house, a commercial building, or the property contained in either. It could fit the needs of a homeowner, the landlord, the tenant, the business owner who owns his building or the business owner who leases his premises. The genius of this policy was that it was general enough in context to apply to almost all Property insurance needs. However, this same attribute was also its greatest weakness. The needs of the consuming public went far beyond the limited definitions and coverages of the Standard Fire Policy. This contract was always sold with endorsements used to *customize* it to fit the needs of a particular Insured. If you insured a business, you might purchase a fire policy with a General Property Building and Contents form attached. If you were a homeowner, you bought it with a Dwelling form or Homeowners form attached.

USING THE STRUCTURE OF THE STANDARD FIRE POLICY AS AN EXAMPLE

2 The Standard Fire Policy is a two page document composed of four main parts **(DICE)**:

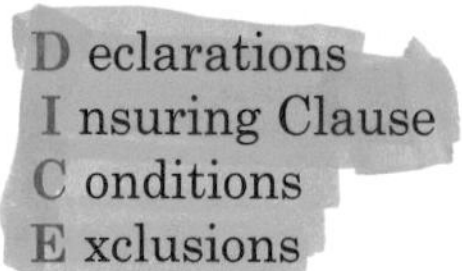

DECLARATIONS

3 The top two-thirds of page one of the Standard Fire Policy is called the Declarations section. It is the **Who, What, When, Where, Which and How Much** of the policy. It is the only section of the policy containing fill-in-the-blanks. Your job as the Agent is to fill in the blanks.

"W's"

THE INSURING CLAUSE

4 The Insuring Clause is the heart of any property insurance policy. It is a **statement by the insurance company that summarizes the promises contained in the policy**, the coverages provided and the conditions and limitations of the coverage in general terms. The Insuring Clause contains the following statements:

promises

- *For the premium listed above (in the Declarations section), the company listed above,*
- *for the policy period listed above,*
- *starting at 12:01 p.m. Standard Time at the location of the property on the date listed above,*
- *insures the property listed above,*
- *to the amount not exceeding the amount listed above,*
- *insures the Named Insured(s) listed above,*

every other policy starts at 12:01 a.m.

- *or their legal representatives (such as their executors, administrators, or guardians),*
- *up to the Actual Cash Value (ACV) of the property at the time of the loss,*
- *but not exceeding the amount that it would cost the company to repair or replace the property with material of a similar kind and quality,*
- *and without regard to any increases in costs of repair or reconstruction as the result of any building ordinances that govern construction or repair,*
- *and without regard for the indirect loss of the interruption of business,*
- *nor in any event for more than the insurable interest of the Insured,*
- *does insure the property against the perils of*
    - *Fire*
    - *Lightning*
    - *Removal*

"whew, that's one sentence"

- *at the location specified above (in the Declarations), or if salvaged from its normal place following a peril, for up to* ***five days*** *at its new storage place.*

1 Notice that the Standard Fire Policy was only intended for property at a fixed location. This is true for most property contracts today – especially in commercial lines.

2 **Assignment** – The next sentence states that the Named Insured cannot assign the policy to another party without the written consent of the insurance company.

The last sentence in the Insuring Clause states that other provisions, conditions,
3 additions or endorsements can be added to the Standard Fire Policy in writing and
made part of the contract.

Summary of the Insuring Clause: The Insuring Clause is a statement made by
4 the insurance company to the Insured which contains the promise that the insurance company will insure the designated property against the designated perils
subject to all the provisions, conditions, extensions, limitations, endorsements and
exclusions contained in the rest of the policy.

ground rules

CONDITIONS

Page two of the Standard Fire Policy contains the policy **Conditions**. The Condi-
5 tions spell out the **terms and stipulations** of the agreement such as cancellation
of the policy, the mortgagee's rights, how and when claims will be paid and the
policyowner's right to sue.

EXCLUSIONS

6 No insurance policy covers everything. There are always some losses that will not be covered – called Exclusions.

STANDARD FIRE INSURANCE POLICY

Standard Fire Insurance Policy for Alabama, Alaska, Arizona, Arkansas, Colorado, Connecticut, Delaware, District of Columbia, Florida, Georgia, Hawaii, Idaho, Illinois, Indiana, Iowa, Kansas, Kentucky, Louisiana, Maryland, Michigan, Mississippi, Missouri, Montana, Nebraska, Nevada, New Hampshire, New Jersey, New Mexico, New York, North Carolina, North Dakota, Ohio, Oklahoma, Oregon, Pennsylvania, Rhode Island, South Carolina, South Dakota, Tennessee, Utah, Vermont, Virginia, Washington, West Virginia, Wisconsin and Wyoming.

No.

RENEWAL OF NUMBER

CAPITAL STOCK COMPANY

AUTHENTIC

SPACE FOR COMPANY NAME, INSIGNIA, AND LOCATION

Insured's Name and Mailing Address

NERO FIDDLER
711 Appian Way
Rome, New York 13440

SPACE FOR PRODUCER'S NAME AND MAILING ADDRESS

July 1, 1969	July 1, 1970	1
Inception (Mo. Day Yr.)	Expiration (Mo. Day Yr.)	Years

It is important that the written portions of all policies covering the same property read exactly alike. If they do not, they should be made uniform at once.

INSURANCE IS PROVIDED AGAINST ONLY THOSE PERILS AND FOR ONLY THOSE COVERAGES INDICATED BELOW BY A PREMIUM CHARGE AND AGAINST OTHER PERILS AND FOR OTHER COVERAGES ONLY WHEN ENDORSED HEREON OR ADDED HERETO.

AMOUNT	RATE	PREPAID TERM PREMIUM DUE AT INCEPTION	ANNUAL PAYMENT DUE UNDER DEF. PREM. PAY. PLAN	PERIL(S) Insured Against and Coverage(s) Provided (Insert Name of Each)
$ 37,500	$ .22 Dwg; $.30 Conts	$ 92.50	$	FIRE AND LIGHTNING
xxxxxxx	$ .13	$ 48.75	$	EXTENDED COVERAGE
	$	$	$	
	$	$	$	
$ 141. TOTAL PREMIUM FOR POLICY TERM UNDER D. P. P. P.	TOTAL(S)	$141.25	$	

Item No.	Amount Fire or Fire and Extended Coverage, or Other Peril	Per Cent of Co-Insurance Applicable	DESCRIPTION AND LOCATION OF PROPERTY COVERED Show construction, type of roof and occupancy of building(s) covered or containing the property covered. If occupied as a dwelling state number of families.
1. -	$ 25,000.	-	Brick, tile roof, two family dwelling, situate 711 Appian Way, Rome New York;
	12,500.		Contents usual to Dwelling described above

Subject to Form No(s). 49D (1-64) INSERT FORM NUMBER(S) AND EDITION DATE(S) **attached hereto.**

Mortgage Clause: Subject to the provisions of the mortgage clause attached hereto, loss, if any, on building items, shall be payable to:

INSERT NAME(S) OF MORTGAGEE(S) AND MAILING ADDRESS(ES)

Augustus Savings and Loan Association, Pontine Marshes, Rome, N.Y.

Agency at

Countersignature Date

________________________ Agent

IN CONSIDERATION OF THE PROVISIONS AND STIPULATIONS HEREIN OR ADDED HERETO AND OF the premium above specified, this Company, for the term of *years specified above* from *inception date shown above* At Noon (Standard Time) to *expiration date shown above* At Noon (Standard Time) at location of property involved, to an amount not exceeding the amount(s) above specified, does insure *the insured named above* and legal representatives, to the extent of the actual cash value of the property at the time of loss, but not exceeding the amount which it would cost to repair or replace the property with material of like kind and quality within a reasonable time after such loss, without allowance for any increased cost of repair or reconstruction by reason of any ordinance or law regulating construction or repair, and without compensation for loss resulting from interruption of business or manufacture, nor in any event for more than the interest of the insured, against all **DIRECT LOSS BY FIRE, LIGHTNING AND BY REMOVAL FROM PREMISES ENDANGERED BY THE PERILS INSURED AGAINST IN THIS POLICY, EXCEPT AS HEREINAFTER PROVIDED,** to the property described herein while located or contained as described in this policy, or pro rata for five days at each proper place to which any of the property shall necessarily be removed for preservation from the perils insured against in this policy, but not elsewhere.

Assignment of this policy shall not be valid except with the written consent of this Company.

This policy is made and accepted subject to the foregoing provisions and stipulations and those hereinafter stated, which are hereby made a part of this policy, together with such other provisions, stipulations and agreements as may be added hereto, as provided in this policy.

Concealment, fraud. This entire policy shall be void if, whether before or after a loss, the insured has wilfully concealed or misrepresented any material fact or circumstance concerning this insurance or the subject thereof, or the interest of the insured therein, or in case of any fraud or false swearing by the insured relating thereto.

Uninsurable and excepted property. This policy shall not cover accounts, bills, currency, deeds, evidences of debt, money or securities; nor, unless specifically named hereon in writing, bullion or manuscripts.

Perils not included. This Company shall not be liable for loss by fire or other perils insured against in this policy caused, directly or indirectly, by: (a) enemy attack by armed forces, including action taken by military, naval or air forces in resisting an actual or an immediately impending enemy attack; (b) invasion; (c) insurrection; (d) rebellion; (e) revolution; (f) civil war; (g) usurped power; (h) order of any civil authority except acts of destruction at the time of and for the purpose of preventing the spread of fire, provided that such fire did not originate from any of the perils excluded by this policy; (i) neglect of the insured to use all reasonable means to save and preserve the property at and after a loss, or when the property is endangered by fire in neighboring premises; (j) nor shall this Company be liable for loss by theft.

Other Insurance. Other insurance may be prohibited or the amount of insurance may be limited by endorsement attached hereto.

Conditions suspending or restricting insurance. Unless otherwise provided in writing added hereto this Company shall not be liable for loss occurring
(a) while the hazard is increased by any means within the control or knowledge of the insured; or
(b) while a described building, whether intended for occupancy by owner or tenant, is vacant or unoccupied beyond a period of sixty consecutive days; or
(c) as a result of explosion or riot, unless fire ensue, and in that event for loss by fire only.

Other perils or subjects. Any other peril to be insured against or subject of insurance to be covered in this policy shall be by endorsement in writing hereon or added hereto.

Added provisions. The extent of the application of insurance under this policy and of the contribution to be made by this Company in case of loss, and any other provision or agreement not inconsistent with the provisions of this policy, may be provided for in writing added hereto, but no provision may be waived except such as by the terms of this policy is subject to change.

Waiver provisions. No permission affecting this insurance shall exist, or waiver of any provision be valid, unless granted herein or expressed in writing added hereto. No provision, stipulation or forfeiture shall be held to be waived by any requirement or proceeding on the part of this Company relating to appraisal or to any examination provided for herein.

Cancellation of policy. This policy shall be cancelled at any time at the request of the insured, in which case this Company shall, upon demand and surrender of this policy, refund the excess of paid premium above the customary short rates for the expired time. This policy may be cancelled at any time by this Company by giving to the insured a five days' written notice of cancellation with or without tender of the excess of paid premium above the pro rata premium for the expired time, which excess, if not tendered, shall be refunded on demand. Notice of cancellation shall state that said excess premium (if not tendered) will be refunded on demand.

Mortgagee interests and obligations. If loss hereunder is made payable, in whole or in part, to a designated mortgagee not named herein as the insured, such interest in this policy may be cancelled by giving to such mortgagee a ten days' written notice of cancellation.
If the insured fails to render proof of loss such mortgagee, upon notice, shall render proof of loss in the form herein specified within sixty (60) days thereafter and shall be subject to the provisions hereof relating to appraisal and time of payment and of bringing suit. If this Company shall claim that no liability existed as to the mortgagor or owner, it shall, to the extent of payment of loss to the mortgagee, be subrogated to all the mortgagee's rights of recovery, but without impairing mortgagee's right to sue; or it may pay off the mortgage debt and require an assignment thereof and of the mortgage. Other provisions relating to the interests and obligations of such mortgagee may be added hereto by agreement in writing.

Pro rata liability. This Company shall not be liable for a greater proportion of any loss than the amount hereby insured shall bear to the whole insurance covering the property against the peril involved, whether collectible or not.

Requirements in case loss occurs. The insured shall give Immediate written notice to this Company of any loss, protect the property from further damage, forthwith separate the damaged and undamaged personal property, put it in the best possible order, furnish a complete inventory of the destroyed, damaged and undamaged property, showing in detail quantities, costs, actual cash value and amount of loss claimed; **and within sixty days after the loss, unless such time is extended in writing by this Company, the insured shall render to this Company a proof of loss,** signed and sworn to by the insured, stating the knowledge and belief of the insured as to the following: the time and origin of the loss, the interest of the insured and of all others in the property, the actual cash value of each item thereof and the amount of loss thereto, all encumbrances thereon, all other contracts of insurance, whether valid or not, covering any of said property, any changes in the title, use, occupation, location, possession or exposures of said property since the issuing of this policy, by whom and for what purpose any building herein described and the several parts thereof were occupied at the time of loss and whether or not it then stood on leased ground, and shall furnish a copy of all the descriptions and schedules in all policies and, if required, verified plans and specifications of any building, fixtures or machinery destroyed or damaged. The insured, as often as may be reasonably required, shall exhibit to any person designated by this Company all that remains of any property herein described, and submit to examinations under oath by any person named by this Company, and subscribe the same; and, as often as may be reasonably required, shall produce for examination all books of account. bills, invoices and other vouchers, or certified copies thereof if originals be lost, at such reasonable time and place as may be designated by this Company or its representative, and shall permit extracts and copies thereof to be made.

Appraisal. In case the insured and this Company shall fail to agree as to the actual cash value or the amount of loss, then, on the written demand of either, each shall select a competent and disinterested appraiser and notify the other of the appraiser selected within twenty days of such demand. The appraisers shall first select a competent and disinterested umpire; and failing for fifteen days to agree upon such umpire, then, on request of the insured or this Company, such umpire shall be selected by a judge of a court of record in the state in which the property covered is located. The appraisers shall then appraise the loss, stating separately actual cash value and loss to each item; and, failing to agree, shall submit their differences, only, to the umpire. An award in writing, so itemized, of any two when filed with this Company shall determine the amount of actual cash value and loss. Each appraiser shall be paid by the party selecting him and the expenses of appraisal and umpire shall be paid by the parties equally.

Company's options. It shall be optional with this Company to take all, or any part, of the property at the agreed or appraised value, and also to repair, rebuild or replace the property destroyed or damaged with other of like kind and quality within a reasonable time, on giving notice of its intention so to do within thirty days after the receipt of the proof of loss herein required.

Abandonment. There can be no abandonment to this Company of any property.

When loss payable. The amount of loss for which this Company may be liable shall be payable sixty days after proof of loss, as herein provided, is received by this Company and ascertainment of the loss is made either by agreement between the insured and this Company expressed in writing or by the filing with this Company of an award as herein provided.

Suit. No suit or action on this policy for the recovery of any claim shall be sustainable in any court of law or equity unless all the requirements of this policy shall have been complied with, and unless commenced within twelve months next after inception of the loss.

Subrogation. This Company may require from the insured an assignment of all right of recovery against any party for loss to the extent that payment therefor is made by this Company.

IN WITNESS WHEREOF, this Company has executed and attested these presents; but this policy shall not be valid unless countersigned by the duly authorized Agent of this Company at the agency hereinbefore mentioned.

Notes

DRAMATIC CHANGES

1 By the late 1970's in the personal lines arena and by the mid 1980's in commercial lines, change began to occur. No longer did it make sense to issue a very narrow coverage contract with a dozen or more liberalizing endorsements. It seemed more user friendly to write a Homeowner's Policy for homeowners, a Businessowner's Policy for a business and so on. However, even though most states do not require a Standard Fire Policy at the bottom of the stack any longer, the influence of the Fire policy is visible on every sheet of paper still found in the stack. The Standard Fire Policy may be a dinosaur in the sense that you may never sell one, but practically everything you learn about this contract will surface again and again in your study of modern Commercial Property contracts and Homeowners policies.

PROPERTY FORMAT

2 In protecting an Insured's property, there are two questions which must be answered:

1. **What property do you want to insure?**
2. **From what causes of loss do you want to insure it?**

What's covered
What's it covered from

3 The answers to these two questions can allow us to insure a modest home or a business as big and complex as IBM.

WHAT?

4 **BUILDING AND CONTENTS** – In a general sense, Property policies are designed to insure buildings (and other structures) as well as the contents of those buildings at a fixed location. It is also possible to insure *betterments* and *improvements* made by the Insured to rented premises. In Commercial Lines Property policies, there is even the opportunity for a businessowner to insure his responsibility for other people's property – e.g. a TV Repair Shop which is responsible for my television. This is a *bailee's-like coverage.* It is further possible for the TV Shop owner to insure his investment of time and materials in his customer's property. If the TV repairman invests $200 in parts and labor into a TV that is destroyed before it is retrieved and the bill is paid, the policy could pay.

5 Regardless of the simplicity or complexity of a given Property risk, the types of property exposures covered by a specific contract will be spelled out on the Dec sheet of that policy.

6 **SPECIFIC VS. BLANKET COVERAGE** – An Inland Marine contract might cover a 1.5 carat diamond in a gold setting as **specific coverage** – that ring and nothing else. A Homeowners policy, on the other hand, might cover up to $50,000 of your personal property on a **blanket basis**. There is no list of personal property required at contract formation. Blanket coverage is also a plus if the insured items could be at any of several locations. . . store #1, store #2 or at the warehouse.

Notes

FROM WHAT?

1 **PERIL/CAUSE OF LOSS** – The specific event that caused the loss. Fire, lightning, windstorm, smoke, hail, falling objects, vandalism, robbery, theft, and flood are examples of perils. In life insurance, the peril is death; in health insurance, the perils are accident and sickness.

2 **NAMED PERIL POLICY** – Property policies can be written in one of two ways: on a Named Peril or an Open Perils ("All Risk") basis. As the name implies, in a Named Peril policy, **each of the covered perils is literally named in the policy**. Example: The company agrees to pay for loss or damage due to Fire, Lightning, Explosion, Windstorm or Hail.

menu

3 You should note that with a Named Peril policy, the *burden of proof* is on the Insured. The fact that Joe's house is destroyed is irrelevant unless it is destroyed by one of the named perils.

4 **OPEN PERILS (*ALL RISK*) POLICY** – The second way to write policies is on an Open Perils basis. This means that the policy does not list the covered perils but, rather, states that the policy will pay for every conceivable peril (even an unusual one) that causes a loss **except for those specifically excluded** in the policy. An Open Perils policy, therefore, provides better coverage (at a higher price) than a Named Peril policy.

everything but...

5 In most cases, the word **Special** indicates Open Perils (All Risk) Coverage.

6 Under an Open Perils policy, the *burden of proof* shifts to the company. If Joe's house is destroyed, the company must pay unless it can show that the cause of Joe's loss is an exclusion under the policy.

7 NOTE: Blanket Coverage is to All Risk...as Specific Coverage is to Named Peril.

8 **HAZARD** – A hazard is any factor or situation that increases or contributes to the probability that a peril will occur. For instance, faulty wiring is a hazard that increases the likelihood that the peril of fire will occur. In the broadest sense, almost any activity of life or business can be viewed as a hazard. Owning a home with a swing set and a swimming pool is a hazard. Owning and operating a motor vehicle is a hazard. Inviting the public into your restaurant or grocery store is a hazard. Manufacturing a product or publishing a periodical is a hazard. Obviously, the only way to avoid hazards altogether is to not own anything and not do anything.

makes it worse

Notes

1 On the other hand, certain hazards can be controlled. Joe can scrape and salt his restaurant parking lot in the winter to reduce the likelihood of a trip-and-fall injury. Within the insurance industry, there are normally considered to be three types of manageable hazards: physical, moral, and morale.

2 A **PHYSICAL hazard** is a visible or tangible condition of the premises that increases the chances of a peril occurring, such as faulty wiring, slippery floors, congested traffic, icy roads, unguarded premises, uninspected boilers, gasoline cans, explosives, and loose items hanging from the ceiling.

3 A **MORAL hazard** concerns the Insured's attempting to defraud the insurance company through **intentional and deliberate destruction** of the insured property. This may occur either by the Insured's intentionally setting fire to his property or hiring an arsonist. The company seeks to determine the probability of a moral hazard by reviewing the proposed Insured's reputation, financial record and past tendency to take advantage of others in business.

4 A **MORALE hazard** has to do with the Insured's indifference, carelessness, laziness, disorderliness, or lack of concern for the insured property. Examples of morale hazards include leaving your keys in your car, smoking in bed, or exceeding the speed limit.

HOW MUCH?

5 **CLAIMS SETTLEMENT OPTIONS** – While claims are most frequently settled with a check from the insurance company, most policies give the company the option to *repair or replace with like kind or quality*. This is the company's option, and they will do what is in their best interest.

6 **VALUATION** - It may surprise you, however, that the value to which an Insured will be indemnified can be defined in several different ways. Some, like Actual Cash Value, strictly adhere to the principle of indemnity, and others, like Replacement Cost, can be much more generous. They all *roughly* fit the concept of indemnity, but several (like Replacement Cost) severely test the limits.

7 Obviously, the more generously we define value in the event of a loss, the more expensive the policy. Just as obviously, each policy must specify how value will be defined under that particular contract.

8 **ACTUAL CASH VALUE (ACV)** – ACV is a formula used to determine the amount the insurance company will pay for a loss.

Replacement Cost - Depreciation = ACV

KNOW THIS:
RC - D = ACV

9 ACV is the most basic method used to determine how much a policy will pay for a loss and is certainly the method for determining value which most rigidly adheres to the principle of indemnity.

Notes

1 Under ACV, value is defined as the **replacement cost** of the destroyed property **at the time of the loss** less an amount that reflects what was used up before the loss (depreciation). **Depreciation** is the decrease in value of property over time as the result of deterioration, or wear and tear. To indemnify a loss on an ACV basis takes into account that the damaged property was partially worn out when the loss occurred. Under an ACV coverage, the insurance company will not pay for the depreciation of the lost or destroyed property, i.e., it will **not** *pay new for old.* However, some policies will pay *new for old*; they are called Replacement Cost policies.

can't collect what's already used

2 **REPLACEMENT COST** – Policies written on this basis will pay the amount it costs to replace the destroyed property. This means that the insurance company will pay to replace the old property with new property of a like kind or quality **without deducting depreciation**. Though you fare better following a loss with a Replacement Cost contract than you would under ACV, a couple of points should be made.

new for old

3 First of all, you paid more premium to get this more generous method of settlement. And, most Replacement Cost contracts have built-in safeguards to keep you from pocketing any profit you might seem to have made. For instance, if your couch has a Replacement Cost of $1,000 and an ACV of $600, most Replacement cost policies would immediately pay $600. When you actually replaced the couch for $1,000, you would be paid the $400 difference. While it would appear that you profited $400 on the loss, you were not able to put the money in your wallet.

4 **FUNCTIONAL REPLACEMENT COST** – Sometimes called **Repair Cost**. Certain buildings, furniture, fixtures, machinery, and equipment are impossible to duplicate or replace. For example, ornate woodwork would require an inordinate amount of labor to reproduce. Obviously, the cost of writing replacement cost coverage for such decorative and expensive work would be prohibitive.

not stained glass ...glass

5 In order to alleviate this problem of expense and still provide a replacement cost-type policy, the Functional Replacement Cost concept was introduced. When the policy is written, the Insured agrees to have the irreplaceable materials replaced with **functionally equivalent** materials, although the decorativeness may be substantially less. While the property will not be exactly replaced, the Insured can obtain replacement cost coverage at a reasonable price, and he will receive materials that are functionally the same as what was destroyed.

6 **STATED VALUE** - Most Property and Casualty policies are written on a Stated Value basis. The Insured tells the company the value of the item and insurance is written for that amount. **Following a loss**, the company can challenge value. If the item can be repaired or replaced for a lesser amount, the company can settle the loss for less than the amount of insurance.

value decided at time of loss

7 **AGREED VALUE** – Another method by which insurance companies can pay losses is on an Agreed Value basis. Under an Agreed Value contract, the insurance company and the Insured agree to a **specific price** for each piece of property **before** the contract is written. The values are *scheduled* on the back of the policy. If there is a loss, the company pays the Agreed Value as specified on the schedule with no regard for depreciation or for the replacement cost of the item. Agreed Value works best for items whose value does not fluxuate greatly. Antiques and artwork – yes; gold and silver – no.

value decided up front

Notes

1 **FAIR MARKET VALUE** – What somebody else will give you in cash for the property at this moment. Fair Market Value is very rarely used in determining property insurance limits because it reflects the value of real estate (land and location) and not just the cost of rebuilding the property itself.

2 In property insurance, what is of importance is the replacement cost of the building and the contents, not the value of the land, because land is not destroyed by most insured perils. Also, the land itself is usually not insured.

COST CONTAINMENT TOOLS IN PROPERTY POLICIES

3 **DEDUCTIBLE** – The deductible is the policyowner's piece of the claim pie. The policyowner always pays the deductible. In property insurance (such as Homeowners and Automobile policies), the deductible is almost always a flat dollar amount, such as $250. In other contracts, it can be a percentage deductible.

4 The primary reason for deductibles is to **stop the overutilization of the policy** (i.e., to control risk by keeping the Insured from using the policy unless there is a substantial loss).

5 **COINSURANCE CLAUSE** – The Coinsurance Clause found in most property policies is designed to encourage the policyowner to insure the property for an amount (at least) approaching the real value of the building. At first glance, a cheapskate policyowner who insures his $100,000 building for only $20,000 would appear to already have an incentive to raise those limits to something more closely reflecting the value of the building. In the event of a total loss, the cheapskate would lose $80,000.

insure to value

not total loss

6 However, what you probably do not know is that the vast majority of property losses are less than 20% of total value. With this in mind, let's structure an example to show why coinsurance is necessary. Suppose Buildings A and B sit side by side. Each is worth $100,000. Joe Cheap insures Building A on a replacement cost basis for only $20,000. Joe Careful insures Building B for $100,000 on a replacement cost basis. A windstorm blows the $20,000 roof off of each building. While Joe Cheap would certainly want the company to pay him the same $20,000 that it will pay Joe Careful, it would not make sense to do so as Joe Careful is paying the company five times as much premium.

7 The purpose of the Coinsurance Clause is to reward the Insureds who purchase adequate levels of insurance and penalize those who do not.

8 The Coinsurance Clause states that if the Insured will agree to insure the property for an agreed percentage of its value (typically 80% **at the time of loss**), then the insurance company will pay 100% of all partial losses, up to the policy limits. If, on the other hand, the Insured fails to carry insurance equal to at least 80% of the value of the property, then the insurance company will penalize the Insured according to an agreed-to formula in the following illustration.

Notes

1 The recommended procedure for calculating coinsurance is for you to answer the following questions:

1. **Is it a partial loss?**

   If ***no*** (i.e., it is a total loss), pay the full claim.

   If ***yes***, go to #2 below.

2. **Did the Insured meet the coinsurance requirement?**

   If ***yes***, pay the entire partial loss.

   If ***no***, then calculate Coinsurance.

"co"-insure – Joe pays part of the claim

2 Example 1:

Coinsurance Requirement	80%
Building Value	$100,000
Amount of insurance in force	$ 60,000
Amount of loss	$ 20,000

3 The first step is to ask whether this is a partial or a total loss. It was obviously a partial loss because the amount of the loss was $20,000 and the building value was $100,000. So go to step number two.

4 The second step is to ask yourself, "Did the Insured meet the coinsurance requirement at the time of the loss?" The coinsurance requirement is 80% of $100,000, or $80,000. The amount of insurance carried was $60,000. Therefore, the Insured did not meet the coinsurance requirement. The formula for determining the amount paid on the loss therefore would be:

$$\frac{\$60{,}000 \text{ carried}}{\$80{,}000 \text{ required}} \times \$20{,}000 \text{ loss} = \text{amount paid}$$

$$\frac{\$60{,}000}{\$80{,}000} \text{ reduces to } \frac{3}{4}, \text{ so}$$

$$\frac{3}{4} \times \$20{,}000 = \$15{,}000 \text{ which is the amount paid}$$

5 Now try one yourself.

Example 2:

Coinsurance Requirement	80%
Building Value	$200,000
Amount of insurance in force	$ 80,000
Amount of the loss	$ 30,000

Amount paid ?

1 The application of the Coinsurance Clause is simple. As long as the Insured carries insurance equal to or greater than the required percentage, the insurance company will pay all partial losses up to the policy limits. However, if the Insured does not maintain the required percentage, then the insurance company will penalize the Insured by only paying a percentage of the Insured's loss according to the coinsurance formula.

2 The theory is that since the property was only partially insured, the company should only pay part of the loss. The purpose of the Coinsurance Clause is to **encourage the policyowner to insure the property to value**.

(The answer is $15,000.)

3 We might summarize coinsurance by saying that it is a mechanism by which the company cheats the policyowner on a claim to the same degree that the policyowner cheated the company when purchasing the insurance in the first place. And while this is a gross oversimplification, it does make the point.

COMMON PROPERTY PROVISIONS

4 **PROOF OF LOSS** – A Proof of Loss is a sworn statement concerning a loss under a Property policy. It must only be submitted when requested by the company, and most claims are settled without one.

sworn

5 **APPRAISAL** – In most property policies there is a provision for appraisal. In situations where the company has acknowledged that a loss is covered by the contract and simply cannot agree with the Insured on a settlement amount, each side hires (and pays for) an appraiser. The two appraisers select an umpire (for whom the two sides split the cost). When two of the three are in agreement as to value, their decision is binding.

only dollars...
...not coverage

6 **RIGHT OF SALVAGE** – When the insurance company pays in full to replace an item, the company gains ownership of the destroyed item. If Joe's auto is totaled, the company has the right to salvage what remains of Joe's car after paying him book value.

company's right

7 **ABANDONMENT** – On the other hand, Joe has no right to abandon his property to the company. After a minor *fender bender,* Joe cannot hand his car keys to the company and demand full book value.

8 **ADDITIONAL COVERAGES AND EXTENSIONS OF COVERAGES** – Most property policies have three or four major coverages and then a list of additional coverages and a list of coverage extensions. Some of these actually add dollars to the total amount payable for a loss, and others merely allow for limited amounts to be paid from the major coverages in circumstances that would otherwise be excluded. Additional coverages are normally **automatic** and the extensions must typically be **earned** by maintaining insurance equal to **eighty** percent of the value of the Insured property.

There's more than meets the eye

Notes

1 VACANCY/UNOCCUPANCY – While these two words are basically synonymous in normal usage, in insurance-ese there is a big difference.

unoccupancy-nobody's home

2 Unoccupancy means that no **people** are there. Most homes and businesses are, therefore, unoccupied for some period every day. Vacancy, on the other hand, means no people are present **and** no furniture, furnishings, or equipment are in place. Obviously, the potential for arson, vandalism, and any number of other perils is greatly increased in a vacant building.

vacancy-they took the furniture with them

COMMON PROPERTY CONDITIONS

Concealment, Misrepresentation or Fraud

3 Your property coverage is void if you intentionally conceal or misrepresent a material fact concerning this coverage.

you lie, you're on your own

Control of Property

4 The negligence of any person beyond your direction or control will not affect your insurance. In fact, even if you violate the terms of this coverage part, it will only affect your coverage at the location involved. Coverage will continue for other locations.

we pay, then chase

Insurance Under Two or More Coverages

5 If you have insured your property under two or more policies, you will not be paid more than the actual loss.

whole not rich

Legal Action Against Us

6 You may not sue the insurance company unless you are in full compliance with your responsibilities and have started the lawsuit within a time limit specified by state law.

Liberalization

7 If the company should revise its policy to broaden coverage in any way without additional premium, those policies already outstanding will be interpreted as if the more liberal provision were included.

No Benefit to Bailee

8 Property policies are two party coverages, and are not designed to protect *Bailee's* obligations.

let him get his own coverage

Notes

Other Insurance

1 If you have a piece of property insured by two Property policies that are identical in peril power (concurrent), each company will pay its share of the claim in the same proportion as its policy limits bear to the total. For example:

pro rata – coverage to claim

	Insurance Limits	Pro Rata Share
Company A	$ 70,000	70%
Company B	30,000	30%
Total	$100,000	100%

2 If there is a $10,000 loss, Company A would pay $7000 and Company B would pay $3000 and each would apply its deductible.

3 However, if we change the example so that the peril power of Company A's policy does not match Company B's (**nonconcurrency**), things could turn out much differently.

	Peril Power	Insurance Limits
Company A	Basic	$70,000
Company B	Basic + Earthquake	30,000

4 If there is a $10,000 earthquake loss, Company A pays zero. Company B would only pay its share, $3000. Remember, Company B is only receiving about one-third of the premium and therefore should not be forced to cover 100% of the loss.

5 NOTE: It would be extremely rare today for a risk to be covered by two separate property policies. It might happen if a building were too expensive for any one company to handle the entire risk. However, **if two property policies do cover the same piece of property, they must be concurrent – the peril power must match**. The major reason that this clause still appears on modern policies is to keep the policyowner from profiting in the event of a loss. Suppose I own a $100,00 building and it is insured with Company A for $100,000 and with Company B for $100,000. I may not be an arsonist, but I am certainly planning to profit if lighting ever does strike. If it does, each would pay its proportionate share of the loss. Company A would pay $50,000 minus a deductible and likewise Company B. In a total loss, I would collect only the $100,000 I lost minus the deductibles.

never more than pro rata

Policy Period and Coverage Territory

6 Obviously, the insurance company only covers losses that occur during the policy period. The coverage territory is defined in the contract.

Notes

Subrogation

(Latin, for *going in place of*) Subrogation is the legal process by which your insurance
company, once it reimburses you for a loss caused by someone else, **assumes your**
1 **legal right to sue the responsible third party**. For example, your next-door
neighbor causes damage to your house and is liable for it. You collect from your own
insurance company for the loss because it is easier than suing your neighbor. Your
insurance company then subrogates against your neighbor in order to recover the
money it paid to you. This is legally possible because you transferred your right to
sue your neighbor to your insurance company when
you accepted payment of the claim.

now, the fun really begins

Transfer of Rights

Subrogation upholds the principle of indemnity
2 (no profit) by preventing you from collecting
twice for the loss (once from your insurance
company and once from your neighbor).

The commercial policies refer to Subroga-
3 tion as ***Transfer of Rights of Recovery***
Against Others To The Insurer.

YOUR DUTIES IN THE EVENT OF A LOSS

- **Notify the police** if a law has been broken.
- **Notify the insurance company promptly.**
- Give the company a **description of the loss**.
- **Protect the property from further damage.**
- If the company requests, **complete an inventory** of the damaged and undamaged property.
- Allow the company to **inspect the damage and your records substantiating the loss**.
- If requested, permit the company to **question you under oath**.
- At the company's request, complete the **Proof of Loss forms** provided by the company, including your sworn signature.
- Cooperate with the company in the settlement of the claim.

Notes

LOSS PAYMENT

1 In the event of a covered loss, the company will do one of the following:

company's choice

- Pay the value of the loss and take the damaged property as salvage.
- Pay the cost to repair or replace the damaged items.
- Repair or replace it with property of like kind and quality.

2 The company will not pay you more than your insurable interest in the damaged property.

3 **VALUATION** – As we have seen, value to which an Insured will be indemnified can be defined in several different ways. Some, like Actual Cash Value, strictly adhere to the principle of indemnity, and others, like Replacement Cost, can be much more generous. Obviously, the more generously we define value in the event of a loss, the more expensive the policy. Just as obviously, each policy must specify how value will be defined under that particular contract.

RECOVERED PROPERTY

4 If either party recovers insured property after payment of a loss, the other party must be notified. It is then your option to return either the dollars or the property to the company.

MORTGAGE HOLDERS

5 The mortgage holder or mortgagee is **the bank** holding an interest in your property as described on the Dec Sheet. The purpose of this section is to protect the banker's rights.

bankers never lose

6 In essence, **the bank never loses**. Even if we catch you burning down the building, we still pay the bank.

7 In fact, if the insurance company pays the bank an amount equal to the entire mortgage, the mortgage note is transferred to the insurance company and the insurance company is now your mortgagee. You can pay the company from whatever federal penitentiary you are residing in while you are serving time for arson.

8 Basically, you can view the bank as the shadow of the policyowner. Any rights or obligations that you fail to exercise become the bank's. If you do not pay the premium, then the bank can (while it simultaneously forecloses on your mortgage). If you don't submit proof of loss within 60 days, then the company will give the bank 60 days to render proof of loss.

9 The Standard Mortgage Clause also protects the mortgagee by requiring that the insurance company give the mortgagee notice in the event of policy cancellation.

Notes

THE CAUSE OF LOSS FORMS: BASIC, BROAD, & SPECIAL

1 As we have discussed, the FROM WHAT? question can be answered with either a list of perils under a Named Peril contract or with an Open Perils (All Risk) contract, which essentially covers anything not excluded.

2 In both Personal Lines and Commercial Lines there are two groups of Named Perils that are nearly identical. They are known as the Basic Perils and the Broad Form Perils. The Basic Perils in Personal Lines contracts are nine in number. In Commercial Lines, the Basic Perils include the same nine plus two more, **for a total of 11 perils**. The Broad Form in each case adds three perils to the appropriate list of Basic Perils.

3 **Memory Hint:** As you look at the Basic Perils in the order presented, you will notice that the first letter of each peril would create a list as follows:

WR ELF VVV SSS

4 Most football fans recognize WR as an abbreviation for Wide Receiver. Therefore, we have a Wide Receiver whose name is ELF, plus three V's and three S's. In Personal Lines, we have the same Wide Receiver ELF plus three V's and only one S. As you move from Dwelling policies to Homeowners to Commercial Property, you will find relatively few other differences, once you have committed this list to memory.

BASIC Cause of Loss Form

Economy model

11 perils

1. **WINDSTORM OR HAIL** covers windstorm (hurricanes, tornadoes, etc.) or hail damage to your building. The interior or contents is not covered for damage by rain, snow, sand or dust driven by the wind unless the building first sustains wind or hail damage that allows the rain, snow, sand or dust to enter. Simply put:

   - If you let Mother Nature in, no coverage.
   - If Mother Nature lets herself in, you're covered.

let herself in

2. **RIOT OR CIVIL COMMOTION** covers acts of striking employees and looting (theft) which occurs during a riot.

not war

3. **EXPLOSION** includes the explosion of gases within a furnace or any fired vessel. It does not include the rupture or bursting of pressurized vessels, like steam boilers. (That's covered elsewhere – Boiler & Machinery / Mechanical Breakdown.)

Purdue exclusion

4. **LIGHTNING** covers the discharge of natural electricity.

not man's electricity

Notes

5. **FIRE** is the oldest and still the biggest risk in property insurance. Actually, this peril is *Fire Plus* because it also covers the results of a fire:

- firefighter damage
- water damage
- smoke damage

more than just fire

Fire can be divided into two subcategories:

- Friendly Fire – a fire you start intentionally to do a job that is in its intended area (like a fire in a fireplace, on a stove, or in a water heater). ***good...***

- Hostile Fire – a fire you did not start intentionally, or a friendly fire which is no longer doing what it was intended to do. ***...bad...***

Damage done by a hostile fire is covered but not damage done by a friendly fire (unless it has become hostile). ***...ugly***

6. **VEHICLES OR AIRCRAFT** provides coverage only for the direct physical contact with insured property by an aircraft, an object falling from an aircraft, spacecraft, missile, vehicle or object thrown up by a vehicle. There is no coverage, however, for damage caused by vehicles you own or operate. ***somebody else's***

7. **VANDALISM** is often called *Vandalism and Malicious Mischief* (abbreviated V&MM) and covers damage done by vandals, but **it does not cover theft**. COVERED IF THEY BREAK IT, BUT NOT IF THEY TAKE IT. Vandalism will cover burglar damage. ***break it – yes*** ***take it – no***

8. **VOLCANIC ACTION** covers the **above ground** damage of a volcano, such as damage from the blast or shock waves, ash, dust or lava flow. ***"A"***

9. **SMOKE** damage is covered as long as it is sudden and accidental. Prolonged exposures are not covered.

Note: Smoke from a hostile fire on your premises is already covered under the peril of fire. Smoke coverage is necessary for smoke damage caused either by someone else's fire or by smoke damage where there was no hostile fire (like due to an overheated stove or furnace). ***sudden... ...accidental***

10. **SPRINKLER LEAKAGE** is covered because we want you to have sprinklers. ***2 Commercial Perils***

NOTE: The only *water coverages* of the Basic form are firefighter water and sprinkler water – water that is there to put out a fire.

11. **SINKHOLE COLLAPSE** is the loss caused by the sinking or collapse of land into underground spaces created by the action of water, limestone or dolomite. This does **not** cover the collapse of land into man-made underground cavities, like a coal mine. ***Florida***

Notes

BROAD Cause of Loss Form

Family sedan

1 This form adds three more perils to the Basic form. It also adds the additional coverage of collapse

14 perils

12. **FALLING OBJECTS** – like a boulder tumbling down a mountainside. Coverage is generally limited to damage of the insured buildings. Contents coverage is only provided if the exterior damage to the building allowed the contents damage to occur.

through the roof

13. **WEIGHT OF SNOW, ICE OR SLEET** provides coverage for a building that is damaged by the weight of snow, ice or sleet.

14. **WATER DAMAGE** broadens the coverage of the Basic form. Before we look at the modifications of the Broad form specifically, let's review the entire picture of water damage in the Commercial Property contracts.

> NOTE: Water damage coverage can be readily understood and remembered if you keep the following three points in mind:
>
> - Firefighter water (and sprinkler water in Commercial policies) is **always** covered.
> - Mother Nature's water in the form of a flood is **never** covered. (Hence the need for Flood insurance.)
> - The Broad and Special forms cover losses due to **intentional water**. That is, water that you bring into the building intentionally in pipes, water heaters, etc. . . . in other words, **plumbing.**

always...

...never...

...broad and beyond

2 Therefore, the Broad form (and the Special form) provides coverage for the damage caused by the **leaking and freezing** of pipes, appliances or systems which contain water. Of course, this only applies if you have done your best to maintain heat in the building. Further, coverage is provided for leakage that is sudden and accidental. Coverage is NOT provided for the appliance or system from which the water escaped.

Notes

Additional Coverage: COLLAPSE

1 The Broad Cause of Loss form provides for the additional coverage of collapse. It is not listed as a peril because there are many perils which can cause a building to collapse. Primarily, **this section provides coverage if any of the Broad form perils damages a building which ultimately collapses**. For example, if fire damages a building and it collapses later, there is coverage. In addition, collapse due to any of the following is covered:

mostly this...

but also...

- Hidden decay
- **Hidden insect or vermin damage**
- Weight of people or personal property
- Weight of rain
- Defective materials or methods of construction if the collapse takes place during the construction or remodeling.

bugs...

people...

...defects...

2 Collapse does not cover outdoor items such as antennas, awnings or guttering, nor does it cover items on the ground such as fences, piers, walkways or roadways. Further, collapse does not cover damage due to settling, cracking, bulging or expansion.

SPECIAL Cause of Loss Form

"everything but"

3 The Special form covers everything covered by the Broad form and more. It is the *All Risk* or Open Perils form. It covers everything except that which is specifically excluded. There are probably two valid questions that can be raised about this and any other all risk coverage:

1. What am I covered for now that I wasn't before?
2. What's excluded?

4 In answer to the first question, the best answers tend to fall into the category of "Weird stuff that happens to me and no one else on earth."

Luxury

- A bear walks into your kitchen and destroys it. *Wild animals* appear on no list of perils, so no named policy would provide coverage. However, since *wild* animal damage is not excluded under an All Risk contract, it would provide coverage.

- You cut yourself at the kitchen sink and bleed on your wall-to-wall carpeting on the way to the bathroom. Not excluded, therefore covered under Open Perils.

- You are preparing to paint the dining room. You have an open 5-gallon can of paint with the electric mixer sitting in it. Your 5-year old turns on the mixer, which creates a splatter pattern worthy of Jackson Pollack – covered under All Risk.

5 The second question is terribly important because an Open Perils contract normally does not list the perils covered. Simply, you are covered for anything not excluded. While it sounds backwards, you can determine the extent of coverage in your All Risk policy by reading the exclusions. Most will fall into the three categories we established earlier:

- Catastrophic losses
- Losses better covered elsewhere
- Predictable losses

	CAUSE OF LOSS	BASIC	BROAD	SPECIAL	Remember
BASIC	1. WIND OR HAIL	X	X	X	...let herself in
	2. RIOT OR CIVIL COMMOTION	X	X	X	not war
	3. EXPLOSION	X	X	X	Purdue Exclusion
	4. LIGHTNING	X	X	X	Mother Nature's Electricity
	5. FIRE	X	X	X	fire, smoke, water, & firemen
	6. VEHICLES OR AIRCRAFT	X	X	X	somebody else's
	7. VANDALISM	X	X	X	break it, but don't take it
	8. VOLCANIC ACTION	X	X	X	Action, Air Ash, Above
	9. SMOKE	X	X	X	sudden ... accidental
	10. SPRINKLER LEAKAGE	X	X	X	good guys
	11. SINKHOLE COLLAPSE	X	X	X	Florida
BROAD	12. FALLING OBJECTS		X	X	through the roof
	13. WEIGHT OF SNOW, ICE, OR SLEET		X	X	weight
	14. PLUMBING		X	X	14 days
	15. **COLLAPSE:** ADDITIONAL COVERAGE		X	X	vermin, people, and more
	16. **EARTHQUAKE:** OPTIONAL COVERAGE	X	X	X	plug in by endorsement
	17. **OPEN PERILS:** "ALL RISK"			X	everything but ...

Notes

CRIME LOSSES

1 Please note that the following are insurance definitions as they relate to crime coverages. They bear little, if any, resemblance to the criminal law definitions.

2 **Robbery** – The taking of property by violence or threat of violence **from a person**.

Robbery... Violence/person

Burglary – The taking of property **from a premises** that is closed and locked tight
3 and leaving marks of forced entry or exit. There must be visible evidence of force
at the point of entry or exit.

Burglary... Violence/building

4 **Theft** – Any act of stealing. Theft is a broad term and includes robbery and burglary, as well as other forms of stealing, such as shoplifting and embezzlement.

Safe Burglary – The taking of property from a locked safe or vault, or the taking
5 of the safe itself. As with burglary, there must be visible marks of force. Cash
registers, cash drawers and cash boxes are not safes.

6 **Disappearance** – Insured property is simply gone. There is no evidence, or even a probability, of theft. Disappearance is covered only in "All Risk" policies.

It was here... ...now it's gone

Notes

Conclusion

In this chapter, you have been introduced to a number of terms and concepts re-
1 lated to Property (two party) contracts. A good group of these fundamentals will be of tremendous value as you begin to examine the specific policies that contain property coverage.

The great-great-granddad of all property insurance is the New York Standard Fire
2 policy of 1943. It standardized the fire policies that had been sold in this country for about 150 years prior to its arrival. The SFP did not do much by today's standards. It covered only three perils – fire, lightning, and removal. And, the coverages it provided were greatly limited by the definitions, provisions and exclusions within the contract. Specific forms and endorsements were developed to *customize* and broaden the coverage for the various subjects of property coverage (business building, homes, contents, etc.). Today, we no longer modify a Standard Fire policy with a stack of endorsements; the major property exposures each have policies written exclusively for use in that area. However, the basic property vocabulary originally developed for the Standard Fire policy is liberally sprinkled throughout theses modern policies.

All Property policies must define **what** property is insured and **from** which perils.
3 Since Property contracts are essentially designed to cover property at specific locations, **buildings** are the perfect subject of a Property policy. On-premises coverage is available for the **contents** of a building. Property coverage can be **specific** – your 1.5 carat diamond ring, or it can be written on a **blanket** basis – all the stuff in your house.

The *from what* question can be answered with a **Named Peril** policy that lists each
4 cause of loss that is covered, or an **Open Perils** contract that covers everything not specifically excluded. A **peril** is an event that causes a loss – fire, lightning, wind and hail. A **hazard** is a factor that increases the likelihood of a peril – oily rags, improper storage of flammable materials, faulty wiring.

To settle a covered loss, the policies can specify any of several ways of establishing
5 the value of that loss. **Actual Cash Value** is the replacement cost at the time of loss minus the depreciation of the insured item. **Replacement Cost** policies do not depreciate the cost of replacement – essentially this is *new for old* settlement. **Functional Replacement Cost** is the amount required to replace damaged property with functionally equivalent materials – plexiglass for stained glass. **Stated Value** is what you say something is worth, but **Agreed Value** is what both you and the insurance company agree that it is worth. **Fair Market Value** is what the property would sell for today. Since Fair Market Value includes the price of the land under the building, this determination of value is seldom used for insurance purposes.

To control costs, Property policies contain **deductibles** – first you pay and then the
6 company will pay. Deductibles reduce the overutilization of the policy. Another cost containment tool is **coinsurance**. It is designed to encourage the policyowner to *insure to value.* There is a reward for those who do and a penalty for those who do not. The penalty can be expressed by the formula

$$\frac{\text{DID CARRY}}{\text{SHOULD CARRY}} \times \text{LOSS} = \text{AMOUNT PAID}$$

Notes

1 Common Property provisions and conditions include some of the following:

- **Appraisal** – two appraiser, one umpire
- **Salvage** – the company keeps the leftovers
- **Abandonment** – you have no right to abandon
- **Unoccupied** – no people
- **Vacant** – no people, no stuff
- **Multiple policies** – covering the same property, pay proportionately if concurrent
- **Subrogation** – company pays you and then sues the at-fault party

2 The list of Named Perils known as the Basic Perils for Commercial risks include WR ELF VVV and SSS. For Personal Lines the Basic Perils are almost identical – WR ELF VVV and S.

Windstorm or hail
Riot or civil commotion

Explosion
Lightning
Fire

Vehicles or aircraft
Vandalism
Volcanic Action

Smoke
Sprinkler leakage
Sinkhole collapse

3 The Broad Form adds three perils to the Basic Perils for both Commercial and Personal Lines contracts.

- **Falling objects**
- **Weight of ice and snow**
- **Water damage (plumbing)**

4 Also, the Broad Form adds the Additional Coverage of **Collapse**.

5 Finally, this chapter defines the important terms of Crime insurance. They include:

- **Robbery** – taking of insured property by violence or threat **from a person**.
- **Burglary** – taking of insured property **from a premises** that is closed and locked tight.
- **Theft** – any act of stealing; includes burglary, robbery and other forms of stealing that are neither burglary nor robbery.

CHAPTER 3
BASICS OF TWO-PARTY COVERAGE

1. Which of the following is essentially the same as repair cost?

   (A) Replacement Cost
   (B) Functional Replacement Cost
   (C) Agreed Value
   (D) Fair Market Value

2. Sidney Smith is the owner-operator of a computer store. He does not worry about cables running across the floor or expensive computers balanced precariously on the edges of tables. He knows that any damage done to the computers or any injury sustained by the customers will be paid by his insurance policy. Sidney is a

   (A) physical hazard.
   (B) psychological hazard.
   (C) moral hazard.
   (D) morale hazard.

3. For insurance purposes, all of the following could be classified as hazards EXCEPT

   (A) The shoddy maintenance of a building
   (B) Hail
   (C) Faulty wiring
   (D) Arsonists

CHAPTER 3 • BASICS OF TWO-PARTY COVERAGE QUIZ

4. Which of the following is the coinsurance formula?

   (A) $\frac{\text{Insurance Carried}}{\text{Insurance Required}} \times \text{Loss} = \text{Amt Ins Co Pays}$

   (B) Coinsurance Percentage x Replacement Cost – Depreciation = Amt Ins Co Pays

   (C) Manual Rate x Experience Credit – Schedule Credit = Coinsurance

   (D) Value – Loss x Coinsurance Percentage = Amt Ins Co Pays

5. Joe has a Property Policy issued by Company A in the amount of $60,000 and a similar policy issued by Company B in the amount of $40,000. Both contain the Broad Cause of Loss form. Both have a $500 deductible. How much would Joe receive following a $10,000 covered loss to his $100,000 warehouse?

   (A) $6000 from Company A and $4000 from Company B
   (B) $5000 from Company A and $5000 from Company B
   (C) $5500 from Company A and $4000 from Company B
   (D) $5500 from Company A and $3500 from Company B

6. Five years ago, you purchased a new machine for $100,000. The replacement cost today for the machine is $120,000. The machine has depreciated by $25,000 during the last five years. The actual cash value of the machine today is

   (A) $120,000
   (B) $100,000
   (C) $ 95,000
   (D) $ 75,000

7. You own a warehouse valued at $100,000 and have it insured under a Property policy containing a 70% coinsurance clause and a $500 deductible. If you have the building insured for $35,000 and suffer a $30,000 loss, you will receive

   (A) $30,000
   (B) $29,500
   (C) $15,000
   (D) $14,500

8. Which of the following is NOT a duty of the Named Insured following a loss to the insured property?

   (A) To notify the police if a law may have been broken.
   (B) To keep a record of any expenses incurred to protect the property, for consideration in the settlement of the claim.
   (C) To send the insurance company a sworn "Proof of Loss" with every claim.
   (D) If requested, permit the company to question you under oath about matters relating to the claim, including a review of your books and records.

9. The Peril of "Fire" covers all of the following losses EXCEPT

   (A) Smoke damage to an insured building caused by a fire in the building.
   (B) Water damage to an insured building caused by firefighters fighting a fire.
   (C) Smoke damage to another's building caused by a fire in the insured's building.
   (D) Damage caused by firefighters fighting a fire in the insured's building.

10. Joe Insured owns a Property Policy on his office building. The Causes of Loss form used is the Special Form, including the Additional Coverage – Collapse. Which of the following collapses would be covered?

   (A) Termites eat through the beams and the building falls down.
   (B) An earthquake causes the building to collapse.
   (C) A local civil authority orders the building to be demolished in order to protect the public from its collapse.
   (D) Beach erosion causes the building to collapse.

11. Coverage for personal property in many different locations would be called

   (A) Specific coverage.
   (B) Broad coverage.
   (C) Non-specific coverage.
   (D) Blanket coverage.

END

QUIZ ANSWERS & EXPLANATIONS ON NEXT PAGE

CHAPTER 3
BASICS OF TWO-PARTY COVERAGE
QUIZ ANSWER KEY

1. B. Repair cost is the personal lines equivalent of functional replacement cost, i.e., you don't get stained glass; you just get glass.

2. D. A subtle, but important distinction, the moral hazards are intentional acts. The morale hazards are the "what the heck, I've got insurance" acts. The cables are physical hazards, but that wasn't the question.

3. B. Hazards increase the likelihood of a loss. Hail is a peril, a cause of loss. The others are hazards which could lead to the peril of fire.

4. A. The co-insurance formula is expressed as "Did over should times the loss"

5. D. The Other Insurance Provision requires if there are two or more policies of the same type, each policy pay its pro rata share of the loss. In a pro rata split each policy will also charge its deductible.

6. C. The formula for Actual Cash Value is replacement cost today minus depreciation.

7. D. The formula to remember is "did over should times the loss." You did have $35,000 of coverage. You should have had 70% of $100,000 or $70,000 (35/70 or 1/2). One half of $30,000 is $15,000. Then subtract the $500 deductible arriving at the amount of the claim, $14,500.

8. C. Proof of Loss, a sworn statement, is only required if requested by the company.

9. C. Two party coverage (property insurance) only provides payments for damage to property in which the insured has an insurable interest. C is an example of a Third Party (liability) loss.

10. A. Collapse of the structure due to hidden insect and vermin damage is a covered loss, collapse due to flood (abnormal beach erosion) and earth movement are excluded, as is governmental action.

11. D. Blanket Coverage can be used to provide insurance in many locations.

BASICS OF THIRD PARTY COVERAGE

4

1 The purpose of all liability policies is to **protect your assets if you injure someone else or their property and are legally obligated to pay for the damage**.

In many respects, this is the opposite viewpoint most people hold as a reason to buy
2 insurance. Most folks buy insurance to protect their property: their building, their business property, their inventory, etc. They are concerned that their *stuff* will be attacked by some peril. Addressing that concern is the function of property insurance as we have studied it. **However, liability is different**. In liability, the risk arises from your property – your building, your inventory, your business activities, etc., and it is the other person who is injured. For example, suppose that the sign over Joe's restaurant falls on a passer-by. In the absence of liability insurance, he would sue Joe for the damages. Liability insurance simply pays on Joe's behalf the damages he is legally obligated to pay.

The Insurance world turned upside down

Notes

1 Notice that a liability policy is not designed to pay you. It does not protect your body or your property. Instead, it **pays to a third party** for damage to his body or property for which you are legally responsible. So, here's your first big legal term: we'll refer to this third party as *the Other Guy*. There are some additional terms which define the damage you might do to the Other Guy.

- **BODILY INJURY (BI)** – the physical destruction or injury of a human being.
- **PROPERTY DAMAGE (PD)** – the physical destruction or damage to *stuff*, which is anything tangible other than human beings. If you hit a cow on the highway, that is property damage.
- **PERSONAL INJURY** – Despite what the name implies, Personal Injury has nothing to do with injury to a person's body (Bodily Injury). Instead, Personal Injury concerns **injury to a person's reputation or mental state**. Personal Injuries include false arrest, false imprisonment, false search and seizure, malicious prosecution, libel, slander, defamation of character, violation of civil rights or right of privacy, wrongful entry or eviction or the invasion of the right of private occupancy. As you can see from the list, not one of the above listed items includes bodily injury but simply relates to mental, reputation or psychological damages to the "injured" person. Please keep in mind the distinction between *Personal* Injury and *Bodily* Injury.
- **ADVERTISING INJURY** - Like personal injury but the victim is a business and not a person.

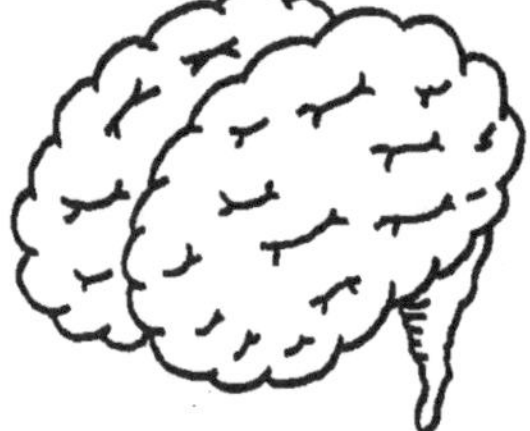

it's all in your mind

copyright, trademark, etc.

2 Notice that we have used the terms legally obligated to pay or legally responsible several times already. It is important to gain an understanding of these phrases.

LEGALLY OBLIGATED TO PAY

3 There are two ways in which you can become legally obligated to pay:

- Settlement – Out of court
- Judgment – In court

4 In either event, the dispute will be resolved under **tort** law. This is the body of law that governs ***wrongs between individuals***. We can contrast tort law with criminal law, which governs wrongs between an individual and society. If the Other Guy walks into your store and you shoot him for not buying enough, that's criminal law. If he slips and breaks his leg on your newly waxed floor, that's tort law. When we say wrongs between individuals, we include persons like you and me and, in this context, we also include companies, associations and even the state and federal government. Any of these entities can be sued as individuals. However, if you want to sue the federal government, you must first obtain its permission. The most common tort, negligence, is the primary concern of liability insurance.

torts – wrongs

Notes

NEGLIGENCE

In a layperson's terms, negligence can be expressed fairly simply. "I was injured
1 because you did not act responsibly." The problem is that several of us could view the same act and disagree vehemently about how responsible or irresponsible it was. Our viewpoint is colored by our own experience and beliefs. If you and I both saw a car drive down the street, we might describe it very differently. You might say the car is big because you drive a Geo. I might say it's small because I drive a Lincoln. I might describe the car that went past us as new and light colored because mine is very old and black. You might see it very differently if yours is brand new and white. Since the law needs to speak with a single viewpoint, tort law has created the concept of the *Reasonable Person* in the form of the men and women that make up a jury. Therefore, we can define negligence a little more precisely. **Negligence is the failure to do or not do what the Reasonable Person would do or not do under the same or similar circumstances.** Under normal circumstances, when a reasonable person is driving his car and encounters a stop sign, he stops. If under the same circumstances, you run the stop sign and injure me, you are negligent.

if you're reasonable, you can never be negligent

Now, it's not really that simple nor that cut and dried. Shortly, we will look at four
2 separate elements that must be established to demonstrate negligence. But before we do, let's observe that **negligence is never an intentional act**. If you draw back your fist and punch me in the nose, that is not negligence. Negligence may be an act of carelessness, ignorance, thoughtlessness, inaction . . . but it is never an intentional act.

omissions... yes

commissions... yes

intentional acts... no

Establishing Negligence

To establish negligence, the injured party must prove four specific elements of neg-
3 ligence. Like a four-legged table, negligence will not stand on three legs, two legs or one leg. All four elements must be established or there is no negligence.

- **DUTY** – You must have a *duty* to the injured party. Most of the duties we have as individuals
4 or as businesses are not duties we have signed up for or agreed to specifically. Most of our duties simply balance the privileges we enjoy in free society. For example, if you enjoy the privilege of operating a motor vehicle, you have a duty to stop when you encounter a stop sign.

If you ever go to law school, you will find that traditionally, there are varying degrees of *duty* depend-
5 ing upon the relationship you have or do not have to the Other Guy. But for our purposes, we can say that the **Standard of Care** is to **act as the reasonable person would act**.

If Joe Insured is a homeowner, he has many privileges
6 and some corresponding duties. For instance, Joe has the right to chop down the 80-foot oak tree in his front lawn. But since the tree is only 40 feet from the street, Joe has a duty to see that when the tree falls, it does not injure a passer-by.

Notes

- **BREACH OF DUTY** – You must fail in your duty to the Other Guy.

  To continue the example, if Joe's tree fell on the Other Guy who was driving down the street, Joe would have failed in his duty to use reasonable care.

- **PROXIMATE CAUSE** – Your breach of duty must be the proximate cause of the Other Guy's injury or property damage. This actually means two things. Your action must be (1) the **direct** and (2) the **foreseeable** cause of the Other Guy's loss. Direct means that there must be an unbroken chain of events from your action to the Other Guy's injuries. Foreseeable means that a reasonable person would have anticipated the occurrence.

  In our example with Joe Insured and the oak tree, most of us would agree that the injuries sustained by the Other Guy and his car were the **direct** result of Joe's action. And, most would also agree that a reasonable person would have anticipated the outcome. However, suppose Aunt Harriet watches this event from her porch two blocks away and suffers a heart attack due to the excitement. That string of events would probably not be foreseeable to most folks, so Aunt Harriet's death could not, therefore, be directly attributed to Joe's negligence.

reasonably forseeable injury to a reasonably foreseeable person

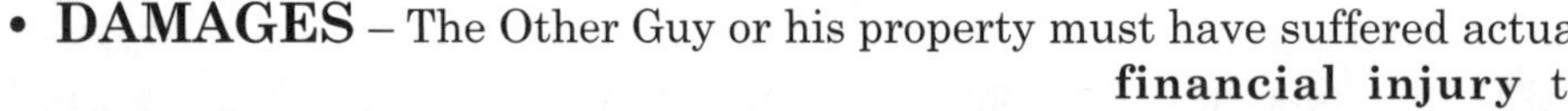

- **DAMAGES** – The Other Guy or his property must have suffered actual **financial injury** to establish negligence. Simply put, if the hurt cannot be translated into dollars, it is not hurt. In our example, the Other Guy's hospital bill, his lost wages and the repair bill for his automobile would be considered damages.

if you can't put hurt into $... you ain't hurt

Notes

Types of Damages

TO COMPENSATE

1 **Compensatory Damages** are those which are designed to, as far as possible, restore the Other Guys to their pre-injury status. There are two types of Compensatory Damages:

- **Special or Economic Damages** are those which are readily identifiable... such as medical bills, lost wages, dented fenders.

- **General or Noneconomic Damages** are those which don't come with a receipt...pain, suffering, loss of enjoyment, embarrassment.

TO PUNISH

2 **Punitive Damages**, unlike Compensatory Damages, are not designed to make the Other Guy whole. Their purpose is to **punish the wrongdoer**. The theory is that such punishment will deter the defendant or similar actors from doing the same type of bad act in the future.

Legal Defenses

3 If the Other Guy alleges that Joe was negligent, there are several potential defenses available to Joe. Only the first fits the oak tree example that we have been developing.

4 **Comparative Fault** – If the Other Guy is even partially responsible for his own injuries, then Joe's financial obligation would be reduced accordingly.

balance the blame

5 If, for instance, Joe could establish that the Other Guy was talking on his cellular phone when the accident happened, maybe the jury would attribute 20% of the fault to the Other Guy and subsequently reduce the award by 20%.

6 **Contributory Negligence** - Comparative fault is **not** the same as contributory negligence. Under contributory negligence the Other Guy collects nothing if **any of the fault** is his own. Not an available defense in most jurisdictions.

7 **Assumption of Risk** – If the injured person knowingly placed himself in a dangerous position, it might eliminate the possibility of negligence on someone else's part.

8 A driver in the Indy 500, for example, would probably not be able to establish negligence on the part of a fellow participant. The Reasonable Man would say that an individual who gets into a bathtub of gasoline and drives it at 240 m.p.h. around a bull ring with thirty-two other drivers assumes his own risk of injury.

9 **Intervening Cause** - Usually there must be a direct relationship between the negligent act and the Other Guy's injuries. If some other factor or force acted to either cause or enhance the damages, then the defendant could be released from liability. This, however, would not occur if the intervening force was reasonably foreseeable. Example: Joe negligently left a broken glass on the floor of his restaurant. Bob trips and knocks Betty down and she is cut by the broken glass. Most courts would still hold Joe liable because actions such as Bob's are reasonably foreseeable.

10 **Statute of Limitations** - Legislatures set the time limits in which the injured party may sue the defendant. After the time runs out, the injured party has no right to pursue a legal action.

Notes

OUTSIDE THE NEGLIGENCE BOX

1 To this point, we have examined the tort of negligence, truly the *pop tort* of liability insurance. Simply put, if you injure the Other Guy and the four elements of negligence can be established, you are liable. It is possible, however, for you to be liable even for things you did not do or for occurrences in which the elements of negligence cannot be established.

Strict Liability

2 ***Strict Liability***, sometimes called ***Absolute Liability***, can make an individual legally liable for damages, even though that individual **has not been negligent**. In other words, under special (**high risk**) circumstances, it is possible for you to become liable for damages to others, even though you have not acted in an imprudent careless manner.

HIGHER STANDARD OF CARE

3 The theory of **Strict Liability** is generally used in inherently dangerous/ultra-high risk situations. Under the law, each right that you have has a corresponding duty. For example, you have a right to drive an automobile, but you have a corresponding duty to keep a proper lookout. The law also attempts **to balance the duty with the risk**. The greater the risk, the greater is the duty to protect others from harm.

4 Very high risk activities impose a **higher standard of care** than imposed under **Negligence**. This higher standard of care is called **Strict Liability**.

5 **Strict Liability** imposes liability on a person even though that person was not at fault/negligent, just because that person was involved in a high risk and dangerous activity. Common situations in which the courts have imposed the concept of Strict Liability include the possession of wild animals, handling and transporting explosives and flammable liquids, abnormally dangerous business activities, such as professional fireworks displays, and, by statute, pollution situations. The defendant can be held liable for damages, simply because an injury has occurred.

Explosives... ...wild animals... ...pollution

6 A classic example of **Strict Liability** applies to the owner of a tiger rehabilitation center. No matter how strong the tiger cages are, and how much care the owner takes in managing their operation, if a tiger causes bodily injury or property damage, the owner is held liable. Another example is handling explosives. No matter how careful the owner is, and **even if the owner is not negligent**, if somebody is injured, the owner is held responsible.

7 Strict Liability is also commonly applied in ***Products Liability*** cases by statute. Even though the manufacturer of a product exercised reasonable care in designing and manufacturing the product, if the product is **unreasonably dangerous**, the manufacturer will be liable.

PRODUCTS LIABILITY

Vicarious Liability

8 When one person does something for the benefit of another, liability is often reaped along with the benefits. For instance, if Joe's secretary, Betty, were driving to the post office for Joe, and she causes an accident, even if she were driving her own car, Joe would be vicariously liable for Betty's acts. This is an example of the most common form of vicarious liability, **the Master-Servant rule**. . . an employer is responsible

MASTER-SERVANT RULE

Notes

for the negligence of his employees during the course of their employment. Vicarious liability can also apply to parents for actions of their children or to employers for acts of independent contractors.

"NO FAULT" BENEFITS

1 Though most casualty contract benefits are available if and only if you are held to be legally liable, there are two huge benefits that are payable without regard to fault.

Medical Payments

2 The Medical Payments section is unusual in that it is the only section of the policy that can pay benefits directly **to the Other Guy** (or his doctor) without establishing a legal obligation to pay.

medical bills only

3 **The Medical Payments section of the policy pays without regard to fault.** If the Other Guy slips and falls on Joe's driveway, Medical Payments (Med Pay) pays. Even if the Other Guy is on roller skates and it appears that he himself is to blame, Med Pay still pays. The limits are rather low (beginning at $1000 per person), but it would certainly pay enough to set the Other Guy's broken arm. Personal Lines contracts will provide Med Pay benefits for up to **three years** from the date of the accident, but Commercial Lines policies limit this benefit to **one year** from the date of the accident.

no fault

4 Obviously, the intent of Medical Payments is to avoid lawsuits. It's like goodwill insurance. If Joe can pay to fix the Other Guy's arm with no hassle, maybe there will be no lawsuit. However, this benefit is limited to bodily injury. Med Pay can pay the doctor, the dentist or even the funeral home, but there is no benefit for lost wages or pain and suffering.

Supplementary Payments

5 Though the word supplementary sounds like an optional add-on, **all liability policies have Supplementary Payments**. They come with the policy–you cannot buy the policy without this benefit.

6 While there are a half a dozen benefits which make up the category of Supplementary Payments, the biggie is **Defense Costs**. For any claim or lawsuit filed against you (to which the insurance applies), the insurance company will provide your legal defense. These costs are paid **in addition to** the limits of liability in most contracts.

expenses for defenses

in addition to the face amount

7 Though it is certainly important that the insurance company provide you with a legal defense in situations where you may be held legally responsible, it may be even more important that a defense be provided if the Other Guy's claim is groundless. Nuisance suits are becoming more common, and it may cost up to $150 - $500 an hour to establish that you are not liable.

8 Other benefits provided by Supplementary Payments include:

- All other expenses incurred in investigating or settling the claim.
- Reasonable expenses you incur at the company's request in assisting their defense efforts, including loss of earnings up to a daily limit.
- The cost of appeal bonds and attachment bonds.
- Any interest awards made to the Other Guy to offset the time between the occurrence or the judgment and the actual payment of damages.

Notes

OTHER LIABILITY POLICIES

COMMERCIAL AND PERSONAL UMBRELLA POLICIES

1 As the size of liability awards given by juries increased to the astronomical, many businesses and some individuals began to want extremely high limits in the liability coverages. To take a basic liability policy and extend it to $1 million, $5 million or more would be prohibitively expensive. The companies would be taking care of all the small claims and would still be responsible for the occasional huge claim. Lloyd's and others stepped in and designed the Umbrella Policy. An Umbrella is designed to augment the limits of primary liability insurance policies.

2 The concept is really quite simple. Suppose you own an Auto policy with limits of $500,000 per person **plus** a $1 million Personal Umbrella. You hit a pedestrian with your car and he is paralyzed for life. The jury awards $1 million. Your Auto policy will pay $500,000 and the Umbrella will pay the $500,000 excess.

3 Surprisingly enough, Umbrella policies are relatively inexpensive. This is because most claims are still small claims. The Umbrella policy gets hit hard when it does get hit, but most claims are adequately covered by the basic policies.

4 **There are really only four basic things to remember about Personal or Commercial Umbrellas:**

- **Excess amounts**
- **No standard form**
- **Uneven at the top**
- **Broadens as well as deepens**

Let's address each in turn.

5 **Excess Amounts** – Umbrellas are written for excessive amounts – $1 million, $5 million, $10 million and more.

Big Bucks

6 **No Accepted Standard Form** – Though Umbrella coverage is readily available today, almost every company writing Umbrellas has a few unique twists in its contracts. Therefore, everything in this discussion should be taken in the most general of terms.

No Standard

7 **Uneven At The Top** – Since the rating of Umbrella policies is dependent upon the underlying coverages absorbing most of the losses, the Umbrella carrier literally dictates which basic coverages you must have if you are to be eligible for the Umbrella.

Add primary to umbrella

8 Joe might have the following Liability coverages:

• Homeowners	$100,000/occurrence
• Auto	$500,000/person
• Boatowners	$100,000/occurrence

9 If he also owns a $1 million Personal Umbrella, then his limits become:

• Homeowners	$1,100,000
• Auto	$1,500,000
• Boatowners	$1,100,000

10 Coverage is **uneven at the top** because it is **uneven at the bottom**.

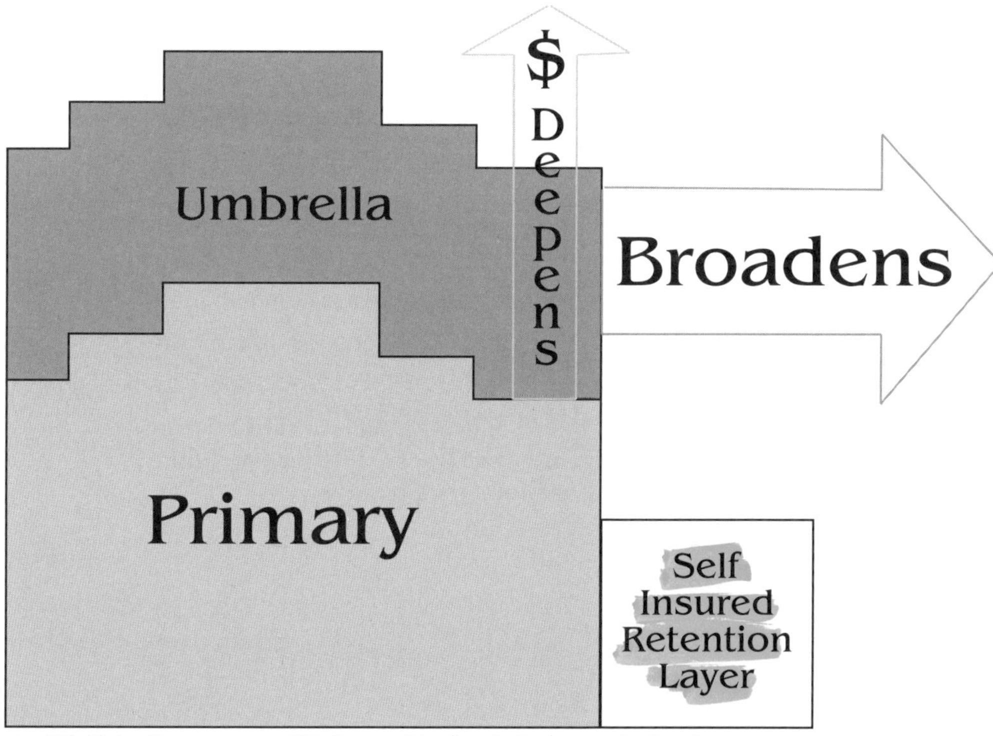

1 **Broadens As Well As Deepens** – Without this final characteristic, there are actually two products that would do everything discussed so far:

- Excess Liability policy
- Umbrella liability policy

2 The difference between these two contracts is that the **Excess Liability policy will never pay unless the underlying policy pays first.**

Suppose that Joe is driving an auto in Germany when he causes a $1 million wreck. His Auto policy defines the coverage territory in the U.S., Canada and Puerto Rico. His Auto policy will not pay and, therefore, an Excess Liability policy will not pay. The Personal Umbrella would, however, **broaden** to cover this loss. Joe would be responsible for first paying a **Self Insured Retention** of, say, $25,000, which functions like a large deductible.

THE CASUALTY ODDBALL

Fire Legal Liability

3 Liability contracts typically exclude coverage for property in your care, custody or control. This is logical because most stuff that is in your care, custody or control is yours – therefore insured under a Property contract, not a Liability contract.

4 But, what about space in a building you rent (and occupy) and accidentally set afire? You probably could not buy property coverage because you don't own the building. If the aforementioned liability exclusion applies, you would have no coverage on the liability side either. Fire Legal Liability provides coverage for tenants who negligently damage the space they occupy in the landlord's building. This is damage done to the **building** - contents are covered under the tenant's property coverage. This coverage is available in both Personal Lines (Homeowners) and Commercial Lines (Commercial General Liability).

Notes

Conclusion

Liability policies are Third Party contracts – you, your company and the unknown, injured third party. The intent of these contracts is to protect your assets if you negligently injure the Other Guy or his property and are legally obligated to pay for the damage.

You can become legally obligated to pay by settlement (out of court), or judgment (in court). In either case, the dispute is resolved under the body of law known as tort law – tort law governs wrongs between individuals.

The central focus of most Liability policies is the tort of negligence – the failure to do or not do what the reasonable person would do or not do under the same or similar circumstances. Negligence is never an intentional act.

To establish negligence, we must show:

- Duty
- Breach of duty
- Proximate cause
- Damages

Compensatory damages are intended to restore the Other Guy to his pre-injury status. Punitive damages are intended to punish the wrongdoer.

If negligence is alleged, the defendant might utilize any of several legal defenses:

- **Comparative fault** – some fault was that of the injured party
- **Assumption of risk** – the Other Guy knowingly placed himself in a dangerous position
- **Contributory negligence** – any fault was that of the injured party
- **Intervening cause** – some other factor acted to cause or enhance the damages
- **Statute of limitations** – too much time has passed

Liability policies contain two important benefits that have nothing to do with fault:

- **Med Pay** benefits can fix the Other Guy's body to avoid a lawsuit

- **Supp Payments** are paid in addition to the policy limits. The most important Supp Payment is the cost of defense.

Personal and Commercial Liability Umbrellas are additional liability benefits that are available after the benefits of the underlying policies have been exhausted. Umbrella characteristics include:

- Written in excessive amounts
- No standard form
- Uneven at the top
- Broadens as well as deepens

Fire Legal Liability provides coverage for tenants who negligently damage the space they occupy in the landlord's building.

CHAPTER 4
BASICS OF THIRD PARTY COVERAGE

1. You can become legally obligated to pay in which of the following ways?

   (A) Settlement
   (B) Judgment
   (C) Neither settlement nor judgment
   (D) Both settlement and judgment

2. Which of the following could NOT be negligence?

   (A) Inaction
   (B) Careless acts
   (C) Thoughtless acts
   (D) Intentional acts

3. All of the following are necessary elements of negligence EXCEPT

   (A) Failing to meet the duties owed the injured party.
   (B) Both parties must be competent to contract.
   (C) There must be a direct and foreseeable link between the act and the injury.
   (D) There must be actual financial injury.

4. Fire Legal Liability would cover damage done

   (A) To a leased office.
   (B) To a leased copier.
   (C) To a leased auto.
   (D) To any Business Personal Property of the insured.

5. In a case where an insured is legally liable, all of the following would be covered losses under his liability coverage EXCEPT:

   (A) The third party's loss of use.
   (B) The insured's loss of use.
   (C) Property owned by the third party, covered by a two party insurance policy.
   (D) Bodily injury to a third party.

CHAPTER 4 • BASICS OF THIRD PARTY COVERAGE QUIZ

6. Which of the following is an example of a Personal Injury?

   (A) A broken arm
   (B) Wrongful death
   (C) Defamation
   (D) Copyright infringement

7. Proximate Cause refers to damage which is:

   (A) caused by an "act of God".
   (B) unintended only.
   (C) intentional only.
   (D) direct and foreseeable.

8. Lost Wages may be classified as all of the following EXCEPT:

   (A) Compensatory Damages.
   (B) Special Damages.
   (C) Economic Damages.
   (D) General Damages.

9. The legal theory which allows the jury to reduce a negligence award because the injured party is partially to blame is:

   (A) Contributory Negligence.
   (B) Comparative Fault.
   (C) Assumption of Risk.
   (D) Intervening Cause.

10. In a third party insurance coverage, the amount of time that the injured party has to bring a claim is set by the:

    (A) Policy Declarations.
    (B) Policy Conditions.
    (C) Insuring Clause.
    (D) Statute of Limitations.

11. The legal theory which states that an employer is responsible for the acts of their employees during the scope of their employment is known as:

    (A) Strict Liability.
    (B) Workers Compensation.
    (C) Vicarious Liability.
    (D) Contractual Liability.

CHAPTER 4 • BASICS OF THIRD PARTY COVERAGE QUIZ

12. In third party coverage, all of the following are true with regard to Medical Payments Coverage EXCEPT

    (A) Fault is not an issue.
    (B) The insured's medical bills are covered if there is no other insurance.
    (C) Lost wages are not covered.
    (D) The pain and suffering are not covered.

13. Supplementary Payments

    (A) Is one of the most common endorsements found in third party policies.
    (B) Pay the expenses of defense.
    (C) Are limited to 25% of the per occurrence limit.
    (D) Pay for the injured party's attorney.

14. Umbrella policies have all of the following characteristics EXCEPT:

    (A) No standard form.
    (B) Uneven at the top.
    (C) Supplementary Payments are deducted from the policy limits.
    (D) Broadens as well as deepens.

15. The tort of Negligence requires that:

    (A) The injured party prove three of the four elements to sustain their case.
    (B) The defendant be insured at the time of the injury to the third party.
    (C) The injury to the third party be caused directly by an act or omission of the defendant.
    (D) There be medical bills and lost wages.

16. Assumption of Risk is best defined as a situation in which an injured party:

    (A) Knowingly places themselves in a situation where injury is likely.
    (B) Is injured by his own negligence.
    (C) Has purchased their own insurance coverage.
    (D) Is partially to blame for their own injuries.

CHAPTER 4 • BASICS OF THIRD PARTY COVERAGE QUIZ

17. Betty owns a nativity scene. It is run over by an out of control forklift truck. This is an example of:

    (A) A bodily injury.
    (B) A personal injury.
    (C) Property damage.
    (D) Potential eternal damnation.

18. Punitive Damages are

    (A) Designed to more fully compensate an injured party.
    (B) Best characterized as noneconomic damages.
    (C) Designed to deter similar conduct.
    (D) Best characterized as special damages.

19. In order for an injured party to collect in a third party claim:

    (A) The insured must be legally liable.
    (B) The injured party must be named in the policy declarations.
    (C) The injuries may not be covered by any other insurance.
    (D) The insured must be negligent.

20. The term "Standard of Care" relates:

    (A) the need to maintain proper insurance coverage.
    (B) only in medical malpractice cases.
    (C) Medical Payments coverage.
    (D) the duty owed to a third party by our insured.

21. Which of the following would NOT generally result in imposition of a Strict or Absolute Liability theory of recovery?

    (A) Damage caused by wild animals kept by the insured.
    (B) Damage caused by the insured's children.
    (C) Damage caused by explosives used by the insured.
    (D) Damage caused by pollution generated by the insured.

END

QUIZ ANSWERS & EXPLANATIONS ON NEXT PAGE

CHAPTER 4
BASICS OF THIRD PARTY COVERAGE
QUIZ ANSWER KEY

1. D. A judgment is a court ordered obligation, while a settlement is a contractual obligation.

2. D. Negligence can be a sin of commission or omission, but intentional negligence is an oxymoron, like jumbo shrimp.

3. B. Legal competency is not required for negligence, e.g. a sixteen year-old driver who runs a stop sign can be negligent, but is not legally competent.

4. A. Fire Legal Liability applies to real property (building) rented (and occupied) by the insured.

5. B. The insured's losses are properly covered by two party contracts. NOTE: Even if the other guy's property is covered by his own two party insurance, there is always the problem of subrogation.

6. C. Personal Injury is damage to an individual's reputation or state of mind. A broken arm and wrongful death fall under Bodily Injury. Copyright infringement is Advertising Injury.

7. D. Proximate cause can be expressed as action, which results in a "reasonably foreseeable injury to a reasonably foreseeable person."

8. D. Lost wages are a type of economic or special damages in that the amount is readily calculated. General damages are those that are not calculable to the last penny, e.g. pain and suffering. Special and General damages are both compensatory, in that they are designed to make the injured party whole.

9. B. Remember: "Comparative fault we balance the blame; Contributory Negligence we wipe out the claim."

10. D. A, B and C are parts of the policy. The injured person is not a party to the contract and cannot be bound by its terms. The Statutes of Limitations on the other hand are set by the legislature.

11. C. Vicarious Liability makes one party responsible for the actions of another; it is most commonly seen in cases involving the "master servant rule," i.e., the employer is responsible for the actions of an employee on the job.

CHAPTER 4 • BASICS OF THIRD PARTY COVERAGE
QUIZ ANSWER KEY

12. B. Third party policies never pay benefits to the insured.

13. B. Third party policies make two promises, not only to pay all sums to which the insured becomes legally obligated to pay, but also to provide a defense. The limits of liability are used to fulfill the first promise, the sums in addition to the policy limits, Supplementary Payments, are used to fulfill the second.

14. C. A, B, and D are three of the four basic characteristics of an umbrella policy. Supplementary Payments are in addition to the limits of liability.

15. C. The four elements of negligence are Duty, Breach of Duty, Proximate Cause and Damages. Answer C expresses the concept of Proximate Cause.

16. A. B and D better fit into the concepts of Contributory Negligence and Comparative Fault. C is irrelevant to establishing legal liability. A fits quite well.

17. C. Property Damage applies to the person's property, Bodily Injury of course relates to damage to their person, Personal Injury applies to damage to reputation or state of mind.

18. C. A, B and D are part of the concept of compensatory damages, making the injured party whole. Punitive Damages on the other hand are designed to punish and deter the bad actor.

19. A. Third Party insurance only pays when the insured is legally liable. Negligence is only one tort theory used to establish legal liability. The injured person is not a party to the contract and thus cannot appear in the declarations. Finally, as stated above, the injured person's own insurance is irrelevant.

20. D. Different levels of duty are defined by the appropriate "Standard of Care." For instance a landowner owes a higher duty to a guest than to a trespasser.

21. B. Strict or Absolute Liability is reserved for ultra hazardous activities, such as wild animals and explosives, or those determined by the legislature, such as pollution and products liability.

Part II
PERSONAL LINES

HOMEOWNERS AND DWELLING POLICIES

5

SOURCE:
ISO HO-2000
ISO DP-2002

1 As we begin to study the Homeowners and Dwelling policies, it is important to recognize the concepts you have learned to this point within the context of the policies themselves. To insure your residence, the insurance company will expect you to have insurable interest and pay premium. You will be encouraged to insure to value and must be able to show proof of loss if requested. In the Personal liability part of the policy, you will buy a coverage that does not pay you but instead pays the Other Guy. In many respects, we are simply applying the principles we developed to insure your home.

How to Insure a House

2 For most of us, our home represents the greatest financial investment we will ever make. Insuring that investment is an absolute necessity, both to us and to the mortgage company that made our purchase a possibility. From the 1700's until the 1950's, you insured your dwelling in the same way you insured most property – under a Fire Policy. Whether it was before 1943 and we are talking about one of the many Fire policies available, or whether it was after 1943 and we are discussing the New York Standard Fire Policy matters little. Under any Fire policy, the coverage was very limited. The insured perils were few (fire, lightning, and removal), and the exclusions and limitations were many.

Notes

There's no place like home

1 By the 1950's, the need for a mechanism that could tailor the Fire policy to more closely fit the needs of the average homeowner became apparent. By adding one of several Dwelling Forms to the Standard Fire Policy, a contract was built that could significantly increase the number of perils covered. Additionally, these Dwelling Forms (or DF's as they were called) expanded the contract to automatically include coverage for other structures on the insured premises, personal property both on and off premises, and additional living expenses if a covered peril rendered a dwelling uninhabitable for a period of time.

2 In time, most companies offered four separate Dwelling Forms. The DF-1 (Basic) could provide coverage on both the buildings and contents that approximated the Basic Cause of Loss Form we studied earlier. The DF-2 (Broad) provided coverage that equaled the Broad Form perils for both buildings and contents. The top of the line was the DF-3 (Special), which gave open perils (All Risk) coverage to buildings but left the contents coverage at the same level as the Broad Form (DF-2). The DF-4 was designed for tenants and, therefore, provided no building coverage whatsoever. The contents coverage was the same as the Basic Form.

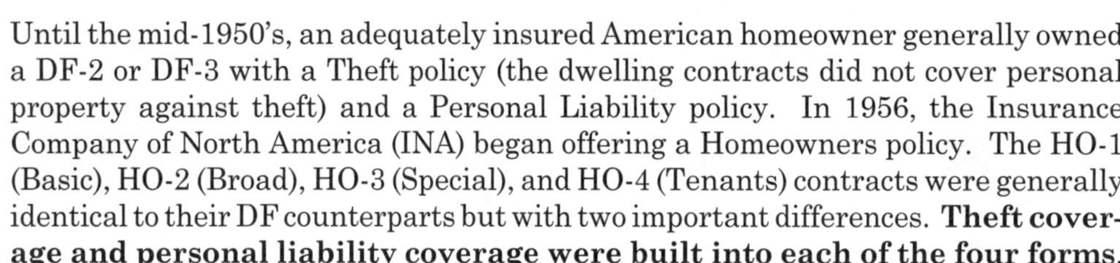

3 Until the mid-1950's, an adequately insured American homeowner generally owned a DF-2 or DF-3 with a Theft policy (the dwelling contracts did not cover personal property against theft) and a Personal Liability policy. In 1956, the Insurance Company of North America (INA) began offering a Homeowners policy. The HO-1 (Basic), HO-2 (Broad), HO-3 (Special), and HO-4 (Tenants) contracts were generally identical to their DF counterparts but with two important differences. **Theft coverage and personal liability coverage were built into each of the four forms.**

ADDED THE PERIL OF *THEFT*

OWNER OCCUPANT

4 As you would expect, within a few years, the number of Dwelling Forms sold began to diminish considerably. Just about anybody who was eligible to purchase a Homeowners policy did so. The continued existence of the Dwelling Forms (or Dwelling Policies as they are called today) is explained by the fact that **not all properties are eligible for a Homeowners policy. One of the fundamental rules of Homeowners is that you must <u>OWN</u> the property and <u>LIVE IN IT</u>**. If you own it, and I rent it, you cannot insure the property under a Homeowners policy. You could, however, use a Dwelling Policy (DP).

5 Although you are unlikely to use Dwelling Policies very frequently as an Agent, they still serve a useful purpose in certain circumstances. While we will expand a little on our discussion of Dwelling Policies at the end of this chapter, for now, a good rule of thumb will suffice: **a Dwelling Policy works approximately like its numerical equivalent in the Homeowners policies except the Dwelling Policies do not have built-in coverage for theft or personal liability**.

DF = DP

The White House homeowners policy covers damage due to the elements. Included are wind, rain, or snow to the roof and hail to the chief.

Notes

HOMEOWNERS

The Homeowners Program

1 As a consumer, you own a Homeowners policy, but as an Agent, you offer to the public a complete Homeowners program – a series of policies that allows your client to select the contract that most closely fits his needs and his ability to pay. In this course, we will examine seven Homeowners policies. While each has some unique characteristics, they all share at least one common attribute. Each packages the property and casualty needs of the consumer into one contract, thus creating a multi-line policy. In the modern Homeowners contract, Part I contains the property coverages and Part II the casualty coverages.

2 The seven forms we will address, in numerical order, are:

- HO-1 Basic Form
- HO-2 Broad Form
- HO-3 Special Form
- HO-4 Tenants (or Contents) Form
- HO-5 Comprehensive Form
- HO-6 Condominium Unit Owners Form
- HO-8 Modified Coverage Form

3 You should notice that, in this sequence, the first four Homeowners forms parallel the four Dwelling policies we mentioned earlier. As you will discover later in this chapter, the similarities do not stop with the name and number. However, at this point, it is more important to look at our seven contracts in conceptual order rather than numerical order.

	Buildings	Personal Property
HO-1	Basic	Basic
HO-8	Basic	Basic
HO-2	Broad	Broad
HO-3	Special	Broad
HO-5	Special	Special
HO-4	N/A	Broad
HO-6	Almost N/A	Broad

What's covered?

From what?

Notes

1 As you examine the chart, you should notice several things. As we move from an HO-1 to an HO-5, peril power gradually increases from the rather limited Basic perils to the extremely generous Special (All Risk) form. Note also that for our purposes, the HO-1 and HO-8 are essentially identical contracts. The only important difference between the two is the method we use to settle the claim, as well as the types of homes covered under the HO-8, and we'll talk about those later.

CONTENTS ONLY

2 Finally, you should see that the HO-4 and the HO-6 are, for all intents and purposes, *contents only* forms. While the logic of this arrangement is apparent to most of us for the HO-4 (Tenants) contract, some of you could be surprised that the HO-6 (Condominium Unit Owners) form is nearly a contents only policy. A word or two describing how a condominium actually works will clear up any confusion.

CONDOs

3 Suppose Joe owns one unit of a 100 unit condominium complex. For simplicity's sake, let's assume that all 100 units are identical. What does Joe actually own? Well, he does not own the walls and roof that enclose his unit. What he actually owns is 1/100 of the entire complex. Therefore, the insurance on the buildings is purchased by the condominium association. The monthly fee that Joe pays to the association goes, in part, to pay the premium for the policy, and Joe is one of 100 Insureds under the contract. Since the buildings are already insured, the nearly contents only coverage offered by the HO-6 is perfectly sensible. If the by-laws of every condominium association were the same, we could stop here . . . but they are not and we won't. Under the by-laws of some associations, Joe has almost no responsibility for the building. Only improvements and betterments that he makes would be his responsibility to insure. However, other associations make Joe responsible for interior walls, permanent fixtures, mechanicals, and appliances. Obviously, pure contents only coverage is inadequate under this arrangement. Therefore, the HO-6 comes automatically with $1000 coverage for the building, and Joe may increase that amount to whatever is necessary to cover improvements he makes and responsibilities imposed upon him by his association's by-laws.

4 At this point, you should have a reasonably good overview of the Homeowners program without the confusion of all the details. You should be aware of the following:

Homeowners in a nutshell

- All Homeowners policies are multi-line contracts . . . Section I is property and Section II is casualty.
- Of the seven Homeowners forms, five are designed to cover both building and contents.
- In progressive order of peril power, these five would be listed as HO-1/HO-8 (same peril power), HO-2, HO-3, and HO-5.
- The two contents only (or nearly contents only) forms are the HO-4 (Tenants) and the HO-6 (Condominium Unit Owners).

5 Using the information you've gained to this point, let's begin to examine the Homeowners policies a little more closely.

Notes

DECLARATIONS SHEET

1 The Declarations page of a Homeowners policy contains typical information about the risk: address of the named Insured(s), location of the dwelling, policy term, coverages, limits, deductible, and the premium. It also contains a reference to any forms or endorsements attached, and the name of the mortgagee (if any).

who, what, when, how much

ELIGIBILITY

2 **Who Qualifies?** – Not every person or every house is eligible for coverage under a Homeowners policy. The primary rule is that **the named Insured must be (or plan to be) the owner-occupant of the insured building**.

Owner Occupied

3 Homeowners Forms HO-1, HO-2, HO-3, HO-5, and HO-8 may be issued to any of the following:

- An **owner-occupant** of a dwelling.
- An intended **owner-occupant** of a dwelling under construction.
- One co-owner of a two-family dwelling that is **occupied** by co-owners.
- A contract-purchaser **occupant** where the seller is retaining title until payments are completed.

Who?

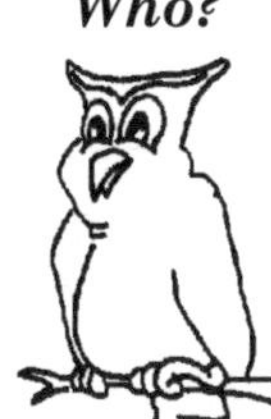

4 An **HO-4** can be issued to any of the following:

Tenants Anyone?

- A non-owner tenant of an apartment or dwelling.
- A non-owner tenant of a mobile home.
- An owner-occupant of a building (e.g., commercial building) which is not eligible for coverage under one of the combined building and contents Homeowners forms.
- An owner-occupant of a condominium unit.

5 An **HO-6** may only be issued to an **owner-occupant** of one of the following:

- Condominium unit
- Cooperative unit

6 Anyone eligible for an HO-6 may purchase an HO-4 instead, but the HO-6 has some extra goodies for condo owners and is better designed to mesh with the building coverage carried by the condominium association.

7 **What Qualifies?** – In all cases (HO-1 through HO-8), the dwelling must be used principally as a residence, but certain low risk business uses are allowed by endorsement. Notice the words *low risk*. A dentist's office or a dance studio would probably qualify – a fireworks stand or liquor store would not. Normally, the kind of business allowed by endorsement is a professional office, private school, or studio. The endorsement is written for a nominal charge to cover the extra traffic in and out of the residence because of the business. It is not designed to substitute for the business coverages needed by that particular business.

Notes

1 Under a Homeowners policy, occupancy of the building is limited to:

- Four families (two in some states)
- Two additional roomers per family

While most companies have separate policies to insure farms and mobile homes,
2 it is possible to modify an HO-2 or HO-3 by endorsement to cover a small farm or
mobile home.

NOTE: If Joe simply owns a house in the country on an acre of ground, he can
3 insure it under an unendorsed Homeowners policy – living in the boondocks does
not make him a farmer.

WHO?

Under a Homeowners contract, there are many potential Insureds – Joe, Jolene,
4 their children, the mortgage company, and even their guests. However, in this
contract (and most other personal lines contracts), the highest rank of Insureds
are the **named Insureds**. They are the people from whom the insurance company
expects to receive premium, and they are the people with whom the company will
settle any claims.

What's in a name?

5 You can acquire the rights of a *named Insured* in two ways:

- Be named on the Dec Sheet.
- Be the spouse of and live with the person named on the Dec Sheet.

Therefore, if the Homeowners policy is written under Joe's name, he is a named
6 Insured. Because Jolene is married to, and living with Joe, she has the rights of a
named Insured. Because we are in the age of the fragmenting family and it is possible for marriage partners to live apart for long periods of time, many companies prefer to name both Joe and Jolene on the Dec Sheet. This makes them both named Insureds regardless of their living arrangements. The Dec Sheet is also where the mortgagee's (first mortgage) interest appears.

. . .more than you think

In cases where a second party (other than the mortgagee) retains interest in the
7 property (e.g., co-owner, contract seller), the second party would also have some
insurable interest in the property. Second party interest can be insured by attaching an Additional Insured Endorsement to the policy.

WHAT?

8 **Dwelling and Other Structures** – Here, coverage is provided for the house, the garage, the swimming pool, the play set, the satellite dish, and the tool shed.

Personal Property and Personal Liability – Coverage is provided in these areas
9 for the named Insured and all residents of the household who are related by blood,
marriage, or adoption. Notice that there is no age limit. If your 40-year-old son lives at home, he is still covered under your policy. As you might guess, a student away at school can still be considered as part of your household.

Notes

1 What about 14-year-old Eskimo Joe who is living with Joe's family as a foreign exchange student? Coverage is provided for **anyone** under age 21 and in the care of any member of Joe's family.

2 **Personal Property of Others** – Suppose Joe's mom (or even a friend) comes to visit for a week with $1,200 worth of personal property in her suitcases. Further assume that when Joe's house is destroyed by a covered peril, it also nails Granny's suitcases. In this situation, Joe's policy could cover Granny's loss, assuming his limits are adequate to do so. (Yes, Granny's own Homeowners policy could pay, but the deductible would nearly eliminate the claim.)

INSURING AGREEMENT

3 This is the **insuring clause** of the policy. The company promises to provide the insurance described in the policy in exchange for the premiums paid by the Insured. Of course, the Insured must comply with all of the provisions in the policy.

we promise

DEFINITIONS

4 The first page of the policy contains the insuring agreement and a number of definitions. Most are self-explanatory. The following two definitions merit special attention since the distinction between them is a key to understanding the application of coverages.

Residence Premises

5 Residence Premises on all forms (except HO-6) means the **dwelling, other structures, and grounds or that part of any building where the named Insured lives that is identified as the residence premises** in the Declarations. With the HO-6, the term *Residence Premises* means the unit where the named Insured lives and is identified in the Declarations.

dwelling. . .
. . .others. . .
. . .and grounds

Part 1

Insured Location

6 *Insured Location* is a much broader definition that primarily applies to **premises liability** coverages. It is identical on all forms and includes all of the following:

- The residence premises.
- Newly acquired premises.
- Any non-owned premises where an Insured temporarily resides.
- Vacant land owned or rented to an Insured excluding farm land.
- Land owned by or rented to an Insured on which a residence is being constructed.
- Cemetery plots of any Insured.
- A premises occasionally rented to any Insured for non-business purposes.

more for Part 2 than Part 1

SECTION I – PROPERTY COVERAGES

WHAT'S COVERED?

1 Section I (Property) of a Homeowners policy subdivides property insured under the contract into four distinct coverages:

Coverage A – Dwelling
Coverage B – Other Structures
Coverage C – Personal Property / Contents
Coverage D – Loss of Use

2 Once we get an idea of what property falls into each of these coverages, we'll turn our attention to answering the second question, "Against what perils do we provide coverage?"

COVERAGE A – DWELLING

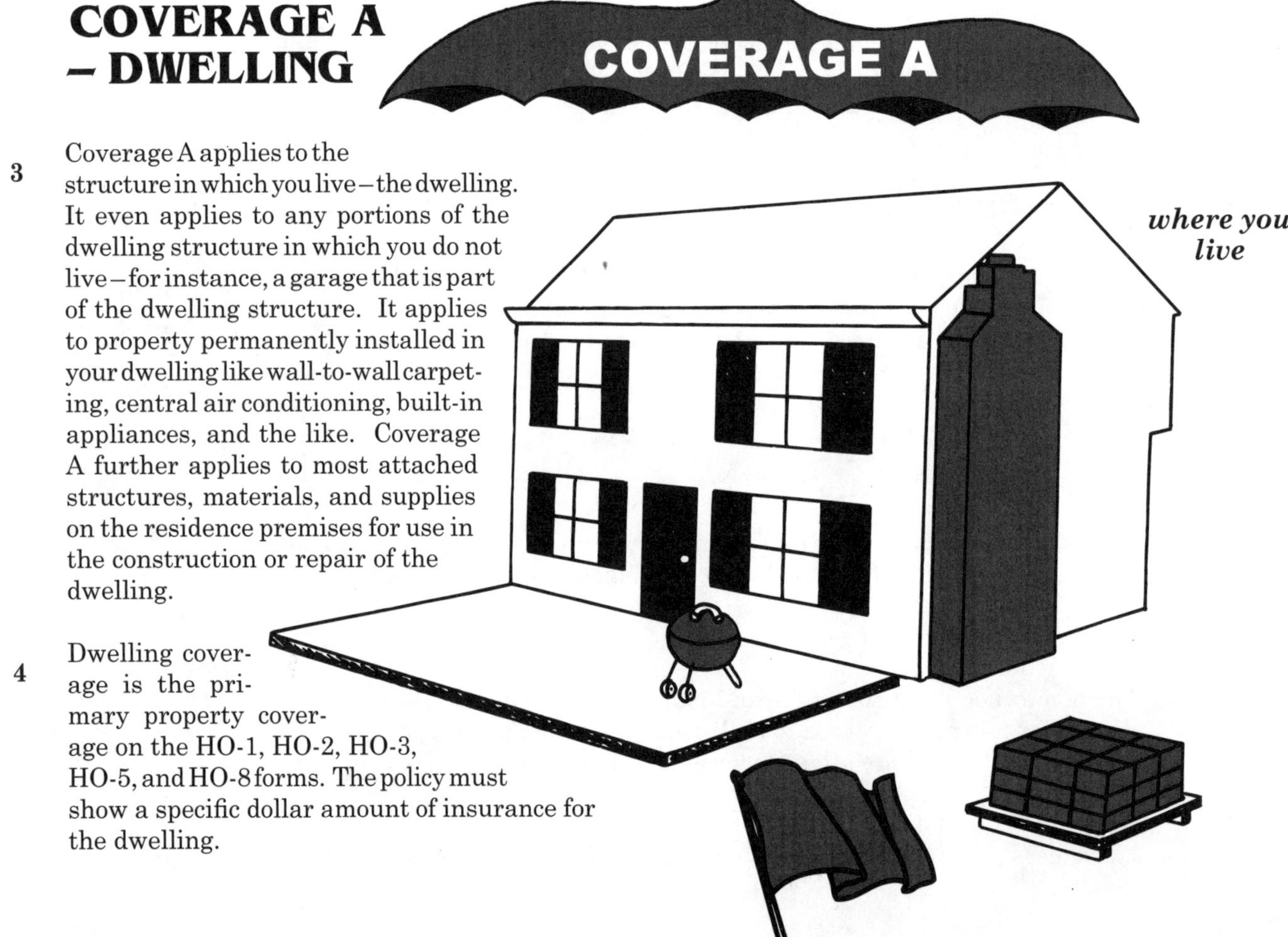

3 Coverage A applies to the structure in which you live – the dwelling. It even applies to any portions of the dwelling structure in which you do not live – for instance, a garage that is part of the dwelling structure. It applies to property permanently installed in your dwelling like wall-to-wall carpeting, central air conditioning, built-in appliances, and the like. Coverage A further applies to most attached structures, materials, and supplies on the residence premises for use in the construction or repair of the dwelling.

4 Dwelling coverage is the primary property coverage on the HO-1, HO-2, HO-3, HO-5, and HO-8 forms. The policy must show a specific dollar amount of insurance for the dwelling.

Notes

1 If you look at the Dec Sheet of an HO-4, you will see no coverage A limits shown at all. In fact, you will see no Coverage A. However, the Tenant's form provides some Coverage A-like insurance for improvements and betterments. With the HO-4, the standard limit is 10% of Coverage C (Personal Property) and is provided as an additional coverage. With the HO-6, the newest Homeowners forms provide Coverage A and it appears on the Dec Sheet. As we have pointed out, the automatic coverage is $1000. As you would guess, the limits in the HO-4 and the HO-6 can be raised by endorsement.

COVERAGE B – OTHER (APPURTENANT) STRUCTURES

2 Coverage for other structures applies to those structures on the residence premises **separated from the dwelling** by a clear space or connected only by a fence, utility line, or similar connection. Typically, other structures include a detached garage or outbuilding, but could also include a swimming pool, tower, tool shed or fence. These other structures can generally have no business use (i.e. used as an office or rented to someone as an apartment), however you could rent your garage to someone for use as a garage and retain coverage.

outbuildings

3 Coverage B is found on all forms except the HO-4 and HO-6.

4 The standard amount of insurance is **10% of the amount written on the dwelling (10% of Coverage A)**, and it is provided as an additional amount of insurance. In other words, if your house is insured for $100,000, then your detached garage is automatically covered for $10,000. If a fire destroys them both, you will receive $110,000. If your garage is worth more than $10,000, you can insure it for a higher amount for an additional charge.

B = 10% of A

Attached - A

Detached - B

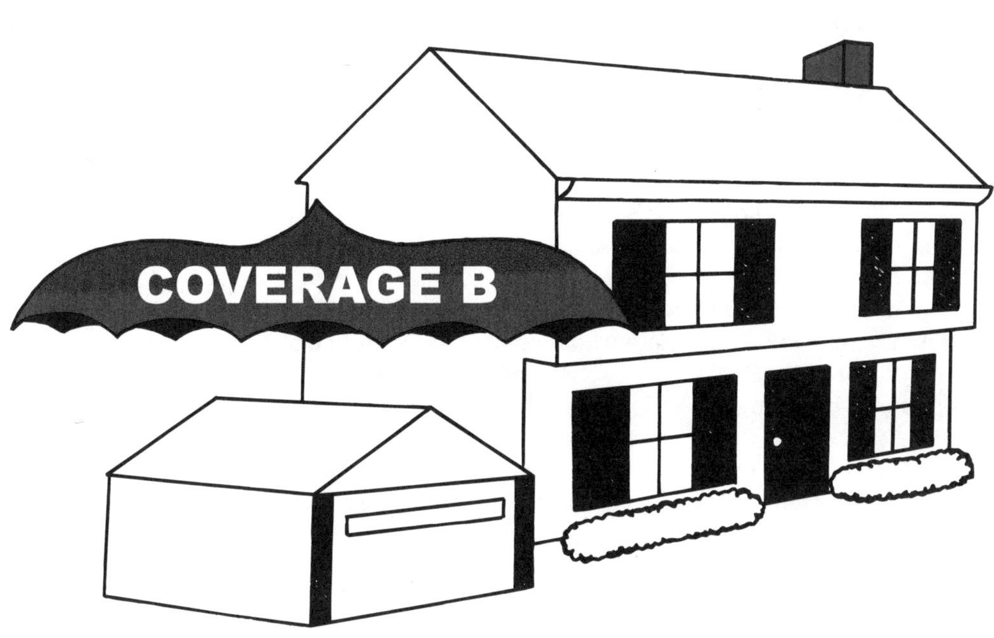

Notes

COVERAGE C – PERSONAL PROPERTY

1 This is coverage for your stuff, and is included on all Homeowners policies. On all forms (except the HO-4, HO-6 and HO-5), the coverage is an additional amount of insurance equal to **50% of the amount written on the dwelling (50% of Coverage A)**. This limit may be increased by endorsement. Recognize that the 50% is a ceiling. If you have a $100,000 house, you have up to $50,000 in coverage on your contents. If you can show a loss of only $22,564 in personal property, that is all the company will pay.

stuff

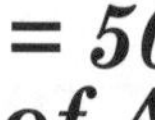

C = 50% of A

2 On the HO-4 and HO-6 forms, personal property coverage is the primary property insurance. The remaining property coverages are based on a percentage of Coverage C.

3 In one respect, Coverage C of Homeowners differs dramatically from the contents coverage of any other property policy. Property policies tend to protect personal property only **on premises**. In the Homeowners policies, personal property owned or used by any Insured is covered while it is **anywhere in the world**. In at least three instances, Coverage C of Homeowners is broader than its counterpart in other property coverages.

worldwide. . . your suitcase on vacation

- Your personal property is covered to the same limits off premises as it is on premises. Therefore, if you took everything you owned on vacation, it would be covered just as it is at home.

- If you own a second residence – say, a fishing cabin – and you permanently locate some of your property at the cabin, you have coverage in an amount equal to 10% of the normal Coverage C limit or $1000 – whichever is greater.

- If you change residences without notifying your company, there is full coverage for your personal property for the first 30 days.

  Obviously, this does not affect those of us who own our home as we could not get a mortgage on the new house without insurance – and very few of us pay cash for our homes. However, this provision could be valuable to an apartment dweller who changes residences without notifying his company.

30 days has September, April, June and Joe's stuff

4 Because Coverage C is so generous, there are certain items of personal property that are not covered at all, and still others that are covered only up to specific dollar limits.

Property NOT covered:

No coverage for:

- ***Better covered elsewhere***
- ***Animals***
- ***Tenants***
- ***Data***

1. Property **better covered elsewhere**, such as automobiles, boats and airplanes
2. Animals, birds, or fish (remember, this is a property exclusion)
3. Motor vehicles and motorized land conveyances, including their equipment and accessories (**but** we will cover vehicles used in the service of the residence and vehicles designed to assist the handicapped)
4. Electronic apparatus designed to be operated solely from the electrical system of a motor vehicle (including accessories and antennas and any tapes, wires, records, or discs intended for use with the electronic apparatus)
5. Aircraft and parts except for model or hobby aircraft
6. Property of boarders or tenants
7. Your property in an apartment on the residence premises rented to others over $2500
8. Your property in an apartment off the residence premises rented to others
9. Business data stored on paper or electronic media
10. Credit card or fund transfer card losses over $500

Property subject to specific dollar limits:

Some coverage

1. $200 for money, bank notes, bullion, gold, and silver
2. $1500 for securities, accounts, deeds, evidence of debt, letters of credit, manuscripts, passports, tickets, stamps, and notes (other than bank notes)
3. $1500 for watercraft including their trailers, equipment and outboard motors
4. $1500 for trailers not used with watercraft
5. $2500 for property on the residence premises used for business purposes
6. $500 for property away from the residence premises used for business purposes
7. $1500 for electronic apparatus (including accessories, antennas, tapes, discs, or other media) **while in or upon a motor vehicle** if the apparatus can be operated from the electrical system of the vehicle while retaining its capability of being operated by other sources of power

Portable GPS

8. $1500 for electronic apparatus not in a motor vehicle but away from the residence premises and which is equipped to be operated by the electrical system of a motor vehicle and is used exclusively for business

Notes

9. $1500 for loss by **theft** of jewelry, watches, furs, precious and semiprecious stones

10. $2500 for loss by **theft** of pewterware, goldware, and silverware

11. $2500 for loss by **theft** of firearms

Limit only applies to theft losses

1 The fact that the standard Homeowners policy does not cover a specific item or limits the coverage on that item does not mean that the item cannot be adequately insured. It only means that a plain vanilla Homeowners policy won't do the job.

Other Personal Property Insurance

All risk Worldwide No deductible

2 We can increase the limits through the use of an Inland Marine contract known as a Personal Property Floater. The coverage is **Open Perils (All Risk)**, meaning that all losses are covered except for those specifically excluded, such as wear and tear, inherent vice, nuclear hazard, and confiscation by the government. The policy territory is **worldwide**, and there is possibly **no deductible**.

3 It is in this area in particular that the distinction between Property insurance and Marine insurance has become blurred. The most common Personal Property Floater **can be written as a separate Inland Marine policy or as an endorsement to the Homeowners policy.**

4 While there are three types of Personal Property Floaters, there is only one used frequently enough to merit any discussion.

Inland Marine

5 **Personal Articles Floater** – This is designed to provide coverage for specific categories of personal property. For years, the customary practice was to issue separate policies to cover the nine categories under the Homeowners scheduled personal property: furs, jewelry, musical instruments, cameras, silverware, golf equipment, fine arts, stamp and coin collections. Currently, insurance companies use a Personal Articles Floater to cover virtually anything. Property is covered up to its full stated value on the basis of a current appraisal or bill of sale. **Depending upon the type of property schedule, recovery may be on the basis of ACV, market value, repair or replacement cost, or agreed value.**

6 One feature of the Personal Articles Floater is that it provides automatic coverage for newly acquired property if there is already coverage for that class of property. This is particularly handy for gift items such as jewelry, furs, cameras, musical equipment, and fine arts. Generally, the automatic coverage is for up to 25% of the amount of insurance already scheduled for that class.

7 There is also a period of time within which the newly acquired property must be reported to the company and the additional premium paid. The time reporting period varies from 30 to 90 days, depending upon the class of property.

Notes

1 It should be noted that unlike most All Risk policies, the Personal Articles Floater has very few exclusions. (Even normal exclusions, like flood, are not on the list.)

- War
- Nuclear hazard
- Wear and tear, deterioration, and inherent vice
- Insects or vermin

Broader than Special

2 There are additional exclusions unique to each class of property. For example, losses to stamp and coin collections are not covered if caused by fading, denting, scratching, or being handled. Damage to musical instruments is not covered if due to faulty repair. Fine arts are not covered while on exhibit or for faulty restoration. Glass, porcelain and other breakables are not covered for breakage unless caused by perils like fire, lightning, explosion, etc. They are not covered if dropped.

COVERAGE D – LOSS OF USE

3 If a covered property loss makes the residence premises uninhabitable, one of the following options would apply:

- **Additional Living Expenses** – meaning any necessary increased expenses incurred so that your household can maintain its normal standard of living.
- **Fair Rental Value** – meaning the market rental value of the portion of the residence premises rented to others.

. . .shelter after the storm. . .

4 If Joe took his family to a motel during this period, he would use the first option. If a portion of Joe's residence premises that is rented or leased to others becomes uninhabitable due to a covered loss, the contract will pay Fair Rental Value.

5 The only event that can trigger these coverages other than a covered peril is if a civil authority (police, fire marshal, etc.) prohibits the use of the residence premises because of direct damage to a neighboring premises by a covered cause of loss.

6 In all cases, payment will be made only for the shortest time required to repair, replace, or rebuild the damaged property.

Notes

AGAINST WHAT?

1 Now that you know that your roof is covered, that you dog is not, and that only $200 of your cash in the cookie jar is covered, it is time to learn **against what perils** all this property is covered.

2 The **good news** is that you can insure your property with a Basic, Broad, or Special Cause of Loss form. The **bad news** is that the Homeowners perils under these forms do not exactly match their counterparts in Commercial Lines. The **good news** is that they **almost** match. Homeowners Basic is WR ELF, VVV,and S.

COMMERCIAL BASIC	HOMEOWNERS BASIC
Wind or Hail	Wind or Hail
Riot	Riot
Explosion	Explosion
Lightning	Lightning
Fire	Fire
Vehicles or Aircraft	Vehicles or Aircraft
Vandalism	Vandalism
Volcanic Action	Volcanic Action
Smoke	Smoke
Sprinkler Leakage	No
Sinkhole Collapse	No
	THEFT
COMMERCIAL BROAD ADDS	**HOMEOWNERS BROAD ADDS**
Falling Objects	Falling Objects
Weight of Ice, Snow, or Sleet	Weight of Ice, Snow, or Sleet
Plumbing	Plumbing
Collapse (Additional Coverage)	Collapse (Additional Coverage)
	Electrical Current Damage
COMMERCIAL SPECIAL	**HOMEOWNERS SPECIAL**
	All Risk
All Risk – first Commercial form to include theft	HO-3 Buildings - yes/Contents - no HO-5 Buildings - yes/Contents - yes

3 As you can see, the Homeowners perils do not differ greatly from the Cause of Loss forms we will study in the Commercial policies. The one truly **important difference is that Homeowners contains theft coverage in all forms.**

Notes

1 In chart form, the build out of peril power would look like the following for our seven policies.

HO Form	Dwelling and Other Structures Coverages A* & B*	Personal Property Coverage C*
HO-1 & HO-8	Basic & **Theft**	Basic & **Theft**
HO-2	Broad & **Theft**	Broad & **Theft**
HO-3	Special & **Theft**	Broad & **Theft**
HO-5	Special & **Theft**	Special & **Theft**
HO-4	N/A	Broad & **Theft**
HO-6	Broad & **Theft**	Broad & **Theft**

ALL FORMS COVER THE PERIL OF *THEFT*

* Coverage D in all forms will pay if a loss covered under A, B or C makes the dwelling uninhabitable.

ADDITIONAL COVERAGES

2 The Homeowners contracts provide some additional coverages. The additional coverages available are listed below. The HO-8 only gets the first nine. The HO-1 and HO-6 only get the first ten. The remaining contracts get not only the first ten, but a choice of flavors on the eleventh additional coverage – chocolate for the HO-2, HO-3, and HO-5, and strawberry for the HO-4.

A - Automatic

1. **Debris Removal** – An additional 5% of the applicable coverage (A, B, or C) can be paid if the damage plus debris removal reaches policy limits. In addition, the company will pay up to $500 to remove one fallen tree that damages a covered building, or blocks the driveway or handicap accessible entrance to the home. Multiple tree damage is capped at $1000.

clean up before fix up

2. **Reasonable Repairs** – to protect from further damage.

plywood

3. **Trees, Shrubs, or Other Plants** – $500 limit for any one plant, and 5% of Coverage A for all plants.

4. **Fire Department Service Charge** – $500, no deductible. This is additional insurance.

5. **Property Removed** – 30 days coverage for property removed from a premises endangered by a covered peril.

6. **Credit Card, Fund Transfer Card, Forgery, and Counterfeit Money** $500 coverage. Does not include unauthorized use by anyone in your household.

7. **Loss Assessment** – $1000 coverage for charges levied against a named Insured by a corporation or association of property owners arising out of direct loss to property owned collectively by members of the association or corporation.

Notes

8. **Collapse** – All forms except HO-1 and HO-8 cover collapse. If any of the named perils result in a collapse of the building, there is coverage. Also, there is coverage for hidden decay, hidden insect damage, weight of contents or people, weight of rain, or use of defective methods or materials in a reconstruction or remodeling which results in collapse.

9. **Glass or Safety Glazing Material** – All forms. On the HO-1 and HO-8, coverage is limited to $100.

10. **Ordinance or Law** – All Homeowners forms except the HO-8 are given an amount up to 10% of coverage A to meet the increased cost of rebuilding or repair due to ordinance or law. This is additional insurance.

11A. **Landlord's Furnishings** – up to $2500 coverage for landlord's furnishings in an area of the residence premises regularly rented to others. Covers losses due to the Broad Form perils and is available only with the HO-2, HO-3, or HO-5.

11B. **Building Additions and Alterations** – For the HO-4 only, the policy will cover additions and alterations made by the tenant in an amount equal to 10% of Coverage C. This is additional insurance.

12. Grave Markers - Up to $5,000 for grave makers (including mausoleums) for loss due to a covered peril.

EXCLUSIONS

1 Because there are actually more listed exclusions in an All Risk contract, we will first look at those common to all three Cause of Loss forms and then turn our attention to those which are unique to the Special form.

2 Those common to all three forms include:

- Ordinance or law (except for that provided as Additional Coverage)
- Earth movement
- Flood
- Sewer back-up and sump pumps
- Off premises power failure
- Neglect
- War
- Nuclear
- Intentional losses
- Government action
- Concurrent causation

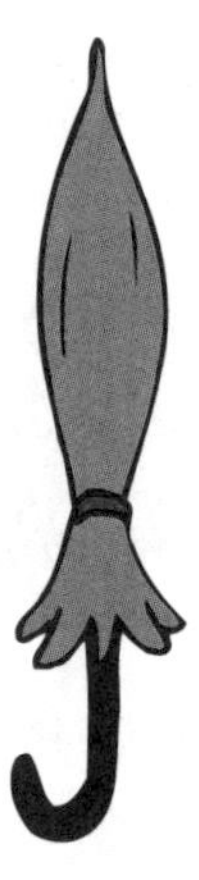

3 Those unique to the Special (all risk) Cause of Loss form include:

everything but. . .

- Collapse not specifically covered by the additional coverage of collapse.
- Freezing of plumbing unless heat is maintained in the building or the water supply is cut off (also true in the HO-2).
- Freezing, thawing, water, or ice damage to pavement, patio, fence, foundation, pier, or dock.
- Theft in or to a dwelling under construction.
- Vandalism after a dwelling has been **vacant for more than 60 consecutive days.**
- Hidden mold or wet rot

- Wear and tear, inherent vice, smog, rust, corrosion, dry rot, or smoke from industrial operations.
- Pollution.
- Settling, shrinking, cracking of patios, foundations, walls, floors, roofs or ceilings.
- Birds, vermin, rodents, or insects.
- Your animals.

CONDITIONS

The Conditions section of Homeowners essentially establishes the rules by which
1 the company and the Insured must play the game. We will reserve the bulk of our
discussion for those conditions unique or different in the Homeowners policy.

- **Concealment or Fraud** – voids the policy
- **Liberalization Clause**
- **Waiver or Change** – must be in writing
- **Cancellation** – The Insured can cancel at any time with written notification. The company can cancel with 10 days notice for nonpayment of premium, 10 days notice for a new policy which has been in effect less than 60 days, or 30 days notice if the policy has been in effect for more than 60 days.

If you're cancelled we tell your mortgage holder

- **Nonrenewal** – 30 days notice required of the company
- **Assignment** – company's consent required
- **Subrogation**
- **Death of the named Insureds** – If a named Insured dies, the executor or legal representative of the named Insured will be covered by the named Insured's policy
- **Insurable Interest** – only pay to your level of insurable interest
- **Duties After a Loss**
  - notify company
  - notify police in the event of theft
  - notify credit card company if appropriate
  - protect property from further damage
  - show the damaged property
  - If we request, send proof of loss within 60 days. Be willing to submit to an examination under oath.
- **Loss Settlement**
  - for Personal Property, structures that are not buildings, awnings, carpeting, appliances, and outdoor equipment, the company pays ACV
  - Buildings under Coverage A or B are covered on a Replacement Cost basis (up to policy limits) **as long as the building is insured for at least 80% of its replacement cost**. If the building is not insured for 80%, then building losses are paid on the basis of ACV or a percentage of the replacement cost as specified in the policy.

stuff = ACV...

Buildings... replacement cost is earned. . .80%

Notes

Note: It is probably a shock to find that a Homeowners policy pays personal property losses on an ACV basis. Many of you are muttering to yourselves, "Not with my policy!" You are probably correct, but it is not because your policy is any different. You have **replacement cost coverage on Coverage C because you bought the endorsement**.

Coverage C replacement cost is endorsed

- **Loss to a Pair or Set** – Loss of an article which completes a pair or a set presents a unique claims settlement problem. For example, let's assume that Jolene owns a pair of enameled earrings designed by Pablo Picasso. Each earring is worth $1000 but the pair is worth $5000. Assume that one earring was destroyed by fire. While Jolene may want $5000 and the company may only wish to pay $1000, neither is fair. The Pair and Set clause says that the company may choose to do either of the following:

  whole worth more than parts

  Value of Set
  -Value Remaining
  =Loss Settlement

  - replace the earring with one of like kind and quality (which is impossible in this case because Pablo is dead).

  - settle on the basis of the following logic.

    Before the loss, Jolene had $5000 in property; after the loss, she had $1000 in property. Her loss is $4000. Therefore, the company should either replace the earring or pay Jolene $4000 less any applicable deductible.

- **Glass Replacement** – Glass damaged by a covered peril will be replaced by safety glazing material when required by ordinance or law.
- **Appraisal** – Two appraisers and one umpire.
- **Other Insurance** – Company will pay pro rata.
- **Suit Against Company** – You must do everything required of you and bring the legal action within two years.
- **Company Option** – Company always has the option of repairing or replacing with like kind or quality rather than writing a check.
- **Loss Payment** – Company pays to the named Insured within 60 days of proof of loss.
- **Abandonment** – No!
- **Mortgage Clause**
- **No Benefit to Bailee**
- **Nuclear Hazard** – No nukes
- **Recovered Property** – You found it after we paid for it? Give it back or give us back the cash.
- **Volcanic Eruption Period** – Any eruptions within 72 hours (3 days) are treated as a single occurrence.

  Vesuvius Clause

Notes

DEDUCTIBLE

1 All Homeowners policies carry a deductible which applies to Section I (Property) losses but not to Section II (Liability) losses. The deductible is applied on an occurrence basis, but does not apply to fire department service charges or to coverage for credit cards, forgery, or counterfeit money.

2 Under current Homeowners policies, the **basic deductible is $250**, which is an increase from the traditional $100 deductible. The Insured has the option of buying back the $100 deductible for additional premium or the Insured may choose a higher deductible of $500, $1000, or $2500 to reduce the premium.

"D-Duck"

3 You might wonder how a deductible would work with property that is also subject to a dollar limit. For example, currency is subject to a $200 limit. If you subtract the deductible, it doesn't leave you with much of a claim. The way it is done, however, is you subtract the deductible from the loss and **then** apply the limit. If you had $1000 stolen from your mattress, we would first subtract the $250 deductible. The policy limit on cash would reduce the claim from $750 to $200.

PROPERTY ENDORSEMENTS

4 **A number of endorsements may be attached to Homeowners policies to alter coverage or increase the policy limits or sub-limits. Naturally, doing so will result in an increased premium. Here are five of the most important endorsements.**

Inflation Guard

5 An Insured can purchase an Inflation Guard endorsement, which will automatically raise the limits for Coverages A & B at periodic intervals. This helps to keep the amount of insurance-to-value for the dwelling at a level adequate to guarantee replacement cost in the event of a loss. The annual percentage increase is pro-rated throughout the year. (e.g. A 6% annual increase would raise the limits by 3% for a loss halfway through the policy period.)

Only A & B

Personal Property Replacement Cost

new for old stuff

6 Personal property replacement cost coverage is available **by endorsement** for all Homeowners policies except the HO-8. The endorsement excludes some types of property such as obsolete articles, antiques, fine arts, and paintings which cannot be easily replaced. Normally, the company will first pay ACV on covered contents losses, and then pay the additional Replacement Cost dollars as the contents are actually replaced.

Scheduled Personal Property

7 Same as a Personal Articles floater except it works as an endorsement to the Homeowners policy rather than as a separate Inland Marine policy. Saves money and saves issuing a separate policy.

Notes

Earthquake

bricks by endorsement

1 Since earth movement is an exclusion in all Homeowners forms, an important endorsement in many areas of the country is Earthquake. It covers only earthquake and volcanic eruption. It is written with a percentage deductible. And, tremors felt within a 72 hour period are treated as a single occurrence.

Limited Fungi, Wet or Dry Rot or Bacteria Coverage

2 This endorsement includes the cost to remove fungi (including mold and mildew) as well as the cost to tear-out and replace damaged parts of the building and the cost to test the air. Coverage only applies when fungi or rot are caused by a covered peril. So faulty construction methods would not be covered.

HOMEOWNER FORM SPECIFICS

As we have moved through the Homeowners policy, we have created a model policy which can be approximated by the following skeletal outline:

Model HO Property Coverage Structure

3

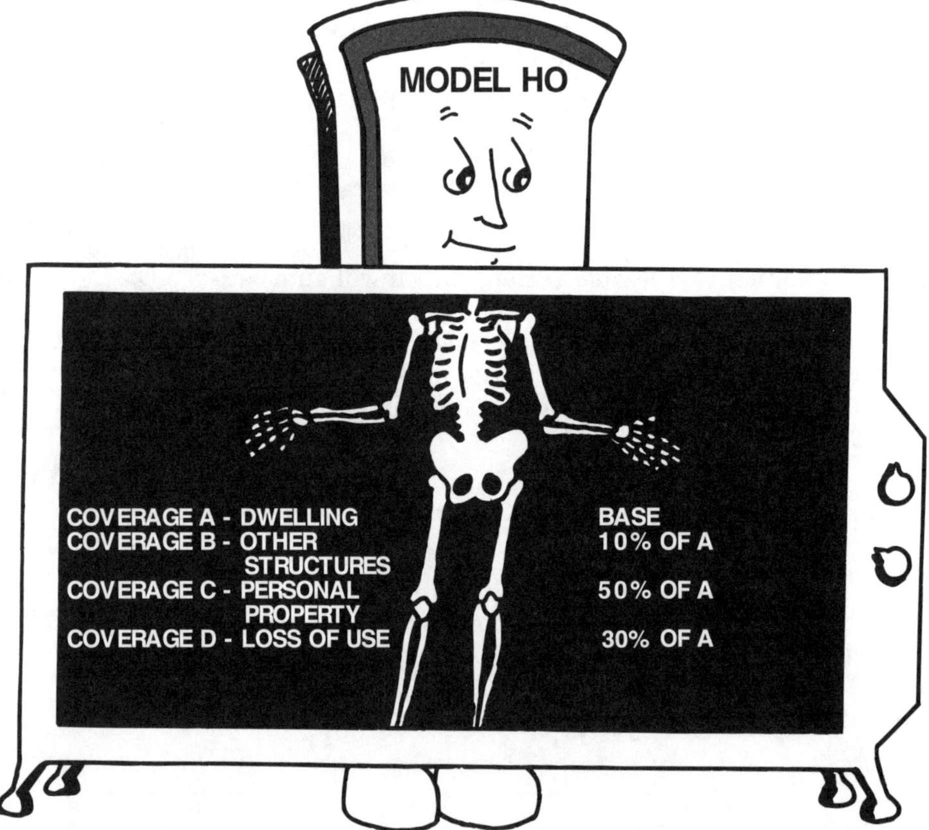

Even with the information you have at this point, you know that our model is not completely representative of all seven forms. The HO-4, for example, doesn't even have Coverage A or B. Therefore, it is important for us to quickly look at each form and notice where it conforms or differs from the bare bones model.

Notes

1 As we walk through that process, we need to point out a few details that have not been important to you up to this time. For instance, we have said that an HO-1 and an HO-8 are nearly identical contracts. That is true, but there are differences or we would only need one of them.

2 You should now have reached the point in your understanding that your mind can accept some of these important details.

BASIC FORM (HO-1)

Property Coverage Structure

BASIC

BASIC

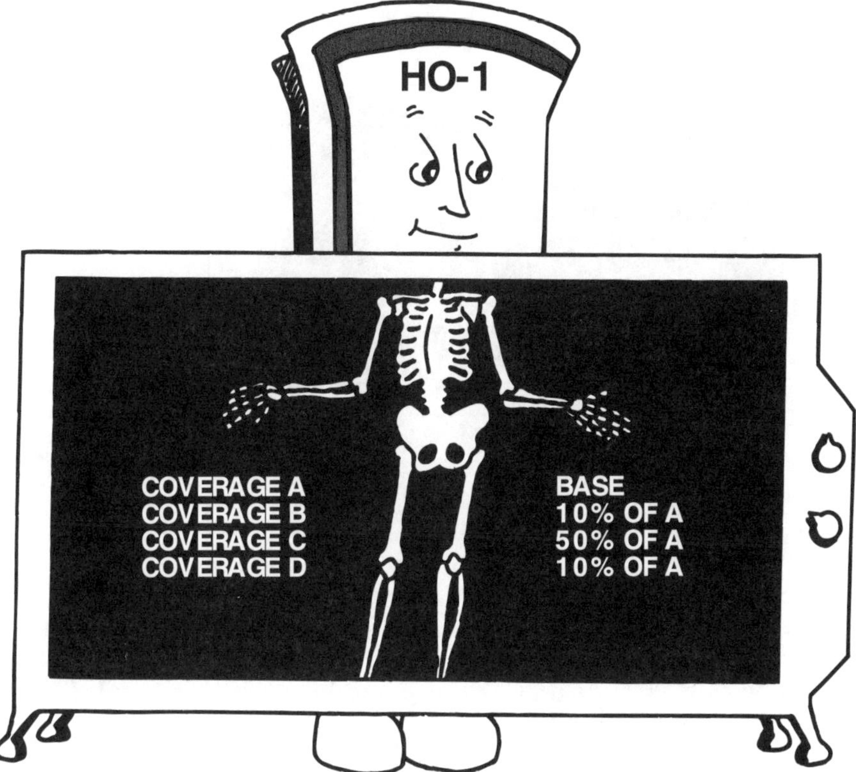

"D" only 10%

Synopsis

3 The skeletal outline of the HO-1 generally follows our model – the one noticeable exception is that Coverage D (Loss of Use) is 10% of Coverage A (Dwelling) as opposed to 30%. You should remember that all HO-1 property coverages are tied to the Basic perils (plus theft), which makes the HO-1 the wimp of the Homeowners program.

Peril wimp

Comment

4 Actually, the HO-1 is even more limited than it first appears. As we've already pointed out, it does not get all of the Additional Coverages. Furthermore, two of the covered perils are defined more restrictively on the HO-1 (and HO-8) than they are on any of the other Homeowners forms.

- Smoke is covered, but not smoke from a fireplace.
- Vehicles driving through your home are covered, but only if the vehicle is not owned by or driven by a member of your household.

don't keep the home fires burning

Notes

1 Many companies do not use an HO-1, and there are jurisdictions that do not allow it to be sold. About the only reason which justifies the continued existence of this policy is that it serves the needs of those who do not qualify for anything else, and perhaps it meets the objectives of the classic cheapskate.

MODIFIED COVERAGE FORM (HO-8)

Property Coverage Structure

FOR OLDER HOMES!

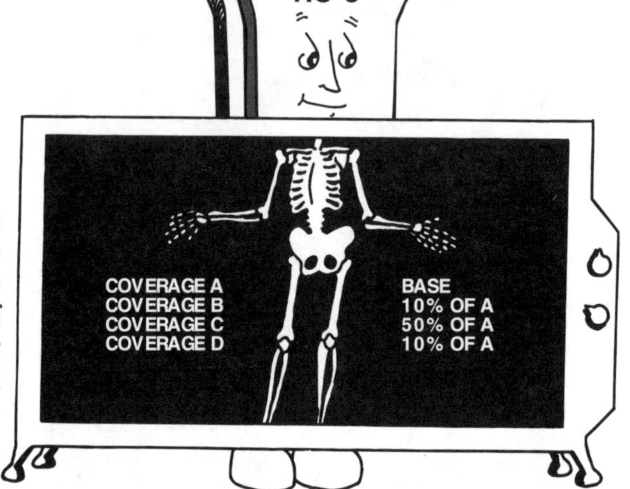

Synopsis

2 As you can see, the bare bones HO-8 simply replicates the structure of the HO-1, and the peril power is still at the level of the Basic form perils (including the limitations we discussed concerning the Additional Coverages, smoke, and vehicles). So why do we need an HO-8?

Still wimpy

3 The HO-8 was developed to insure **older homes** whose replacement costs far exceed their market value. In most cities, you can find homes built in the 1930's or 1940's that, because of their ornate design or the way they were built (use of a labor-intensive method of construction or building materials that today are unavailable or prohibitively expensive), they would cost $200,000 to $500,000 to replace. But, because these homes are often located in older, declining neighborhoods, their market value may be only $60,000 to $100,000. As we've learned, dwelling losses are settled on a replacement cost basis if, and only if, the Insured carries insurance equal to 80% or more of the value. If you bought a house for $80,000, you probably would not want to insure it for $200,000. And, if you did, no company would want to write the coverage because you would have a $120,000 incentive to burn down the house.

FOR OLDER HOMES!

4 The HO-8 is designed to solve this dilemma. With the HO-8, you would insure your house for the fair market value, say, $80,000. In its original version, and still today in most states, losses would be settled as follows:

- Total Building Loss – Policy Limits
- Partial Building Loss – ACV
- Contents – ACV

5 Some states allow the HO-8 to be written on a repair cost basis. The repair cost version is more expensive than the ACV approach, but there is no depreciation in the event of a partial building loss. Therefore, if your roof is destroyed, you get another roof. However, the policy only requires that the replacement or repair be made with "functionally equivalent materials." As an example, the slate roof on your old mansion might be replaced with asphalt shingle.

glass - not stained glass

Notes

Comment

1 For the most part, an HO-8 could be viewed as the equivalent of an HO-1 with a different method of settling building losses. The peril power is the same and the basic structure and limits of the policies are the same with only a couple of differences.

- With the HO-8, there is a $1000 limit on all theft losses.
- Off premises losses to personal property are limited to 10% of Coverage C or $1000, whichever is greater.
- Debris removal cannot cause the claim to exceed the face amount.
- The tree, shrub, or plant limit is $250 rather than $500.
- The standard deductible is $100.

BROAD FORM (HO-2)

Property Coverage Structure

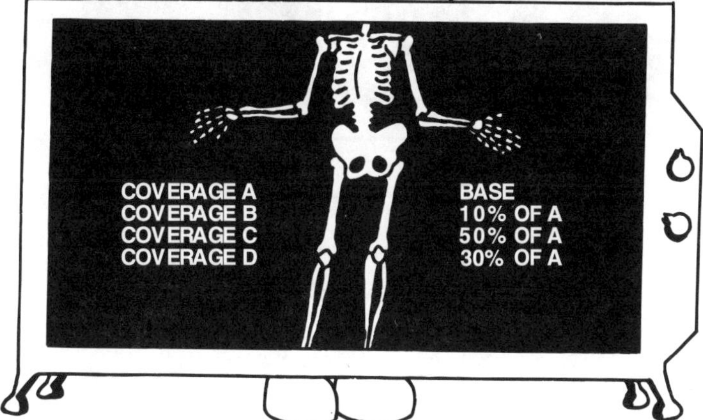

BROAD

BROAD

Synopsis

2 The HO-2 exactly parallels the skeletal structure of our model Homeowners. With the HO-2, all coverages are tied to the Broad form perils so losses due to collapse, weight of ice and snow, plumbing, falling objects, and damage from artificially generated electrical current are now covered.

a little more muscle

Comment

3 The HO-2 is a much better policy than the HO-1. Beyond the fact that it covers more perils, the restrictive definitions of the HO-1 (and HO-8) are now gone for good. Smoke from a fireplace is covered, and there is coverage for those of you who plan to drive a vehicle through your living room. Probably the biggest limitation of the HO-2 is that coverage is still provided on a **named peril basis**. If it is not on the list, it is not covered. The burden of proof is still on the Insured.

Notes

SPECIAL FORM (HO-3)

Property Coverage Structure

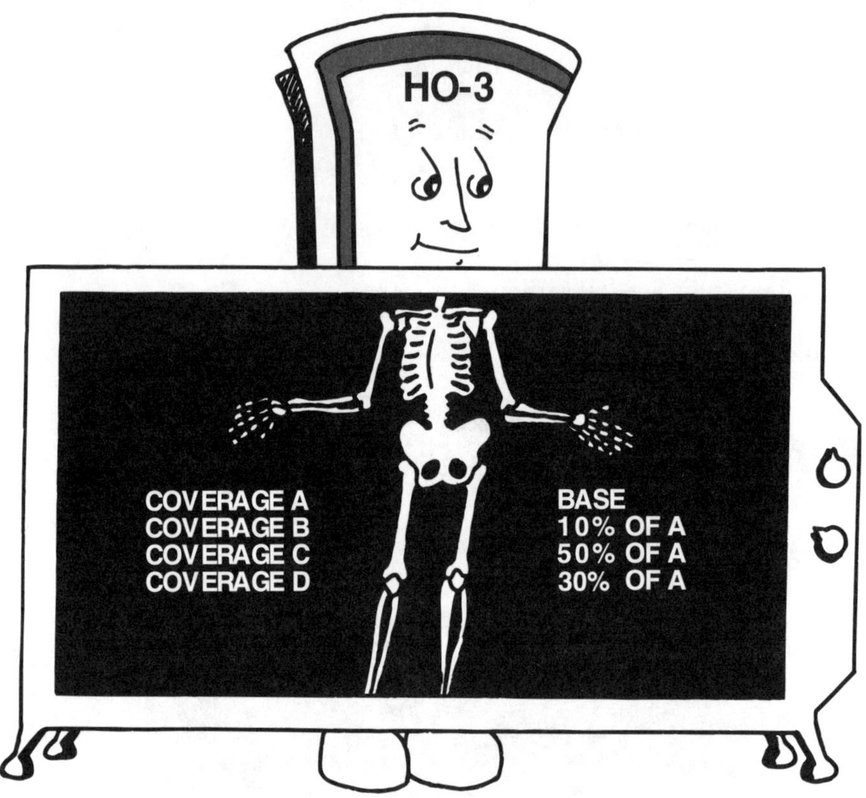

SPECIAL

BROAD

Synopsis

1 As you can see, the HO-3 property coverage structure matches our model exactly. The HO-3 is unique in that Coverages A and B are written using the Special Cause of Loss form, and Coverage C still uses the Broad form perils.

Comment

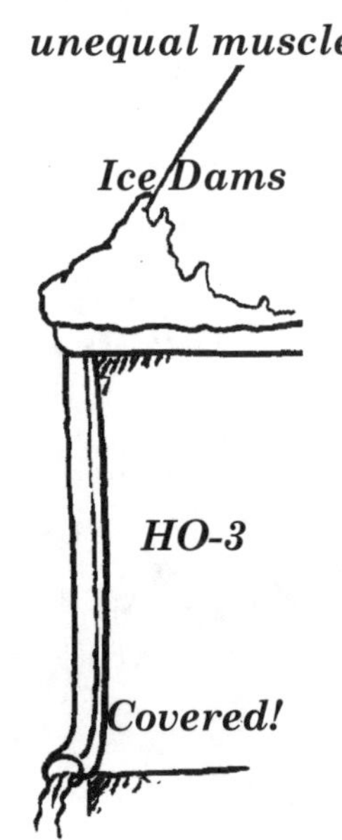

2 The big change with the HO-3 is that **coverage on the dwelling and other structures becomes Open Perils**. Now, if it is not excluded, it is covered. A great example that differentiates the coverage offered by an HO-3 as opposed to an HO-2 occurs in parts of this country every winter. Snow builds up on a rooftop, ice clogs the gutters, and then we have a 36° day with the sun out. The surface of the snow layer begins to melt. If you are lucky, the water runs over your gutters and onto the ground. If you are not, it seeps into your house and does interior damage. What about coverage under the HO-2 or HO-3?

- The HO-2 will **not** cover this loss because Mother Nature made no hole or opening into the structure to allow the water to enter.
- The HO-3 will provide coverage because this loss is not excluded.

Notes

COMPREHENSIVE FORM (HO-5)

Property Coverage Structure

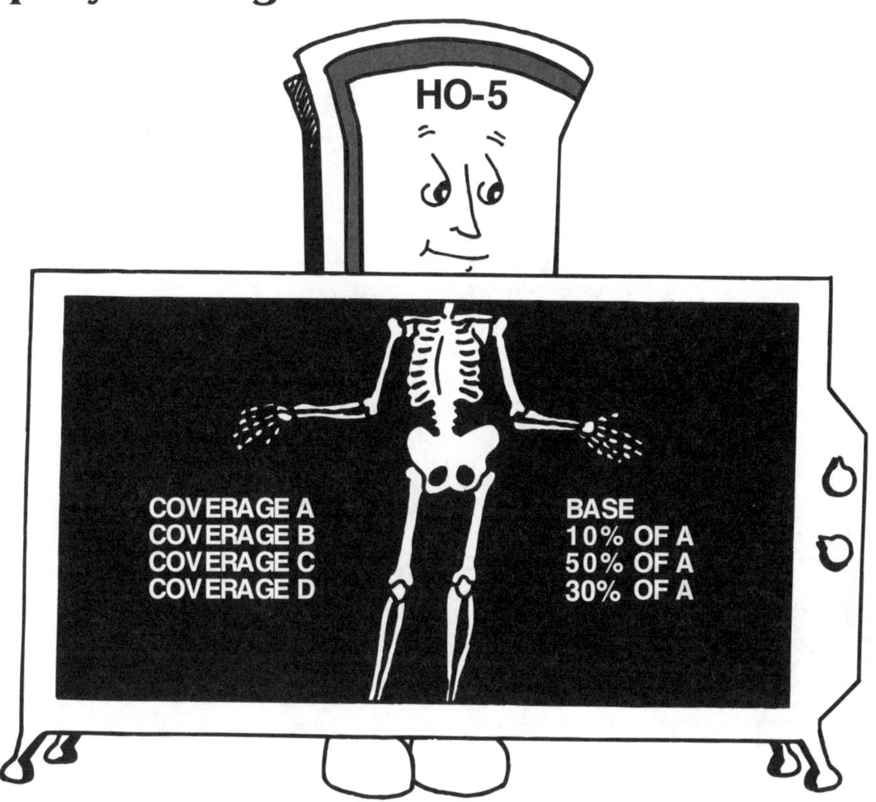

SPECIAL

SPECIAL

Synopsis

1 The HO-5 almost matches the structure of our model; however, Coverage C is 50% of Coverage A. It improves upon the HO-3 in the only way possible – it boosts the peril power on personal property (Coverage C) to Open Perils. The Dwelling and Other Structures coverage is the same as on an HO-3.

Comment

2 Obviously, the big news in the HO-5 is that **Coverage C (Personal Property) also becomes Open Perils**. Coverage for theft of personal property is expanded somewhat by an HO-5. The special sub-limits of coverage for theft of jewelry, watches, furs, precious stones, silverware, goldware, pewterware, and firearms remain the same, but the limits are made to apply to "loss by misplacing or losing" as well as theft. This makes the HO-5 the only Homeowners form which insures personal property that you simply lose or misplace.

HO-5 ate his spinach

$1500 for theft of jewelry and $1500 if you lose or misplace it

3 About the only unique exclusions that apply to an HO-5 center around certain fragile personal items such as eyeglasses, glassware, and porcelain items that are too delicate for all risk coverage. These items are only covered if lost to specific perils, such as fire, lightning, wind, hail, smoke, explosion, and theft.

Notes

TENANT BROAD FORM (HO-4)

Property Coverage Structure

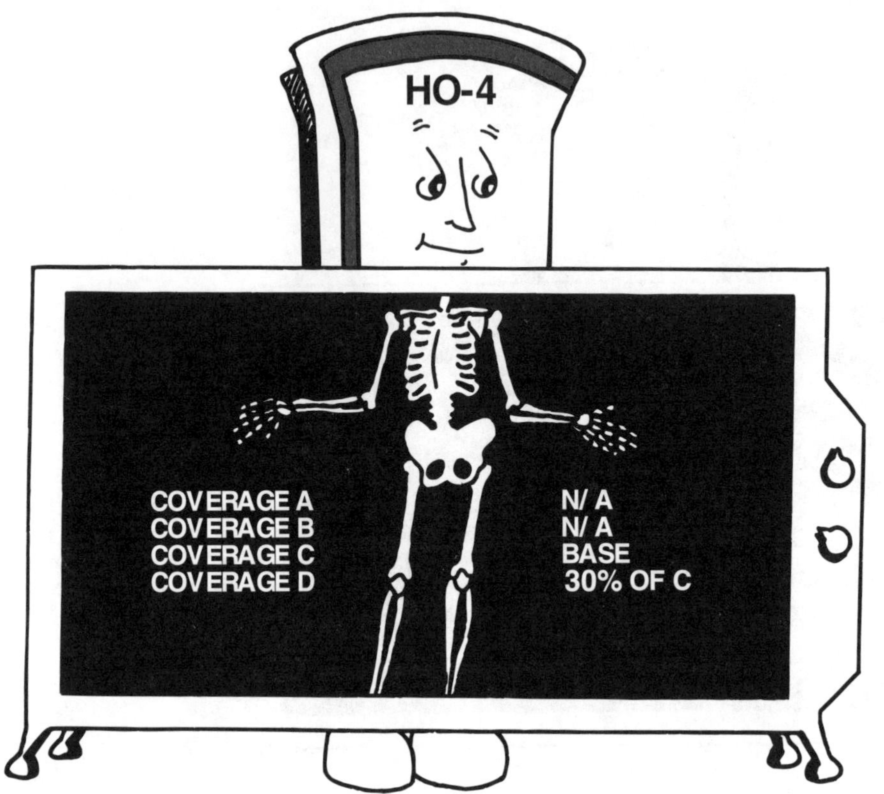

D = 30% of C

Synopsis

1 The HO-4 (Tenant Broad Form) deviates significantly from the model Homeowners contract. Since there is no Coverage A or B, Coverage C becomes the base and Coverage D becomes 30% of C. As the name implies, the plain vanilla HO-4 is written with the Broad form cause of loss. As you might guess, it can be endorsed to cover personal property on a Special cause of loss basis.

only stuff

Notes

CONDOMINIUM OWNERS FORM (HO-6)

Property Coverage Structure

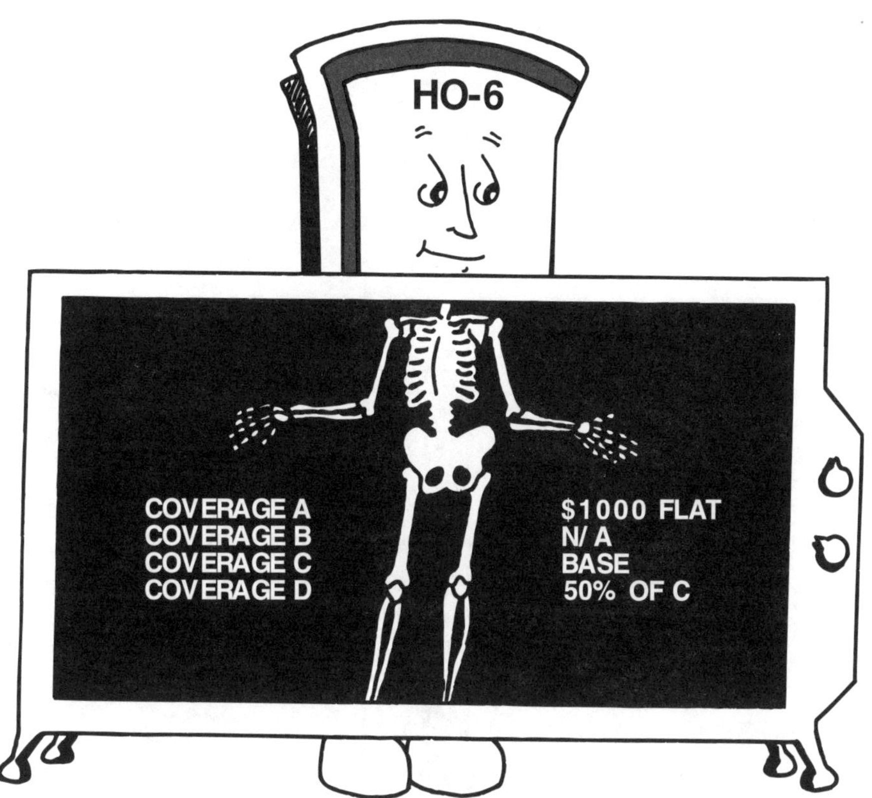

D = condo owners must live better

Synopsis

1 Like the HO-4, the HO-6 is designed to insure personal property against the same perils as the HO-2: the Broad form perils.

Comment

2 For the most part, the **HO-6 functions like an HO-4**. There are only two important differences. On an HO-6, there is $1000 coverage for alterations and other owned building items listed as Coverage A. Secondly, an HO-6 is designed to provide a standard limit of 50% of Coverage C for Loss of Use (Coverage D) whereas the HO-4 uses 30% of Coverage C as its Coverage D limit.

Notes

HOMEOWNERS PROPERTY COVERAGE REVIEW

1 Most of the important points we have made about the Homeowners property coverages are summed up nicely on the following chart.

HOMEOWNERS PROPERTY COVERAGES

HO Form	Dwelling and Other Structures Coverages A* & B*	Personal Property Coverage C*
	REPLACEMENT COST	ACTUAL CASH VALUE
HO-1 & HO-8**	Basic & Theft	Basic & Theft
HO-2	Broad & Theft	Broad & Theft
HO-3	Special & Theft	Broad & Theft
HO-5	Special & Theft	Special & Theft
HO-4	N/A	Broad & Theft
HO-6	$1000 . . . Broad & Theft	Broad & Theft

* Coverage D in all forms will pay if a loss covered under A, B or C makes the dwelling uninhabitable.

** HO-8 settlement on buildings is ACV or Repair Cost.

MOBILEHOME ENDORSEMENT

Eligibility

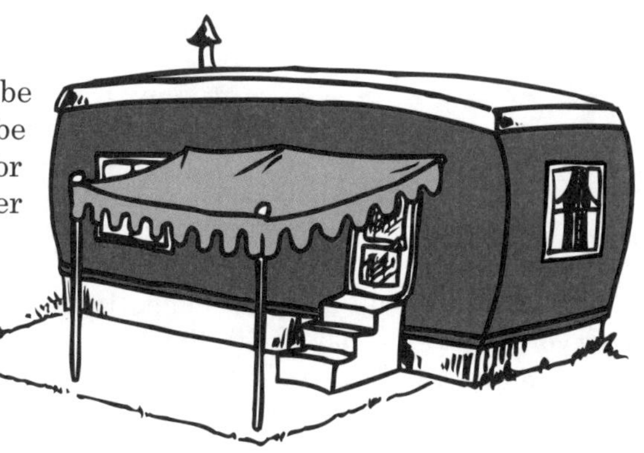

1 The **Mobilehome Endorsement** may be added to either the **HO-2** or the **HO-3**. To be eligible, a mobilehome must be designed for portability and year round living. In order to be covered under this endorsement, the mobilehome must be at least 10 feet wide and 40 feet long. Otherwise, the basic HO eligibility rules, such as owner occupancy, apply.

HO-2 or HO-3

Coverages

2 The Mobilehome Endorsement covers about the same property as a regular HO. Coverage A includes the mobilehome, attached structures, utility tanks, and permanently installed items such as appliances, cabinets and floor coverings. This coverage is written on a **replacement cost** basis. Items such as permanently installed awnings, outdoor antennas and other outdoor equipment are also covered, but on an **ACV** basis. The other coverages look a lot like those available under any other HO.

Policy Limits

3 Coverage A is again the *lead domino*. Coverage B is 10% of A, with a minimum limit of $2,000. **Coverage C is 40% of A**. Coverage D is 30% of A.

C = 40%

Definitions, Conditions and Additional Coverages

4 The *residence premises* is modified to include the mobilehome as well as the land owned or **leased** by the Insured.

5 The *pair set clause* is expanded to include *panels*, should it be impossible to match lost or damaged body panels.

6 Under the coverage additions, there is up to $500 available for moving the mobilehome to avoid damage. Assume that Joe's mobilehome is parked just south of Miami, and Hurricane Ichabod is winging its way to the coast. The policy will pay up to $500 to move Joe's mobilehome inland, and no deductible will apply.

Options

7 The most important of the Mobilehome Endorsement options is the Transportation or Permission to Move Endorsement. It is actually an endorsement to an endorsement. Without it, we don't cover damage to a mobilehome sustained while it's being mobile.

8 With it, however, the Insured has protection from the perils of collision, upset, and sinking. Sinking applies to losses while the mobilehome is being transported on a licensed ferry boat. The coverage lasts for 30 days, and applies anywhere in the continental United States and Canada.

Notes

SECTION II – CASUALTY COVERAGES

THE PERSONAL LIABILITY POLICY

1 Up to this point, the portions of the Homeowners policy that we have studied have been primarily concerned with insuring your property – your house, your kid's stereo, your living room furniture, even the clothes in your closet. Section II of Homeowners concerns itself with an entirely different problem. In Section II, you, your spouse, your kids, or even your stuff gets you into trouble by injuring someone else or their property. Your son chops down the tree in your front yard and it damages a neighbor's auto. Your dog bites the mail carrier. Section II of Homeowners is designed to protect you in situations very much like the ones just mentioned.

2 The same principles that we established in Chapter Four of this text will guide us in this portion of the Homeowners policy. A short review is probably in order.

LIABILITY REVIEW

3 As with most liability coverages, the Homeowners policy is primarily concerned with **negligence**. Negligence is the failure to do or not do what the **reasonable person** would do or not do in the same circumstances.

4 To prove negligence, four specific elements must be established:

- Duty
- Breach of Duty
- Proximate Cause
- Damages

5 You can become legally responsible for damage to someone else or their property in two ways:

- Settlement
- Judgment

6 In either event, this policy will never pay you; it pays the injured third party – the Other Guy. As you might guess, where there is liability, there is also Med Pay – our way of avoiding lawsuits. And, if there is no way to avoid legal action, there are Defense Costs.

Notes

COVERAGE E – PERSONAL LIABILITY (BI AND PD)

1 In the Homeowners policies, the phrase Personal Liability is used to describe a homeowner's potential legal liability for negligence resulting in bodily injury or property damage to a third party. (Notice that there is no personal injury coverage provided.) The **basic limit is $100,000 per occurrence**, and there is no aggregate limit. While this coverage applies separately to each Insured, total liability coverage resulting from any one occurrence may not exceed the Coverage E limit stated in the policy. Of course, limits higher than $100,000 are available for additional premium.

E = $100,000 per occurrence

2 It is important to note that the Personal Liability coverage protects the members of the Insured's household, both **on and off insured locations** unless they are involved in activities that are specifically excluded (such as driving a car, which should be covered under an auto policy).

COVERAGE F – MEDICAL PAYMENTS TO OTHERS

3 Unlike Coverage E (Personal Liability), the Medical Payments To Others section does not require that legal liability be established. Negligence does not have to be established. If someone is injured at your house or is injured due to the activities of you or one of your family, it pays – even if the accident is not your fault. It covers necessary medical expenses incurred within **three years** of an accident which causes bodily injury. Of course, an accident is covered only if it occurs during the policy period. **The basic Medical Payments limit is $1000 per person**, but higher limits may be purchased. The obvious purpose is once again to avoid lawsuits. However, suppose an injured party collects $1,000 under Medical Payments and still sues for lost wages, pain and suffering, etc. If they are ultimately awarded $50,000, they will receive $49,000. **You cannot add Med Pay to the Liability limits**.

F = $1000 per person

4 This coverage does not apply to expenses related to injuries of the named Insured or any regular resident of the Insured's household, except **residence employees**. At the insured location, coverage applies only to people who are on the insured location with the permission of the Insured. Away from the insured location, coverage applies only to people who suffer bodily injury caused by an Insured, an animal owned by the Insured, a residence employee in the course of employment by an Insured or losses which arose out of a condition in the insured location.

Notes

EXCLUSIONS FOR SECTION II – LIABILITY

The coverage statements for liability and Med Pay are very broad. The only way to
1 know for sure that something is covered is to see what is excluded. Losses not covered
by Coverage E (Personal Liability) or F (Med Pay to Others) include the following:

1. War
2. **Intentional acts**
3. **Professional liability**
4. **Business pursuits** that are full time, part time, or occasional are excluded--unless the business earns less than $2,000 per year

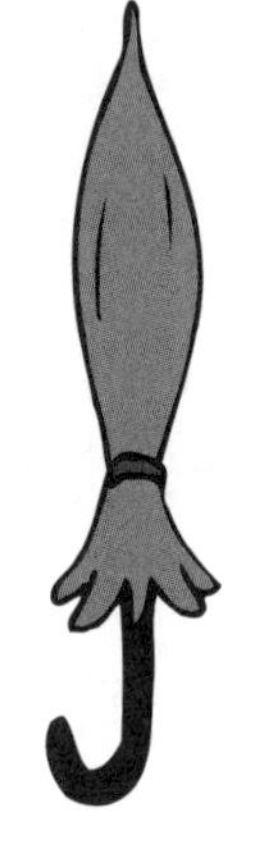

5. Damage to property rented or occupied by an Insured except for negligent **fire**, smoke or explosion damage (Fire Legal)
6. Losses stemming from a premises that is not an insured location
7. Bodily injury to any person covered by **Workers Compensation**
8. Bodily injury or property damage to any resident of the household other than a residence employee
9. Transmission of a communicable disease
10. Sexual or physical abuse, including molestation and corporal punishment

11. Losses due to the use, sale, manufacturing or delivery of a controlled substance (illegal drugs)
12. Ownership, maintenance, use, loading, or unloading of an excluded **vehicle, watercraft, or aircraft**
13. Vicarious liability imposed on a parent for the use of an excluded vehicle, aircraft or watercraft by a minor

Comment

Excluded vehicles means most motor vehicles, motorized land conveyances, and
2 trailers towed or carried on motorized vehicles that are owned, operated by, rented,
or loaned to an Insured. Coverage is provided for the following: unregistered
vehicles, vehicles in dead storage, vehicles used to service an Insured's residence,
vehicles designed to assist the handicapped, and motorized golf and recreational
vehicles designed for use off public roads.

off road OK

Excluded watercraft – While there is some liability protection for watercraft
3 under a Homeowners policy, it is extremely limited coverage. Primarily, the size
and speed (horsepower) of a boat are the critical factors in determining the liability
exposure. The following is a thumbnail sketch of the excluded watercraft under
Section II of the Homeowners policy.

Section I - $1500 limit

Section II - size

Notes

1 There is only liability coverage for a(n):

- Outboard you own under 25 horsepower.
- Sailboat under 26 feet in length which you own or rent.
- Inboard powerboat under 50 horsepower that you rent.

on a slow boat to China

Therefore, a person with a major watercraft exposure is not fully covered under a
2 Homeowners policy. Those who need broader coverage should purchase a Boatowners or Yacht policy to provide adequate coverage. See Chapter 7 for details.

3 Excluded aircraft means any device used or designed for flight, other than model or hobby aircraft.

SO WHAT IS COVERED?

Now that you've been through a couple of laundry lists of exclusions, you may be
4 wondering, What is covered? Well, most of the things you would expect to be . . .
the trip and fall injuries on your sidewalk, your dog biting the mailman, one of your
kid's playmates knocks out a tooth while skating in your driveway. Notice, however,
that these two coverages are not restricted to your premises. If you are out on the
golf course and mow someone down with your cart, there is coverage. If you put
your golf ball through someone's window (or into someone's head), there is coverage.

The liability section of a Homeowners policy is like a little bubble of protection that
5 follows you and your family around wherever you go or whatever you do. About the
only time coverage collapses is when you are:

- On the job.
- In your car, boat, or airplane.

6 In these situations, you are better covered elsewhere.

7 Additionally, there is one very valuable coverage in Section II of Homeowners that the policy never mentions by name. Due to its importance, we will mention it by name.

Fire Legal Liability

It is customary in a liability policy to eliminate coverage for other people's property in
8 your **care, custody, or control**. For example, if you rent a house or apartment, we
are not going to pay your landlord under the liability section of your policy because
you are a neglectful, slovenly, or malicious tenant – these losses are preventable.

Accordingly, you might remember that in the Homeowners policy, we excluded li-
9 ability coverage for property in your care, custody, or control . . . **except** for damage
done by fire, explosion, or smoke. These exceptions give you Fire Legal Liability
coverage. This is especially important to people with an HO-4. A grease fire in your
apartment kitchen could easily result in $10,000 worth of damage to your apartment.
The apartment owner would file a claim under his Commercial Property policy, his
company would pay, and then subrogate against you. Your Fire Legal Liability
would cover you on this loss.

Notes

can't beat food cooked over an open fire

1 Those of us who do not rent our dwellings but own them (along with the mortgage company) do not have the same problem. A $10,000 fire in your home would be paid by Section I of Homeowners. Your rates might go up, but your company cannot subrogate against you.

2 However, even someone like Joe who owns an HO-3 can benefit from this coverage. Suppose Joe rents a lakeside cottage for a month. The same kind of kitchen fire can cause the same kind of damage. Again, the property owner will file with his property carrier, and that company will subrogate against Joe.

3 This coverage may not be obvious as you read the policy, but it might well save your bacon if a nonfictional kitchen fire ever pays you a visit.

ADDITIONAL COVERAGES

4 Each Homeowners policy provides three important coverages in addition to the stated limits of liability for Section II of the contract.

- Claim Defense
- First Aid to Others
- Damage to the Property of Others

5 **Claim Defense** coverage includes the costs of defending a claim, court costs charged against an Insured in any suit the insurance company defends, and premiums on bonds which do not exceed the Coverage E – Personal Liability limit and that are required in a suit defended by the insurance company. When the insurance company requests the assistance of an Insured in investigating or defending a claim, reasonable expenses of the Insured, including loss of earnings of up to $50 per day, are covered.

6 Expenses for **First Aid to Others** are covered when the charges are incurred by an Insured and when the charges result from bodily injury to a covered third party. If a social guest is injured at your house and you call the paramedics or take your friend to the emergency room of a hospital, the cost is covered. If you, as the Insured, submit the bill, First Aid to Others pays. If the injured party submits the bill, Med Pay pays. As you would guess, this coverage is not available to you or the residents of your household.

First Aid

others' stuff

7 If **Damage to Property of Others** is caused by an Insured, the policies provide replacement cost coverage of up to $1000 per occurrence. Of course, damage done intentionally by an Insured (who is 13 or older) is excluded. Notice that property that is rented is not covered in this section. Property that is rented is considered to be in your care, custody or control. For insurance purposes, it is your property, and is, therefore, insured under Section I of the Homeowners policy.

OPTIONAL COVERAGES

8 Homeowners policies may be endorsed to extend the Personal Liability and Medical Payments coverages to include insurance for people, property, situations or activities which are not normally covered. Endorsements may be used to cover the interest of an additional Insured or to cover the exposure related to an additional premises.

Notes

1 Although certain incidental businesses are permitted, an endorsement must be used to cover the liability exposure of having an office, professional, private school or studio in your house. Optional liability coverage may be written to include the business pursuits of the named Insured (other than a business owned or controlled by the Insured) and such coverage for teachers may be written to include or exclude liability for the corporal punishment of students. Liability for bodily injury and property damage arising out of the ownership, maintenance or use of usually excluded watercraft may also be covered by endorsement. Various other optional coverages are also available.

endorse that business

POLICY CONDITIONS

2 Due to the differences between property and liability coverage, certain conditions apply only to the liability section of Homeowners policies. One provision declares that bankruptcy of the Insured does not relieve the insurance company of its obligations under the policy.

3 The Insured's duties in the event of a covered liability occurrence are a little different and a little broader than with a property loss. They include providing written notice identifying the Insured, the policy, names and addresses of claimants and witnesses and information about the time, place, and circumstances of the accident or occurrence. The Insured is also required to promptly forward every notice, demand, or summons related to the claim and, when requested, to assist in the process of collecting evidence, obtaining the attendance of witnesses, and reaching settlement. The Insured is not supposed to assume any obligations or make any payments (other than first aid to others following a bodily injury), except at the Insured's own expense.

with a little help from our friends

4 Another clause states that payment of Medical Payments to Others is not an admission of liability by the Insured. When Medical Payments are made, the Insured or someone acting on the behalf of the injured person is required to provide written proof to support the claim, and to authorize the insurance company to obtain medical reports and records. The injured party must submit to a physical examination if it is requested by the insurance company.

LIABILITY ENDORSEMENTS

- **Business Pursuits** - Provides Premises Liabiliry and Med Pay coverage for the in-home business.

- **Day Care** - The Home Day Care Endorsement is an option available for those who might operate a day care business on the residence premises. Normally, the coverage under the basic endorsement is for up to three individuals in the care of the Insured. Larger numbers can be handled on an individual underwriting basis. This endorsement provides coverage for exclusions found in the liability coverages under Coverage E of the policy itself, e.g., abuse, corporal punishment, and sexual molestation. On the property side, an unendorsed Homeowners would not provide coverage for a separate structure (e.g. a garage) used for a business. This endorsement would provide coverage.

"Relative Daycare": my mom watching my kids at her house (even for pay) does not need this endorsement

Notes

- **Permitted Incidental Occupancies** - Another business endorsement. Works like Home Day Care for any other kind of in-home business - like a beauty parlor or a music teacher. Also includes coverage for Business Personal Property.

- **Personal Injury** - For extra premium, gives Personal Injury coverage under Homeowners. Includes false arrest or imprisonment, malicious prosecution, libel, slander, defamation, invasion of privacy, wrongful eviction and entry. Ideal for landlords.

- **Watercraft** - Provides Liability and Med Pay for boats exceeding the limits under the basic policy. The specifics of the insured craft are spelled out on the Dec sheet and companies vary about how big or powerful a boat can be and adequately be covered in this manner.

BACK TO THE CHART

1 Let's see what our Homeowners summary chart looks like with the two liability coverages we've just discussed included.

2 Although Coverages E and F greatly impact the value of the Homeowners policy you own, they impact the summary chart very little. On all seven Homeowners contracts, the basic Section II limits are the same.

HOMEOWNERS

Section I Property			Section II Casualty	
HO Form	**Dwelling and Other Structures Coverages A* & B***	**Personal Property Coverage C***	**Liability Coverage E**	**Med Pay Coverage F**
	REPLACEMENT COST	ACTUAL CASH VALUE		
HO-1 & HO-8**	Basic & Theft	Basic & Theft	$100,000/ Occurrence	$1,000/Person
HO-2	Broad & Theft	Broad & Theft		
HO-3	Special & Theft	Broad & Theft		
HO-5	Special & Theft	Special & Theft		
HO-4	N/A	Broad & Theft		
HO-6	$1000 . . . Broad & Theft	Broad & Theft		

* Coverage D in all forms will pay if a loss covered under A, B or C makes the dwelling uninhabitable.
** HO-8 settlement on buildings is ACV or Repair Cost.

Notes

THE DWELLING POLICY BACK TO THE BASICS

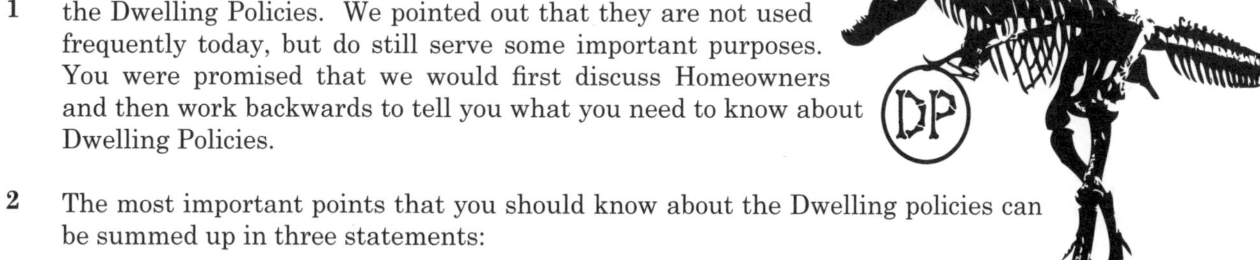

Dwelling Policy is a Dinosaur

1 In the opening pages of this chapter, we talked briefly about the Dwelling Policies. We pointed out that they are not used frequently today, but do still serve some important purposes. You were promised that we would first discuss Homeowners and then work backwards to tell you what you need to know about Dwelling Policies.

2 The most important points that you should know about the Dwelling policies can be summed up in three statements:

- Dwelling policies **do not automatically cover theft**.
- Dwelling policies **do not automatically provide liability coverage**.
- There are now **only three Dwelling policies**: DP-1 (Basic), DP-2 (Broad), and DP-3 (Special).

3 Therefore, our chart can be easily modified to make it a Dwelling policy chart instead of Homeowners.

DWELLING ~~HOMEOWNERS PROPERTY~~ COVERAGES

DP ~~HO~~ Form	Dwelling and Other Structures Coverages A & B	Personal Property Coverage C
	REPLACEMENT COST	**ACTUAL CASH VALUE**
DP ~~HO~~-1 & ~~HO-8~~	Basic & ~~Theft~~	Basic & ~~Theft~~
DP ~~HO~~-2	Broad & ~~Theft~~	Broad & ~~Theft~~
DP ~~HO~~-3	*Special (which includes Theft)	Broad & ~~Theft~~
~~HO-5~~		
~~HO-4~~		
~~HO-6~~		

* The DP-3 would provide theft coverage on the Dewlling and other structures because it is not excluded. Therefore, a DP-3 would cover theft of your copper gutters, your front door or your entire house.

OTHER DIFFERENCES ‡

SFP + EC + V&MM = Basic

- The DP-1 automatically covers only the perils of fire, lightning and internal explosion (e.g. furnace, water heater). By adding the **Extended Coverage Endorsement** and the **V&MM Endorsement**, it provides coverage for the group of perils we have been describing as the **Basic Perils**.

- **Coverage C** in all DP's limits off premises coverage to 10% of the on premises coverage.

- **In all DP's,** Coverage C must be specifically selected by the policyowner. It is not automatically 50% of Coverage A like in Homeowners.

- Because DP's are often used by landlords to cover a rental property, **Coverage D is listed as Fair Rental Value**. It simply pays the landlord for the amount he loses in rent if the building is damaged by a covered peril.

- For those living in a structure that they choose to insure with a DP, **Coverage E becomes the familiar Additional Living Expenses**.

Coverage A	Dwelling
Coverage B	Other Structures
Coverage C	Personal Property
Coverage D	**Fair Rental Value**
Coverage E	Additional Living Expenses

- **A separate policy** has been required historically to provide theft coverage or liability coverage with a Dwelling policy. In 1989, changes were made to allow either of these additions to be made with an endorsement to the DP form.

no theft or liability without endorsement

- **Theft coverage** can be obtained in two ways. Both cover theft, attempted theft, and vandalism as a result of a theft or attempted theft. The **Broad Theft Coverage Endorsement** is for owner-occupied dwellings and covers both on premises and off premises theft. The **Limited Theft Coverage Endorsement** is for landlords and only covers on premises theft.

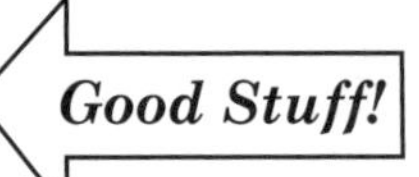

- **Liability coverage** can also be added in two ways. The **Personal Liability Endorsement** is for owner-occupants and essentially duplicates Section II of Homeowners. However, in the DP program liability is known as Coverage L and Med Pay to Others as Coverage M. The **Premises Liability Endorsement** is for landlords and provides premises liability coverage at the insured location only.

- **Dwelling Under Construction** endorsement covers a residence that is being built.

1 With these as the major exceptions (and, admittedly, some of these are very minor), the DP's tend to function much like the HO's. The standard deductible is $250; the Additional Coverages, the exclusions, and the conditions are identical or nearly identical to the Homeowners policy language.

Conclusion

1 In this chapter, we have examined the Homeowners program and the Dwelling Policies.

2 The **Homeowners** program packages both the property and casualty needs of your client into a single policy. Section I of the policy contains the property coverages, and Section II contains the liability coverages. The forms, numbered from HO-1 through HO-8 (but there is no HO-7), cover varying amounts of perils. With Forms 1, 2, 3 and 5, the perils covered continue to increase with each higher-numbered form.

3 Except for the HO-4 (Tenants Form) and HO-6 (Condominium Unit Owners Form), a Homeowners policy covers not only the building, but also its contents. Because tenants and condo owners do not insure the buildings they live in, the HO-4 and HO-6 are designed to cover contents; coverage on the structure is generally limited to betterments and improvements.

4 The primary rule on eligibility for a Homeowners policy is that the named Insured must be (or plan to be) the owner-occupant of the insured building. Also, the dwelling must be used principally as a residence, although certain low risk business uses, such as a private dance studio, are allowed by endorsement.

5 The policy distinguishes a named Insured from an Insured. The named Insured is the one who pays the premium and the one to whom the claim is paid. The spouse of the named Insured, if living at the same address, is given the rights of a named Insured. In addition to the named Insured(s), a Homeowners policy also covers the Insureds – kids of the named Insured(s) (no age limit) who live there, the mortgage company, and in some cases, even guests.

6 Section I (Property) of a Homeowners policy subdivides the property insured into four distinct coverages:

Coverage A – Dwelling
Coverage B – Other Structures
Coverage C – Personal Property
Coverage D – Loss of Use

7 The amount of coverage provided under the subsections varies depending upon which Homeowners form it is, and standard limits and exclusions can generally be increased or plugged up by endorsement. For example, a Personal Articles Floater could be used to provide adequate coverage for an expensive piece of jewelry.

8 The perils covered under a Homeowners policy will vary depending on which Cause of Loss form is used: Basic, Broad, or Special. Unlike Commercial Lines, in the Homeowners program, all three Cause of Loss forms cover theft.

9 The Homeowners program also includes Additional Coverages, such as debris removal, reasonable repairs, trees, shrubs, or other plants, fire department service charge, collapse, etc. Two of the most important optional property coverages that can be added for additional premium are Inflation Guard and Replacement Cost. The exclusions and conditions were set out in detail in this chapter. The standard deductible in Homeowners is $250. It applies to Section I (Property), but not to Section II (Liability).

1 Liability (Section II) of Homeowners has two coverage parts:

Coverage E – Personal Liability (BI and PD)
Coverage F – Medical Payments to Others

2 Personal Liability (Coverage E) is designed to pay the Other Guy for an Insured's negligence which results in bodily injury or property damage, and the basic limit is $100,000 per occurrence. Personal Liability coverage exists both on and off premises. Med Pay (Coverage F) is also designed to pay the Other Guy, but it doesn't require that negligence be established. You should think of it as goodwill insurance. It pays for medical expenses due to bodily injury that occur within three years of the accident, regardless of who is at fault, and the basic limit is $1000 per person. Remember that neither Coverage E nor Coverage F pay the Insured – they pay to a third party.

3 Excluded under the Liability section of Homeowners are losses better covered elsewhere (such as Workers Comp, Professional Liability, Automobile Liability, Aircraft and Watercraft), losses within the control of the Insured (such as intentional acts), catastrophic losses (such as war and nuclear hazards), and various other exclusions. Homeowners does, however, provide coverage for Fire Legal. Fire Legal liability coverage is especially important to tenants as it will pay for damage caused by fire, explosion, or smoke from property in the care, custody, or control of the tenant – like the grease fire in the apartment kitchen.

4 Additional Coverages under Section II of Homeowners include: Claim Defense, First Aid to Others, and Damage to Property of Others. Remember that these Additional Coverages pay in addition to the policy's stated limit of liability. There are also Optional liability coverages that can be purchased for additional premium.

5 The **Dwelling Policies** (or Dwelling Forms as they used to be called) were designed to be attached to the old Standard Fire Policy to cover the needs of the average homeowner. The Dwelling Policies are not used much today, although they do still serve the needs of the homeowner who isn't eligible for a Homeowners policy. The program consists of the DP-1, DP-2, and DP-3, and the policies work approximately like their numerical equivalents in the Homeowners program except that they don't have built-in coverage for theft or liability.

CHAPTER 5
HOMEOWNERS

1. A house has an actual cash value of $35,000 and a replacement cost of $50,000. The Replacement Cost Provision of a Homeowners policy will only apply if the minimum policy face amount is

   (A) $35,000
   (B) $40,000
   (C) $45,000
   (D) $50,000

2. Coverage F (Med Pay) would pay for all of the following EXCEPT

   (A) Injury sustained in your home by a visitor.
   (B) Your dog bites a cyclist in the park.
   (C) Your live-in nanny is injured escorting your children home from school.
   (D) An independent contractor is injured while repairing your roof.

3. Miss Parton owns a Homeowners policy. She has a set of two irreplaceable crystal goblets. Each is valued at $100, but the set is worth $500. One goblet is destroyed by a covered peril. The company would pay which of the following amounts?

   (A) $100
   (B) $250
   (C) $400
   (D) $500

4. A home with a commercial Photo Studio in the basement

   (A) Cannot be covered by a Homeowners policy.
   (B) Can be covered by an unendorsed Homeowners policy.
   (C) Can be covered by a Homeowners policy with the proper endorsement attached.
   (D) Can be covered by a Commercial Package policy.

CHAPTER 5 • HOMEOWNERS QUIZ

5. Which of the following accurately describes the differences between Homeowners Coverage E (Personal Liability) and Coverage F (Medical Payments)?

   (A) Liability need not be established under Coverage E, but must be established under Coverage F.
   (B) Coverage E pays for bodily injury to the insureds family, while Coverage F pays for medical bills of others.
   (C) Coverage E could pay for pain and suffering while Coverage F could pay for Funeral Expenses.
   (D) Coverage E limits are normally much smaller than Coverage F limits.

6. Mike Sullivan owns an HO-2. During the winter, ice blocks his gutters and melting snow seeps down the interior walls. When all of the walls in Mike's house are ripped out for replacement, he calls his Producer to see if his policy will cover the costs of debris removal. The Producer should tell Mike that the policy will:

   (A) not pay.
   (B) pay.
   (C) pay, but Mike must pay an additional deductible.
   (D) pay if Mike purchased the Additional Coverages section.

7. No deductible would be charged if a loss were paid under which of the following Homeowners coverages?

   (A) Coverage B
   (B) Coverage C
   (C) Coverage D
   (D) Coverage E

8. Mary Bradley rents an apartment and is insured under an HO-4. The apartment owner has a Commercial Property Policy on the buildings. Mary accidentally causes a fire which severely damages the kitchen ceiling. The subsequent claims would <u>ultimately</u> be paid by which of the following?

   (A) Section I of Mary's policy
   (B) Section II of Mary's policy
   (C) The Building and Personal Property Coverage Part of the Commercial Property Policy.
   (D) The Fire Legal Liability section of the Commercial Property Policy.

9. Mary Garcia owns a Homeowners policy with a Coverage A limit of $100,000. She suffers a total loss of her property by an insured peril. Her losses are as follows:

Dwelling Structure	$100,000
Personal Property	$ 50,000
Detached Garage	$ 10,000
Automobile	$ 10,000

Her Homeowners policy will pay up to which of the following amounts?

(A) $100,000
(B) $150,000
(C) $160,000
(D) $170,000

10. A policyowner is considering upgrading his HO-2 to an HO-3. In agreeing that he should upgrade, your most compelling argument is which of the following?

(A) He would have all-risk coverage on his personal property under the HO-3.
(B) Any restriction concerning vacancy and unoccupancy are eliminated with an HO-3.
(C) In the event of a dwelling loss, the burden of proof would be on the company.
(D) Policy limits on property, such as jewelry, furs, cash and firearms, are higher on an HO-3.

11. Susan owns an HO-2. Her hot water heater system accidentally discharges 40 gallons of hot water onto her $1,800 mink coat. Under the terms of the policy, which of the following best describes what will happen when she files her claim?

(A) The company will deny the claim because this is not a covered peril.
(B) The company will deny the claim because mink coats are not covered under the basic policy.
(C) The company will pay only $1,500 because this is the limit for furs under any policy.
(D) The company will pay the full amount of the claim less any applicable deductible.

CHAPTER 5 • HOMEOWNERS QUIZ

12. Which of the following best expresses the differences between a Homeowners Basic Form 1 (HO-1) and a Homeowners Special Form 3 (HO-3) in regards to the Part 2 (Liability) section of the policy?

    (A) An HO-3 has higher bodily injury limits.
    (B) An HO-3 has higher property damage limits.
    (C) An HO-3 has higher medical payments limits.
    (D) None of the above.

13. The basic limits for the Medical Payments to Others coverage found in an Homeowners policy is best expressed as which of the following?

    (A) $ 500 per accident
    (B) $ 500 per occurrence
    (C) $1,000 per person
    (D) $1,000 per occurrence

14. Randy Montgomery owns an HO-3 with $100,000 liability limits. His neighbor is injured in Randy's garage and files a lawsuit against Randy. The court awards the neighbor $100,000 for his injuries. Additional costs include: $5,000 in defense costs, $500 in investigative costs, $200 in travel and lost wages during the 10 day hearing. Randy's policy will pay which of the following?

    (A) $100,000
    (B) $105,000
    (C) $105,500
    (D) $105,700

15. If you own an HO-5 and wish to determine if coverage is provided for a specific loss to your personal property, you should look at which of the following sections of your policy?

    (A) Declarations.
    (B) Insuring Clause.
    (C) Conditions.
    (D) Exclusions

CHAPTER 5 • HOMEOWNERS QUIZ

16. All of the following are true concerning Homeowners policies EXCEPT

    (A) They automatically cover direct damage by a volcano.
    (B) They must be endorsed to cover earthquakes.
    (C) Additional coverages include credit cards as well as trees, shrubs and other plants.
    (D) They go into effect at 12:01 P.M.

17. Arlene Smith owns an unendorsed HO-3 and an expensive coat. The coat is destroyed by a covered peril. The insurance company would pay:

    (A) up to $1,500
    (B) the actual cash value of the coat less the deductible.
    (C) the replacement value of the coat less the deductible.
    (D) nothing

Questions 18-20 will deal with the following types of Dwelling policies. You may use a choice once, more than once or not at all.

(A) DP-1
(B) DP-2
(C) DP-3
(D) DP-4

From the Dwelling policies above, select the minimal form necessary to provide coverage for the losses described below.

18. Joe's neighbor's car damages Joe's living room.

    (A) (B) (C) (D)

19. The accumulated weight of ice and snow causes the roof of an insured premises to collapse.

    (A) (B) (C) (D)

20. Someone steals your front door.

    (A) (B) (C) (D)

CHAPTER 5 • HOMEOWNERS QUIZ

21. A woman removes her ring to wash the dishes and places it next to the sink. Later, she returns to find it missing. It was there last week, but today it cannot be found. This is considered to be which of the following?

    (A) Burglary
    (B) Robbery
    (C) Theft
    (D) Mysterious Disappearance

22. Red owns a mobile home insured under an HO-3 with a mobile home endorsement. Which of the following is not true concerning his coverage?

    (A) Coverage A is written on an all risk, replacement cost basis.
    (B) Coverage C is written on an all risk, replacement cost basis.
    (C) Losses to outdoor equipment, such as awnings, would be settled ACV.
    (D) The policy will pay to move the mobile home inland if it is threatened by a coastal hurricane.

23. Section I of an HO-3 would NOT cover

    (A) Debris removal.
    (B) Weight of ice and snow.
    (C) Falling objects.
    (D) Pets.

24. An HO-8 policy is written specifically for a (an)

    (A) New home.
    (B) Mobile home.
    (C) Older home.
    (D) Multi-family dwelling.

END

QUIZ ANSWERS & EXPLANATIONS ON NEXT PAGE

CHAPTER 5
HOMEOWNERS QUIZ ANSWER KEY

1. B. Maintaining coverage of at least 80% of replacement cost triggers the Replacement Cost Provision for damage to the dwelling.

2. D. Medical Payments Coverage does not cover claims involving Workers Compensation.

3. C. The Pair Set Clause formula is: "The value of the set minus the value of the remainder."

4. C. The Homeowners policy will provide coverage when there is a small low risk business in the home. However the policy must be endorsed to allow for the increased Section II (third party) risk (additional traffic on the premises).

5. C. Coverage E (Liability) and F (Medical Payments to Others) are both third party coverages. Coverage E limits are higher than those found in F. Medical Payments are made without regard to fault, and are limited to doctor, dental, hospital and funeral expenses.

6. A. Debris removal will only be covered if the debris is caused by a covered peril. The HO-2 offers broad form perils for damage to the dwelling. The broad form ice and snow coverage is limited to damage caused by the "Weight of Ice and Snow." The debris was not caused by a covered peril. An HO-3 would cover the loss and the debris.

7. D. Deductibles are found in two party coverages. Coverage E is a third party coverage.

8. B. As a tenant Mary has no insurable interest in the apartment, thus there is no coverage under Section I. There is coverage under Fire Legal Liability, found in Coverage E, Section II. Even if the landlord's two party policy covered the loss, Mary's policy would protect her in the event of a subrogation action being filed.

9. C. The car is excluded as being "better covered elsewhere", Auto. The Homeowners policy would cover the balance of the loss; the dwelling is covered under Coverage A for $100,000. The detached garage is covered under "B" for up to 10% of the "A" limit, or $10,000. The personal property is covered under "C" for up to 50% of "A" or $50,000.

CHAPTER 5 • HOMEOWNERS QUIZ ANSWER KEY

10. C. The HO-2 offers Broad Form for all of Section I. The HO-3 offers All Risk for Coverage A, but still retains Broad Form for Coverage B. In all other facets the policies are alike. When moving from named peril to open perils (All Risk) the burden of proof shifts from the insured (requiring proof that the loss was caused by a covered peril) to the company (requiring proof that the loss was caused by an excluded peril).

11. D. The loss was caused by a covered peril (water damage). The $1500 limitation on furs only applies to theft claims.

12. D. Section II is the same in every form.

13. C. Medical Payments utilizes a per person limit, while liability has a per occurrence limit.

14. D. The liability limit controls the amount used to pay the "other guy." The expenses for defense, including up to $50 per day in lost wages, are funded by Supplementary Payments, which have no limit on the Dec Sheet and further are in addition to the Limits of Liability.

15. D. The HO-5 is All Risk throughout Section I. All Risk (everything but) coverage is defined by exclusion.

16. D. Standard ISO forms are effective at 12:01 A.M.

17. B. The inside limit on coats only applies to fur coats in a theft loss. Replacement Cost is obtained by endorsement for Coverage C in the ISO Homeowners policies; otherwise, ACV.

18. A. The DP-1 offers the Basic perils. Damage caused by vehicles driven by a third party is a Basic peril.

19. B. The DP-2 offers the Broad perils. The Weight of Ice and Snow is one of the Broad form perils.

20. C. Although theft is not automatically covered in a DP, the DP-3 is an All Risk form for the building, and theft is not specifically excluded.

21. D. The remaining three are specific crime coverage definitions.

22. B. Remember that the HO-3 Coverage C is written on a Broad Form basis. The HO-3 is called the Special Form, but "it ain't that special."

23. D. Pets are not covered items under Section I of the Homeowners policy. Damage caused by pet is however covered under Section II.

24. C. The HO-8 is a modified form of the HO-1 specifically designed for older homes.

6

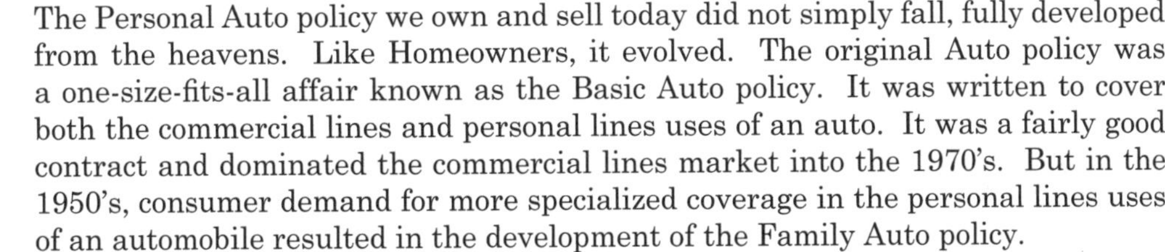

PERSONAL AUTO POLICY

SOURCE:
ISO PAP 2005

"...come away with me, Lucille..."

1 The Personal Auto policy we own and sell today did not simply fall, fully developed from the heavens. Like Homeowners, it evolved. The original Auto policy was a one-size-fits-all affair known as the Basic Auto policy. It was written to cover both the commercial lines and personal lines uses of an auto. It was a fairly good contract and dominated the commercial lines market into the 1970's. But in the 1950's, consumer demand for more specialized coverage in the personal lines uses of an automobile resulted in the development of the Family Auto policy.

2 The Family Auto policy revolutionized personal lines auto in much the same way as Homeowners revolutionized personal lines property insurance. Where the Basic Auto policy was written to insure an automobile, the Family Auto policy was written to cover the American family and the problems that can result from the family's use of an automobile. While a few companies offered a low budget cousin called the Special Auto policy (which discounted both price and coverage), the Family Auto policy dominated the personal lines auto market for nearly three decades.

3 In the late 1970's, three new policies were introduced: the Personal Auto policy, the Business Auto policy, and the Garagekeepers policies. All three were written in simplified language and streamlined format. They have largely replaced all previous auto policies. The Personal Auto policy was written to cover the exposures created by personal or family use of an auto. The Business Auto policy is the Commercial Auto module of the Commercial Package policy and is designed to cover the business uses of an automobile. The Garagekeepers policies are written for businesses that are in the automobile business – selling, leasing, repairing, storing, or parking. We will discuss both the Business Auto policy and the Garagekeepers policies in the commercial lines portion of this text. Therefore, in this chapter, we will only discuss the workings of the Personal Auto policy.

4 As a guide to your thinking in this chapter, we would suggest that you not worry too much about *what's covered*. Just about any reasonable loss resulting from the ownership or use of an auto is covered. **Your attention should be directed to answering the question, *Where is a loss covered?*** Knowing what coverage section covers which specific losses is the beginning of a solid understanding of the Personal Auto policy.

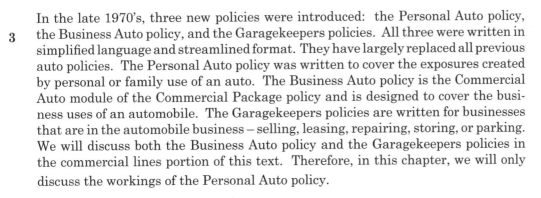

Notes

Who can buy a Personal Auto Policy?

- An individual
- A husband and wife residing together
- Two non-related individuals who reside together and jointly own a car
- By endorsement, two related individuals are not husband and wife. Example: Mother and son, brother and sister etc., as long as they reside together

What can be insured under a Personal Auto Policy?

- Private passenger vehicles, with **four or more wheels**, owned or leased by the Insured for more than six months. Vehicles that can be covered include: Private passenger automobiles of all types, including SUVs, vans and pick-up trucks (under 10,000 pounds and not used as delivery vehicles).
- By endorsement, the Personal Auto Policy can cover motorcycles, RV's, and golf carts.

POLICY STRUCTURE

1 The Personal Auto policy has eight parts, four of which are the four coverage sections.

Zeus Says, "All Auto is divided into four parts"

- Declarations
- Definitions
- **Part A – Liability**
- **Part B – Medical Payments**
- **Part C – Uninsured and Underinsured Motorists**
- **Part D – Coverage for Damage to Your Auto** (Physical Damage)
- Part E – Duties After an Accident or Loss
- Part F – General Provisions

2 The coverage sections (Parts A, B, C, and D) operate much like mini-policies. Each has its own insuring agreement, coverages, limits, and exclusions. While in reality each coverage section is one part of a single policy, thinking of each as a separate agreement working in harmony with the others is helpful in learning what each section does and in answering the question posed earlier, *Where is it covered?*

DECLARATIONS

3 The Declarations section does what it always does . . . fits the policy to the Insured and gives us a picture of the Insured's needs.

makes it fit

NOTE: As you can see by looking at the sample Dec Sheet following, we will work under the assumption that a family with more than one vehicle can insure all of their vehicles under one policy. Some companies prefer to issue a separate policy for each insured auto.

Personal Auto Policy Declarations

POLICYHOLDER: David M. and Joan G. Smith
(Named Insured) 216 Brookside Drive
Anytown, USA 40000

POLICY NUMBER: 296 S 468211

POLICY PERIOD: **FROM:** January 3, 20XX
TO: July 3, 20XX

But only if the required premium for this period has been paid, and for six-month renewal periods if renewal premiums are paid as required. Each period begins and ends at 12:01 A.M. standard time at the address of the policyholder.

INSURED VEHICLES AND SCHEDULE OF COVERAGES

	VEHICLE	COVERAGES	LIMITS OF INSURANCE		PREMIUM
1	2012 Honda CRV B		ID #JT2AL21E8B3306553		
		Coverage A—Liability	$ 300,000	Each Occurrence	$
		Coverage B—Medical Payments	$ 50,000	Each Person	$
		Coverage C—Uninsured Motorists	$ 300,000	Each Occurrence	$
				TOTAL	$
2	2014 Chevrolet Camaro		ID #1FABP3OU7GG212619		
		Coverage A—Liability	$ 300,000	Each Occurrence	$
		Coverage B—Medical Payments	$ 50,000	Each Person	$
		Coverage C—Uninsured Motorists	$ 300,000	Each Occurrence	$
		Coverage D—Other Than Collision	Actual Cash Value Less $ 250		$
		—Collision	Actual Cash Value Less $ 500		$
				TOTAL	$

POLICY FORM AND ENDORSEMENTS: PP 00 01, PP 03 06

COUNTERSIGNATURE DATE: January 3, 20XX

AGENT: Chris Toball

Notes

DEFINITIONS

1 Although the Auto policy defines a great many terms used in the contract, many of them, like bodily injury or property damage, are quite familiar to us already. We will, therefore, simply define the terms that are somewhat unique to auto insurance.

2 **Named Insured** – The person named on the Declarations. **A spouse**, if living at the same address, is given the same rights as the Named Insured. If a spouse moves out, they remain a named Insured for 90 days unless they obtain coverage elsewhere. In the simplified language of the Personal Auto policy, the named Insured is simply **You**.

Theory of Relativity

3 **Family Member (or Relative)** – A person related to the named Insured by blood, marriage, or adoption (including a foster child) **and** living at the same address. A student, although away at school, is still considered a relative.

4 **Occupying** – This means more than just riding down the road. It can also mean being on, getting in, getting on, getting off of, or out of an automobile.

5 **Trailer** – A vehicle designed to be pulled by a private passenger vehicle. It can also mean a farm trailer or farm implement that is being towed.

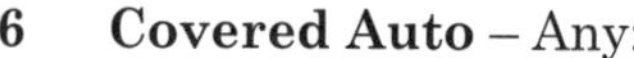

6 **Covered Auto** – Any:

- Vehicle named in the Declarations.
- Trailer owned by the named Insured (liability only).
- Newly acquired **additional** vehicle. You keep car #1 and purchase car #2. Without notification to the company, you get the same coverage on #2 as you had on #1, but **only for 14 days**. If you did not have physical damage on car #1, you get 4 days of physical damage coverage subject to a $500 deductible.

- Newly acquired **replacement** vehicle. Here, the company is a bit more generous when you trade in car #1 to acquire car #2. The broadest coverage you have on the policy will apply to car #2 (**except** Physical Damage) until the end of the policy period. If you have Physical Damage coverage on #1, you have it on #2, but only for 14 days without notification. If you did not have physical damage on car #1, you get 4 days of physical damage coverage subject to a $500 deductible.
- A non owned vehicle or trailer being used as a **temporary substitute** due to the unavailability of the covered vehicle due to breakdown, repair, servicing, loss or destruction.

7 GENERAL AUTO POLICY EXCLUSIONS

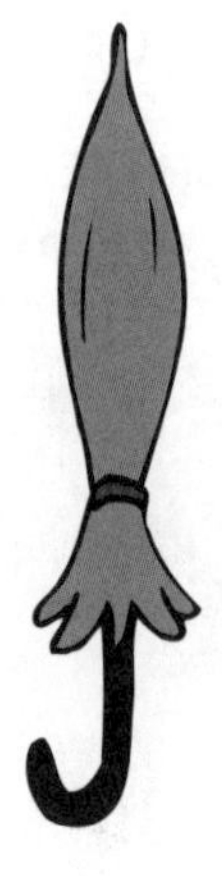

While the Personal Auto policy does not contain a *General Exclusions* section, the authors of this text believe it should. As we pointed out already, each coverage section in the contract is set up as a mini-policy with its own insuring clause, coverages, and exclusions. However, many of the exclusions are repeated two or three times, and this can greatly complicate your study of the policy. Therefore, we will address the repetitive ones here – once – and talk about those that are truly unique to each coverage section in turn.

Notes

1 There is no coverage for:

- War
- Nuclear Energy or Radiation
- Intentional Acts
- Using a vehicle without a reasonable belief that you were entitled to do so
- Vehicles with less than four wheels
- Vehicles used as public or livery conveyances (car for hire / taxi / limo)

EXCLUSIONS

No "cycles"

GENERAL AUTO POLICY GUIDELINES

2 As with the exclusions we just outlined, there is no section in the policy called General Guidelines. However, once again, there are some concepts that come up over and over again.

- **Primary coverage goes with the car** – Assume I have an auto policy and you have one as well. If I am driving your car, either policy can pay. Whose policy pays first? The rule is simple. The car's! It's your car; your policy is primary . . . for everything . . . damage done to the car or by the car . . . for bodily injury sustained by those in the car or outside of the car. If your limits are inadequate (or if your policy just expired), my policy can pay as excess coverage.

Primary coverage goes with the car

- Given the point that we just made, I should never never drive my car nor should you ever drive yours. If you and I have equal policies, I have twice as much coverage (given the primary and excess discussion) driving your car as I do driving my own and vice versa. Obviously, insurance companies are not staffed with idiots. Therefore, I have coverage driving your car as long as it is **not provided for my regular and frequent use**. If I am putting 100,000 miles a year on your car, my policy provides no coverage. Nor would it provide coverage for a company car provided for my use.

Regular & Frequent Usage

- **We make you whole, not rich.** If circumstances are such that you could collect under more than one section of the policy, you only get paid once.

To Indemnify

- The hired car exclusions do not generally apply to **car pooling**.

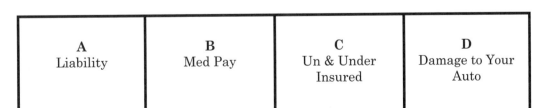

COVERAGE OVERVIEW

3 As we pointed out in the beginning of this chapter, your primary task with the Personal Auto policy is to learn what each coverage section does. Before we get consumed in the detail of the four sections, let's get a quick overview of what each does and how they work together. Once again, we'll develop a chart to track the important points. The four coverage sections are:

A Liability	B Med Pay	C Un & Under Insured	D Damage to Your Auto

Notes

COVERAGE A (LIABILITY)(BI & PD)

1 Coverage A (Liability) pays for damage you do to the Other Guy's body (BI) or to the Other Guy's property (PD). It doesn't cover you or your stuff. While it is possible for a passenger in your car to collect under Coverage A, the majority of claims stem from people and property outside of your auto. You hit a pedestrian in a crosswalk; you drive through my living room; you run a stop sign and collide with a passing vehicle – these are all Coverage A (Liability) claims. As you might guess, since we have liability coverage, we also provide Supplementary Payments (Defense Costs being the biggie) in addition to the dollar limits of the policy.

The Other Guy

COVERAGE B (MED PAY)

2 Coverage B (Med Pay) works a bit differently in Auto than it does in most other policies. In the Homeowners policy, for example, Med Pay never paid you. It paid the Other Guy to get his body repaired with the hope that a lawsuit could be avoided. In the Auto policy, **Med Pay will pay to you and your family if:**

- You're injured while occupying a vehicle.
- You sustain bodily injury as a pedestrian due to an automobile.

Insured

3 In addition, Med Pay will pay for injuries sustained by **anybody *occupying your car***. Obviously, *occupying* is the key to this coverage.

4 Assuming that you and your family are the primary occupants of your vehicle, then we find in the Auto policy a situation where **Med Pay pays you and yours**. For the most part, Med Pay in Auto does not exist to avoid lawsuits since you cannot sue yourself anyway.

our guy

5 Most of the other things we've learned about Med Pay, however, remain true. Med Pay pays without regard to fault, and it only pays to fix your body – doctors, dentists, hospitals, funeral homes. It does not pay for *pain and suffering* or lost wages.

COVERAGE C (UN & UNDERINSURED MOTORISTS)

6 There are a few states with a no-fault auto system in place, but in the majority of states, the basic automobile liability rule is quite simple: **He who is at fault pays for everything.** Well, that rule can present a problem. What if the Other Guy cruises a stop sign and hits you broadside? He is legally liable, you suffered bodily injury and property damage, but he has no insurance . . . or not enough.

our guy. . .

7 Your first reaction might be that such a situation is impossible in your state because your state has mandatory auto liability insurance requirements. Well, here's a flash: in such mandatory environments, it is generally estimated that 25% of the population is without insurance and that this 25% is involved in 35% of the accidents. They can't afford insurance, and they can't drive.

8 **Uninsured Motorists coverage is essentially a policy you purchase for the Other Guy so that he will have the funds to pay you when he injures you with his auto.** It is primarily designed to cover your body and the bodies of your family and passengers. In some states, you can cover damage to your auto as well, Uninsured Motorists Property Damage (UMPD).

UN

Notes

*Under*insured Motorists coverage is for situations where the Other Guy has enough
1 liability insurance to be legal, but not enough to pay for the damage he did. Again,
you are buying him a liability policy so that he can pay for the damage to you for
which he is legally liable.

UNDER

In this text, we will examine these two coverages together as they are both address-
2 ing different angles of the same problem – an at-fault driver who does damage he
cannot pay for.

COVERAGE D (COVERAGE FOR DAMAGE TO YOUR AUTO)

Though many of the *Old Geezer* elements of the P&C industry still refer to this sec-
3 tion as **Physical Damage**, the simplified language of the modern contract refers to
this as ***Coverage for Damage to Your Auto***. This coverage section insures your
automobile . . . your property. Therefore, it works like most property policies. You
must be concerned with the level of peril power (named perils or open perils), you
expect to see exclusions, and you should anticipate a deductible.

our guy's car

There are two coverages in this section: **Collision and Other Than Collision.**
4 **Collision** is a named peril – it covers nothing but collision. **Other Than Collision**
coverage is ***all risk*** and essentially covers everything else. Again, the *Old Geezers*
give themselves away by referring to Other Than Collision as Comprehensive coverage. The courts disliked the word *Comprehensive* as it implied that everything
is covered against any peril. As you should certainly know by now, such is not the
case, and the Open Perils protection provided by the Other Than Collision coverage certainly has exclusions. First on the exclusion list is Collision as it is better
covered elsewhere.

INSURANCE LITE

"The other car collided with mine without giving warning of its intention."

"I was on my way to the doctor's with rear end trouble when my universal joint gave way, causing me to have an accident."

"The guy was all over the place. I had to swerve a number of times before I hit him."

"I was driving my car out of the driveway in the usual manner, when it was struck by the other car in the same place it had been struck several times before."

"Coming home, I drove into the wrong house and collided with a tree I don't have."

"The pedestrian had no idea which direction to go, so I ran him over."

Notes

1 At this stage, you should have a reasonably good feel for what each of the four coverage sections is designed to do. A reasonable summary in chart form follows.

A **Liability**	B **Med Pay**	C **Un & Under Insured**	D **Damage to Your Auto** (Physical Damage)
Other Guy's Bodily Injury (BI) Property Damage (PD) Supp Payments pays in addition to limits	Pays: 1) Those **occupying** your car 2) Your family **occupying** or as pedestrians 3) No fault	**Other Guy legally at fault . . .** Pays You & Yours for: • Bodily Injury (BI) • Maybe Property Damage (PD)	Collision Named Peril Other Than Collision (Comprehensive) *All Risk*

2 **NOTE**: Until this point in the course, we could have used the words *physical damage and property damage* more or less interchangeably. In auto insurance, however, this is not the case. If you use the old-fashioned words *physical damage* to describe Coverage D, you must not confuse it with the *property damage* coverage found in Section A. An easy way to keep them separate is to see the *o* in property damage and think *O*ther Guy's property. Then, see the *i* in phys*i*cal damage and think *I*nsured's property.

Checkpoints

3 Assume you have every coverage of the Personal Auto policy we have discussed as you answer the following questions.

1. You smash your car into a tree. Damage to the auto is covered under Section ____________________. Injuries you sustain are covered under Section ____________________.
2. You hit a pedestrian at a crosswalk. Your policy would pay for his injuries out of Section ____________________.
3. A driver without insurance hits you in a pedestrian crosswalk. You suffer bodily injury, pain and suffering, and lost wages. Which of your coverages would pay for any or all of these losses? ____________________
4. Your car is vandalized. Section ____________________ would pay for the damage.
5. You drive your car through someone's living room. Section ____________________ of your auto policy would cover the damage to the house.

1. D (Damage to Your Auto); B (Med Pay)

2. A (Liability)

3. B (Med Pay) – bodily injury; C (Uninsured Motorist) – bodily injury, pain and suffering and lost wages

4. D (Damage to Your Auto)

5. A (Liability)

Notes

PERSONAL AUTO COVERAGES – A CLOSER LOOK

1 Now that you have a handle on the generalities of the Personal Auto policy coverage sections, we can more closely examine each for the specifics of the coverage provided.

COVERAGE A (LIABILITY)

2 While the minimums vary from state to state, most jurisdictions require by law that you meet a minimum available cash requirement in order to drive legally in that state. Some states actually require insurance, and others give some alternatives. For most of us, Coverage A (Liability) is the only reasonable way for us to meet our financial responsibilities while operating a motor vehicle. Therefore, this section is generally considered mandatory in all states.

3 The insuring agreement consists of two parts:

- The promise to pay claims – money
- The promise to defend and settle claims – Supplementary Payments

4 In the insuring agreement, the company agrees to pay for **bodily injury or property damage**, up to the **policy limits**, for which an **insured person** is legally responsible because of an auto accident. Further, the company agrees to **settle or defend** any claims to which the **coverage applies**. These defense costs are **in addition to the policy limits.**

5 Let's take the company's promise apart phrase by phrase.

6 **Bodily Injury or Property Damage** – Whose body and whose property? The Other Guy's.

7 **Up to the Policy Limits** – The dollar limit to which the company will pay on your behalf is stated on the Dec Sheet in one of two ways:

- **Single Limit** – This is a flat dollar amount, like $60,000 or $400,000, which is the most in damages that the company will pay for any one accident. The damage can be 100% bodily injury or 100% property damage or some combination of both. With a single limit of, say, $100,000, it does not matter how badly someone is injured, how many were injured, nor the extent of the property damage – the company will not pay over $100,000. If the total damage is $150,000, then the company pays $100,000 and you pay the $50,000 difference.

Single Limit

Split Limits

- **Split Limits** – Another way of defining limits is to put a maximum dollar amount upon each of the types of liability losses possible in any one accident:

  – Maximum BI per person
  – Maximum BI per accident (may be several persons)
  – Maximum PD per accident

Notes

1 Essentially, the split limit format creates three inside limits as well as a total policy limit. Split limits are written in the following manner:

2 BI per person/BI per accident/PD per accident

SPLIT LIMITS

3 Assume the minimum limits of liability in State A were $25,000 for BI to any one person, $50,000 for BI for all the injured persons in any one accident and $10,000 for PD in any one accident. We could express these limits in insurance shorthand as 25/50/10.

4 Assume that a person living in State A wants limits of $100,000 BI for any one person, $300,000 BI for any one accident and $100,000 PD for any one accident. These limits would be expressed as 100/300/100.

5 Translating split limits into single limits is really quite simple. If a state had minimum limits of 25/50/10, the maximum the policy could possibly pay for BI losses is $50,000, and the maximum it could pay for PD losses is $10,000. The state would accept a $60,000 single limit policy as an equivalent policy.

6 25/50/10 = $60,000 single limit

7 For those of you who worship formulas, **DROP** the first number – POOF /50/10 – and **ADD** the last two.

SINGLE LIMIT

8 You should be able to solve simple claims problems with what you know to this point. Assume you own a policy with limits of 25/50/10. Further assume that you run a stop sign and injure only the driver of the other car in the amount of $32,000. You also destroy his car worth $12,000. To calculate what the policy will pay, we suggest you follow this procedure: write down the limits we gave you to work with and then organize the damage under BI or PD.

25/50/10

BI	PD
$32,000	$12,000

9 Then, using the limits given, reduce the damage to what the policy will actually pay.

10

25/50/10

BI		PD
~~$32,000~~ $25,000	+	~~$12,000~~ $10,000

= $35,000 Company will pay (+ defense costs)

Notes

1 Now let's illustrate a more complex problem involving several claimants, still assuming coverage of 25/50/10. We will start by solving it like most people do – the **wrong way!**

2 There is a natural inclination to add the BI claims, get $54,000, compare it to the second number in the limits and reduce the BI payment to $50,000. But, like many natural inclinations, that is wrong!

Notes

1 We cannot ignore the first limit of $25,000. We must first make certain that we pay no more than $25,000 for any one body. Second, the total BI must not exceed $50,000. Finally, we apply the $10,000 limit to the total PD. See the following correction.

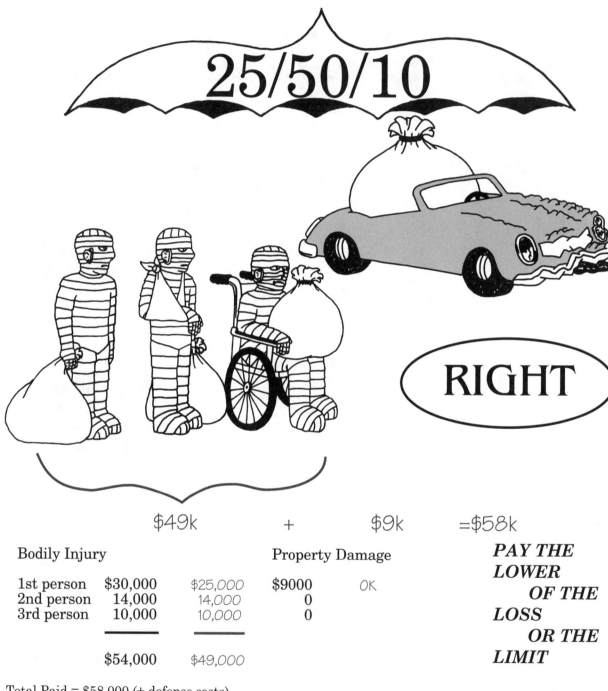

25/50/10

RIGHT

$49k + $9k =$58k

Bodily Injury			Property Damage	
1st person	$30,000	$25,000	$9000	OK
2nd person	14,000	14,000	0	
3rd person	10,000	10,000	0	
	$54,000	$49,000		

PAY THE LOWER OF THE LOSS OR THE LIMIT

Total Paid = $58,000 (+ defense costs)

Notes

1 **Insured Persons** – Up to this point, the insuring agreement has said that we will pay for BI and PD up to the policy limits caused by a legally responsible **insured person**. What do we mean by insured person? You will notice that the term is not limited to named Insureds, specific automobiles, or even licensed drivers. **Insured persons** include the following two important groups:

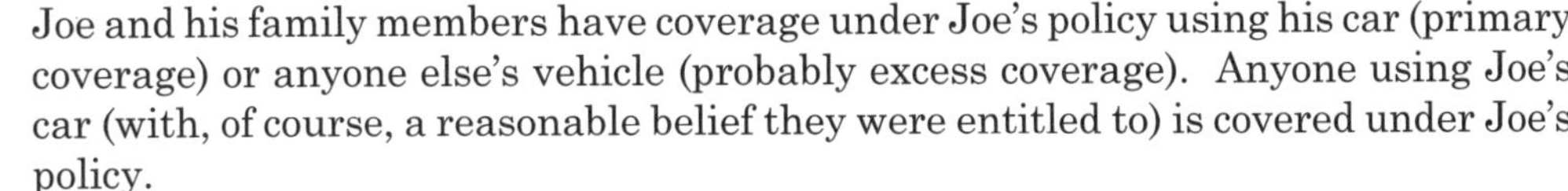

- The named Insureds and any family member using **any auto**.
- Any persons using the named Insured's covered auto.

A bunch of Insureds

2 Joe and his family members have coverage under Joe's policy using his car (primary coverage) or anyone else's vehicle (probably excess coverage). Anyone using Joe's car (with, of course, a reasonable belief they were entitled to) is covered under Joe's policy.

3 **Settle or Defend** – The second promise of the insuring agreement was settle or defend any claim. The major benefit here is **defense costs.** The other **Supplementary Payments** include:

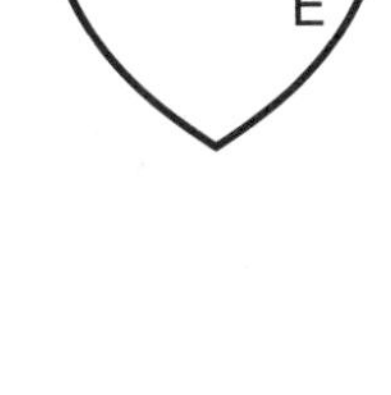

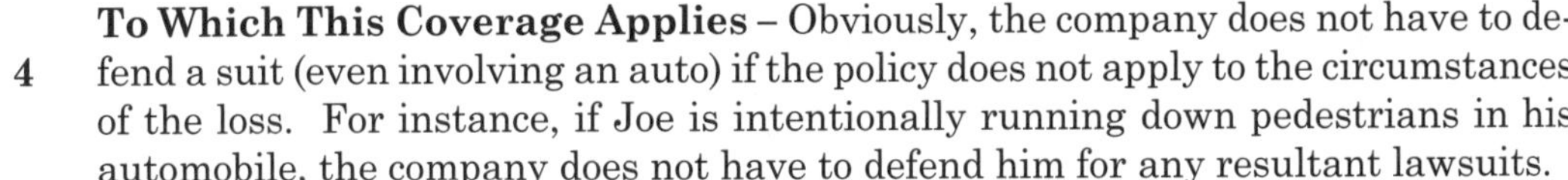

- Bail bond premiums following an accident
- Premiums on appeal bonds and bonds to release attachments
- Interest accruing after a judgment (Prejudgment interest is part of the liability limits.)
- Loss of earnings to attend trial ($200/day max.)
- Other reasonable expenses

4 **To Which This Coverage Applies** – Obviously, the company does not have to defend a suit (even involving an auto) if the policy does not apply to the circumstances of the loss. For instance, if Joe is intentionally running down pedestrians in his automobile, the company does not have to defend him for any resultant lawsuits.

5 **In Addition to the Limits of the Policy** – Defense costs and all other Supplementary Payments are paid by the company over and above the liability limits of the contract. For example, assume Joe has liability limits of 100/300/100 and hits a pedestrian. A jury awards the pedestrian $100,000. The company spent $25,000 in defense costs and another $5,000 in miscellaneous Supplementary Payments expenses. The total bill for the company is $130,000.

PART A (LIABILITY) EXCLUSIONS

6 The liability section of the Personal Auto policy has a number of exclusions, the majority of which were discussed earlier in *the General Auto Policy Exclusions* section. We need only to look at two additional exclusions.

- Liability coverage is not provided for your **employees injured on the job**. If Joe backs over his dishwasher who was carrying trash to the dumpster, Joe's employee is covered under **Workers Compensation**, not the liability coverage of Joe's automobile insurance.

WORKERS COMP

COMP IS KING

- Even with permission, you **cannot extend your auto policy to cover a garage**. Suppose Joe's car is in Delbert's Garage for brake repair. If the chief mechanic, Roy Bob, takes it out for a test drive and hits a pedestrian, Joe's policy will not protect the garage, Delbert, or Roy Bob. This is a commercial exposure and **should** be covered under Delbert's Garage policy.

In the business

Notes

COVERAGE B (MEDICAL PAYMENTS)

1 Since Coverage B generally covers you and your family – the most likely occupants of your automobile – it is not a requirement in the vast majority of states that the public buy this coverage or that you, the Agent, offer it.

2 The Coverage B insuring agreement tells us that the company will pay for reasonable and necessary **medical and funeral expenses** incurred by **an Insured** because of bodily injury caused by an automobile accident. Only expenses incurred within **three years** of the accident are covered. This coverage applies without regard to fault.

No Fault

Med Expenses Only

3 While most of this promise has been discussed already in this text, there are a few portions which merit a second look.

4 **Medical and Funeral Expenses** – This coverage is only designed to offset the costs of medical treatments or funeral expenses. Doctors, dentists, hospitals, and funeral homes are in; pain and suffering and lost wages are *out*.

5 **Incurred by an Insured** – In the Medical Payments section, an *Insured* can be anyone who fits into either of the following categories:

- Named Insured or family member *occupying* or, as a pedestrian, *struck* by **any motor vehicle** (including trailers) primarily designed for use on public roads.
- Any other person while occupying your covered auto.

Us

occupiers

6 Therefore, Joe's Med Pay coverage protects Joe and his family in his or any vehicle and as pedestrians struck by any vehicle. Joe's Med Pay coverage extends to other people only if they are *occupying* one of Joe's covered vehicles. Remember that *occupying* is in it, on it, getting into it, getting out of it, or getting off of it.

7 **Incurred Within Three Years** – The normal Med Pay rules hold – one year for Commercial Lines and three years in Personal Lines.

COVERAGE B (MEDICAL PAYMENTS) EXCLUSIONS

8 As with Liability, the Med Pay section has numerous exclusions, most of which were discussed earlier in the *General Auto Policy Exclusions* section. There is only one brand new one to discuss, but there is a different application of one we first encountered in Coverage A (Liability).

- Med Pay coverage does not apply if you are **using your vehicle as a residence**. Remember, we could endorse the policy to cover recreational vehicles. Therefore, if you are living in your RV, stumble and break an arm, Med Pay will not pay. If you are injured while living in your RV, health insurance can pay for medical bills. If someone is visiting you and is injured in your RV, Homeowner's can extend coverage. If you are living in your RV, it is not being used as an automobile, and therefore, Automobile Med Pay would not cover your medical bills.
- We saw earlier that there is no liability coverage for your employees injured on the job. Likewise, there is no coverage under Med Pay if you are the employee injured on the job. Assume that Joe is running his cash deposit to the bank when he backs into a tree. If his **Workers Comp** coverage will pay, then the Med Pay section of his Personal Auto policy will not pay.

WC

Notes

COVERAGE B (MEDICAL PAYMENTS) LIMITS

1 Med Pay coverage is purchased on a ***per person* basis**. Suppose that Joe has limits of $5000/person and he and Jolene are both injured in the same accident. The company could pay out as much as $10,000. If Joe has five people in his five passenger sedan, the amount could be as much as $25,000.

per/person

2 You should keep in mind one of our general auto policy guidelines. *We make you whole, not rich.* Suppose Joe is driving with liability limits of 100/300/100 and a Med Pay limit of $5000/person. Assume Joe is driving recklessly when his passenger, Joe Kool, gets hurt. Kool collects $5000 in Med Pay benefits, sues Joe for negligence in the amount of $100,000 and wins. He will recover only $95,000 from the liability section as he has already received $5000.

ours. . . If

COVERAGE C (UN & UNDERINSURED MOTORISTS)

3 In tort states where the responsible party is supposed to pay for all the damage in an auto accident, it is generally a requirement that UN and UNDER coverage be offered to every Insured. It can be declined by a written waiver, but it must be offered.

4 The insuring agreement in this section says that the company agrees to pay compensatory damages, **up to the stated limits** of the contract, for **bodily injury or property damage** that an **insured person** is **legally entitled to receive** from an **uninsured motorist** caused by an accident.

BI & PD

5 If we again take this promise apart phrase by phrase, we find that this section, like the previous two, has stated dollar limits. In most states, the law says that the amount of **UM coverage cannot be less than the state minimum limit nor more than the Coverage A (Liability) limit** selected under the same policy. Therefore, assume Joe lives in a state where the minimum legal limit is 25/50/10. Further assume his Coverage A limits are 100/300/100. Joe could purchase any coverage amount he wants between these two extremes. Because Joe values his body (and the bodies of his family) as highly as he values the Other Guy's, his first two numbers for his UM Bodily Injury coverage (UMBI) will likely be 100/300. The third number depends upon the **value of Joe's automobile**. Let's assume that he is adequately protected with UM limits of 100/300/20.

the Other Guy is at fault AND Uninsured

What's UMBI?

6 Uninsured Motorists coverage is available nationwide for bodily injury and in most jurisdictions for property damage. The need for bodily injury coverage is fairly obvious. If Joe is injured through the negligence of an uninsured motorist, without this coverage, his policy can only pay medical bills. If Joe is off work for six months, his medical bills may pale in comparison to his lost wages. If Joe is very seriously injured, his Med Pay limits may be exhausted rather quickly.

7 The need for **property damage coverage** under UM is not so obvious. **If Joe has collision coverage with a low deductible, he probably does not need UMPD.** On the other hand, if he has no collision coverage or has it with a very high deductible, UMPD could make sense for him. In some states, UMPD must be at least offered with no deductible at all, which makes it even more attractive.

UMPD

Notes

1 In all states where UMPD is available, the rules that regulate what you can buy under this section are fairly standard. Your choices are:

- Buy nothing
- Buy UMBI only
- Buy UMBI and UMPD

2 **You cannot purchase UMPD without UMBI.** A person who is unconcerned about his body but very concerned about his automobile is probably an accident waiting to happen.

3 An **insured person** in the UM section must fit into one of the following three groups:

- The named Insured and family members are covered if injured by an uninsured motorist while they are occupying any auto or if they are pedestrians.

- Any other person who is injured while occupying a covered auto.

- Any other person who is legally entitled to recover damages. This last group could include people not even involved in the accident. For example, if a passenger in your car is killed by an uninsured motorist, the spouse and family of the deceased could be entitled to damages and file a claim under your Uninsured Motorists coverage.

4 Obviously, no benefits can be paid from this section unless the Uninsured Motorist is legally responsible for the damage – settlement or judgment.

5 We have been using the term **Uninsured Motorist** for some time now without defining it. While it may seem self-evident, it is not. For UMBI claims, there are four ways in which the negligent party can be considered an Uninsured Motorist. Despite the way the word *uninsured* sounds to our ears, you should notice that in three of the four definitions, the uninsured motorists may actually have some insurance:

UN
illegal

- Person with no insurance.

No Insurance

- Person with insurance but with liability limits less than the state minimum.

. . .or too little. . .

- Person with auto liability coverage but his company denies the claim or is insolvent.

or won't or can't pay. . .

- Hit-and-run driver. (**BI Only**)

or, hit and run

6 For UMPD coverage, an uninsured motorist can be any of the above except the hit-and-run driver. The logic here is fairly straightforward. If an Insured chose not to buy collision coverage (which is pretty expensive), he might be tempted to claim that any collision loss is the result of a hit-and-run driver and file a UMPD (pretty cheap coverage) claim.

PD not hit and run

Notes

UNDERINSURED MOTORISTS

1 We've made the point that an **uninsured motorist is one without insurance or with insurance less than the state's minimum limits of liability**. An underinsured motorist, on the other hand, is one with enough insurance to be driving legally, but not enough to cover the damage resulting from an accident he caused. The Other Guy, then, can be an uninsured or an underinsured motorist, **but he cannot be both**.

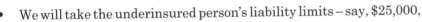

UNDER
legal, but inadequate

2 As we've pointed out, the ISO Auto policy requires that you add Underinsured coverage as an endorsement. However, a great many companies have already built Underinsured coverage directly into the Uninsured section. The companies that have not yet done so are preparing to do so. To accomplish this process easily, it is a requirement that the limits match the limits of the policy's Uninsured Motorists coverage. Therefore, if Joe is driving with Uninsured Motorists limits of 100/300/20, he should have Underinsured limits of 100/300/20.

3 The promise made to the policyowner by Underinsured Motorists coverage is one of the most commonly misunderstood concepts in Auto insurance. What is promised by limits of 100/300/20 with only one person injured is as follows:

dead beet

- We will take the underinsured person's liability limits – say, $25,000,
- And add enough dollars to cover your injury
- Up to a total of no more than $100,000.

4 In other words, with the limits we've just used in our example, the most that could be paid by your Underinsured coverage is $75,000.

$100,000 Limit
– 25,000 from the Other Guy
$75,000 from your Underinsured coverage

5 If the Other Guy has limits of $50,000 per person, then the most your policy could pay is $50,000.

Your Under
- His BI
=Most that your policy will pay

$100,000 Limit
– 50,000 Other Guy's
$ 50,000 Yours

6 If his limit equals yours, your policy could pay nothing.

$100,000 Limit
– 100,000 Other Guy's
$0 Yours

7 The mistake made by many people is in the event you are injured $125,000 worth. They want to take his limit of $25,000 and add to your limit of $100,000 and pay a total of $125,000. As we saw earlier, with these numbers, the most that could be paid is $75,000 ($100,000 – $25,000). The rule is simple: with **Underinsured Motorist, you never add The Other Guy's limits, you subtract them.**

Notes

COVERAGE C (UN AND UNDERINSURED MOTORISTS) EXCLUSIONS

1 In addition to the general exclusions discussed earlier, there is one new exclusion:

- We will not provide bodily injury coverage if the Insured settles the claim without company permission.

For example, suppose you are hit by an uninsured motorist. You apparently suffer
2 minor injuries, and he offers you $200 to forget it happened. If you accept, you have closed the door to future recovery if your injuries turn out to be more expensive than you first thought.

COVERAGE C (UN AND UNDERINSURED MOTORISTS) ARBITRATION

Since all of Coverage C has to do with your company paying for your body (or maybe
3 your car) and the bodies of your family or passengers, it is certainly possible for there to be a disagreement between you and your company over the value of your body. To avoid court, this coverage outlines a system to resolve disputes that is similar to the appraisal process in property insurance.

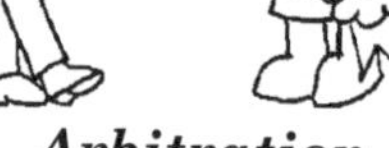
Arbitration

- Either party can make a demand for arbitration.
- Each side selects and pays for a qualified arbitrator.
- The two arbitrators select a third and his cost is split 50/50
- The arbitrators decide:
  - if the Insured is entitled to damages
  - **and** the amount of the damages.
- If the amount determined is less than state minimum limits, the decision is binding.
- If the amount exceeds state minimum limits, either party can demand a trial.

COVERAGE C (UNINSURED MOTORISTS) SUBROGATION

As you've probably guessed by now, when you accept payment from your own com-
4 pany under Coverage C for injuries or damages for which the Other Guy has legal responsibility, you give your company the legal right to pursue the Other Guy to recover the damages. This process does two things:

- It allows your company to recover from the legally responsible party.

- It keeps you from recovering twice. When you give your company the right to go after the Other Guy, you give up the right to go after him yourself.

- Subrogation does not happen with Underinsured Motorists because you must release the Underinsured Motorist to recover the limits of his policy.

Notes

COVERAGE D (DAMAGE TO YOUR AUTO)

1 Making the somewhat unrealistic assumption that you own your car outright, this coverage is totally optional. There is no state law that says you must purchase Coverage D, and there is no waiver to sign if you don't want it.

2 Realistically, this is the only auto coverage that a policyowner should view as optional regardless of what the state law says about it. Trying to save money by cutting liability limits is very shortsighted in today's legal climate, and failing to adequately protect yourself and your family by scrimping on Coverages B and C would be a terrible mistake. Most of your premium dollars go into Coverage D and there are several ways to save significant dollars without setting yourself up for financial disaster.

- If you are extremely wealthy, don't buy Coverage D – you can afford to replace your car.
- If you are moderately wealthy, take very high deductibles.
- If you drive a beater worth $800, you might bypass Coverage D altogether, or you could drop just the Collision coverage, which is by far the more expensive coverage in this section.

COLLISION

3 The Coverage D (Damage to Your Auto) insuring agreement is straightforward. It says that the company will pay for direct and accidental loss to **your covered auto** or any covered **non owned auto** caused by **Collision** or an **Other Than Collision** type loss. Obviously, if you have chosen not to buy either one or both coverages in this section, the company has no obligation in the event of such a loss.

4 **Covered auto** means the car listed on your Dec Sheet, a newly acquired additional or replacement vehicle, or a non owned auto. These coverages also apply (probably as excess insurance) to any non owned private passenger auto or trailer that is not available for your regular use. The coverage available for a non owned auto is simply the same as what you have on your own vehicle. **If Joe has Collision and Other Than Collision on his own car, then he has the same coverage driving his neighbor's car**. If Joe owns two automobiles, one with Collision and Other Than Collision coverage and the other with no Coverage D at all, the Auto policy applies the broadest coverage provided for any covered auto shown in the Declarations. In this case, Joe would have both Collision and Other Than Collision coverage driving a non owned auto.

Collision. . .

5 In defining **Collision**, the policy says that it is the **upset of a covered auto** or non owned auto **or** their **impact with another vehicle or object.** Notice that the vehicle does not have to be moving to have a collision, nor does the collision have to be with another vehicle. If Joe's car is sideswiped in the parking lot – collision. If Joe runs into a tree – collision. If somebody rear-ends Joe – collision.

. . . or upset

6 Collision losses are paid **without regard to fault**. If the accident is Joe's fault, the policy pays. Joe pays the deductible (and the rate increase upon renewal), but the policy pays without regard to fault. If the accident is the fault of the Other Guy, Joe's policy could pay to speed the settlement process and then subrogate against the Other Guy and his company.

Notes

1 As we have noted, the Dec Sheet will tell us what coverages (if any) Joe has purchased in this section. While the ISO forms do not specifically prohibit it, many companies have underwriting rules that forbid the purchase of collision only in Coverage D. Their reasoning is that to do so could be encouraging collision losses. For example, if Joe has collision only coverage and a neighborhood vandal keys his car, there is no legitimate coverage. Joe might be inclined to sideswipe a tree (a certifiable collision) simply to get coverage.

2 With most companies, your choices in Coverage D are as follows:

- Buy nothing.
- Buy both Collision and Other Than Collision.
- Buy only Other Than Collision.

3 As we have pointed out, Collision is by far the more expensive coverage of the two and invariably carries the higher deductible. It would not be unusual to find a situation where the Collision deductible is $250 and the Other Than Collision deductible is $100. In every respect, the policyowner is better off with an Other Than Collision loss than with a Collision loss. A rate increase in the Other Than Collision section is less expensive and the deductible is lower. If a policyowner has any coverage at all in this section, he probably has Other Than Collision.

4 **Other Than Collision** coverage is open perils coverage. Any damage to a covered or non owned auto that is not excluded is covered. Unlike any other open perils contract we have examined, the Auto policy gives you a *for instance* list of specimen coverages. The contract does not say that **only** these perils are covered – it says that all of these fit under the Other Than Collision heading. The specimen coverages include:

- Missiles or falling objects
- **Fire**
- Explosion or earthquake
- Windstorm
- Hail, water, or **flood**
- Malicious mischief or vandalism
- Riot or civil commotion
- **Theft** or larceny
- **Contact with a bird or animal**
- Breakage of glass

"ALL RISK," OTHER THAN COLLISION

Comprehensive

5 Most of these sample coverages are self-explanatory, but the last three bear some discussion. **Theft** surely fits into the Other Than Collision category, but what if someone steals your car and then wrecks it? We still consider this to be an Other Than Collision loss as the theft started the chain of events leading to the loss.

6 **Contact with a bird or animal** is considered an Other Than Collision loss. Now, if you hit a deer, it may feel like Collision to you, but it is not. Even if you hit an elephant, it is not Collision.

Bumping Bambi

7 **Glass breakage** is an Other Than Collision coverage, but if the glass breakage is the result of a collision, the Insured can elect to have the glass considered as part of the Collision coverage. Without this option, you could be hung for two deductibles on one loss – one for the collision damage and one for the glass.

Can you see through it?

Notes

Coverage D also provides **transportation expenses** for an Insured following the
1 **loss or destruction** of a covered auto or non owned auto. The company will pay up to $20 per day (to a maximum of $600) to offset transportation expenses the Insured may incur or, in the case of a non owned auto, be legally responsible to pay. This coverage does not start until 24 hours following the loss. If the loss is due to **theft**, the waiting period is **48 hours**. Though one might argue that there is a **time deductible**, there is no dollar deductible in transportation expense coverage.

COVERAGE D (DAMAGE TO YOUR AUTO) EXCLUSIONS AND LIMITATIONS

2 The only unique exclusions found in this section are as follows:

- **Wear and Tear** – We cover tires as part of the loss if a vehicle is *totaled* in a collision, but we won't replace them because you've worn them out or if they suffer road damage.
- **Mechanical or Electrical Breakdown**
- **Freezing** – If you put water in your radiator in the middle of winter, there will be no coverage when your engine cracks.
- **Electronic Equipment** – The Auto policy excludes just about all electronic equipment except equipment and accessories designed for the reproduction of sound if the equipment is permanently mounted in the auto. If not permanently mounted, the policy excludes radios, stereos, tape decks and CD players. Further excluded are CB radios, navigational systems (GPS) radar detectors, telephones, two-way mobile radios, scanning monitors, TV's, VCR's, personal computers, and radar detection equipment. In addition, the contract excludes tapes, discs, and records used with sound equipment. There is an endorsement available which can broaden the coverage to include most electronic equipment (permanently installed or not) and will cover CD's, tapes, and records up to a specified limit.

- **Government Confiscation** – If you are dealing cocaine out of your auto and the DEA takes it – no coverage.
- **Customized Equipment** – If your van has Lazy Boy chairs and a hot tub, those items are not covered.
- **Autos Used for Racing**
- **Nonowned Trailer** – Property damage limit is $1500.

COVERAGE D (DAMAGE TO YOUR AUTO) SETTLEMENT

3 Damage to Your Auto losses are settled for the lower of the:

- ACV of the damaged or stolen property.
- Amount necessary to repair or replace the property.

Appraisal may be necessary if you and your company
4 disagree over the value of your auto. The process is the same as we have encountered before . . . two appraisers and one umpire.

Notes

1 This completes our discussion of the coverage sections of the Personal Auto policy. The following chart should serve as a good summary of the important information about Coverages A, B, C, and D of the contract.

A **Liability**	B **Med Pay**	C **Un & Under Insured**	D **Damage to Your Auto** (Physical Damage)
Other Guy's Bodily Injury (BI) Property Damage (PD) State Minimum* ____________. Adequate** ____________. Supp Payments pays in addition to limits **+**	Pays: 1) Those **occupying** your car 2) Your family **occupying** or as pedestrians 3) No fault $/person For instance, $10,000/person	**Other Guy legally at fault . . .** Pays You & Yours for: • Bodily Injury (BI) • Maybe Property Damage (PD) Un must be between ____________.Un Under match Un ____________.Under	Collision Named Peril More expensive Higher deductible Other Than Collision (Comprehensive) *All Risk* Less expensive Lower deductible

***Minimum liability limits vary from state to state.**
****Adequate limits can vary from client to client.**

PART E – DUTIES AFTER AN ACCIDENT OR LOSS

2 Part E of the contract outlines the policyowner's responsibilities following an accident or a loss. The company has no obligation to pay a claim unless there is full compliance under this section. If there is an Uninsured Motorists loss or a Damage to Your Auto loss, there are additional duties imposed.

- Prompt notice
- Cooperation with the company
- Prompt submission of any legal papers
- Physical exam and examination under oath
- Authorization for medical records
- Proof of loss, if required

3 Uninsured Motorists losses also require:

- Notify the police if a hit and run driver is involved
- Submission of legal papers

You might have to call the police

4 Damage to Your Auto losses also require:

- Prevent further damage
- Notify the police of a stolen auto
- Inspection and appraisal

PART F – GENERAL PROVISIONS

1 These are the general conditions that apply to the entire policy.

- **Bankruptcy of the Insured** does not relieve the company of its obligations.
- **Policy Changes** must take the form of a written endorsement.
- **Fraud** on the Insured's part eliminates coverage.
- **Legal Action** against the company cannot be taken until the Insured has fulfilled his obligations under the contract.

- **Insurer's Right to Recover** simply gives the company subrogation rights.
- **Policy Period and Territory** The policy period is typically six months and the policy territory is the U.S., its possessions, Puerto Rico, and Canada.
- **Termination**
  - Insured can cancel at any time with written notification
  - company must follow state laws concerning reasons for cancellation and notification periods
- **Transfer of Rights (Assignment)** – requires company's written consent
- **Two or More Policies** – maximum company limit of liability is the highest applicable under any one policy. Assume Joe has two policies with Company A. The limits on one are 25/50/10 and 100/300/100 on the other. While driving his neighbor's car, Joe has limits of 100/300/100. The two policies cannot be *stacked*.

PERSONAL AUTO POLICY ENDORSEMENTS

- **Extended Nonowner Coverage for Named Individuals** - Covers nonowned auto provided for the use of the Insured. Joe has only a company car. Since he has no car of his own, he has no Personal Auto policy. Therefore, he would have no coverage driving a neighbor's car. This endorsement allows him to buy a Personal Auto policy, even without a car, and provides coverage for Joe driving any non-owned auto. Notice, the coverage works for the named individual only, not his family members.

- **Joint Ownership** - Allows unrelated named Insureds who own a car together to buy an auto policy together (the sin surcharge).

- **Miscellaneous Type Vehicles** - Allows you to cover vehicles like snowmobiles, dune buggies, motor homes, and golf carts under your Personal Auto policy. Also incorporates the joint ownership modifications of the previous endorsement.

- **Towing and Labor** - Pays the cost of moving a stranded automobile to a *safe harbor*, either through towing or emergency roadside repair. Note that the coverage is not designed to solve the car's mechanical problems, merely enough to get the vehicle out of *harm's way*.

Notes

NO-FAULT INSURANCE

1 Throughout this century, it has been generally true that if you were involved in an automobile accident that resulted in damage to your body or your property, your primary avenue of recovery was through tort law and the establishment of legal liability. No award could be paid to you until the fault (legal liability) of the responsible party was established. Certainly, your own policy could have provided some limited benefits under the Medical Payments or Uninsured Motorists coverage, but claims for disability, lost wages, pain and suffering and major property damage generally required legal action against the person at fault for the accident.

Like, you know, if we, like, all love one another, and, like, didn't argue about, like, the blame, you know. . .

2 Since the early 1950's, the number of claims and the amounts of those claims have skyrocketed each year. Attorneys have taken a lot of the blame as they normally collect 30% to 40% of any award made to you (the accident victim), or if they defend the company, they are earning $150 to $200 an hour for their efforts. Of course, the cost of automobile insurance has gone up with every claim, has accelerated faster as the size of the claims has increased, and has picked up even more momentum as the costs of the legal processing have skyrocketed. By the late 1960's, numerous critics were charging the whole system with being too slow, too expensive, and too fat for everyone but the victim.

3 It was at this time that the idea of no-fault insurance developed. Under true no-fault insurance, fault is not a consideration. You simply collect under your own policy for any damages you suffer. Essentially, true no-fault auto insurance is a two party contract like property insurance – everything is between you and your company.

4 Partly because there is a strong belief by most Americans that the responsible party, not the victim, should pay for damages, there are no true no-fault auto plans operating in this country.

5 However, many states have adopted **modified no-fault** plans. These allow the injured party to collect damages from his own policy, like true no-fault, but they preserve his right to sue for certain damages or in instances where his injuries are so serious that they result in his death or disability. A few states have adopted optional no-fault plans which do not affect the victim's right to sue at all. These optional plans simply increase the immediate benefits a victim could claim under his own policy while the legal liability of the responsible party is being established.

Conclusion

In this chapter, we have taken a look at the Personal Automobile policy. Most any
1 individual or individuals living in the same household can purchase a Personal Auto policy. This policy is primarily designed to cover a private passenger automobile operated for personal use. The policy structure, in addition to the Declarations, Definitions, General Provisions, and Duties After an Accident or Loss, is comprised of four main coverage parts:

- **Part A – Liability**
- **Part B – Medical Payments**
- **Part C – Uninsured and Underinsured Motorists**
- **Part D – Coverage for Damage to Your Auto** (Comprehensive and/or Collision)

Coverage A (Liability) pays for **bodily injury or property damage** you do **to**
2 **the *Other Guy*** up to the policy limits. The policy limits may be stated as either a single limit or as split limits. A single limit is a flat dollar amount that is the most in damages that the company will pay for any one accident. A **split limit** is a format which sets three inside limits as well as a total policy limit. For example, a person with limits of 25/50/10 would have coverage for up to $25,000 for bodily injury to any one person, up to $50,000 of coverage for all bodily injury in any one accident, and up to $10,000 of coverage for property damage in any one accident. In addition to paying for damage to the Other Guy, Coverage A provides **Supplementary Payments**, which include **defense costs** and various other legal expenses. The Supplementary Payments pay in addition to the limits of the policy.

Coverage B (Medical Payments) pays medical and funeral expenses incurred
3 within **3 years** of the accident by an Insured because of bodily injury caused by an automobile accident. In other words, **Med Pay will pay to you, your family, or anybody *occupying your car*** if you're injured while occupying a vehicle, or to you and your family if you sustain bodily injury as a pedestrian due to an automobile. For anyone other than your family, *occupying* is the key to this coverage. This coverage pays without regard to fault. An *Insured* is not only the named Insureds, but also any family member using any auto and any persons using the named insured's covered auto.

Coverage C (Un & Underinsured) is primarily designed to pay you for your bodily
4 injury in situations where the Other Guy is legally liable for the auto accident but doesn't have insurance or has inadequate insurance. An **uninsured motorist** is one without insurance or with insurance less than the state's minimum limits of liability. It could also be a person with auto liability coverage but whose company denies the claim or is insolvent, or a hit-and-run driver. An **underinsured motorist** is someone with enough insurance to be driving legally, but not enough to cover the damage resulting from an accident he caused. The Other Guy, then, can be uninsured or underinsured, **but he cannot be both**. Most states not using a no-fault system require that Coverage C be offered to every Insured. If not declined by a written waiver, you can choose **Uninsured Motorists Bodily Injury (UMBI)** limits up to your Coverage A limits, but not less than the state minimum limit. In most states, you can also cover damage to your auto – with Uninsured Motorists Property Damage (UMPD). However, **you cannot buy UMPD without UMBI**.

Notes

1 **Coverage D (Coverage for Damage to Your Auto)**, formerly known as *Physical Damage*, is property insurance coverage for your car. It has two coverage sections: **Collision**, which covers nothing but collision and is therefore a named peril coverage, and **Other Than Collision**, formerly known as *Comprehensive*, which essentially covers everything else and is therefore an open perils coverage. The insuring agreement of Coverage D says that the company will pay for direct and accidental loss to **your covered auto** or any covered **non owned auto** caused by Collision or an Other Than Collision type loss. **Covered auto** means the car listed on your Dec Sheet, a newly acquired additional or replacement vehicle, or a temporary substitute auto. A **non owned auto** is a private passenger auto or trailer that is not available for your regular use but which you happen to be driving. **Collision** is defined as the upset of a covered auto or non owned auto or their impact with another vehicle or object. Keep in mind that the vehicle does not have to be moving to have a collision, nor does the collision have to be with another vehicle. Also, Collision losses are paid without regard to fault. With most companies, you cannot buy Collision without also buying Other Than Collision. **Other Than Collision** coverage is open perils coverage, and would pay, for example, for damage to your car caused by:

- Missiles or falling objects
- Fire
- Explosion or earthquake
- Windstorm
- Hail, water, or flood
- Malicious mischief or vandalism
- Riot or civil commotion
- Theft or larceny
- Contact with a bird or animal
- Breakage of glass

2 A couple of overriding general guidelines in automobile insurance are that **coverage goes with the car,** and the company will make the Insured whole – not rich. For the details on the Personal Auto policy declarations, definitions, general provisions, exclusions, and duties after an accident or loss, please refer back to those sections of this chapter.

3 Finally, we took a brief look at no-fault. Under a pure **no-fault** plan, fault for who caused the automobile accident is not a consideration – you simply collect under your own policy for any damages you suffer. Although there are no true no-fault auto plans operating in this country, many states have adopted ***modified no-fault*** plans. These allow the injured party to collect damages from his own policy, like true no-fault, but they preserve his right to sue for certain damages or in instances where his injuries are so serious that they result in his death or disability.

CHAPTER 6
AUTO

1. A court orders claim payments of $35,000, $30,000 and $20,000 for bodily injury plus $12,500 for property damage. Defense costs total $6,000. What is the total amount the company would pay under $25,000/$50,000/$10,000 Automobile liability coverage?

   (A) $ 60,000
   (B) $ 66,000
   (C) $ 85,000
   (D) $103,500

2. All of the following could be considered an insured under a Personal Auto policy EXCEPT

   (A) The named insured's seven year old son.
   (B) The named insured's daughter while away at college.
   (C) The named insured's houseguest with permission.
   (D) The named insured's spouse while driving her company car.

3. Personal Auto Medical Payments would pay for which of the following?

   (A) Bodily injury you inflict on a pedestrian with your car.
   (B) Bodily injury you sustain while crossing the street to get to your car when struck by a bus.
   (C) Bodily injury you sustain when hit by a riding lawn mower.
   (D) Bodily injury you sustain when you're involved in a boating mishap.

Questions 4 through 7 refer to the following Automobile coverages:

(A) Supplementary Payments
(B) Other than Collision
(C) Uninsured Motorists
(D) Collision

From the coverages listed above, choose the one that best fits the following descriptions. Each coverage may be used once, more than once or not at all.

4. The coverage which protects the insured against losses due to vandalism.

   (A) (B) (C) (D)

CHAPTER 6 • AUTO QUIZ

5. The coverage which helps pay for the cost of appeal bonds, bail bonds and attachment bonds.

   (A) (B) (C) (D)

6. Damage to glass caused by a meteor.

   (A) (B) (C) (D)

7. Mr. Jones' car is hit from behind by a hit-and-run driver. His property damage claim would be covered by

   (A) (B) (C) (D)

8. At intersection "A", Joe Insured hits a pedestrian with his car, causing the person bodily injury in the amount of $25,000. Later the same day, Joe strikes 3 pedestrians at intersection "B". Bodily injuries sustained in the second accident are $30,000, $10,000, and $5,000. Joe's policy has liability limits of 25/50/10. What will his company pay for the total bodily injury claims at intersections "A" and "B"?

   (A) $50,000
   (B) $65,000
   (C) $70,000
   (D) $75.000

9. Which of the following persons would have liability coverage under their Personal Auto policy while driving a nonowned automobile?

   (A) A little league mother car-pooling with a car borrowed from a friend.
   (B) A salesperson driving a company car which is provided for her regular use.
   (C) A person on vacation driving a rental car in Mexico.
   (D) A truck driver driving a semi-trailer on business.

CHAPTER 6 • AUTO QUIZ

10. All of the following are true concerning Personal Auto Medical Payments EXCEPT

    (A) It covers all reasonable medical expenses up to the policy limits that are incurred within 3 years after an accident.
    (B) It is no fault.
    (C) It can cover someone not related to the insured, who is riding in the insured's car.
    (D) Med Pay always pays to a third party, never to the insured.

11. A deductible is usually found in

    (A) Collision and Other than Collision coverage.
    (B) BI and PD Liability.
    (C) Medical Payments.
    (D) Collision, but not Other than Collision coverage.

12. Which of the following Auto coverages pays only if the policyowner is found to be legally liable?

    (A) Bodily Injury
    (B) Supplementary Payments
    (C) Medical Payments
    (D) Uninsured Motorists

13. Joe Insured has an Automobile policy with Bodily Injury limits of \$50,000/\$100,000. Three persons hit by the insured's car were awarded \$5,000, \$60,000 and \$25,000. What is the total the insured's policy will pay?

    (A) \$80,000
    (B) \$80,000 plus the insured's court and defense costs
    (C) \$90,000
    (D) \$90,000 plus the insured's court and defense costs

14. A.J. accidentally crashes his Tarantula 180 into his boss's home. Repairs to the house would be covered under which section of A.J.'s Auto policy?

    (A) Property Damage Liability
    (B) Physical Damage
    (C) Collision
    (D) Uninsured Motorists

15. In question 14 above, which section of A.J.'s policy would pay for damage to A.J.'s car?

    (A) Property Damage Liability
    (B) Supplemental Payments
    (C) Collision
    (D) Uninsured Motorists

16. In Question 14 above, which section of A.J.'s policy would pay for damage to A.J.'s body?

    (A) Property Damage Liability
    (B) Physical Damage
    (C) Collision
    (D) Medical Payments

17. Which of the following loss categories would the collision of a stolen vehicle best fit?

    (A) Collision
    (B) Other than Collision
    (C) Property Damage
    (D) Uninsured Motorists

18. Which of the following is NOT true concerning Personal Auto policies?

    (A) Collision is named peril coverage
    (B) Other than Collision (Comprehensive) is all risk coverage.
    (C) Collision is excluded under Other than Collision.
    (D) Striking an animal is considered a collision.

19. Joe is involved in a collision with Fred. Fred is at fault. Fred's bodily injury limits are 50/100. Joe's Underinsured Motorists limits are 100/300. What's the maximum Joe's Underinsured Motorists limits would pay for his injuries as a result of this accident

    (A) $50,000
    (B) $75,000
    (C) $100,000
    (D) $150,000

CHAPTER 6 • AUTO QUIZ

20. A Personal Auto policy provides coverage

    (A) In the USA only.
    (B) In the USA and Canada only.
    (C) In the USA, Canada and Puerto Rico only.
    (D) In the USA, Canada, Puerto Rico and Mexico.

21. A car is parked on a hill, the parking brake slips and the car rolls into a tree. This is

    (A) A comprehensive loss.
    (B) A collision loss.
    (C) A preventable loss and is therefore excluded.
    (D) A violation of policy conditions and is therefore excluded.

22. Which of the following would be covered under collision coverage?

    (A) Vandalism
    (B) Falling objects
    (C) Overturn
    (D) Fire

END

QUIZ ANSWERS & EXPLANATIONS ON NEXT PAGE

CHAPTER 6
AUTO QUIZ ANSWER KEY

1. B. In all claims questions we must remember to apply the rule of 3L's: Always use the Lower of the Loss or the Limit. The per person BI limit is $25K. The first person is hurt 35K, thus we pay $25K. The second victim is hurt $30K, thus we again use $25K. The final victim is hurt $20K, we use this number as it is lower than the per person limit. The total of the BI in the accident is $70K, but the per accident limit is $50K. Again apply the rule of 3L's, the policy will only pay $50K. The PD limit in the policy is $10K; the total property damage is $12,500. We add the total BI claim $50K, to the PD claim, $10K, for a grand total of $60K in damages. Defense cost are covered under Supplementary Payments, which are in addition to the liability limits, giving a total of $66K paid out under the policy.

2. D. The Personal Auto Policy (PAP) does not provide coverage while driving a nonowned auto "provided for the insured's "regular and frequent" use.

3. B. Coverage B, Med Pay, provides coverage for the insured and the insured's resident relatives injured by an automobile as pedestrians. The only third parties that are afforded coverage are those occupying a covered auto. C and D do not involve auto accidents.

4. B. This is a covered loss by the Other than Collision Coverage.

5. A. Supplementary Payments pays for the cost of the defense of claims brought by Coverage A, including the premiums on bonds.

6. B. Glass is an Other than Collision loss.

7. D. In the case of a hit and run driver, the insured's BI is Coverage C; his car is Coverage D, Collision.

8. B. The trick here is to remember that the BI limit applies separately to each accident. The BI claim for the first accident is $25K. The calculations start with fresh limits for the second accident. BI claims for this accident total $40K. (Again using the rule of 3L's, the per person payments will be $25K, $10K & $5K). The total for both accidents is $65K.

9. A. The PAP does not provide protection when driving a nonowned auto provided for the insured's regular and frequent use. The policy territory is limited to the USA, its possessions and Canada. The PAP does not cover business uses. The mother in A would have coverage, even though the car's coverage would be primary.

10. D. The PAP Med Pay is primarily a two party coverage. The only third parties entitled to benefits are those occupying a covered auto.

11. A. Deductibles are found in both of the types of claims covered under Coverage D.

12. A. Both Medical Payments and Supplementary Payments are triggered without regard to fault. Uninsured Motorist requires that the other guy be at fault. Only BI in Coverage A requires that the insured be at fault.

13. B. Using the rule of 3L's the individual BI claims were $5K, $50K and $25K, for a total BI claim of $80K. As the damages were awarded, there would be court and defense costs paid under Supplementary Payments.

14. A. Property Damage Liability would pay for any property owned by a third party damaged by the insured.

15. C. Collision pays for our insured's auto, without regard to fault.

16. D. Med Pay covers our insured's injuries as a result of an auto accident, without regard to fault.

17. B. There was a loss as soon as the car was taken; the fact that it suffered additional losses as a result of a collision is irrelevant.

18. D. Collision with a bird or an animal is an Other than Collision (Comprehensive) loss.

19. A. In determining what the limit for any particular Underinsured claim would be, one must subtract the other guy's Coverage A limit from the insured's Coverage C limit.

20. C. This is the ISO PAP coverage territory.

21. B. This is a collision loss even though the car was not occupied at the time of the impact.

22. C. The overturning, sometimes called "Upset," is a Collision loss.

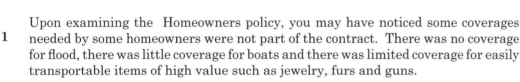

SPECIALTY POLICIES

1 Upon examining the Homeowners policy, you may have noticed some coverages needed by some homeowners were not part of the contract. There was no coverage for flood, there was little coverage for boats and there was limited coverage for easily transportable items of high value such as jewelry, furs and guns.

2 In this chapter, we will show how these coverages can be obtained in our discussion of Flood insurance, Personal Watercraft coverage, and Marine insurance. Further, we will briefly address the methods through which a house which is ineligible for a Homeowners policy can qualify for coverage under the FAIR Plan.

FLOOD INSURANCE

3 It is a fundamental principle of good underwriting for an insurance company to seek the **geographic dispersion** of exposure units. Simply, the company does not want all of its policyowners clustered together. The reason for this is that a peril, such as fire, could strike one policyowner and spread to many others before it could be stopped. With the peril of flood, this is an inherent problem. Flood, by its very definition, does not cause a loss to only one property. Flood damages hundreds or thousands of properties in one geographic area, which makes it very difficult for an insurance company to spread the risk.

4 Compounding this problem is the concept of **adverse selection**. Adverse selection is the tendency for people who have a high need for a particular coverage to buy, while those who have a lesser need do not buy. With respect to flood insurance, adverse selection means that people living in low elevations alongside rivers want to buy, whereas people living in high elevations and in dry areas are not interested. This makes it difficult for insurance companies to spread the risk, control their exposure, and keep their premiums affordable. Prior to 1968, very few companies accepted flood insurance risks. Flood insurance simply was not profitable.

Notes

THE NATIONAL FLOOD INSURANCE PROGRAM (NFIP)

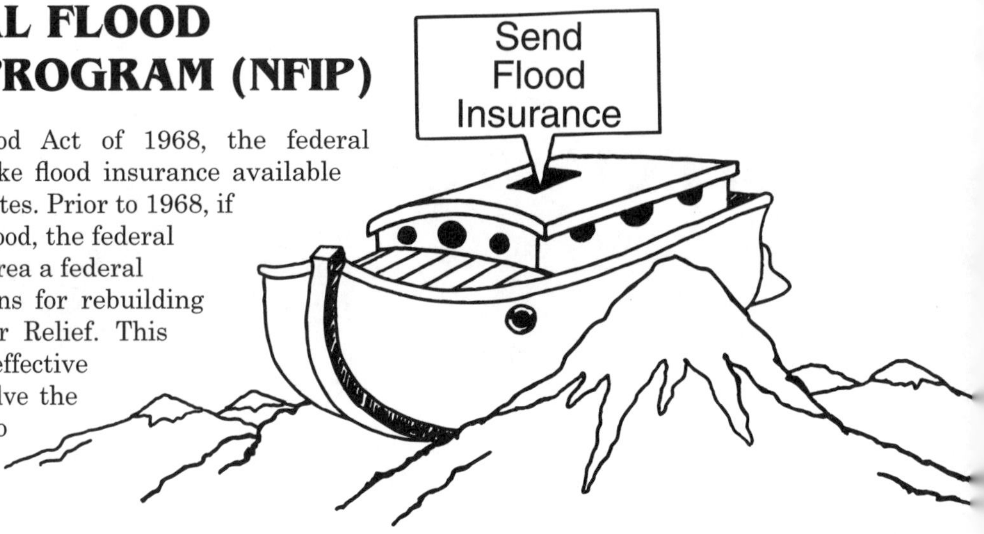

1 Under the National Flood Act of 1968, the federal government sought to make flood insurance available nationally at reasonable rates. Prior to 1968, if an area suffered a major flood, the federal government declared the area a federal disaster and provided loans for rebuilding through National Disaster Relief. This program was rather ineffective because it didn't really solve the problem, which was to reduce the risk of future flooding by investing in flood control projects, such as canals, levees, dredging and building ordnances designed to control construction in flood prone areas.

2 The program introduced in 1968 is called the National Flood Insurance Program (NFIP). This program is administered by the Federal Emergency Management Agency (FEMA). Under the Flood insurance program, the **federal government is the insurer and takes all of the insurance risk**. But the program is as much about **the reduction of future flood risks** as it is about insurance.

3 For the first 15 years of the Flood program, the federal government also did the marketing and sales, which was not so successful. So in 1983 the federal government started the "Write-Your-Own" program which allows private insurance companies and their Agents to write and sell flood policies under their private insurance company names in order to take advantage of the insurance industry's marketing channels. Under NFIP about 90 private insurance companies market Flood insurance, collect the premiums, keep a certain percentage of the premium to cover their expenses, earn a small profit, and administer claim payments. If there is not enough money to pay the claims, the NFIP/federal government provides the difference. While the private insurance companies are not assuming the risk in the NFIP, they are responsible for adjusting losses and writing the claims checks.

4 The NFIP combines both insurance protection against Flood, and a floodplain management program aimed at the mitigation / reduction of flood risk, whereby the community and the federal government work together to rebuild the community in order to reduce the vulnerability to Flood damage. Both residential and commercial buildings and contents may be insured in those communities that agree to adopt and enforce floodplain management ordinances to reduce future flood damage. Nearly 20,000 communities across the USA participate in the NFIP in order to protect their homeowners and businesses against Flood.

5 **Flood is the most common natural disaster** in the United States. Yet only a very small percentage of U.S. homes and businesses are covered by Flood insurance.

Companies -sell

6 In summary, the National Flood Insurance "Write-Your-Own" Program is a federal insurance program whereby private insurance companies sell the Flood policies, collect the premiums and administer the payment of claims, but ultimately the federal government assumes all of the risk.

Government - takes the risk

Notes

THE FLOODING RISK: A FLOOD FOR ALL SEASONS

1 Flooding can happen any time of year. Some of the more frequent causes are:
1. Tropical Storms and Hurricanes
2. Spring Thaws
3. Heavy Rains
4. West Coast Threats
5. Levees & Dams breakage
6. Flash Floods
7. New Developments

VOLUNTARY OR MANDATORY?

2 As you know, the peril of Flood is EXCLUDED under all Homeowners and Commercial Property policies. So do you have to buy Flood insurance?

If you live in a NFIP designated community (see below for an explanation), and you
3 do not have a mortgage on your home, purchasing Flood insurance is Voluntary/ Optional. However, if you have a mortgage from a federally regulated or insured financial institution (which is almost all financial institutions), or federal financial assistance, such as a FHA or VA backed mortgage, and you live in the flood plain, then **purchasing Flood insurance is mandatory**. By federal law, lenders must notify borrowers, prior to the closing, that their property is located in a high-flood-risk area, and that purchasing Flood insurance is therefore required. It is your responsibility as an Agent to determine if your Insured Policyowner lives in a designated Floodplain. If so, you should recommend the purchase of Flood insurance. To determine if property is in a Floodplain, just go to WWW.FLOODSMART.GOV.

FLOOD DEFINED

4 NFIP Flood insurance covers only the direct physical loss caused by Flood. Indirect Loss coverage for Additional Living Expenses is NOT covered by Flood insurance.

5 In simple terms, **a Flood is an excess of water on normally dry land**. But the official definition is as follows.

The peril of FLOOD is defined by FEMA as: "A general and temporary condition
6 of the partial or complete inundation (coverage by water) of **two or more acres of normally dry land**, or of **two or more properties** (including your own) from:

Temporarily wet

1. The unusual and rapid accumulation or run-off of surface waters from any source; or

2. The overflow of inland or tidal waters; or

3. A Mudflow (defined as "A river of liquid and flowing mud on the surface of a normally dry land area, as when earth is carried by a current of water" / a river of mud made fluid and mobile by heavy rain or a rapid snowmelt); or

4. The collapse or subsidence (sinking) of land along the shore (shoreline) of a lake or similar body of water (bay or ocean) as the result of erosion, or as the result of the undermining caused by waves or currents of water exceeding the anticipated cyclical levels (extra high tides), that result in a flood as defined above." ***mudflow - yes***

7 In simple terms, a Flood is an excess of water, accumulating through natural causes, covering normally dry land. Translation: Mother Nature's water in excess. ***landslide - no***

LOSSES NOT COVERED BY "FLOOD"

1 Coverage is EXCLUDED for:

1. Landslides

2. Mudslides

2 Note: **Mudflows are covered, but Mudslides are not**. A Mud FLOW is a river of mud. On the other hand, a Mud SLIDE is like a Land slide, but caused by excessive amounts of rain. The wet heavy earth just slides down the hillside.

3. Sewer Backup, unless the sewer backup is the direct result of flooding.

4. Flooding that is within the control of the Insured. For example, if a farmer drains his own lake and accidentally floods his own home, it would not be covered by his Flood policy.

5. Wind Driven Rain Is not covered by "Flood", but it IS covered under the Homeowners peril of Windstorm or Hail. However, to make matters even more confusing, please note that "Wind Driven Surface Water", known as **Storm Surge** (when the high winds of a storm blow the ocean waters onto the land, such as during Hurricane Katrina of 2005), IS covered by Flood insurance.

Note: Flood experts suggest that one way to think about the coverages under Home-
3 owners as contrasted with Flood insurance is: If the water is coming DOWN, the coverage is Homeowners. If the water is coming UP, the coverage is Flood.

4 Memory device: If the rain is coming down, HO, HO, HO ! But if the river is coming up, run from the Flood!

KEY DEFINITIONS

1. SPECIAL FLOOD HAZARD AREA (SFHA) A Special Flood Hazard Area is an area of normally dry land that would be flooded/inundated in a "100 Year Flood". A Special Flood Hazard Area is the technical name for floodplain.

2. 100 YEAR FLOOD / 100 YEAR STORM The term "100 Year Flood" is confusing. The term infers that a flood will occur only once every 100 years, which is NOT the case. Rather the term is referring to water elevation, and the percentage chance that the water will rise above a certain level on an annual basis. So the definition is: "The flood water elevation that has a 1% chance of being equaled or exceeded in any given year."

5 A 100 Year Flood may also be referred to as a 100 Year Storm. The area of land inundated by water during a 100 Year Flood is called the Floodplain.

6 Translation: A Floodplain is land that has a 1% + chance of being flooded each year.

Notes

3. FLOODWAY A floodway is the part of the floodplain where the water is likely to be the deepest and run the fastest. It is the area of the floodplain that should be reserved/kept free of obstructions. This allows the floodwaters to move downstream with the least resistance which avoids the backup of excess water, thereby reducing flooding.

4. BASEMENT The area of a building, with a floor, that is below ground level on all sides. Therefore, a "walk out" "basement" is NOT a basement according to the NFIP.

1 NFIP does NOT consider a basement as "living quarters", but instead merely as the place upon which the structure rests. Therefore, there is a major difference between how a Homeowners policy insures a finished "basement" and how NFIP insures it (which is minimal). For example, the NFIP flood coverage for a basement does NOT insure finished basement improvements, such as finished walls, floors, cabinets, home theaters, ceilings, etc. Also NOT covered by Flood insurance are any Personal Property/Contents in the basement. Translation: When the water level starts rising, grab the Big Screen TV(plus all of your other Personal Property), and head for higher ground!

ELIGIBILE COMMUNITIES

2 Flood insurance is only available in NFIP designated and approved communities, of which there are about 20,000 across the country. The NFIP accepts the communities into the Flood program, administers the plan, enforces the plan rules, and sets the premium rates. To qualify for NFIP, a community must agree to a **flood control program designed to significantly reduce future flood losses**. This includes constructing river dikes and levees, adding storm drain systems, and building "flood proof" buildings. In addition, there are numerous zoning and building code requirements that must be met. Thus, the flood program not only provides coverage for losses, but it also invests in future loss prevention.

3 To summarize, a community establishes its eligibility to participate in NFIP in two ways:

1. By adopting and enforcing floodplain management measures to regulate new construction; and

2. By ensuring that substantial improvements are made to existing buildings within the identified flood plain.

Designated area. . .

Property owners in NFIP communities, but who DO NOT live in the flood plain, can
4 still purchase flood insurance. In fact, 30% of all flood claims come from properties OUTSIDE the high-flood-risk (SFHA) areas.

. . .local plan

Before a community becomes a designated NFIP area, the community must apply to
5 the NFIP. During the application stage, the community is said to have "Emergency" status, which is Phase One of the flood program. When the community has fulfilled its application requirements, it is accepted into the regular flood program. During the "Emergency" status, the community is eligible to purchase flood insurance, but the benefit limits are lower than when accepted in to the regular program.

Notes

ELIGIBLE PROPERTIES & BENEFIT LIMITS

1. Residential Dwellings & Contents	$250,000	&	$100,000
2. Commercial Buildings & Contents	$500,000	&	$500,000

1 **Note**: Dwelling coverage during the "Emergency" status phase is limited to $35,000, and Contents coverage is limited to $10,000.

Emergency. . . doesn't mean the water is rising

2 EXCLUSIONS – PROPERTY NOT COVERED BY "FLOOD"
1. Land
2. Other Structures/Appurtenant Structures, UNLESS coverage is purchased. The Flood program offers coverage for one detached garage.
3. Crops
4. Vehicles
5. Damage caused by moisture, mildew, or mold that the Insured could have avoided.
6. Paper worth something.
7. Living Expenses/ Consequential Losses
8. Other Exclusions typically found in Homeowners policies, such as Better Covered Elsewhere.

FLOOD POLICY FORMS

3 There are three Flood policy forms provided by FEMA.

1. Dwelling Form	for Homeowners, Renters & Condo Owners
2. General Property Form	for commercial properties
3. Condominium Form	for Condo Associations

COVERAGES: BUILDING AND CONTENTS

4 All residential dwellings, farms and commercial buildings are eligible for Flood insurance. Contents/Personal Property coverage is also available. However, the contents must be located inside the insured building to have coverage.

If you don't buy flood. . . . . .you might be all wet

FLOOD DETAILS

1. STANDARD DEDUCTIBLE - Is $1000. The Deductible is applied twice: once on the Building loss, and again on the Personal Property/Contents loss.

2. 30 DAY WAITING PERIOD - There is a 30 Day Waiting Period from the date of application and premium payment to the beginning of Flood coverage. (Different rules apply in situations of refinancing a home.)

3 NO BINDING COVERAGES - The NFIP Flood program does NOT allow Agents to bind Flood coverage. Actual policies must be issued in order to have Flood coverage.

4 ADDITIONAL LIVING EXPENSES - If a flood makes an insured residence uninhabitable, the additional living expenses incurred by the Insured Policyowner are not covered, as there are NO Loss of Use benefits in Flood insurance.

5. LOSS SETTLEMENT

   a. Building - Is settled on a Replacement Cost basis IF the building is insured for at least 80% of the Replacement Value, or is the maximum available for the property under NFIP. Otherwise, settlement is on an ACV basis. (Different rules apply for "Second Homes").

   b. Personal Property/Contents - Is always settled on an Actual Cast Value (ACV) basis.

6. POLICY PERIOD - The Flood insurance Policy Period is one year. Policy renewal does not require a new Application.

1 For more Flood details, changes in the Flood program, and to determine if your
Insureds are in Floodplains, please go to the FEMA website @

WWW.FLOODSMART.GOV

Or call FEMA @ 888. 379. 9531

PERSONAL WATERCRAFT

Joe and Jolene have reached a point in their lives where they have some discre-
2 tionary income, a little free time, and a yen for the great outdoors. Like so many
Americans, they have chosen to do some boating. They start out with a simple
boat – like a small outboard or a small sailboat. Insurance coverage for these basic
boats is usually available in a Homeowners policy. If not, the Homeowners policy
can be endorsed to cover the risk.

***BOAT:* A hole in the water into which you pour money**

A couple years later, Joe and Jolene trade up to the next level – they buy a runabout,
3 ski boat, or bass boat. Their coverages need to be upgraded to a Boatowners policy,
which is an automobile-type policy for boats.

Then, one day, Joe and Jolene win the lottery and become instant millionaires.
4 They buy a *BIG* boat . . . a yacht. Another upgrade in their insurance coverage is
necessary. They now need a Yacht policy.

Notes

1 In this section, we are going to discuss watercraft – privately owned boats used for pleasure purposes only. (This text will not address coverages for commercial marine risks, such as ocean-going ships on the high seas, or boats operated for profit.)

DF
NO THEFT
NO LIABILITY

DWELLING POLICIES

2 The Dwelling Policies (DP's) provide almost no coverage for boats. There is a small amount of **property** coverage for rowboats and canoes, but only up to $1000. If the boat has a motor or a sail, there is no coverage. Keep in mind also that the Dwelling Policies have **no liability coverage** and **no theft coverage**.

NOT OK

HO covers SMALL, SLOW, CHEAP, LOW RISK BOATS

HOMEOWNERS

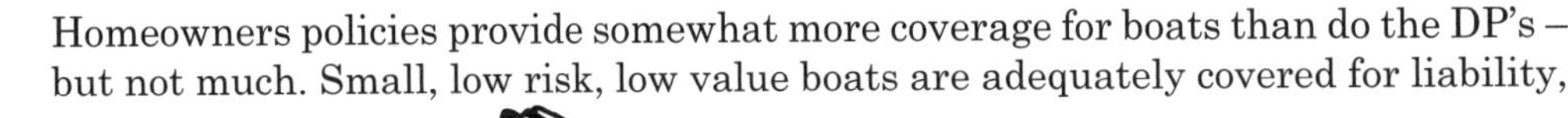

3 Homeowners policies provide somewhat more coverage for boats than do the DP's – but not much. Small, low risk, low value boats are adequately covered for liability,

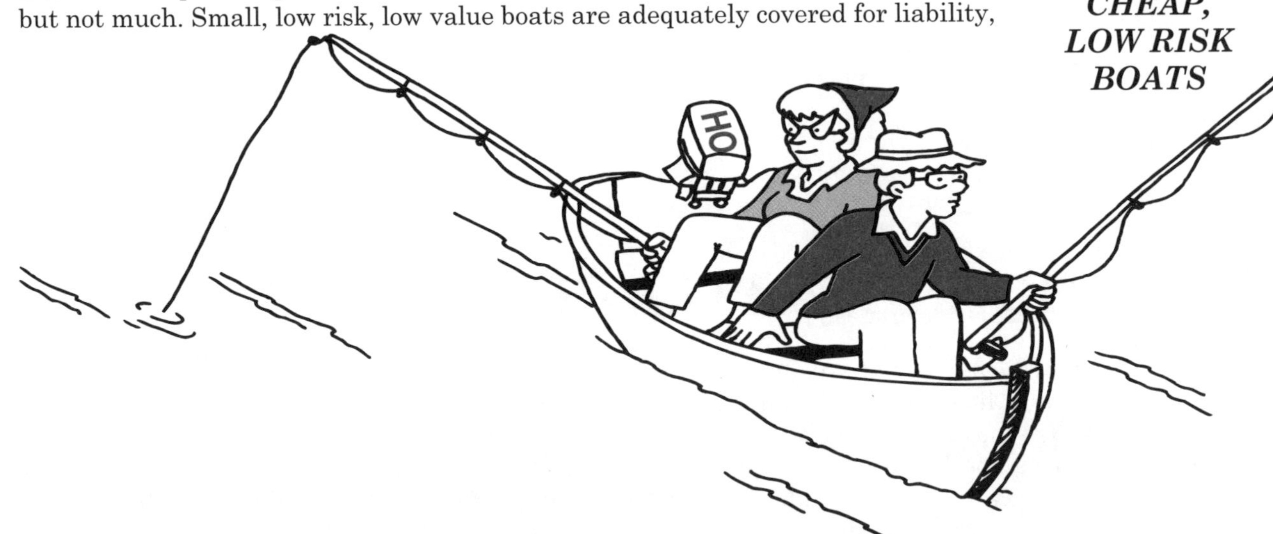

but there is only limited property coverage of up to $1500.

4 Section I (Property) of a Homeowners policy covers all of your watercraft, including your trailers, equipment, and outboard motors, but only up to the policy limit of $1500. Also, there is no coverage for the most frequent (and high risk) perils:

- **Theft away from premises**
- **Wind damage** (unless the boat is inside of an enclosed building)

Notes

1 Personal Liability (Section II) of a Homeowners policy provides **very limited liability coverage** for watercraft. A Homeowners policy generally provides adequate liability coverage only for the following low risk (*slow*) boats:

small. . .

- Sailboats up to 26 feet in length
- Outboard powerboats owned by the Insured under 25 horsepower
- Inboard (or inboard/outboard) powerboats under 50 horsepower *that the Insured rents*

. . .slow

2 You should notice that all of the above boats are ***small*** and ***slow***. Homeowners has such limited liability coverage for boats that as a general rule, the only way it's covered is if Joe and Jolene can outrun the boat. In other words, Homeowners will provide adequate liability coverage only if your boat is powered by paddles, oars, sails, or a mini-outboard and you and your spouse can throw it on top of your van. If you have a more serious boat, then you have two policies to choose from: Boatowners or a Yacht policy.

BOATOWNERS

3 If Joe and Jolene own a trailerable-size watercraft, then the appropriate coverage is a Boatowners policy. As we approach this policy, it is important to note that **there are no standard forms**. Insurance companies that write Boatowners policies do so in a variety of ways, so our discussion will be full of *generally* and *usually*. Also, a Boatowners (or Personal Watercraft Policy) is very similar in design to the Personal Automobile Policy. You might think of Boatowners as a *marine version of Auto*. It's a package policy that includes property, liability, med pay, uninsured boaters, and collision coverages.

BOATOWNERS

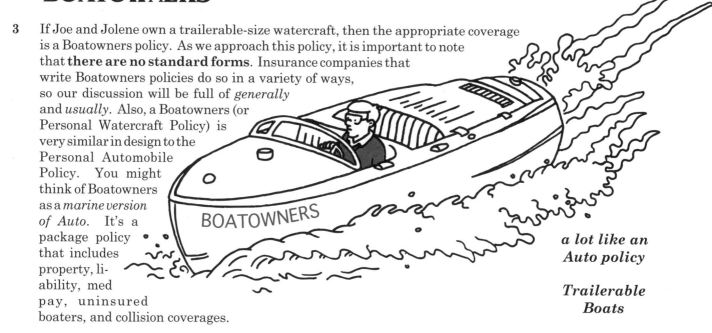

a lot like an Auto policy

Trailerable Boats

4 Eligibility

Generally, Boatowners policies are written to cover trailerable boats, such as sailboats, bass boats, runabouts, and other open cockpit boats that are less than 26 feet long. These types of boats are normally stored on a trailer and can be towed behind the family automobile.

Property Coverages

- Includes boat, motor(s), trailer, equipment, and accessories as specified on the Dec Sheet. Values for each will probably be stated on the Dec Sheet.
- Excludes cameras, personal property and all sporting and fishing equipment.
- Excludes any loss arising out of the use of the boat for commercial purposes or racing of powerboats. (Sailboat racing is okay.)
- "All Risk" (including collision damage to the boat)
- Loss settlement is ACV, but better policies often use Replacement Cost.
- Some policies pay for the cost to recover a sunken or stranded boat.
- The normal exclusions still apply - war, nuclear, **mechanical breakdown**, etc.

Liability Coverages

- Essentially the same as Auto: pays BI and PD. Collision liability is covered.
- Also covers your use of a borrowed boat with the owner's permission.
- Exclusions – standard, plus powerboat racing, commercial activities, and losses caused by or to the employees of boat yards (maintenance facilities).

Med Pay – Same as Auto

- Water-skiers may be covered.

Uninsured Boaters – Same as Auto

Territorial Limits

- The policy will limit the waters in which the boat can be operated, such as the *inland waters of the U.S. and Canada only. Others will also include coastal waters within 15 miles of shore.* The policyowner can **warrant** that the boat will only be operated in a more restricted area and be rewarded by a reduction in premium.

15
mile
limit

Notes

if you have to ask. . . you can't afford it

No Ordinary Joe

YACHT POLICY

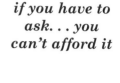

1 For the serious boater with a serious (and expensive) "boat jones", a Yacht policy is appropriate. Yachts usually have enclosed cockpits and sleeping and cooking facilities. They must carry safety equipment, such as **lifeboats, fire extinguishers, and flares**. Yachts are docked in marinas when it is warm. When it gets cold, they are hauled out of the water by large mechanized cranes and are stored for the winter on land in boat yards. If they travel on the highway, they do so on specialized trailers towed by trucks.

2 A Yacht policy is a package policy that includes all of the Boatowners coverages, plus some additional special coverages, such as Workers Comp for a paid crew, coverage for the *tenders* (dinghies), and a discount on the premium while the boat is in dry dock (storage).

Differences

- Settlement is generally **Agreed Value** on total losses and **Replacement Cost** on partial losses.
- Deductibles are usually a percentage of the hull amount, like 1% or 2%.
- **Workers Comp** is included for a paid captain or crew (called **Longshore and Harbor Workers Compensation**).
- Navigation/cruising limits are stated **as warranties** on the Dec Sheet.
- Tenders are usually covered.
- Hull (boat) values may be in the hundreds of thousands of dollars.

SUMMARY: THREE TYPES OF BOATS

1. **TOYS** - small, slow, inexpensive, **low risk** boats.
   A. *Coverage: HOMEOWNERS* policy OK because it covers *Toy Boat* Liability
2. **TRAILERABLE** - medium-size, high-speed, expensive, dangerous, **high risk** boats.
   A. *Coverage: BOATOWNERS* policy
3. **TRUE** - big, very expensive yachts, paid crews.
   A. *Coverage: YACHT* policy (includes Workers Comp)

Notes

OCEAN AND INLAND MARINE

BACKGROUND

1 One of the major segments of property insurance is marine (transportation) insurance, which is concerned with the perils of property **in transit** as opposed to property at a fixed location.

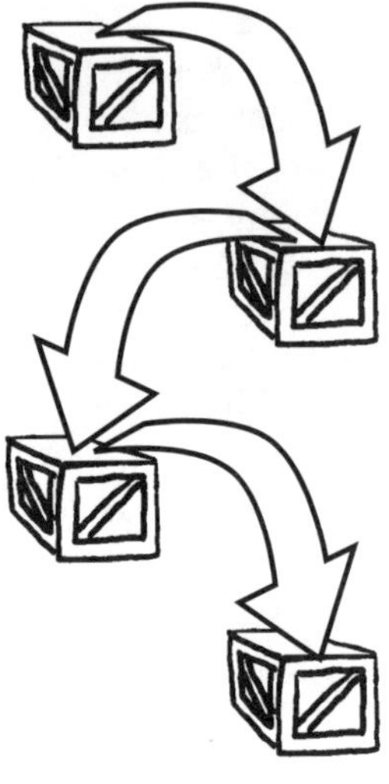

goods in transit

2 Marine insurance began in the 14th century and is the oldest type of insurance still in existence today. The process began when Greek shipowners financed their commercial voyages by borrowing the necessary capital from moneylenders and pledging their ships as collateral. The loan agreements, however, contained a clause that stated that if a ship were lost at sea, the moneylenders would give up any rights to collect their loan. Since this provision shifted the entire risk of the loss of the ship from the shipowners to the moneylenders, the lenders insisted on being heavily compensated for taking on this risk. As compensation, they charged a **premium**, or a higher amount, for taking on this risk in addition to the normal interest on the loan. This was the beginning of insurance as we know it today.

3 Originally, only the ships (not the cargoes) were insured. By the 15th century, the concept of ocean marine insurance spread west to Spain and England, and for the next 300 years it was just about the only type of insurance available.

wet – ocean
dry – inland

4 The marine underwriters then got involved with insuring land-based items that were related to marine activities, such as cargo storage, warehouses, piers, docks, bridges, tunnels and eventually the shipment of cargo over land to its final destination. **These land-based, or *dry*, risks were classified as inland marine as opposed to ocean marine, or *wet*, insurance.**

5 By the 18th century, the concept of insurance was being applied to buildings (real property) that were not mobile. This was the beginning of what we usually think of as property insurance — coverage for real property at a fixed location. The nature of this insurance is very different from that of marine insurance. Fire is the main peril in property insurance. Marine (transportation) perils include such risks as pirates, assailing thieves and sinking. **The Standard Fire Policy was designed to cover property at a fixed location while marine insurance was designed to protect property that is either moving, capable of being moved or that aids in movement.**

6 Land-based movable property was naturally passed on to marine underwriters because such risks were more closely related to transportation than to fire insurance.

7 At the turn of the 20th century, the marine insurers became more directly involved with the American public by offering marine floater policies that covered the personal effects of traveling salesmen. Then, they expanded their markets by insuring *fixed location* storage buildings at low rates by merging these storage risks with the related transportation risks. The fire and casualty insurers became alarmed by the rapid growth of marine insurance and its infringement into their sacred fixed location field. The marine underwriters, free from control by the rate bureaus, could adjust rates at will and were thus more competitive than the fire and casualty companies. The 1929 economic crash aggravated the situation, and by 1933, the fire and casualty companies sought to legally restrict the encroachment of the marine insurers by supporting the issuance of the first nationwide definition of marine insurance. The definition was revised in 1953 and again in 1976.

1976 NATIONWIDE MARINE DEFINITION

1 The purpose of this definition is to restrict the areas in which marine underwriters can write coverages. Today marine underwriters are limited to six categories:

- Imports
- Exports
- Domestic Shipments
- Bridges, Tunnels, Docks, and other Instruments of Transportation and Communication
- Personal Property Floaters
- Commercial Property Floaters

2 **IMPORTS** – Property being shipped from another country for delivery in the United States. When the import reaches its destination, it ceases to be a proper subject for marine insurance.

coming...

3 **EXPORTS** – Property being shipped from the U.S. for delivery in another country. An export becomes a proper subject for marine insurance once it is designated as an export or is being prepared for export.

...going...

4 **DOMESTIC SHIPMENTS** – Property being shipped from one location to another within the U.S. Trip Transit, Motor Truck Cargo and Parcel Post are typical policies. After a limited period of time specified in the contract, the domestic shipment is no longer considered "in course of transportation" and therefore is no longer a proper subject for marine insurance.

...staying

5 **BRIDGES, TUNNELS, DOCKS, and other INSTRUMENTS OF TRANSPORTATION and COMMUNICATION** – Includes piers, marine railways, pipelines and pumping equipment, power transmission lines, telephone lines, radio and TV broadcasts (the theory being that they "transport" words and messages), and outdoor cranes/loading bridges used to load and unload ships. These are classified as marine insurance in recognition of a long standing practice in the business. Such coverages had been written by marine underwriters for years, mainly since fire underwriters did not want to give broad protection on this type of property.

things that help movement

6 Excluded are buildings used in connection with bridges and other instruments of transportation or communication. **Neither ships nor boats are mentioned specifically in the definition since tradition made it obvious that they are eligible for marine coverage.**

7 **PERSONAL PROPERTY FLOATER RISKS** – Mobile property that is excluded, limited or inadequately covered under a Homeowners or Dwelling policy can be covered with a Personal Property Inland Marine Floater.

8 **COMMERCIAL PROPERTY FLOATER RISKS** – *All Risk* policies covering mobile property pertaining to a business, profession, or occupation.

Notes

FAIR PLAN COVERAGE

1 **FAIR (Fair Access to Insurance Requirements)** Plans are designed to make **property insurance available to individuals living in high risk urban areas**. FAIR Plan coverage is available in the vast majority of states. Over thirty five states offer some form of FAIR Plan Coverage.

2 **How does it work?**

3 FAIR Plan policies are **issued by a servicing insurer**, but the risk is underwritten by a **pool of the property insurers** doing business in a particular state. Some states pass the additional costs of FAIR Plan coverage to the other property owners in the state by means of a surcharge.

4 **Is the FAIR Plan available to everyone?**

5 In short, no. Some states require that the property be located in certain geographic areas. Some states will not cover commercial risks or farms. Some states require that the applicant be turned down by private insurance companies, while others require that the insurance merely be too expensive through normal channels. With almost all FAIR Plans, coverage is **unavailable if the property fails to meet basic underwriting requirements**, is vacant, or has a property tax bill which has not been paid.

6 **NOTE: No applicant may be turned down, however, simply because the property is located in a high risk location.**

7 **What Coverage is available under the FAIR Plan?**

8 Most FAIR Plans provide only two party (property coverages); a few state's FAIR Plans offer full blown HO policies. In most cases, the Cause of Loss Form used is similar to a Standard Fire Policy with what are known as Extended Coverages. This is similar to an DP-1. Most FAIR Plans **do not cover theft.**

Aha! . . . another use for DPs.

Conclusion

Flood Insurance

Both Personal Lines and Commercial Lines Property policies **exclude the peril**
1 **of flood.** This is due to the fact that flood losses are geographically concentrated,
and the people that purchase flood coverage typically need it very badly. To cover
flood under a standard property policy would be to encourage **adverse selection**
at its worst.

Under the **National Flood Insurance Program,** your company can sell flood
2 insurance, collect the premiums, retain some monies for profit and expenses, and
utilize the balance to pay claims. If claims exceed this surplus, the NFIP will
provide the difference. Essentially, private companies **sell the policies for a fee,**
but the Federal government assumes all the risk.

Buildings and contents coverage is available in qualified communities across the
3 country. To qualify, a community must implement a flood control program designed
to reduce further flood losses. **The effective date of coverage is 30 days after**
the application.

4 **The standard deductible is $1000, which is applied twice – once on the building, and again to the contents.**

5 The NFIP's Dwelling Form offers:

- Building coverage of up to **$250,000**, and
- Personal Property (Contents) coverage up to **$100,000**.

Personal Watercraft

6 Personal watercraft can be covered under any of four policies. As an overview, if you:

- Take the boat to the lake on top of your car, a **Dwelling policy** or **Homeowners policy** may be adequate.
- Haul the boat to the lake on a trailer, you probably need a **Boatowners policy.**
- If your boat is too big to haul and lives at the marina, you need a **Yacht policy**.

7 DP's – Property only, boats and canoes up to **$1000**

HO's – Property: **$1500** limit; no theft away from premises, no wind damage unless
8 boat is in an enclosed building.
Casualty – Sailboats under **26 feet,** outboards under **25 horsepower,** rental boats with engines under 50 horsepower.

Boatowners – Trailerable boats up to 26 feet in length.
9 Property – Boats, motors and accessories as spelled out on the Dec Sheet.
Settlement – ACV or RC
Exclusions – powerboat racing, mechanical breakdown.
Casualty – Similar to Personal Auto – BI, PD and Med Pay.

Notes

Yacht policy – Boats with enclosed cabins, usually with sleeping and cooking facilities.
Property – settlement is Agreed Value or total losses, and RC on partial losses.
Casualty – Includes Longshore and Harbor Workers Compensation.

Ocean and Inland Marine

Ocean and Inland Marine contracts are principally written to cover goods in transit. If moved by water (ship, boat or barge), an Ocean Marine contract is used. If moved by air or land (airplane, truck or train), an Inland Marine contract is appropriate. The 1976 Nationwide Marine definition includes six categories:

- Imports
- Exports
- Domestic shipments
- Bridges, tunnels and docks
- Personal property floaters
- Commercial property floaters

FAIR Plans

Plans operate in most states to provide property coverage for risks uninsurable (at reasonable rates) through the private insurance market. Typically, all companies writing property insurance in a given state must proportionately underwrite this pool in that same state. While some states exclude commercial buildings and farms, most do include homes. The mandated coverage may be at the Dwelling policy, or, in other states, the required coverage may be at the level of an HO-1 or HO-2.

CHAPTER 7
SPECIALTY POLICIES

1. Which of the following would NOT be included in the Nationwide Marine definition?

   (A) Tunnels
   (B) Oil Pipe Lines
   (C) Barges
   (D) Exports

2. In Flood Insurance the deductible is applied:

   (A) Once for each occurrence.
   (B) Once for the building and once for the contents.
   (C) Once for direct losses and once for indirect losses.
   (D) Once each policy period.

3. Characteristics of a Personal Articles Floater include all of the following EXCEPT:

   (A) Worldwide coverage.
   (B) Maybe no deductible.
   (C) All risk coverage.
   (D) Supplementary Payments.

4. A Boatowners policy is most similar in structure to a

   (A) Personal Auto Policy.
   (B) Marine Policy.
   (C) Homeowners Policy.
   (D) Standard Fire Policy.

5. A Boatowners policy will offer a premium reduction for boats

   (A) Less than 26 feet in length.
   (B) Without living quarters.
   (C) Used only in inland lakes, rivers and streams.
   (D) Having both bows and sterns.

6. Which of the following best describes the watercraft coverage found in a Dwelling Policy?

   (A) Limited two party coverage
   (B) Limited two and third party coverages
   (C) Limited two party coverage and broad third party coverage
   (D) Broad two and third party coverages

7. In Flood Insurance, the Federal government generally

   (A) Markets the coverage.
   (B) Underwrites the coverage.
   (C) Both markets and underwrites the coverage.
   (D) Neither markets nor underwrites the coverage.

8. Which of the following would be covered by NFIP insurance?

   (A) A residential dwelling in which the basement has been flooded by the backup of a basement floor drain.
   (B) A dock which collapses because of abnormal beach erosion.
   (C) A farmer's corn crop which has been washed away by excessive rainfall.
   (D) A factory which is destroyed when a dam bursts upstream.

9. A 36 foot boat, with a full galley and six berths would best be covered by

   (A) A standard Homeowners policy.
   (B) An Ocean Marine policy.
   (C) A Boatowners policy.
   (D) A Yacht policy.

END

QUIZ ANSWERS & EXPLANATIONS ON NEXT PAGE

CHAPTER 7
SPECIALTY POLICIES QUIZ ANSWER KEY

1. C. Even though barges are marine risks they are not specifically mentioned in the 1976 Nationwide Marine Definition.

2. B. The flood deductible is applied separately for the building and the contents.

3. D. Supplementary Payments are not found in a two party coverage, such as the Personal Articles Floater.

4. A. The typical Boatowners policy has Liability, Med Pay, Uninsured Boaters and Physical damage.

5. C. This must be warranted on the application.

6. A. The DP only covers damage to rowboats canoes and kayaks.

7. B. Flood coverage is marketed through private carriers, but underwritten by the Federal government.

8. D. Flood covers only buildings and contents. It is available for residential, commercial and farm risks, but growing crops are not covered. A sewer back up does not meet the definition of a flood.

9. D. A yacht policy is best used for boats over 26 feet in length with living quarters.

Part III
COMMERCIAL LINES

THE COMMERCIAL PACKAGE POLICY

8

... pick and choose...

1 The insurance needs of modern businesses are varied and complex. A business may own numerous different kinds of property, such as buildings, business property in those buildings, automobiles, computers, inventories, airplanes and data banks. Also, businesses deal with the public in numerous different ways, such as selling products to the public, providing services to the public, selling through direct mail, inviting the public into its buildings. To write one comprehensive policy to handle all of these hundreds of variables is a monumental task. If you write a contract that will work for the most complex business, it will be substantially more complicated than need be for a simple business, so the policy designers face a major challenge.

Modules

2 The solution is to design units of coverage, or **modules**, that can be used as needed. If the business owns property, then it requires property coverage. If the business has a liability exposure, then it needs liability coverage. If the business has automobiles, then it requires automobile coverage. The modular concept allows the Insured to pick and choose — to buy a coverage form for each type of risk that the business may encounter. The Insured simply selects those modules for which the business has a need.

Notes

1 To date there are seven **coverage parts**, or coverages, that have been adopted in the modular concept. They are:

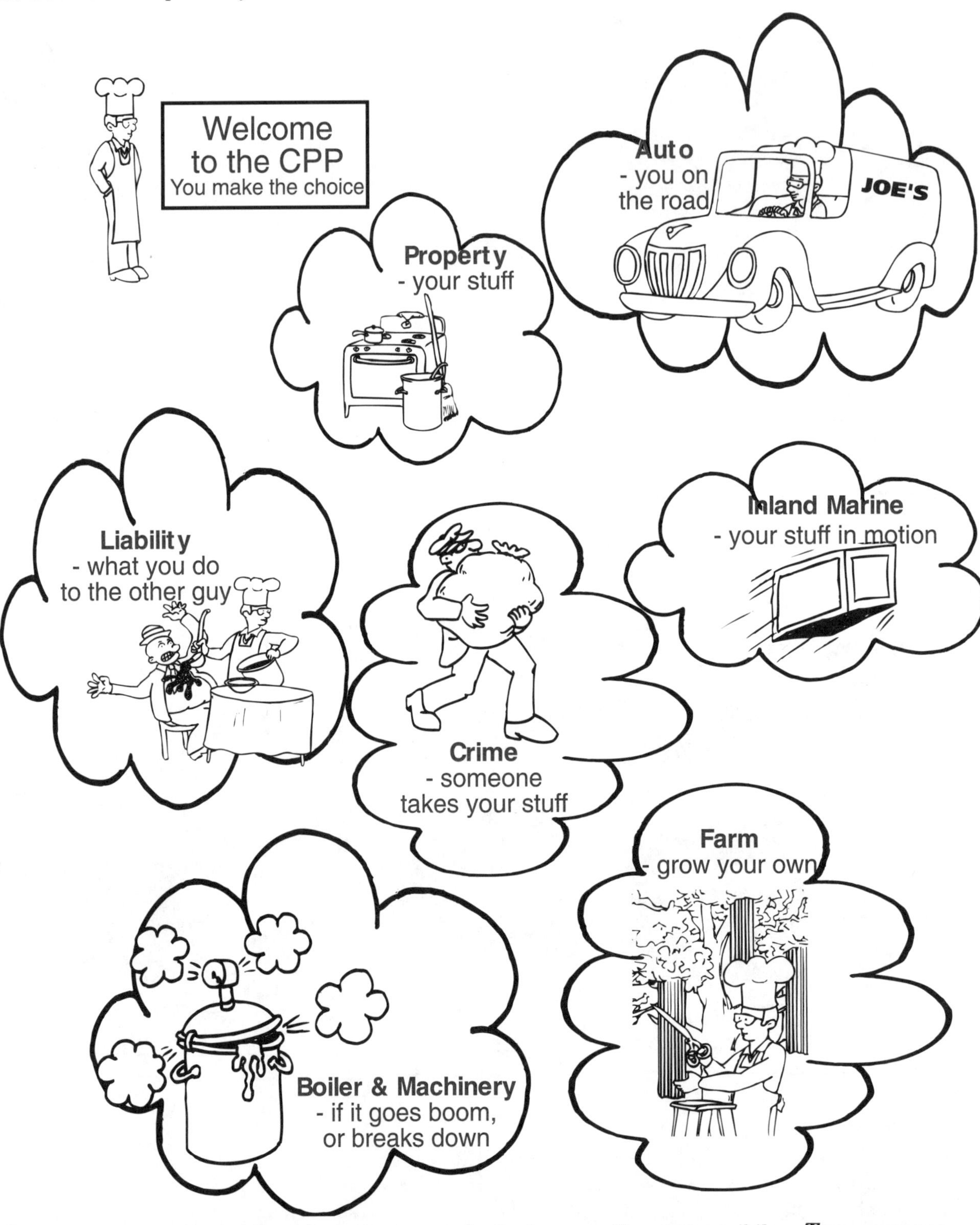

2 These seven coverages are the primary coverages for businesses. Your responsibility as the Agent is to recommend those coverages which are required according to each business customer's needs. You will select one or more than one as the need demands. Each can be written by itself as a **monoline policy**, or you may combine any two or more of the seven into a **package policy**.

Two or more. . .
. . .package

only one. . .
. . .monoline

Notes

THE COMMERCIAL PACKAGE POLICY (CPP)

1 The Commercial Package Policy is built out of the modules, or units, listed above. Anytime you take two or more of the seven coverages and staple them together, you have a Commercial Package Policy. The only time it exists is when you make one. Understanding the Commercial Package Policy is simply a matter of understanding the seven parts of which it may be comprised.

2 The beauty of the Commercial Package Policy lies in its simplicity. All of the coverage parts are updated to reflect changes in technology, legal and social developments and business conditions. The policy structure allows policy rates to be more sensitive to inflation as well as to the actual risks involved. Also, we now have more standardization in the coverages which makes understanding the contracts much less complicated.

COMMON POLICY DECLARATIONS AND CONDITIONS

3 For businesses that need to package several coverage modules together, there is certainly the likelihood of much repetition of basic information from one coverage module to the next. To avoid this duplication and possible contradiction, all common elements have been extracted from the coverage parts and printed once in the **Common Policy Declarations** and the **Common Policy Conditions**. *Both of these forms must appear in every policy, whether it is written as a monoline policy or as a package policy.*

COMMON POLICY DECLARATIONS

"in common"

4 As you can see from your copy of the Common Policy Declarations Page (included in this chapter), it lists the First Named Insured, his/her mailing address and the policy period. Please note that the policy period starts at **12:01 a.m. Standard Time** (1 minute after midnight) **at the Insured's mailing address** as shown on the Policy Declarations Sheet. There is also a description of the business followed by an insuring clause which states that in return for the payment of the premium and subject to all the terms and conditions of the policy, the insurance company agrees to provide the coverages as listed. The next section contains a list of the seven coverage parts that can be made part of this policy. If a premium amount is shown alongside any coverage module, you can assume there is coverage. If no premium is indicated, there is no coverage.

It will always be dark out when coverage begins

Package

COMMON POLICY DECLARATIONS

POLICY NO. ____________________

COMPANY NAME AREA	PRODUCER NAME AREA

NAMED INSURED ______________________________

MAILING ADDRESS ______________________________

____

POLICY PERIOD: **From** ________ **to** ____________________ **at**
12:01 a.m. Standard Time at your mailing address shown above.

BUSINESS DESCRIPTION ______________________________

IN RETURN FOR THE PAYMENT OF THE PREMIUM, AND SUBJECT TO ALL THE TERMS OF THIS POLICY, WE AGREE WITH YOU TO PROVIDE THE INSURANCE AS STATED IN THIS POLICY.

THIS POLICY CONSISTS OF THE FOLLOWING COVERAGE PARTS FOR WHICH A PREMIUM IS INDICATED. THIS PREMIUM MAY BE SUBJECT TO ADJUSTMENT.

NOTE: The Dec shows premium not limits

	PREMIUM
Equipment Breakdown COVERAGE PART	$ ________
COMMERCIAL AUTO COVERAGE PART	$ ________
COMMERCIAL CRIME COVERAGE PART	$ ________
COMMERCIAL GENERAL LIABILITY COVERAGE PART	$ ________
COMMERCIAL INLAND MARINE COVERAGE PART	$ ________
COMMERCIAL PROPERTY COVERAGE PART	$ ________
FARM COVERAGE PART	$ ________
____________________	$ ________
TOTAL	$ ________

Premium shown is payable: $ ________ **at inception.** **$** ________ ________

____

____

Forms applicable to all Coverage parts: ______________________________
(show numbers)

____

____

COUNTERSIGNED ____________________ **BY** ______________________________
(Date) **(Authorized Representative)**

NOTE: OFFICERS' FACSIMILE SIGNATURES MAY BE INSERTED HERE, ON THE POLICY COVER OR ELSEWHERE AT THE COMPANY'S OPTION

Notes

COMMON POLICY CONDITIONS

"in common"

The Conditions section of any policy is the **"If . . ., then . . ."** section. *If* there is a
1 loss, *then* you must do this and we must do that. *If* you want to change the policy, *then* we must approve it and put it in writing.

ground rules

The only unique feature of the Common Policy Conditions is that they apply to all of
2 the subparts of the package policy. Again, they must be included even if the contract is a monoline policy. As we have discussed, the ranking Insured in Commercial policies is the **First Named Insured**. Therefore, every time the policy requires an action on the part of the policyowner, the policy language reads, *The First Named Insured must . . .*

Cancellation

- You, as the **First Named Insured**, may cancel the policy simply by giving the company written notice; no lead time is required.
- If the company wants to cancel, it must give you written notice and a reasonable lead time. The lead times vary depending upon which subform is involved. The rules for Commercial Property, for example, are different from those for Commercial Auto.
- No matter who cancels, you will get some refund of unused premium.

notice. . .

. . .refund

Changes

This section says that the policy contains the entire agreement between the company
3 and the policyowner. Changes requested by the First Named Insured can be made with the company's consent. These changes take the form of a written endorsement attached to and made a part of the policy.

Most commonly, an endorsement is written to modify but one module of coverage -
4 like Commercial Property. If an endorsement is written to cover several modules **or lines of insurance** it is called an **interline endorsement**.

Examination of Your Books and Records

5 The company reserves the right to examine your books and records at any time during the policy period and for up to three years afterwards.

Look at your books

Inspections and Surveys

The company has the right (not the obligation) to make inspections and surveys at any
6 time during the policy period. The company will give you reports and recommended changes. These inspections are only for the purpose of establishing insurability and calculating the premium. In no way is the insurance company warranting that conditions are safe or healthful nor that you are in compliance with laws, regulations, codes or standards applicable to your business or building.

Look at your business

Notes

Premiums

1 The First Named Insured is responsible for paying premiums and will be the person to whom the company will return any unearned premiums.

Transfer of Your Rights and Duties

2 This policy can be transferred only with the company's written consent. The only exception is in the event of death of a named Insured, in which case all rights will be transferred to his/her legal representative. *company's consent*

Nonrenewal

3 As with Cancellation, the company must give written notice on a timely basis. Again, the length of the notice can depend upon which subform is being nonrenewed as well as upon the laws of the state in which your business is located.

COMMERCIAL PACKAGE POLICY (CPP)

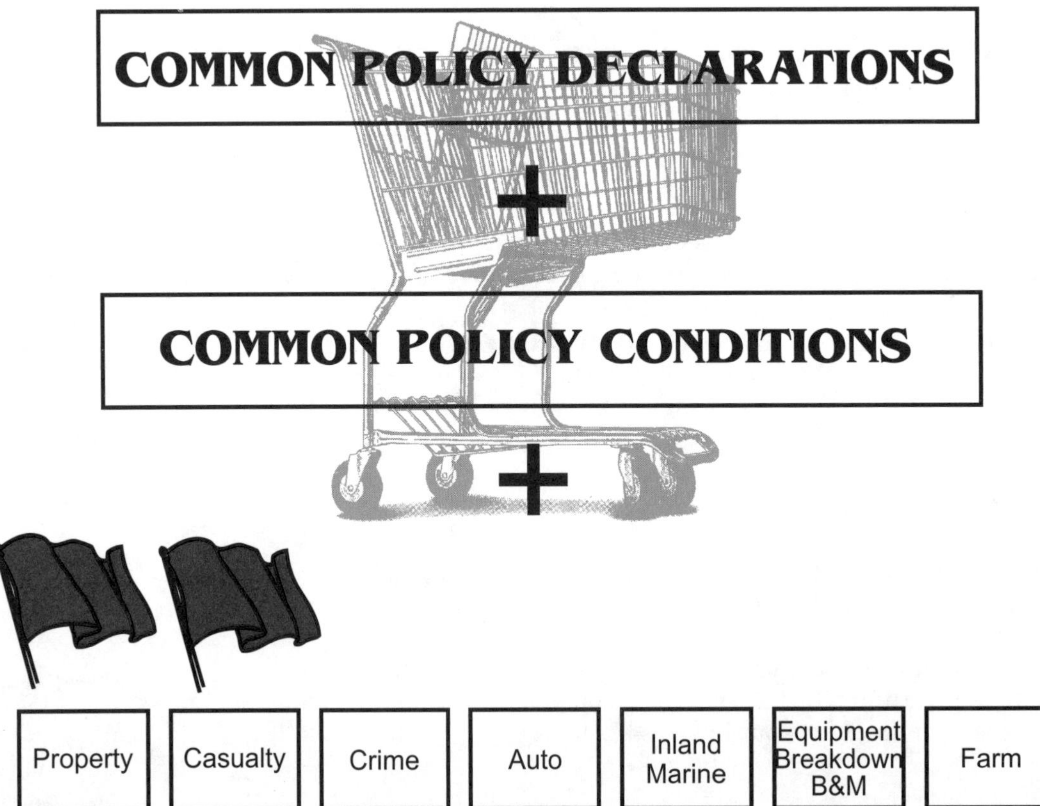

Notes

Conclusion

There are seven coverages that are part of the Commercial Package Policy concept.
1 Each of those modules can be written by itself (as a monoline policy) in which only one coverage is provided. If you wish to combine two or more of the modules into one policy, it is referred to as a Commercial Package Policy. A Commercial Package Policy is nothing more than a combination of two or more of the modular parts.

Whether you are writing a monoline policy or a Commercial Package Policy, you
2 must use a Common Policy Declarations page and a Common Policy Conditions page. The Common Policy Declarations page, most importantly, determines who is the First Named Insured and what policy coverages have been written. The Common Policy Conditions page contains policy conditions that apply to each and every coverage part that is written.

3 We will examine each of the seven coverage modules individually in the following chapters. We hope that you appreciate the simplicity of these forms!

The Chapter 8 Quiz is combined with the Chapter 9 Quiz, and can be found at the end of Chapter 9 on page 9-34.

COMMERCIAL PROPERTY POLICY

9

SOURCE:
ISO-CP 2007

1 Now that you have had a look at the overall structure of the Commercial Package Policy, let's explore each of its subparts.

2 The most important of the modules are the Commercial Property and the Commercial Liability coverages. Very few of your customers will have risks that do not entail some property coverages and some liability coverages, so we will discuss those two coverage forms first. This chapter will deal with the property coverages.

3 If your client has any commercial property, then you would use the coverages described in this chapter - the Commercial Property policy. This policy can be used alone, as a monoline policy, or in conjunction with one or more of the other policy forms to form a Commercial Package Policy. In any event, this section of the policy would be the same, whether monoline or a package.

Joe's stuff

Notes

COMMERCIAL PACKAGE POLICY (CPP)

COMMON POLICY DECLARATIONS

COMMON POLICY CONDITIONS

Property	Casualty	Crime	Auto	Inland Marine	Equipment Breakdown B&M	Farm

COMMERCIAL PROPERTY POLICY FORMAT

1 One of the beautiful features of the Commercial Property policy is that we have one contract that can be used for **almost all** commercial property. Whether you are insuring a thimble factory, manufacturing plant, retail drug store, warehouse, oil refinery or a condominium association, you use the same basic contract – the Commercial Property policy. This flexibility exists because the structure of the Commercial Property policy raises only two basic questions:

1. **What property do you want to insure?**

2. **From what perils do you want to insure it?**

2 The answers to these two questions can allow us to insure a business as big and complex as IBM or as small and as simple as Pop's Lawnmower Repair.

WHAT?

1 In answering this question, the proposed Insured has thirteen subforms (categories of property) from which to choose. He may need one or more than one of these. For example, if he needs to insure his buildings and personal property, you would use the Building and Personal Property Form. If the customer owns a 20-story glass and steel structure, you would also add the Glass Form. If the customer has a business income risk, then you would add the Business Income Form as well, and so on. The thirteen property subforms are:

1. **Building and (Business) Personal Property**
   a. **Building**
   b. **(Business) Personal Property**
   c. **Personal Property of others**
2. **Business Income**
3. **Extra Expense**
4. **Business Income (with Extra Expense)**
5. Glass
6. Builder's Risk
7. Leasehold Interest
8. Condominium Association
9. Condominium Commercial Unit - Owner's
10. Legal Liability
11. Mortgage Holders Errors and Omissions
12. Tobacco Sales Warehouse
13. Standard Property Form

2 The first three are the most common coverage forms and the ones we will discuss in detail.

FROM WHAT?

3 Defining what **Causes of Loss** (perils) covered property is insured against is critically important to the value of any property policy. We started with fire as the only peril and as the needs of the public demanded, we increased the number of named perils. Ultimately, it became simpler to offer *All Risk* coverage to the clients willing to pay for the most extensive coverage. Under the All Risk (or *Open Perils*) concept, every peril is covered except those specifically excluded.

4 One of the most flexible features of the Commercial Property policy is that you can select the peril power appropriate to each category of property listed on the Dec Sheet. For example, you might suggest that a client obtain All Risk coverage on his warehouse as it is exposed to almost every conceivable peril, but the contents of that warehouse are greatly protected by the structure itself. Therefore, you might propose a less expensive named peril form for the contents.

Notes

1 The three choices of peril power under the Commercial Property policy are:

- **Basic** – covers eleven perils — ***Economy Model***
- **Broad** – covers fourteen perils — ***Family Sedan***
- **Special** – covers all perils not specifically excluded (sometimes referred to as Open Perils or All Risk) — ***Luxury Model***

2 The more perils that are covered, the better the contract, but also the more expensive.

3 It is the job of the Agent to guide the Insured in selecting the peril power that is consistent with his or her needs and ability to pay.

WHEN DOES IT PAY?

4 Following a loss, a claim is paid only if you get a *yes* to both questions posed below:

Two Questions

WHAT'S COVERED

DIRECT

Building
(Business) Personal Property
Personal Property of Others

INDIRECT

Business Income
Extra Expense

FROM WHAT

BASIC (11)
BROAD (14)
SPECIAL (all except)

Notes

1 Suppose your building is insured under a Special Cause of Loss form. If it is destroyed by fire, you get a yes to both questions and the claim is paid. But suppose the building is destroyed by earthquake. Now the building is insured, but not from the peril of earthquake – no valid claim. Now suppose that the building is insured by a Special Cause of Loss form, but there is no Business Income coverage. If the building is destroyed by fire, you get two yes answers on the building loss itself and the claim is paid. But no loss of income benefits would be paid while the building is being rebuilt. The "From What?" answer is yes, but the "What's Covered?" answer is no – no benefits.

PROPERTY DECLARATIONS & PROPERTY CONDITIONS

As you learned in the last chapter, all seven of the coverages that could be found in
2 a Commercial Package Policy are subject to the Common Declarations and Common Conditions. The logic was that it made more sense to say something once rather than repeat it seven times.

That same logic is applied again within the Property module that we are addressing
3 now. There are thirteen kinds of property that can be insured under the Commercial Property policy and they can be insured against the perils of the three major Cause of Loss forms. If we can say something once instead of several times, we should do so. For this reason, we have a set of **Property Declarations and Conditions** in addition to the **Common Declarations and Conditions** we have already discussed. The former deals with all of the **property** coverages contained in the policy while the latter deals with all of the policies under the common umbrella of the Commercial Package Policy.

4 Therefore, if you are constructing a Commercial Property policy (monoline or as part of a package), the first four pages you would assemble would be the following:

- Common Policy Declarations
- Common Policy Conditions
- Commercial Property Declarations
- Commercial Property Conditions

CUSTOMIZING ENDORSEMENTS

There are scads of endorsements that can be used to customize a property policy
5 according to the needs of your customer. Examples of customizing endorsements include coverage for outside signs, radio/television antennas, burglary and property protection systems, protective safeguards like sprinkler systems, alcoholic beverage tax exclusions, etc. Many of these endorsements buy back coverages that are excluded in the basic property policy. Over time, you will become familiar with these endorsements as the need arises. However, we will not deal with them to any great extent in this book.

Notes

NEXT STEPS

1 Let's review where we are. There are seven major coverage forms in the Commercial P&C business, such as Commercial Property, Commercial Liability, Crime, Inland Marine, and Automobile. It's possible to write each of these as a separate coverage . . . as an individual policy. It's also possible to combine two or more of these coverages into one policy, which would then be called a Commercial Package Policy. Each of these individual coverages may have its own Declarations and Conditions section and there's also a Common Declarations and Conditions section that covers all of the subparts of the policy.

2 We are now going to explore the Commercial Property coverages in further detail. The Commercial Property coverages can be subdivided into eleven coverage forms, such as Building and Personal Property, Business Income, Extra Expense, Glass, Condominium Association, Tobacco Sales Warehouses, etc... We will dissect the first three of these forms in detail, and you will become familiar with the remaining forms in the future as the need arises. We will also look at the four Cause of Loss forms in the process.

COMMERCIAL PROPERTY COVERAGE PART
DECLARATIONS PAGE

POLICY NO. EFFECTIVE DATE 1 / 1 / This Year

☐ "X" IF SUPPLEMENTAL DECLARATIONS IS ATTACHED

NAMED INSURED

There may be more than one "Named Insured"

DESCRIPTION OF PREMISES

PREM. NO. BLDG. NO. LOCATION, CONSTRUCTION & OCCUPANCY

COVERAGES PROVIDED INSURANCE AT THE DESCRIBED PREMISES APPLIES ONLY FOR COVERAGES FOR WHICH A LIMIT OF INSURANCE IS SHOWN.

PREM. NO.	BLDG. NO.	COVERAGE	COVERED CAUSES OF LOSS	COINSURANCE	RATES
		BUILDING	SPECIAL	80%	
		BUS. PERS. PROP	BROAD	100%	
		PERS. PROP OTHERS	BASIC	70%	
		BUSINESS INCOME	SPECIAL	50%	

* IF EXTRA EXPENSE COVERAGE, LIMITS ON LOSS PAYMENTS

OPTIONAL COVERAGES APPLICABLE ONLY WHEN ENTRIES ARE MADE IN THE SCHEDULE BELOW

PERM.NO.	BLDG. NO.	AGREED VALUE EXPIRATION DATE COVERAGE	AMOUNT	REPLACEMENT COST (X) BUILDING	PERSONAL PROPERTY	INCLUDING STOCK
1	1	1-1-NEXT YEAR BLDG.	$500,000		X	

INFLATION GUARD (PERCENTAGE) BUILDING	PERSONAL PROPERTY	*MONTHLY LIMIT OF INDEMNITY (FRACTION)	*MAXIMUM PERIOD OF INDEMNITY (X)	*EXTENDED PERIOD OF INDEMNITY (DAYS)
12%	10%			90

*APPLIES TO BUSINESS INCOME ONLY

MORTGAGE HOLDERS

PREM. NO. BLDG. NO. MORTGAGE HOLDER NAME AND MAILING ADDRESS

Note: This is the standard deductible

DEDUCTIBLE

$500. EXCEPTIONS

FORMS APPLICABLE

TO ALL COVERAGES

TO SPECIFIC PREMISES/COVERAGES FORM NUMBER

Notes

COMMERCIAL PROPERTY CONDITIONS

DICE

you lie, you're on your own

- **Concealment, Misrepresentation or Fraud** – If you lie, you lose.
- **Control of Property** – If somebody else is responsible, we'll pay and then...
- **Subrogation** – We'll get him.

we pay, then chase

whole not rich

- **Insurance Under Two or More Coverages** – We only make you whole.
- **Legal Action Against Us** – You must do your part and then take action against the company within **2 years**.
- **Liberalization** – It can get better, but not worse.
- **No Benefit to Bailee** – This policy is for your benefit, not the benefit of someone holding or doing work on your stuff.

let him get his own coverage

- **Other Insurance** - As we have said, if you have a piece of property insured by two Commercial Property policies that are identical in peril power (concurrent), each company will pay its share of the claim in the same proportion as its policy limits bear to the total. For example:

pro rata - coverage to claim

	Insurance Limits	Pro Rata Share
Company A	$ 70,000	70%
Company B	30,000	30%
Total	$100,000	100%

If there is a $10,000 loss, Company A would pay $7000 and Company B would pay $3000 and each would apply its deductible.

Remember, however, if we change the example so that the peril power of Company A's policy does not match Company B's (**nonconcurrency**), things could turn out much differently.

	Peril Power	Insurance Limits
Company A	Basic	$70,000
Company B	Basic + Earthquake	30,000

If there is a $10,000 earthquake loss, Company A pays zero. Company B would only pay its share, $3000. Company B is only receiving about one-third of the premium and therefore should not be forced to cover 100% of the loss.

Same policy

Primary - Secondary

A very different situation exists within the Commercial Package Policy. There are a few places where two of the seven modules could cover the same loss. For instance, burglar damage is covered by both the property module and the crime module. To coordinate claims in this event, the policies have established an additional rule. **If a loss is covered by two different policy forms, the Property policy is excess; the other module pays 100% first.**

Notes

Therefore, if you owned a $70,000 Property policy and a $30,000 Crime policy and you suffered a $10,000 burglar damage loss, the Crime policy would pay the entire $10,000 claim. If you suffered a $31,000 loss, the Crime policy would pay to its limit, $30,000, and the Property policy would pay the excess, $1000.

- **Policy Period and Coverage Territory -** Obviously, the insurance company only covers losses that occur during the policy period. The coverage territory is:
  - The United States and its possessions
  - Canada
  - Puerto Rico

BUSINESS

BUILDING AND PERSONAL PROPERTY COVERAGE FORM

1 Almost all Commercial Package Policies will include this form because almost all businesses own some property. The basic coverage selections that can be chosen on the Property Declarations Page are as follows:

- Building
- Business Personal Property
- Personal Property of Others

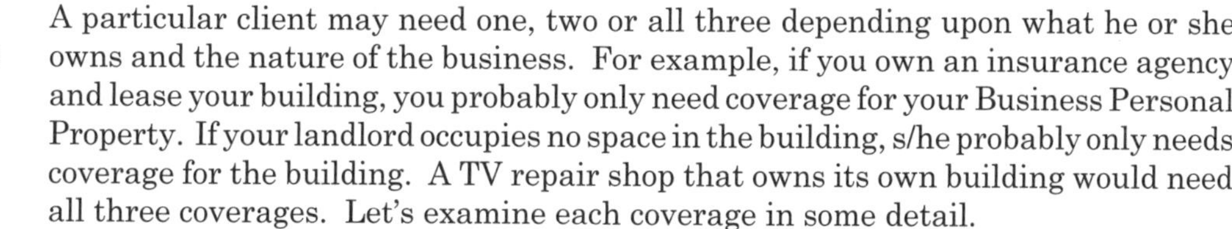

2 A particular client may need one, two or all three depending upon what he or she owns and the nature of the business. For example, if you own an insurance agency and lease your building, you probably only need coverage for your Business Personal Property. If your landlord occupies no space in the building, s/he probably only needs coverage for the building. A TV repair shop that owns its own building would need all three coverages. Let's examine each coverage in some detail.

What's A Building?

3 The term *building* not only includes the building listed on the Declarations Page, but also encompasses more. It includes:

- Completed additions and additions under construction
- Permanently installed fixtures, machinery and equipment
- Outdoor fixtures (flagpole, fountain, hotel swimming pool)
- Personal property owned by the Insured and used in the service or maintenance of the building, such as:
  - lawn mowers or snow blowers
  - fire extinguishing equipment
  - outdoor furniture
  - appliances used for cooking, laundering, refrigeration and ventilation whether permanently installed or not

but may not be covered

some "stuff" is part of the building

Notes

NOTE: While it might seem silly to classify a snow blower as a building, remember that a landlord really only wants to purchase coverage on the building. By including items used in the **service** of the building in this coverage, the nonresident landlord only needs this coverage.

100ft.

- Materials, equipment and supplies within 100 feet of the premises used for making repairs, alterations or additions.

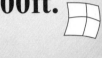

What's BUSINESS Personal Property?

bubble of protection

NOTE: All property can be classified as either
1 *real* property (immobile – like a building, or real estate) or *personal* property (movable – like furniture). The term *Business Personal Property* therefore means **movable** property that a **business** owns, i.e., desks, chairs, computers, copy machines. This does **not** include the personal belongings that employees often bring into an office, such as a radio, coat, briefcase, or set of golf clubs. Personal belongings of employees are ***Personal Effects*** and are **not** covered under a Business Personal Property form. (Don't worry – Personal Effects are covered elsewhere.)

This coverage, Business Personal Property, is for your **business stuff**.
2 It is covered while in the building described in the Declarations or outside of the building (or outside of the building in a vehicle) if within 100 feet of the building. Your Business Personal Property includes the following:

100ft.

- Furniture and fixtures
- Machinery and equipment
- *Stock*, which can include inventory, raw materials or finished product

inventory

- All other personal property owned by you and used in your business
- Your investment of time and materials **in someone else's property**. For example, you, as a TV repairman, could have $50 in parts and $100 in labor invested in a client's TV when your shop burns to the ground.
- Your *use interest* as a tenant in permanent improvements in a rented building

Notes

What's Personal Property of Others?

1 This section provides coverage for you if you are responsible for someone else's property that is in your care, custody or control. Businesses like TV repair, computer servicing, dry cleaners and furniture repair need this coverage. In *insurancese*, we say this is a *bailee's-like* coverage. Coverage is provided if the property is inside your premises or out in the open (or in a vehicle) within 100 feet of your building.

PROPERTY NOT COVERED

2 Not every kind of property important to every type of business is covered by the basic policy. This is good for us as consumers because it keeps insurance affordable. As an example, the first exclusion eliminates coverage for cash. Most businesses do not need this rather expensive coverage. Those that do can purchase it separately. In fact, almost anything can be covered for a price. The fact that it is excluded here does not mean that it cannot be covered; it simply means that the standard policy does not cover it.

DICE

3 The excluded property is as follows:

1. **Paper worth something**: cash, deeds, evidence of debt (IOUs), notes or securities
2. **Animals**, unless your business is boarding or selling animals

   no guard dog
3. **Autos** held for sale
4. Bridges, roadways, patios or other **paved surfaces**
5. **Contraband**

   not a Central American musical group
6. Cost of excavations, grading and backfilling
7. **Foundations** below the lowest basement floor
8. **Land**

   NOTE: It might seem a little weird that land is not covered and really weird that foundations are not covered. However, if you think for a moment, you will realize that a $1,000,000 commercial building might have $300,000 of its purchase price in the land and $200,000 of its building cost in the foundation. Since most perils would only do damage from the ground up, excluding the land and foundations allows the client to buy half as much insurance. If you want to cover your foundation and are willing to pay for it – no problem.

Rule of thumb: nothing below ground

9. Personal property that is **airborne** or **waterborne**

   inland marine
10. Pilings, piers or docks
11. **For property covered by another specialty coverage and this general property form, the other policy pays first and this one pays as excess**
12. Retaining walls if not part of the building

Notes

13. **Underground** pipes, flues or drains

14. **Electronic data** – Including data and programs, except as provided under coverage Additions

15. The Cost to Replace or Restore information -- including valuable papers, and records, except as provided in coverage Extensions.

16. **Cars, trucks, boats and airplanes** are not covered here – better covered elsewhere. However, we do cover:

    autos - no

    - Mobile Equipment – bulldozers, farm equipment and forklift trucks (vehicles designed for use off public roads)

      mobile equipment - si´

    - Rowboats and Canoes – if out of the water at your described business premises.

17. **Crops** that have been harvested but that are outside the walls of building

18. **Outdoor property**, such as fences, radio or TV antennas (including masts, towers and satellite dishes), trees, shrubs and plants. The upcoming Extensions of Coverage can give a small amount of coverage for these items. Note: If you are in the tree and shrub business, your trees and shrubs are your inventory and can be covered.

    don't worry - you'll get it back

ADDITIONAL COVERAGES

1 These extras are automatically built into the contract. You do not purchase them separately nor do you pay extra to get them.

Automatic and free

Debris Removal – If a building is destroyed, there are often major costs associ-
2 ated with the clean-up. This coverage is provided as long as the debris is caused by a covered peril.

after a covered loss

3 If you could buy a policy without the Additional Coverages, you would find debris removal to be limited in two ways:

- Debris removal costs must be no more than **25% of the loss**.
- Debris removal cannot cause the policy to pay out more than the policy limits.

4 This Additional Coverage called debris removal enhances the coverage provided in two ways:

- Debris removal can exceed 25% by **$10,000**
- Debris removal can exceed policy limits by **$10,000**

5 **Fire Department Service Charge** – If your business is in an area where the fire department charges for a call, we will pay up to $1000 for your liability for that service charge. This is an additional amount of insurance over the policy limits, and no deductible applies.

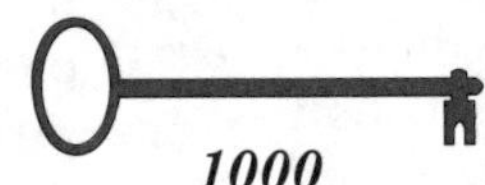

1000

1 **Pollutant Clean-up and Removal** – We will pay up to $10,000 in addition to the policy limits to extract pollutants from land or water at your premises caused by or resulting from a covered cause of loss.

2 **Preservation of Property** – If it is necessary to move insured property from the described location to protect it from a covered peril, we will cover it for any direct loss at its new location for 30 days. This coverage **will not** increase the applicable limits of insurance.

30 days all risk

3 **Increased Cost of Construction** – If the building is insured on a Replacement Cost basis, this Additional Coverage applies. Assume that following a covered loss, the Insured discovers that to comply with local law or ordinance he will have to modify his building in some way (e.g. sprinklers, handicapped access) as the rebuilding or repairs are completed. This coverage adds $10,000 or 5% of his building limit (whichever is less) to cover repairs to the damaged building. This is additional insurance above the policy limits. If the owner had been informed before the loss occurs that these modifications were necessary and had failed to make them, then this coverage does not apply.

4 **Electronic Data - $2500 to restore data destroyed or corrupted by a covered peril.**

COVERAGE EXTENSIONS

5 Unlike the Additional Coverages, these Coverage Extensions must be earned. You only get these if your coinsurance percentage on the *Dec Sheet* is 80% or more. All of these Extensions of Coverage are in addition to the stated policy limits.

Earned

only if. . .not free

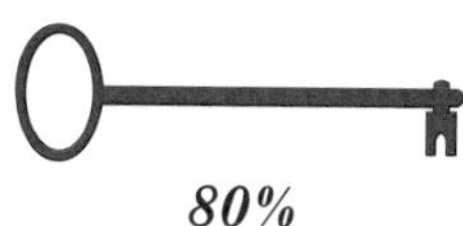

80%

6 **Newly Acquired or Constructed Property** – We will provide coverage for new buildings constructed upon the described premises or new buildings acquired at other locations.

- The limit for this extension is $250,000.
- This extension can also apply to your Business Personal Property contained in the new building. The limit for contents is $100,000.
- This coverage is valid for only 30 days after you acquire the new building or begin to construct the new building.
- You pay from day one.

30 days coverage

billed from day 1

7 **Personal Effects and Property of Others** – This Coverage Extension is particularly valuable as it gives you a couple of coverages you have not had yet under this policy.

- **Personal Effects** – These are your or your employees' personal belongings that happen to be at the office, such as golf clubs, jogging shoes, purses, pictures of kids, bowling trophies, etc. This Coverage Extension covers these personal effects for everything except theft.

truly personal

Notes

- **Property of Others** – This Coverage Extension is important for businesses that choose **not** to get the Personal Property of Others coverage under the Building and Personal Property Form. This is because a business could have an exposure of damage to clients' property, even though it does not normally take in customers' property to repair, service, store, etc. For example, suppose you have an insurance agency. You don't take in customers' property to repair, store, etc., (like a TV repair shop owner or a dry cleaner does) but you may have a client drop by, hang up an overcoat, leave a briefcase, and walk across the street with you for lunch. If, during your absence, your building burned down and your client's stuff were destroyed, this Coverage Extension would cover the loss of this client's property – **even for theft**.

1 The limits on this Coverage Extension are fairly low – **$2500**. Therefore, it would not be wise for a TV repair shop to **not** buy the Personal Property of Others coverage and count on this Coverage Extension to cover the 25 televisions belonging to his customers.

2500

2500

2 **Valuable Papers and Records — (Other than Electronic Data)** – As indicated in Exclusion #14, we generally do NOT pay for the cost of recovering lost information. Under this extension, we throw you a bone – a very tiny bone. We'll pay up to $2,500 for the cost of lost information.

100ft.

3 **Property Off-Premises** – For the most part, the policy covers property at or within 100 feet of the described location. This extension provides coverage for your business property away from your premises for up to **$10,000**. This does not apply to property in a vehicle, in the custody of a salesperson or property at a fair or exhibition.

4 **Outdoor Property** – Exclusion #18 eliminated coverage for outdoor property such as fences, radio and TV antennas, satellite dishes, trees, shrubs and plants. This extension gives you a tiny bit of coverage for these items if the damage is caused by:

Here you get your outdoor stuff. . . told you not to worry

- Fire
- Lightning
- Aircraft
- Riot
- Explosion

5 The dollar limit for any of these items is $1000 and no more than $250 for any one tree, shrub or plant.

take your trees home at night

LIMITS OF INSURANCE

6 **The company will pay the amount of each loss up to the policy limits.** Therefore, if you have limits of $100,000 and suffer a $90,000 covered loss, the company will pay $90,000; if you have a loss of $110,000, the company will pay $100,000. The only exceptions to this rule are the Extensions of Coverage; the Fire Department Service Charge, Debris Removal, Pollution Clean-up coverage and Increased Cost of Construction, which can obligate the company to pay more than the policy limits.

***L** ower **L** oss **L** imit*

7 The Commercial Property policy limits coverage for signs to $2,500. This is the amount of coverage for either an attached or detached sign. Larger limits are provided by endorsement or by purchasing an Inland Marine policy.

DEDUCTIBLE

- The deductible is found on the Dec Sheet.

- The company will only pay losses that exceed the deductible and then only up to the applicable limit of insurance.

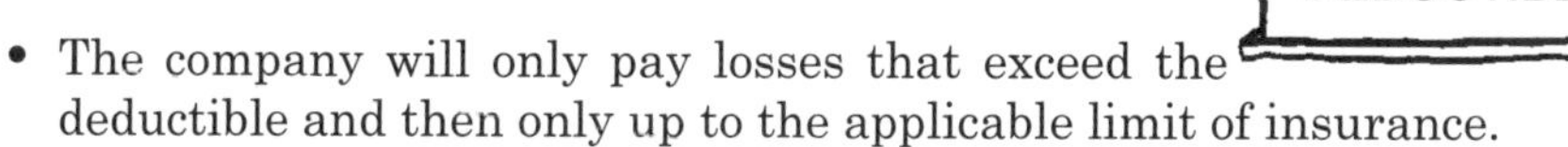

LOSS CONDITIONS

1 **Abandonment** – If you suffer a partial loss, you may not abandon your property to the company in order to collect the full insured value.

Appraisal – If you and your company disagree over the value of insured property,
2 either side can request appraisal. Each party will select an appraiser and the two appraisers will select an umpire.

- A decision reached by any two of the three is **binding**.

binding

- Each party will pay for its own appraiser, the costs of the appraisal and its half of the cost for the umpire.

- The appraisal process is used to determine the value of damaged property. It is not used to decide if coverage exists.

only dollars

YOUR DUTIES IN THE EVENT OF A LOSS

- **Notify the police** if a law has been broken.

- **Notify the insurance company promptly.**

- Give the company a **description of the loss.**

- **Protect the property from further damage.**

- If the company requests, **complete an inventory** of the damaged and undamaged property.

- Allow the company to **inspect the damage and your records substantiating the loss.**

- If requested, permit the company to **question you under oath**.

- **If the company requests**, complete the Proof of Loss forms within **60 days**.

- Cooperate with the company in the settlement of the claim.

Notes

LOSS PAYMENT

1 In the event of a covered loss, the company will do one of the following:

company's choice

- Pay the Actual Cash Value of the loss and take the damaged property as salvage.
- Pay the cost to repair or replace the damaged items.
- Repair or replace it with property of like kind and quality.

2 The company will not pay you more than your insurable interest in the damaged property.

3 The company will pay (or refuse to pay) within 30 days after receiving your written Proof of Loss.

4 To summarize, the sequence is as follows:

- **Notice** – Promptly
- **Proof of Loss** (if required) – 60 days from date of company's request
- **Payment of Claim** – 30 days

Done in 90 days

RECOVERED PROPERTY

5 If either party recovers insured property after payment of a loss, the other party must be notified. It is then your option to return either the dollars or the property to the company.

VACANCY

6 In most states, it is the option of the company to simply cancel insurance altogether on vacant buildings. However, there could be vacant buildings upon which the company is willing to continue coverage.

If a building has been vacant for more than **60 consecutive days** before a loss, the company will not pay for loss by the following perils under any Cause of Loss form.

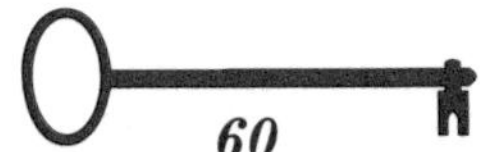

- Vandalism
- Sprinkler leakage (unless you have protected the building from freezing)
- Building glass breakage
- Water damage
- Theft
- Attempted theft

fewer perils

Any claims the company **does** pay for perils still covered will be reduced by 15% of what the company would ordinarily pay.

fewer dollars

Notes

VALUATION

1 The no-frills Commercial Property Policy is designed to pay losses on an Actual Cash Value (ACV) basis. Other rules include:

- **If a building loss is under $2500, the company will pay on a Replacement Cost basis.**

- Inventory is valued **wholesale**, not retail. If Betty buys refrigerators for $300 and sells them for $500, then ten units are valued at $3,000.

no profits

- Improvements made by an insured tenant will be settled ACV if the repairs are made immediately. If repairs are not made immediately (or not at all), the company will pay in proportion to the percentage of the lease that remains prior to expiration. For example, if an insured restaurant owner spent $10,000 to build a lunch counter in a leased space and it were destroyed in the eighth year of a ten year lease, the company would pay only $2000 if the Insured chose not to replace the counter.

use interest

COINSURANCE

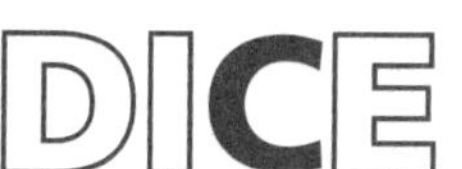

As you learned in Chapter Three, coinsurance is a device used by insurance compa-
2 nies to encourage policyowners to insure their property for amounts that are close to the value of the property. There is a reward if you do and a penalty if you do not. The *standard* coinsurance requirement is 80%, but there is nothing magic about this figure. It could be 90% or 100%. Typically, you can reduce your rates if you agree to a higher coinsurance percentage. To review:

insure to value

- **Coinsurance does not apply to total losses.** If you grossly underinsure a building that burns to the ground, the company will pay the dollar limits you purchased. Essentially, you have established your own penalty.

partial losses only

- If you suffer a partial loss and **have met the coinsurance requirement**, there is no penalty. The company rewards you by paying the entire partial loss.

. . .we're not tyrants after all

- If you suffer a partial loss and **did not meet the coinsurance requirement**, the company will penalize you in accordance with the following formula:

$$\frac{\text{Did Carry}}{\text{Should Carry}} \times \text{Loss} - \text{Deductible} = \text{Amount Paid}$$

3 Assume a $100,000 building, 80% coinsurance, a $40,000 policy, a $10,000 loss and a $500 deductible.

Remember - always start with what it's worth today

$100,000
.80
$ 80,000 Should Carry

$$\frac{\$40{,}000 \text{ Did Carry}}{\$80{,}000 \text{ Should Carry}} \times \$10{,}000 \text{ Loss} = \$5{,}000$$

$ 5,000 Subtotal
- 500 Deductible
$ 4,500 Amount to be paid

Notes

DICE

MORTGAGE HOLDERS

1 The mortgage holder or mortgagee is **the bank** holding an interest in your property as described on the Dec Sheet. The purpose of this section is to **protect the banker's rights**.

2 Basically, you can view the bank as the shadow of the policyowner. Any rights or obligations that you fail to exercise become the bank's. If you do not pay the premium, then the bank can (while it simultaneously forecloses on your mortgage). If you don't submit proof of loss within 60 days, then the company will give the bank 60 days to render proof of loss.

Mortgage Holders NEVER Lose!

3 **NOTE**: A variation on this theme is the **Loss Payable Clause**. The Loss Payable Clause also allows the proceeds to be paid to someone other than the Named Insured. However, unlike the Mortgagee Clause the third party under the Loss Payable Clause is not immune from the bad acts of the Insured. For example, suppose Joe bought his restaurant under a land sale contract, and the seller was listed under a Loss Payable Clause. If Joe commits arson, then under the Loss Payable Clause the policy would **not pay** the proceeds to the seller.

4 The Standard Mortgage Clause also protects the mortgagee by requiring that the insurance company give the mortgagee notice in the event of policy cancellation. In most jurisdictions the requirement is 10 days notice if the cancellation is due to nonpayment and 30 days for any other reason.

OPTIONAL COVERAGES

5 The following Optional Coverages can be selected by marking the appropriate spots on the Dec Sheet.

6 **Inflation Guard** – You select a percentage (like 6% or 8%) which will automatically cause your policy limits to increase by that percentage over the year. This is particularly important if your property is in a rapidly appreciating area, or if you have purchased just enough insurance to meet your coinsurance requirement.

"It's gonna cost ya. . ." $

7 The inflation-guard idea works reasonably well in keeping the amount of insurance appropriate for the value of the building. However, if inventories fluctuate dramatically during the year (e.g. toy store) then adjustments must be made by notifying the company on a **reporting form**.

8 One version of this endorsement is referred to as the **Peak Season Endorsement**; it would work well with risks like the toy store mentioned above.

9 The **Full Value Reporting Form** imposes a strict duty of compliance with the reporting clause stated in the policy. The reports must be made within **30 days** after the end of the reporting period.

10 **Replacement Cost** – This option insures your property on a Replacement Cost basis (as opposed to the plain vanilla policy that pays on an Actual Cash Value (ACV) basis).

11 **Agreed Value** – In most areas of insurance, the concept of agreed value is useful in insuring expensive, irreplaceable items like artworks and antiques. Though a business can use this option in the same way, more commonly, the Commercial Property Contract is written on an Agreed Value basis for an entirely different purpose.

Suppose that you own a factory built 20 years ago. To replace it as it stands would
1 cost $20 million, but you could build an equivalent factory using state-of-the-art
technology for $12 million. To meet an 80% coinsurance requirement on your existing
building would require that you purchase $16 million of coverage. However, if you
could get your company to issue an Agreed Value contract for $12 million, you would
have funds to do what you intend if a loss occurs and you would save thousands in
premium if no loss occurs. In issuing the Agreed Value form, the insurance company
is agreeing to **waive coinsurance** in the event of a partial loss. Therefore, partial
property losses would be paid in full.

Whether the Agreed Value is used to cover irreplaceable items or to dodge coinsur-
2 ance, it is important that this agreement be updated annually as it is not automatically part of the policy renewal process.

3 **Spoilage** - This is coverage for spoilage of perishable stock. Perils that can be covered include: power outage, breakdown and contamination.

BUSINESS INTERRUPTION INSURANCE

4 The next two Commercial Property coverages available from the thirteen Property subforms are the **Business Income** and **Extra Expense** coverage forms. You will also see that it is possible to buy both in one contract.

Up to this point, our concentration has been on direct loss coverage. That is, if your
5 restaurant burns to the ground, we will replace it. Now, we turn our attention to
what may be an even bigger problem. What about the money you fail to earn dur- *loss of use*
ing the six months that it takes to rebuild the restaurant? This loss of income is an
indirect loss and can be covered by business interruption insurance. Note: An
indirect loss can't happen by itself; it must follow a direct loss.

6 Let's suppose that we could divide all the businesses in the world into two categories:

- Those that would close temporarily if their building were destroyed, and
- Those that would continue operations despite it all.

The assignment of a particular business into one category or the other
7 would be based on several criteria. Could the business relocate
(even temporarily)? A hotel, bowling alley, restaurant or
factory might be hard pressed to find suitable temporary facilities in which to relocate. Would the business lose its customer base forever if it were closed for five months? An insurance agency, a bank, a doctor or dentist, a newspaper or a lawyer might not ever recover from being unavailable to their clients for such a lengthy period. Is it even possible to shut some businesses down if you tried? A farmer could not stop a harvest nor could a dairy keep the cows from producing milk.

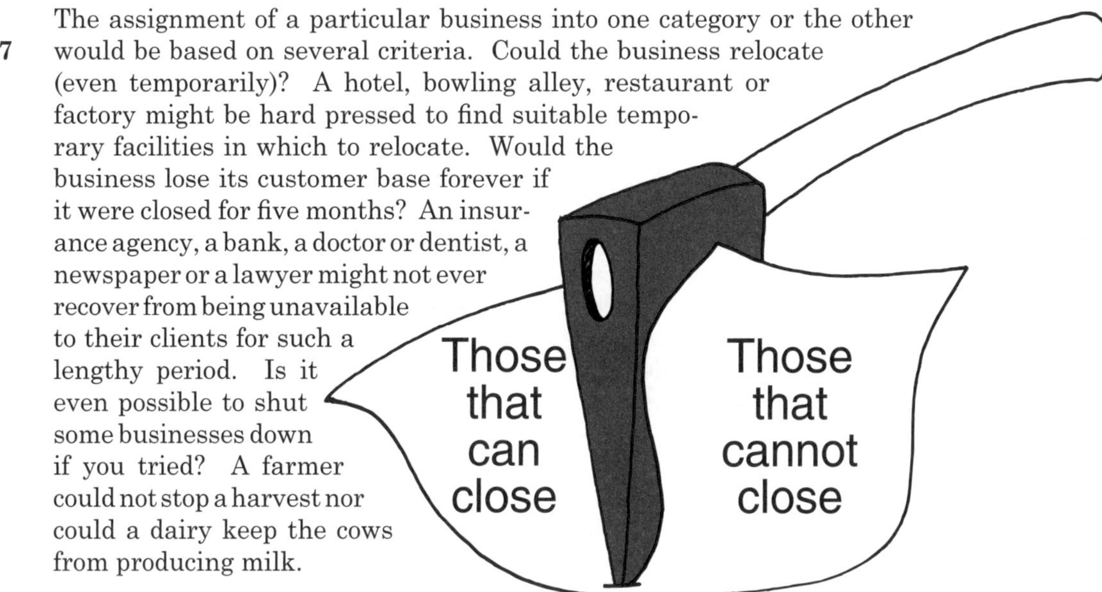

Notes

1 A partial listing might be as follows:

Those Which Would Close	Those Which Would Not
Restaurant	Dairy
Hotel	Insurance Agency
Bowling Alley	Bank
Shopping Mall	Newspaper Publisher
Grocery Store	Doctors, Lawyers, Accountants

Either... pay lots more, or keep the doors open

Businesses that fall on the *Would Close* list need to purchase the **Business Income**
2 **Coverage Form**. This coverage is essentially designed to pay the business what it would have earned had no loss occurred. Businesses that *would not close* may not lose income. The newspaper on the above list would continue to sell subscriptions and advertising. Its problem would be the **extra costs** involved in continuing to operate: finding temporary quarters, immediately buying or leasing presses, purchasing ink and paper under exceedingly tight time constraints and maybe subcontracting some of its printing. To cover these additional costs of staying in business, the newspaper needs the **Extra Expense Coverage Form**.

BUSINESS INCOME COVERAGE FORM

For those businesses that would temporarily close if their building were destroyed,
3 the Business Income coverage will pay for the actual loss of **business income** during the **period of restoration** up to the limits of the policy. Let's examine that promise in a little more detail.

after direct losses only

- You have to prove you lost income – usually on the basis of the past performance of your business.

History important

- Business income is defined as **net income plus continuing operating expenses** (lease, lawyer, accountant, insurance, **payroll**, etc.)

net + continuing expenses

- The period of restoration is the time elapsed from the date of the loss until the building is or should be repaired with reasonable speed and similar quality.

Since most businesses that have been closed for several months could not simply
4 re-open and immediately do business at the volume that they were before the loss, this coverage automatically provides for a 30 day start-up time called the **Extended Business Income Period**. If a longer period is needed, it can be indicated on the Dec Sheet.

up to speed

As with the Building and Personal Property coverage form, Business Income only
5 pays if the original damage done to your business **is caused by a covered cause of loss**. The fact that nobody wants to buy your product anymore or your employees are all on strike is not enough to trigger payment. As before, you can choose the Basic, Broad or Special Cause of Loss form. While there is no rule that the coverage on a client's building must match the peril power of his or her Business Income coverage, most good Agents insist upon it. How would you like to inform a client that his building that collapsed in an earthquake was covered because it was written on the Broad form plus earthquake, but his Business Income will not pay a dime during the rebuilding because it was written on the Broad form? That would be tough to explain. It's probably better that the two coverages match in peril power.

Notes

1 The only additional situation in which coverage could be triggered under the Business Income form is by action of a **Civil Authority**. If access to your property is prohibited by civil authority because of direct physical loss to nearby property that was caused by a covered cause of loss, you have up to three weeks coverage. (No, this would not work for a street repair problem.)

not street repair

Like the Building and Personal Property form, the Business Income form has a
2 coinsurance requirement that will penalize you if you are underinsured. However, the **coinsurance requirement in Business Income is typically only 50%**. Therefore, if your business income (net profit plus continuing expenses and payroll) is $1 million each year, you must purchase at least $500,000 of Business Income if we assume a 50% requirement. This arrangement is excellent for many businesses as the only two limits of this coverage written with coinsurance are:

Oh, no, not coinsurance again

- The company will pay no more than your losses.
- The company will pay no more than $500,000.

There is no limit on how much the company would pay in any one month nor on
3 how many months the company would pay. If your business is so seasonal that you lost $450,000 in the one month you were closed, the company would pay it. If your building took eight months to replace, the company would continue paying if the limits had not been exhausted.

Some businesses, however, do not like the coinsurance approach. Suppose an insured
4 restaurant owner had these concerns: "Since I have business income of $1 million, I am supposed to buy $500,000 of Business Income, but I don't think I need that much. Most losses are small losses and I think the odds are pretty good that I could be back in business in 30 to 60 days. Therefore, I could get by with, say, $200,000 of Business Income coverage, and I do not want to pay a coinsurance penalty for
5 underinsuring." For that person, the company will waive coinsurance requirement if he will accept any of the following three alternatives:

- **Maximum Period of Indemnity** – The company will pay for up to **120 days**, not to exceed the policy limit.

Time

6 - **Monthly Limit of Indemnity** – The company will pay up to the limits of insurance, but will pay no more than a specific amount each month.

1/4 same as 25%

  Example: Suppose our client's total insurance coverage is $200,000. On the Property Dec Sheet, he can choose one of three fractions: 1/6, 1/4 or 1/3. If he chooses 1/4, then we multiply that by the limit to get the monthly limit.

  1/4 x $200,000 = $50,000 monthly limit

Now we have two dollar limits. The company will pay no more than $50,000 in any one month, nor more than $200,000 total.

- **Agreed Value** – The company and you agree in advance what limits you must carry and what the company will pay. Only if you fail to do what was agreed upon could you be subject to a coinsurance penalty.

we know up front

Notes

EXTRA EXPENSE COVERAGE FORM

Extra cost to keep the "doors open" during restoration

1 This form pays businesses that cannot go out of business for the **extra expenses actually incurred** during the **period of restoration** following a direct physical loss caused by a **covered cause of loss** or **action of a civil authority**. As you can tell, the approach of the Extra Expense form almost duplicates the Business Income form. The major difference is that Extra Expense is NOT designed to replace income – it is written only to pay extra expenses.

2 About the only difference in structure is the way limits are expressed in the Extra Expense form. As before, the company will not pay more than you can prove you lost nor will it pay out more than the policy limits. However, with Extra Expense, the company will further limit payment by a percentage of the total limit depending upon the length of the period of restoration.

If the period of restoration is ...	The company will pay up to ...
30 days or less	40% of limit of insurance
60 days or less	80% " " " "
More than 60 days	100% " " " "

3 Therefore, if you had a limit of $100,000 and suffered extra expenses of $50,000 during a period of 25 days, the company would pay $40,000 (40% of $100,000). Of course, if your losses were only $30,000, then that is all the company would pay.

BUSINESS INCOME COVERAGE FORM (INCLUDING EXTRA EXPENSE)

4 Okay, okay . . . we admit it. We lied. Not all of the businesses on earth fit neatly into Business Income or Extra Expense. (Actually, we didn't lie. We said, "Let's suppose . . .") There are some businesses that need both and can buy both under this form. Since you've already studied both forms separately, there is really nothing new to learn. About all that we should do is give you an example of a business that needs both forms.

5 Assume we have a client that has a commercial print shop. Fifty percent of his income stems from walk-in traffic with almost no repeat customers. For this part of his business, our client needs Business Income. However, the other half of his income comes from one contract printing job. Our client prints the Sunday Magazine section of the Chicago Tribune. Since he cannot afford to disrupt this part of his business and must meet his contract with the Trib at any cost, he needs Extra Expense for this portion of his business. We should provide the Business Income form (with Extra Expense).

Notes

THE CAUSE OF LOSS FORMS: BASIC, BROAD, & SPECIAL

The coverage section of the Building and Personal Property coverage form we re-
1 viewed earlier in this chapter says, "We will pay for direct physical loss to covered
property resulting from any **covered Cause of Loss**." The Business Income form
and the Extra Expense form that we just finished discussing say that the company
will replace income or cover extra expenses necessitated by the direct physical loss
2 of property caused by a **covered cause of loss.** Essentially, these three forms
contain half of the insuring clause. We've addressed what's covered; now we need
to define **from what.** We complete the insuring clause and form the contract by
selecting an appropriate Cause of Loss form. There are two named peril forms and
one open perils form as follows:

Basic – 11 perils
Broad – Basic + 3 more = 14 perils
Special – Open Perils (All Risk)

Our approach will be to review the eleven Basic perils, discuss the additional three
3 of the Broad form and then briefly look at the extra coverages you get from the
Special form. As you might guess, all of these forms have exclusions and we will
analyze the exclusions after we are comfortable with the peril power of each form.

BASIC Cause of Loss Form

economy model

But, unlike Homeowners, Theft coverage is not automatic

1. WINDSTORM OR HAIL
2. RIOT OR CIVIL COMMOTION
3. EXPLOSION
4. LIGHTNING
5. FIRE
6. VEHICLES OR AIRCRAFT
7. VANDALISM
8. VOLCANIC ACTION
9. SMOKE
10. SPRINKLER LEAKAGE
11. SINKHOLE COLLAPSE

Notes

BROAD Cause of Loss Form

1 This form adds three more perils to the eleven of the Basic form. It also adds the additional coverage of collapse.

family sedan no Theft

12. **FALLING OBJECTS** – like a boulder tumbling down a mountainside. Coverage is generally limited to damage of the insured buildings. Contents coverage is only provided if the exterior damage to the building allowed the contents damage to occur.

through the roof

13. **WEIGHT OF SNOW, ICE OR SLEET** provides coverage for a building that is damaged by the weight of snow, ice or sleet.

14. **WATER DAMAGE** broadens the coverage of the Basic form. Before we look at the modifications of the Broad form specifically, let's review the entire picture of water damage in the Commercial Property contracts.

> NOTE: Water damage coverage can be readily understood and remembered if you keep the following three points in mind:
>
> - **Firefighter water** and sprinkler water (even sprinkler leakage) is **always** covered.
> - **Mother Nature's water** in the form of **a flood** is **never** covered. (Hence the need for Flood insurance.)
> - The Broad and Special forms cover losses due to **intentional water**. That is, water that you bring into the building intentionally in pipes, water heaters, etc. . . . in other words, **plumbing.**

always. . .

. . .never. . .

. . .broad and beyond

Therefore, the Broad form (and the Special form) provides coverage for the damage caused by the **leaking and freezing** of pipes, appliances or systems that contain water. Of course, this only applies if you have done your best to maintain heat in the building. Further, coverage is provided for leakage that is sudden and accidental. Coverage is NOT provided for damage due to seepage or leakage that occurs over a period of **14 days** or more, nor for the appliance or system from which the water escaped.

Notes

Additional Coverage: COLLAPSE

1 **This section provides coverage if any of the 14 Broad form perils damages a building which ultimately collapses.** For example, if fire damages a building and it collapses later, there is coverage. In addition, collapse due to any of the following is covered:

- Hidden decay
- **Hidden insect or vermin damage** *bugs. . .*
- Weight of people or personal property *people. . .*
- Weight of rain
- Defective materials or methods of construction if the collapse takes place during the construction or remodeling. *. . .defects. . .*

"everything but. . ."

SPECIAL Cause of Loss Form

2 The Special form covers everything covered by the Broad form and more. It is the *All Risk* or Open Perils form. It covers everything except that which is specifically excluded. There are probably two valid questions that can be raised about this and any other all risk coverage:

1. What am I covered for now that I wasn't before?

2. What's excluded?

luxury finally . . . Theft

3 Both questions are important to your understanding of the Special Cause of Loss form, so we will answer each in turn.

What New Coverages Do I Have?

4 If you study the fourteen perils of the Broad form, you would be hard pressed to think of any major peril that is not already covered. However, if you attempt to upgrade a client from Broad to Special, you had better have at least one or two examples on the tip of your tongue. There are numerous minor improvements, but the most important addition is **THEFT**. It's not full theft protection because this policy does not cover money, securities, stocks or bonds and, as you will see later, high-target items like jewelry or furs have very low dollar limits. This theft protection is no substitute for the Crime module of the Package Policy. However, for businesses that have little to steal except their furniture, fixtures and inventory, this may be enough.

sticky fingers

What's not covered?

5 Oddly enough, anytime you go from a Named Peril form to All Risk, the number of listed exclusions actually increases. While this may be contrary to what you would expect, there is a certain logic to it. The exclusions under a Named Peril contract exist primarily to protect the company against a misinterpretation of a covered peril. However, in an All Risk form, the company has literally thrown the doors wide open and will cover everything except what is specifically excluded. For example, if the Insured lost property as the result of a scam, the loss would be covered unless scams were specifically excluded.

Notes

1 In examining the exclusions of the Basic, Broad and Special Cause of Loss forms, we will first look at those that are found in all three forms. We will then point out those that are unique to the Special form.

EXCLUSIONS COMMON TO ALL

DICE

- **Building Ordinance or Law** – If the costs of rebuilding an insured building would be increased by local ordinances requiring sprinkler systems or fireproof buildings or special facilities for the handicapped, this policy will not cover those additional costs, except for those provided in the Additional Coverages.

This would make you better than whole

- **Earth Movement** – such as an earthquake.

elsewhere

- **Government Action** – seizure or destruction of property by governmental authority is excluded.

- **Nuclear Hazard** – If it glows, it goes.
- **Power Failure** – off premises that causes a loss. For example, food which spoiled in a restaurant freezer that shut down because a power line collapsed down the street.
- **War and Military Action**
- **Flood**, **Mudslides** and **Sewer Backup**
- **Leakage or seepage** – of over 14 days or resulting from your failure to maintain heat in the building.
- **Artificially Generated Electrical Current**
- **Explosion of steam boilers**
- **Mechanical Breakdown**

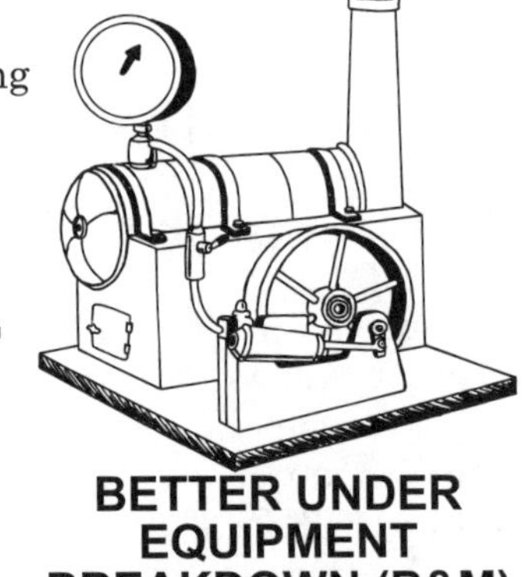

BETTER UNDER EQUIPMENT BREAKDOWN (B&M)

EXCLUSIONS UNIQUE TO THE SPECIAL FORM

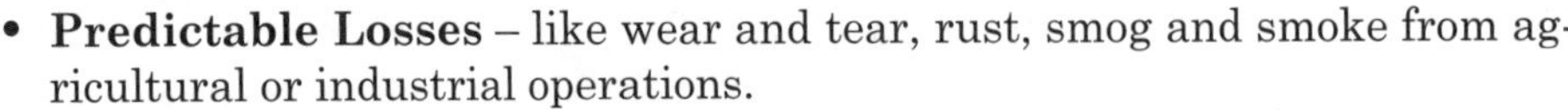

- **Predictable Losses** – like wear and tear, rust, smog and smoke from agricultural or industrial operations.
- **Dishonest Acts** – by you or your employees

This stuff makes sense

- **Voluntary Parting** – with insured property as in a scam
- **Rain, Snow or Ice** – damage to personal property left out in the open
- **Concurrent Causation** – if a loss is caused by a covered peril and an excluded peril, we will only cover the damage attributable to the covered peril regardless of the sequence of events.

Notes

1 NOTE: **Because theft is covered** under the Special form, there are some unique exclusions and limitations relating to theft.

- **Theft** – of building materials not attached to the building
- **Inventory Shortage** – with no physical evidence of theft
- **Theft Limitations** – for the following property loss by theft provides coverage only up to the limits indicated:

  - Furs $2500
  - Jewelry, watches, precious stones and precious metals $2500
  - Patterns, dies, molds and forms $2500
  - Stamps, tickets and letters of credit $250

minor theft

EARTHQUAKE ENDORSEMENT

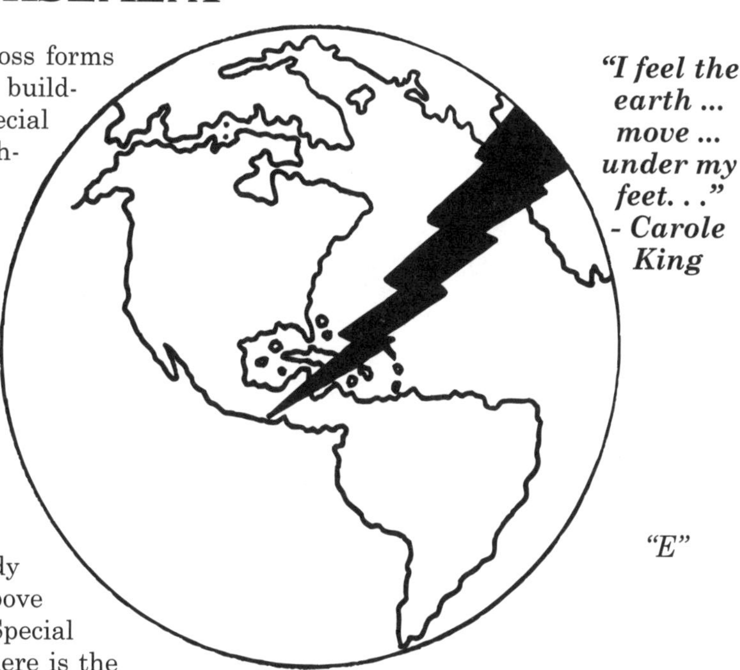

2 As we have noted, all three Cause of Loss forms exclude earth movement. Whether your building was covered by the Basic, Broad or Special perils, you would have no coverage for earthquake. As was the case in Homeowners, the peril of earthquake can be added by endorsement.

"I feel the earth ... move ... under my feet. . ." - Carole King

3 While the name would imply that this endorsement adds only the peril of earthquake, such is not the case. This is a two peril form adding the perils below:

- Earthquake
- Volcanic Eruption

"E"

4 You should remember that we have already provided coverage for Volcanic Action (above ground damage) in the Basic, Broad and Special forms. The Volcanic Eruption covered here is the **underground damage** done by a volcano.

5 Beyond this, there are only a few minor things to know about Earthquake.

- Everything except Earthquake and Volcanic Eruption is excluded.
- All earthquake shocks or volcanic eruptions that occur within a **168 hour** period (seven days) will be treated as a single occurrence.
- The deductible is a **percentage deductible** as shown on the Property Dec Page. If you bought earthquake coverage with a 5% deductible on a $100,000 building, then you have a $5000 deductible. If your loss is $20,000, the company will pay $15,000. The deductible applies separately to each insured building and to the contents of each building.

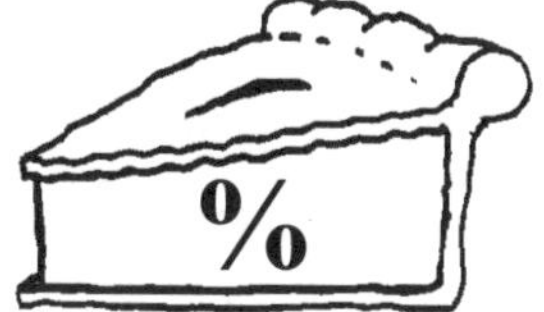

THE REMAINING PROPERTY COVERAGE FORMS ‡

1 To this juncture, we have examined the most important Commercial Property Coverage Forms. Most businesses have some property they need to insure; most have some liability exposure; and most cannot afford to be out of business very long.

2 As you will recall, there are nine other forms that a commercial client may need. We will look at those briefly.

3 **GLASS** - This form provides glass coverage to the levels required by many modern businesses. A glass schedule is used to describe the insured glass, identify its location in the building and to describe any lettering or ornamentation. Usually glass is written on an ACV basis and there are two causes of loss. The policy will pay for direct physical loss or damage to covered property caused by or resulting from:

- Breakage of glass
- Chemicals accidentally or maliciously applied to the glass.

4 As you can see, this is practically all risk coverage. The only exclusions are:

- Fire
- Nuclear
- War and military action.

5 In addition to the very broad coverage we have described, the Glass Form provides for debris removed and for temporary repairs in an emergency.

6 **BUILDERS RISK** - This form provides coverage for a **building or structure under construction**. It covers the building, foundation, temporary scaffolding and any material supplies and equipment that will become part of the building either within the building or within 100 feet of the building.

7 This coverage is tied to the Basic, Broad or Special Cause of Loss form and settlement is on an ACV basis.

8 While this coverage is normally written on a completed value basis, the underwriting assumption is that the average exposure from start to finish is about 50% of the completed value. Therefore, the coverage is relatively inexpensive. Oddly enough, there is no condition called *Coinsurance*, but most companies effectively require 100% coinsurance under a condition titled *Need for Adequate Insurance.*

9 Coverage under Builders Risk ceases when any of the following transpire:

- The builder's interest ceases.
- The purchaser accepts the building.
- The insured builder abandons the project with no intention to finish it.
- 60 days after the building is occupied (fully or partially), or 90 days after the construction is complete.

10 While the builder is normally the policyowner, it is possible for the ultimate building owner to purchase this coverage.

Notes

1 **LEASEHOLD INTEREST** - The Leasehold Interest Form is designed to offset the financial damage done to a commercial tenant if a favorable lease is cancelled as the result of physical damage done to the property by a covered cause of loss.

2 Perhaps an example will help. Suppose Joe pays $5000 a month to lease the building that houses his restaurant and has 36 months left on his lease. Further assume that in today's marketplace Joe would have to spend $8000 a month for a similar building. If the building were destroyed by fire today, and the owner chose to build a high rise apartment building in that location, Joe would suffer a major financial loss over the next 36 months. If he had spent $50,000 on betterments and improvements that have not been fully amortized, he is in even worse shape. The purpose of the Leasehold Interest Coverage Form is to offset this risk.

3 Obviously the mathematical calculations required to establish the amount of insurance needed and to compute the claim in the event of a loss are quite complex. On the first day of a 60 month lease the exposure is probably enormous. By the 60th month it is almost nonexistent.

4 For purposes of this course, we will suffice it to say that Joe can cover this exposure with the Leasehold Interest Coverage Form.

5 As with most of the commercial property coverages Joe can choose either the Basic, Broad or Special Cause of Loss form.

6 **CONDOMINIUM ASSOCIATION COVERAGE** - This form is purchased by the residential or commercial condominium association to insure the buildings, hallways, stairways and facilities that the unit owners own jointly.

7 It has the same coverages as the Building and Personal Property form - building, business personal property and property of others. It also has the same Additions, Extensions and Exclusions. It is linked with the Basic, Broad or Special form.

8 **CONDOMINIUM UNIT OWNERS COVERAGE** - A commercial condominium is a condominium for businesses instead of residents. This coverage does for the commercial unit owners what the HO-6 does for the unit owner of a residential condominium. It insures the business personal property of the business housed in the condominium.

9 **LEGAL LIABILITY COVERAGE** - This form is very unique in that it gives you a way to insure property that **you do not own**. Suppose that Joe leases his restaurant space and negligently destroys it in an explosion. His landlord would file a claim with his property carrier who would, in turn, subrogate against Joe. This coverage would pay on Joe's behalf.

10 Like the liability coverages we will study in the next chapter, this form will pay **in addition to the policy limits** for defense costs, investigative costs, bonds required by the court and even Joe's expenses (up to $100 a day) of being in court rather than at work.

11 As we will discuss in Chapter 10 of this text, there is another, narrower approach to this problem available as part of the Commercial General Liability policy. It is called *Fire Legal*. It is narrower in the sense that it only covers negligent fire damage caused by a tenant. The Legal Liability Coverage Form would cover any negligent damage done by the tenant business that is covered by the Cause of Loss form shown on the Dec Sheet.

Notes

MORTGAGE HOLDERS ERRORS AND OMISSIONS COVERAGE - This form
1 is designed for lending institutions who hold mortgages on property. If the mortgage holder errs and fails to purchase insurance on a mortgaged property (or, more likely, fails to verify that the mortgagor did so), this coverage protects the lender, the mortgagor and (for specified perils) the property itself. It also pays damages for which the lender becomes legally liable if real estate taxes are not paid as agreed on behalf of the mortgagor.

TOBACCO SALES WAREHOUSE COVERAGE - This coverage is for the business
2 that receives tobacco from the growers and auctions it to the cigarette manufacturers. It only covers the tobacco for the short period in which it is in the warehouse. Coverage may be written on a Basic, Broad or Special Cause of Loss form.

STANDARD PROPERTY COVERAGE - This form is a *no choices* version of the
3 Building and Business Personal Property Form that we examined in depth. This form contains the same coverages, conditions and exclusions as the earlier form, but none of the options. While it is theoretically possible to use any of the Cause of Loss Forms with this coverage, it is generally written with a Basic Cause of Loss Form to provide what we used to call *Fire Coverage* for an older building.

Difference in Conditions Coverage ‡

A Difference in Conditions (DIC) form is not technically a property form, nor is it
4 a part of the Commercial Package as it is normally written. So, why discuss it at this point? Well, this Inland Marine form is often purchased by large commercial property risks who purchase the Commercial Property Form with the Basic Cause of Loss form. By adding the DIC form they not only add most of the Broad Form Causes of Loss but also (at their option) earthquake, flood, property in transit and business income for these new exposures.

Full coverage recipe: Take a "Basic CPP" and add a DIC

Essentially, then, the DIC form fills in some rather significant coverage gaps in
5 the Commercial Property contract. As you would suppose, it excludes the perils already covered by the Commercial Property Basic Cause of Loss form in that these exposures are already covered.

One unique underwriting aspect of the DIC coverage is that **there is no coinsur-**
6 **ance** requirement. Therefore, commercial Insureds using this form need only purchase the amount of coverage they believe necessary for the perils added by the DIC. If the Insured owns a $1 million building but believes that the potential damage that could be done by a flood is only $200,000, then only $200,000 in flood coverage needs to be purchased.

No coinsurance

Notes

The New Peril - Terrorism

1 Up to 9/11/01, commercial property policies essentially covered acts of terrorism at no charge... it was considered to be a rather improbable event. But with losses of $32.5 billion attributed to the events of 9/11, commercial insurers began to exclude "losses due to acts of terrorism." Congress acted to discourage companies from this reaction by passing the Terrorism Risk Insurance Act (TRIA) in 2002. In 2005, this law was renewed for another two years. In 2007, this law was renewed for another seven years.

2 TRIA defines an act of terrorism as any act certified by the Secretary of the Treasury (in concurrence with the Secretary of State and the Attorney General) which is dangerous to human life, property or infrastructure within the U.S. or on the premises of a U.S. mission outside the U.S. or upon a U.S. flagged vessel. To be certified:

- Damage must be in excess of $100 million

3 In essence, the Federal Government acts as an unpaid reinsurer when losses exceed an indexed amount. To qualify, a company must offer terrorism coverage to its Commercial Property policyowners. The policyowners may, of course, reject the coverage.

4 Commercial P&C companies pay losses up to a certain level based on size and thereafter "share" losses with the Federal Government in accordance with an indexed coinsurance percentage.

5 The government's cost cap on this program is $100 billion per year, but the feds can recoup some or all of its expenditures from the Commercial P&C industry as a whole. Companies participating in this repayment will do so by levying a surcharge (capped at 3%) on policies covered by this program.

Notes

Conclusion

1 Commercial Property policies cover your business stuff: the building you own, the business property you own or lease, and other people's stuff in your possession at your business. Let's take a quick look at what we can cover and what we won't.

2 —If you want to cover the structure you own that houses your business, you'd need to buy **building** coverage. A building is the walls, roof, floor, wall to wall carpeting, permanently installed stuff (central air, lunch counter), construction materials within 100 feet of the building, and a fire extinguisher or snowblower. Maybe even a microwave oven.

3 —If you want to cover your business property (fax machines, copiers, computers, office furniture, inventory, parts, etc.), you'd buy **Business Personal Property** coverage. It covers your business stuff inside the business or within 100 feet of your business.

4 —If in your business you take custody of other people's property - say you are in the dry cleaning business, or you operate a TV repair shop - you have a responsibility for your customer's property. You need to purchase **Personal Property of Others** coverage. It covers other people's stuff in your care, custody or control that's either inside your business or within 100 feet of your business.

5 —If you want to still have some money coming in while your business is closed due to damage by a covered peril you'd buy **Business Income** coverage.

6 —If your building is damaged by a covered peril and you must relocate and stay open while the damage is being fixed you'd buy **Extra Expense** coverage to pay for the unanticipated expenses you'll incur.

7 —Some of the things not covered by a **Commercial Property policy** are spelled out here in lovely poetic form.

You have no coverage for animals or money,
Your car is not covered, so sorry honey.
Foundations are excluded, as is your land,
And we never cover your contraband.
We exclude fences, your tree and your shrub,
But extensions can cover them, so don't sweat it, Bub.

Notes

1 When you buy a Commercial Property policy you get some **additional coverages** absolutely free. There are only 5 additional coverages. They are **Debris Removal, Preservation of Property, Fire Department Service Charge, Pollutant Clean-Up and Removal, and Increased Cost of Construction**. To help remember the **additional coverages** just think of the 1960's Western, Rawhide as you sing, "Clean it up, put it up, put it out, build it up, mop it up....*Rawhide*"

2 Remember that a **Commercial Property policy** also offers coverage **Extensions.** You only get these if you are **80%** insured to value. Some of the Extensions are: **Coverage for a New Building and/or Property, Coverage for Personal Effects and Property of Others ($2500), Coverage for Business Property Off Premises ($10,000),** And **Coverage for Outdoor Property, Trees and Shrubs ($1000 max, only $250 for a tree).**

3 **Commercial Property** losses are settled on an **Actual Cash Value** basis. Both the building and contents are covered **Actual Cash Value** on an unendorsed policy. One important exception: If a building loss is under $2500 the company pays on a **Replacement** cost basis.

4 If you have a loss you must notify the company **promptly**. If the company requests, you must submit proof of loss within **60 days**. The company then must pay or reject your claim within **30 days**. Therefore, the whole claims process will be completed within **90 days**.

5 Know your perils. There are **11 perils covered with the basic form, 14 perils plus collapse** are covered by the **broad peril form and** the **special peril** form **covers everything except for what is excluded.**

CHAPTERS 8 & 9
COMMERCIAL PACKAGE & COMMERCIAL PROPERTY

1. Which of the following statements is true concerning the Commercial Package Policy?

   (A) The Commercial Package Policy has two specific mandatory coverage sections and five optional sections.
   (B) The subsections of the Commercial Package Policy, such as the Commercial Property Form, may not be sold separately as independent policies.
   (C) The Commercial Package Policy is a standard form that is printed in its entirety, with all of its subsections present and it cannot be subdivided.
   (D) The Commercial Package Policy has common declarations and common conditions that apply to all of the subsections of the policy.

2. Which of the following statements about the Commercial Property Policy is true?

   (A) The Commercial Property Policy cannot be sold as a monoline policy.
   (B) The Commercial Property Policy cannot be purchased without containing both Building and Business Personal Property coverage.
   (C) The Commercial Property Policy will not pay for cash that's stolen, but it will pay for cash that is destroyed.
   (D) The Commercial Property Policy may be used for any commercial property risk with almost no exceptions.

3. William Shakespeare owns Stratford Glove Factory. He is insured under a Commercial Property policy issued by Curtain Call Casualty Company. The replacement cost of Will's building is $120,000. The policy has a building limit of $90,000, which satisfies the coinsurance requirement on the dec sheet. Will puts up a new glove drying shed on his premises. Which of the following best describes coverage on the new shed?

   (A) Will would have $120,000 of coverage for 30 days.
   (B) Will would have $250,000 of coverage for 30 days.
   (C) Will would have coverage equal to the cost of labor and materials to build the new shed.
   (D) Will would have no coverage on the new shed.

CHAPTERS 8 & 9
COMMERCIAL PACKAGE & COMMERCIAL PROPERTY QUIZ

4. A business is insured with Broad Cause of Loss form coverage on its building and business personal property. If a hammer falls off a 20 foot high shelf and destroys a copy machine owned by the business, the insurance company will most likely

   (A) Pay the Actual Cash Value of the loss.
   (B) Replace the copy machine.
   (C) Pay the claim and then subrogate.
   (D) Deny the claim.

5. You own a business that's insured with a Commercial Property Policy, with a Basic Cause of Loss form. One day the building next door to you catches on fire. If while putting out the fire, the fire department sprays water into your building and damages your inventory, would the loss be covered?

   (A) No, the insurance company would classify it as a flood loss.
   (B) Yes, but only up to a maximum of $1000.
   (C) No, there is no coverage for any water damage in the Commercial Property Policy with a Basic Cause of Loss form.
   (D) Yes, because firefighter water damage is covered.

6. Under the Commercial Property policy, which of the following is NOT true concerning the Debris Removal coverage additions?

   (A) Claims can exceed 25% of the loss by $10,000.
   (B) If necessary, the insurance company can pay up to $10,000 over the limit of the policy to pay for debris removal.
   (C) If the loss isn't covered, neither is the cost of removing the debris.
   (D) The insurance company will provide up to 30 days, All Risk coverage, for debris removed to a new location.

7. The amount of the deductible printed on the Property Declarations page is

   (A) $ 100
   (B) $ 250
   (C) $ 500
   (D) $1000

CHAPTERS 8 & 9
COMMERCIAL PACKAGE & COMMERCIAL PROPERTY QUIZ

8. You have insured a pet store under a Commercial Property Policy. All of the following items would be covered under the Building and Personal Property Coverage Form EXCEPT

(A) The inventory of pets that are for sale.
(B) Cash receipts.
(C) A fire extinguisher.
(D) Your business personal property which is located in your delivery truck parked within 100 feet of the insured building.

9. Under the Building and Personal Property Coverage Form of the Commercial Property module, the First Named Insured has a duty to notify the insurance company of a loss within how long?

(A) Promptly.
(B) Five days.
(C) Ten days.
(D) Sixty days.

10. Under the Building and Personal Property Coverage Form, which of the following would NOT be classified as part of the building?

(A) Outdoor fixtures.
(B) Materials and supplies within 100 feet of the building used for making additions to the building.
(C) A microwave oven in the employee dining room.
(D) The foundation of the building.

11. Under the Building and Personal Property Coverage Form, which of the following would NOT be classified as part of your Business Personal Property?

(A) Your stock in the building.
(B) Your use interest as tenant in the improvements in the building.
(C) Your labor and materials invested in the repair of the personal property of others that is in your care, custody or control.
(D) Your personal effects that are located in the building.

CHAPTERS 8 & 9
COMMERCIAL PACKAGE & COMMERCIAL PROPERTY QUIZ

12. Under the Building and Personal Property Coverage Form, there are three options for establishing value. Which of the following is NOT one of the options?

    (A) Fair Market Value
    (B) Agreed Value
    (C) Actual Cash Value
    (D) Replacement Cost

13. Which of the following is true concerning the Commercial Property Policy?

    (A) You must select one Cause of Loss Form that will apply to every subpart of the policy.
    (B) The Broad Form covers more perils than the Special Form.
    (C) The Earthquake Form must be used in conjunction with one of the other three Cause of Loss Forms.
    (D) The Special Form covers earthquake losses.

14. Jack Frick owns a large apartment complex which is insured under a Commercial Property Policy with the Basic Causes of Loss form. Which of the following perils would not be covered by his policy?

    (A) Sprinkler leakage
    (B) Weight of snow, ice, or sleet
    (C) Sinkhole collapse
    (D) Vandalism

15. J.T. Jones has a boat manufacturing plant insured under a Commercial Package Policy with the property coverages written using a Basic Cause of Loss Form. One day, while the large overhead doors are open, a gust of wind blows four bushels of sand into the building and destroys an expensive boat that is in production. Which of the following is true concerning this loss?

    (A) The loss will be covered because windstorm is a covered peril.
    (B) The loss will not be covered because boats are specifically excluded under this Causes of Loss Form.
    (C) The loss will be covered because the business frequently operates with the overhead doors open.
    (D) The loss will not be covered because the insured let the sand enter the building.

CHAPTERS 8 & 9
COMMERCIAL PACKAGE & COMMERCIAL PROPERTY QUIZ

16. Under the Business Income Coverage Form, business income is defined as:

    (A) Gross profit plus normal operating expenses.
    (B) Net income plus continuing normal operating expenses, including payroll.
    (C) Net profit before taxes plus extra expenses.
    (D) Net income plus expediting expenses, including overtime.

17. Under the Business Income Coverage Form, a Period of Restoration would end on which of the following dates?

    (A) The expiration date of the policy.
    (B) The last day of the twelfth month following the date of the loss.
    (C) The date when the property is or should be repaired, rebuilt, or replaced with reasonable speed and similar quality.
    (D) The date the business is ready to operate at the same level as before the loss.

18. Under the Business Income Coverage Form, which of the following best describes the Extended Business Income Period?

    (A) The period of time from the end of the policy period until the property is replaced and ready to resume operations.
    (B) Up to 30 days, starting on the date that the property is repaired and operations are resumed through the date that the business could be back in the condition that it was in before the loss occurred.
    (C) A period of time immediately following a direct loss when extra expenses are paid.
    (D) None of the above.

19. Under the Business Income Coverage Form, an insured elects the Monthly Limit of Indemnity and uses a fraction of one-fourth on the Declarations Page. If the limit of insurance is $120,000, and the loss of income for the first month is $40,000, then the insured will collect

    (A) $40,000
    (B) $30,000
    (C) $20,000
    (D) None of the above

CHAPTERS 8 & 9
COMMERCIAL PACKAGE & COMMERCIAL PROPERTY QUIZ

20. Which of the following statements is NOT true regarding Agreed Value?

    (A) Agreed Value is an option that can be selected on the Declarations.
    (B) The Coinsurance Clause does not apply to property covered under Agreed Value.
    (C) The Agreed Value option is only good for one policy year at a time.
    (D) Under the Agreed Value option, the insurance company will pay the replacement cost for any total loss.

END

QUIZ ANSWERS & EXPLANATIONS ON NEXT PAGE

CHAPTERS 8 & 9
COMMERCIAL PACKAGE & COMMERCIAL PROPERTY QUIZ ANSWER KEY

1. D. The Commercial Package Policy has seven modules - the insured may choose any two or more. There are no mandatory coverages. Each module may be purchased as a separate monoline coverage. There are common declarations and common conditions that apply to each selected module.

2. D. The Property coverage is available as either part of the Package or as a monoline coverage. A tenant could purchase Personal Property Coverage without Building Coverage. Cash receipts are excluded from coverage. There are enough forms available to provide almost any coverage that the insured needs.

3. D. Coverage for "a newly acquired or constructed premises" is an extension. Extensions must be earned by maintaining 80% coverage. The insured only maintained 75% of value, thus he did not earn the extensions. Coinsurance could be set at 70%.

4. D. To cover damage inside the premises from a falling object, the object had to fall from outside the premises (through the roof).

5. D. The peril of Fire includes damage caused by firefighter's water.

6. D. The policy covers the cost to remove debris caused by a covered peril, but does not cover the debris itself. Do you insure your trash?

7. C. This can of course be raised.

8. B. Cash receipts are not covered property.

9. A. Notice of Claim must be prompt. Proof of Loss, if requested, must be made within 60 days of the request.

10. D. The building includes outdoor fixtures, incidental cooking equipment, building materials stored within 100 feet of the premises, but not the foundation. NOTE: The Commercial Property policy excludes all parts of the building under the lowest building floor.

CHAPTERS 8 & 9
COMMERCIAL PACKAGE & COMMERCIAL PROPERTY
QUIZ ANSWER KEY

11. D. Coverage for personal effects is available as an extension.

12. A. Fair Market Value is not an option.

13. C. Earthquake coverage cannot be purchased on its own.

14. B. The Weight of Ice and Snow is a Broad Form peril.

15. D. To cover damage inside the premises caused by the peril of Wind and Hail, "Mother Nature had to let herself in."

16. B. The measure of a business income loss is the net plus continuous operating expenses, including the payroll.

17 C. The operative word is "should" be ready to reopen.

18. B. The Extended Business Income Period, which follows the restoration period, allows the insured's business to get back up to speed.

19. B. Multiply the fraction times the limit (1/4 x $120K = 30K) to find the monthly limit. Using the Rule of 3L's, compare the monthly limit to the monthly loss ($30K to $40K).

20. D. Agreed Value is typically used for items that cannot be readily replaced.

COMMERCIAL GENERAL LIABILITY

10

SOURCE:
ISO CGL-2007

1 The second key element of the Commercial Package Policy is the Commercial General Liability module. As with Commercial Property, it can be sold as part of the Commercial Package, or it can be sold as a monoline contract. As we look at the policy, we need to remember the basic concepts of legal liability that we discussed earlier in this text.

COMMERCIAL LIABILITY

2 As we begin to examine liability insurance from the Commercial Lines viewpoint, it would be helpful for you to think as a businessowner. Forget about your dog biting the neighbor – we've done that. Now, you need to think like a businessowner or a professional and about all of the ways your activities could create major liability exposures. Actually, even a partial list looks fairly ominous:

1. Premises
2. Operations
3. Products
4. Completed Operations
5. Independent Contractors
6. Contractual
7. Fire Legal
8. Personal Injury
9. Advertising Injury

at the Insured's connection to what happened

Notes

1 These nine liability hazards are normally classified by the insurance industry as **General Liability exposures** and can be covered (mercifully) by one super-duper policy – the Commercial General Liability (CGL) policy. Actually, an unendorsed CGL automatically covers these exposures as well as two very important extras. Your study of the CGL will be greatly advanced if you first gain some insight into each of these exposures, the extras provided by the contract and an overview of what a plain vanilla CGL does not cover. Let's begin with the nine covered exposures.

Premises Liability

2 Simply owning or occupying business premises can get you into trouble. Retail stores, professional offices, public buildings . . . even ballparks fall into this category. Suppose Joe owns a restaurant. If the Other Guy trips over an extension cord and breaks his arm, Joe **may** be liable.

Rule of thumb: Doing something on premises . . . it's premises

3 NOTE: You will notice a lot of *maybe's* and *could be's* in this discussion. The reason for this is that we cannot predict with accuracy what a jury will decide. If the Other Guy in the example above wants to sue, Joe will surely be named in the lawsuit. If Joe leases the restaurant, his landlord might also be named. If he leases through a property management company, it could be named in the lawsuit as well. This concept is sometimes called the ***Rule of Deepest Pocket***. It says, "Sue everyone possible and get the money from the guy with the most money". As an Agent, your job is **not** to decide whether your client is liable; **it is your responsibility to see that he or she is covered for any *potential* exposure, no matter how far fetched.**

Operations Liability

4 Unlike the *premises-oriented* businesses we've just described, other businesses earn money by performing operations. Many of these businesses do not even have premises into which the public is invited. A roofing or lawn care company performs its operations entirely off premises. If Joe caters a dinner away from his restaurant and a huge pot of soup turns over and burns several guests, that is Operations Liability. Carpenters, plumbers, demolition companies and baby-sitting services fall into this category.

. . . doing something off premises. . . it's operations

5 NOTE: An exception to the *off premises* rule is a manufacturer. Obviously, a manufacturer performs an operation on its own premises and would need this coverage. However, 99.9% of the time, someone injured in a factory is an employee and is, therefore, excluded from coverage – making this a relatively unimportant exception to the off premises rule for you at this point.

Products Liability

6 If you **manufacture, distribute or sell** a product, you have a potential Products Liability exposure. Notice that you do not have to manufacture the product to have an exposure. Anyone in the distribution chain has an exposure. The general rule is that **Products Liability begins** (and Premises Liability ends) **when the product leaves your premises and enters the stream of commerce.**

made. . .
. . .or sold

7 About the only significant exception to this rule of thumb is food consumed in a restaurant. By endorsement, the rules are changed so that food is covered by Products Liability **as soon as it is served.**

Notes

1 For example, suppose Joe has a gift shop in his restaurant and a customer injures himself trying out a veg-a-matic. Since the product **has not entered the stream of commerce**, Joe's Premises Liability would cover this event. If the customer bought the veg-a-matic and the **same thing happened at his home**, Joe's Products Liability would cover the accident if Joe were held to be legally responsible. Notice that the item does not have to be sold. The rule of thumb for Products Liability is *left the premises and entered the stream of commerce.* Even if Joe had given the customer the veg-a-matic as a promotional gimmick, everything would still work the same way.

. . .enters the stream of commerce. . . leaves the Insured's premises

2 Products Liability is actually a stricter form of liability than negligence. Essentially, the message is: *If you are going to make, distribute or sell a product, it should not injure people or damage their property.* Generally, Products Liability cases are based upon one of two types of warranties:

Strict Liability

- **Expressed Warranties** – are guarantees in writing, like "This transmission is guaranteed for 12 months or 12,000 miles," or "These tires are guaranteed for 40,000 miles."

promises. . . . . .written. . .

- **Implied Warranties** – are guarantees that are not in writing but which the Reasonable Man would assume, like the product is fit for its intended use. Ford never said in writing that the Pinto would not explode when hit from the rear at speeds in excess of 25 m.p.h. but the Reasonable Man would not expect the car to explode under such conditions.

. . .unwritten

3 As you might guess, most Products Liability cases are argued on the basis of Implied Warranties. Normally, the arguments center on bad design, improper manufacture or failure to warn through proper labeling.

Completed Operations Liability

4 Many of the same kinds of businesses that need Operations Liability coverage need Completed Operations Liability coverage. **Operations** Liability provides protection **while** the work is being done; **Completed Operations** offers protection **after** the work is done. Keep in mind, Completed Operations offers protection for bodily injury or property damage caused by the work itself. Suppose the Other Guy is hit on the head by a hammer that a carpenter dropped while installing a chandelier. The carpenter's Operations Liability coverage would be operable. However, if the carpenter had finished his work and then the chandelier dropped on the Other Guy, the carpenter's Completed Operations Liability section would provide coverage.

work done

5 Completed Operations Liability coverage begins (and Operations Liability ends) when:

1. The job is completed, or

2. **The Insured's** part of the job is completed, or

3. The job is partially completed and the completed portion is being put to its intended use.

3 triggers

6 The first two triggers are fairly obvious, but the third requires some explanation. Imagine a strip shopping center under construction. The first space is completed and a Seven-Eleven is operating in that space while the remaining spaces are still under construction. From the contractor's viewpoint, the Seven-Eleven is covered by Completed Operations and the unfinished spaces still fall under Operations Liability.

Notes

Independent Contractors Liability

1 Joe has coverage under his own policy for his acts and those of his employees, but what about the acts of any independent contractors Joe might engage, such as a carpenter paneling the restaurant? The independent contractor should have his or her own insurance - either a CGL to cover an ongoing business or an **Owners and Contractors Protective** to cover this one job only. Independent Contractors Liability protects Joe if he is held legally responsible for the actions of an independent contractor. Remember the Rule of Deepest Pocket.

other than employees

Contractual Liability

2 If you voluntarily assume someone else's liability by contract, you need this coverage. While assuming someone else's liability might seem like a dumb idea, it is often necessary in business.

3 The CGL recognizes five common situations where a business is almost forced to enter into a contract and assume someone else's liability. The policy provides coverage for these five situations, which have come to be known as the *insured contracts*. These five ***insured contracts*** are:

L Lease
E Easement
A Agreement to indemnify a municipality
S Sidetrack agreement
E Elevator maintenance agreement

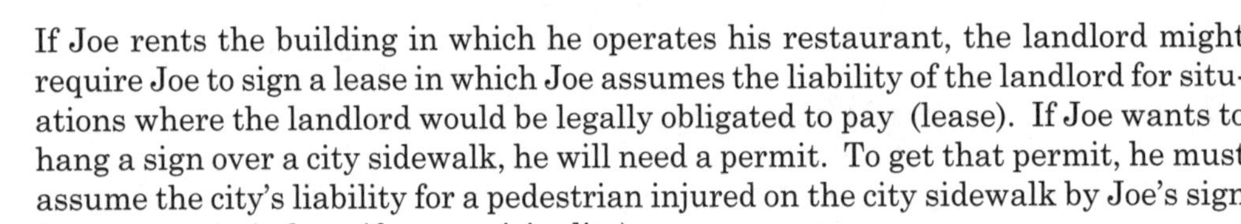

4 If Joe rents the building in which he operates his restaurant, the landlord might require Joe to sign a lease in which Joe assumes the liability of the landlord for situations where the landlord would be legally obligated to pay (lease). If Joe wants to hang a sign over a city sidewalk, he will need a permit. To get that permit, he must assume the city's liability for a pedestrian injured on the city sidewalk by Joe's sign (agreement to indemnify a municipality).

5 In addition to the CGL providing coverage for the above situations, the policy provides contractual coverage any time the Insured enters into an agreement where there would have been tort liability in the absence of a contract or agreement. For example, let's suppose Joe wins a bid with the local stadium to run the food concessions at all the home football games. The stadium requires Joe to sign a contract in which Joe assumes the liability of the stadium with respect to Joe's food and operations at the stadium. At the game, Wimpy purchases one of Joe's burgers, bites down into it, breaks a tooth and sues the stadium. As Joe has assumed the stadium's liability, Joe's CGL would pay for this loss. The key words are *where there would have been tort liability in the absence of a contract or agreement.* Even without the contract in place, Joe has responsibility for the broken tooth (tort liability). The CGL realizes that contracts are used often in business and extends the coverage to pay on behalf of others when it is the Insured's action that caused the loss.

Notes

Fire Legal Liability

Fire Legal provides coverage for negligent fire damage the Insured does to a **building**
1 **he occupies as a tenant**. Suppose that Joe **rents** the first story of a commercial building to house his restaurant. The second story is occupied by his landlord. If Joe is responsible for a fire that destroys the entire building and all the contents, what will happen? Joe will file a claim for his contents under his Commercial Property policy. The landlord will file with his property carrier for his contents and for the building. The landlord's company will subrogate against Joe as he is responsible. Joe's CGL will pay for the landlord's contents and for the second story of the building.

The first story of the building, however, presents a problem. As you will see in a few
2 pages, a standard exclusion in the CGL says that we do not cover property that is in your "**care, custody or control**." (This is logical as most property in Joe's control is his and should be covered by his Property policy) The Fire Legal coverage *gives back* some of what the exclusion takes away. It will pay (up to the separately stated Fire Legal limits on the Dec Sheet) for negligent fire damage done to premises that Joe occupies as a tenant. Therefore, the Fire Legal coverage of Joe's CGL pays for the damage to the first floor.

3 C's

Care
Custody
Control

Personal Injury Liability

As you may recall from Chapter 4 in this text, Personal Injury has nothing to do with
3 injury to a person's body (Bodily Injury). Instead, Personal Injury concerns **injury to a person's reputation or mental state**. Personal Injuries include false arrest, false imprisonment false search and seizure, malicious prosecution, libel, slander, defamation of character, violation of civil rights or right of privacy, wrongful entry or eviction or the invasion of the right of private occupancy. As you can see from the list, not one of the above listed items includes bodily injury but simply relates to mental, reputation or psychological damages to the "injured" person.

Slander: Joe has a bad day

Notes

Advertising Injury Liability

business not person

1 This is closely related to Personal Injury Liability except a business is harmed rather than an individual, like the banker. It provides coverage if Joe inaccurately represents the quality of a competitive restaurant in an advertisement.

2 This coverage can also help Joe if he is sued for stealing another business's logo, trademark, advertising slogan or symbol of business. For instance, he would need this coverage if he erected golden arches over his restaurant and began advertising as McJoe's. Advertising Injury Liability also includes coverage for Joe if he infringes on a copyright **or title belonging to another business.**

---

3 **NOTE:** This is a good time to point out a rather important fact. You may be wondering why it is important to know all about these coverages since the CGL includes all of them anyway. One reason is that it will be necessary to know them when we get to our discussion of limits later on. As a practicing Agent, it's important because of **cost**. By endorsement, you can eliminate any or all of the following:

- Advertising Injury
- Advertising and Personal Injury
- Fire Legal
- Medical Payments (see below)
- Products and Completed Operations

4 In addition, you can reduce Contractual Liability from its blanket-type coverage to where it applies only to the *insured contracts*. Any elimination or reduction in coverage will, of course, save premium dollars. However, as an Agent, you must understand these coverages very well before you could risk eliminating one of them to save a client some money.

NO FAULT! NO FAULT!

5 Now that we have studied the nine basic coverages that are provided by the CGL, we can turn our attention to a couple of extra goodies built right into the CGL (or any other liability policy, for that matter). Though they are two separate and distinct benefits and will be addressed individually, they share one common denominator. Unlike everything else in the CGL that you have studied, **these coverages are not triggered by your legal obligation to pay**.

6 One of these extras is **Medical Payments**. By covering the Other Guy's medical costs following an injury without even questioning who was at fault, the company is attempting to avoid a lawsuit and the issue of legal responsibility altogether.

7 The second extra is **Supplementary Payments**. Amongst several benefits included is one of major importance – Defense Costs. If you are sued, the company provides a lawyer and assumes the costs of defense. Essentially, the company is attempting to establish that you are not legally obligated to pay for damages suffered by the Other Guy. Let's take a closer look at each.

Notes

Premises or Operations Medical Payments

The Medical Payments section of the policy pays without regard to fault. If
1 the Other Guy slips and falls in Joe's restaurant, Medical Payments (Med Pay) pays.
Even if the Other Guy is on roller skates and it appears that he himself is to blame,
Med Pay still pays. The limits are rather low (beginning at $5000 per person), but
it would certainly pay enough to set the Other Guy's broken arm.

no fault

2

Obviously, the intent of Medical Payments is to avoid lawsuits. It's like goodwill insurance. If Joe can pay to fix the Other Guy's arm with no hassle, maybe there will be no lawsuit.

There are, however, several limitations of Med Pay. The **limits are low**, the benefits are restricted to **medical costs** (no payment for lost wages or pain and suffering) and the policy provides only **Premises or Operations** Med Pay benefits. In other words, the cause of the injury must be a Premises type of loss or an Operations type of loss. If the Other Guy slips and falls (Premises), Med Pay pays. If the Other Guy buys a bad hamburger at Joe's restaurant and gets violently ill (Products), Med Pay does NOT pay. In this latter case, the Other Guy would have to establish Joe's legal liability and then Joe's Products Liability coverage would pay.

must be premises / operations

Supplementary Payments

Though the word *supplementary* sounds like an optional add-on, **all liability policies have Supplementary Payments**. They come with the policy – you cannot buy the policy without this benefit.

3 While there are a half a dozen benefits that make
up the category of Supplementary Payments, the
biggie is **Defense Costs**. For any claim or lawsuit
filed against you (to which the insurance applies), the
insurance company will provide your legal defense.
4 **These costs are paid in addition to the limits of
liability of the policy**.

expenses for defense

in addition to the face amount

Though it is certainly important that the insurance company provide you with a legal defense in situations where you may be held legally
5 responsible, it may be even more important that a defense be provided if the Other
Guy's claim is groundless. Nuisance suits are becoming more common, and it may
cost up to $150 - $500 an hour to establish that you are not liable.

Other benefits provided by Supplementary Payments include:

6 • All other expenses incurred in investigating or settling the claim.

• Reasonable expenses you incur at the company's request in assisting their defense efforts, including loss of earnings of up to $250 per day.

• The cost of appeal bonds and attachment bonds.

• Any interest awards made to the Other Guy to offset the time between the occurrence or the judgment and the actual payment of damages.

Notes

NOT COVERED

1 As broad as the CGL is, not every liability exposure for every business is included.

2 The remaining hazards must be covered by the purchase of a separate policy. These include:

- Commercial Auto Liability
- Liquor Liability (for those in the liquor business)
- Nuclear Energy Liability
- Pollution Liability
- Professional Liability
- Employee Injury Liability
- Employee Benefit Liability
- Director & Officer's Liability
- Commercial Aircraft or Watercraft Liability

NEXT STEPS

3 Now that you have a basic grasp of the concept of liability and a general understanding of what the CGL is designed to cover and not cover, it is time to look at the policy in detail. As with Commercial Property, the CGL requires a separate Dec Sheet in addition to the Common Dec Sheet already discussed. However, the CGL does not have a separate Conditions section like Commercial Property does. The conditions relevant to the CGL are built right into the coverage form itself.

COMMERCIAL GENERAL LIABILITY DECLARATIONS

POLICY NO. ______________________________

COMPANY NAME AREA	PRODUCER NAME AREA

NAMED INSURED ______________________________

MAILING ADDRESS ______________________________

____

POLICY PERIOD: **From** ____________ **to** ____________ **at 12:01 A.M. Standard Time at your mailing address shown above.**

IN RETURN FOR THE PAYMENT OF THE PREMIUM, AND SUBJECT TO ALL THE TERMS OF THIS POLICY, WE AGREE WITH YOU TO PROVIDE THE INSURANCE AS STATED IN THIS POLICY.

LIMITS OF INSURANCE

GENERAL AGGREGATE LIMIT (Other Than Products - Completed Operations)	$ ____________	
PRODUCTS - COMPLETED OPERATIONS AGGREGATE LIMIT	$ ____________	
PERSONAL & ADVERTISING INJURY LIMIT	$ ____________	
EACH OCCURRENCE LIMIT	$ ____________	
FIRE DAMAGE LIMIT	$ ____________	**ANY ONE FIRE**
MEDICAL EXPENSE LIMIT	$ ____________	**ANY ONE PERSON**

RETROACTIVE DATE (CG 00 02 only)

Coverage A of this insurance does not apply to "bodily injury" or "property damage" which occurs before the Retroactive Date, if any, shown below

Retroactive Date: ______________________________

(Enter Date or "None" if no Retroactive Date applies.)

Form of Business:

- ☐ **Individual**
- ☐ **Partnership**
- ☐ **Joint Venture**
- ☐ **Organization** (Other than Partnership or Joint Venture)

Business Description: ______________________________

Location of All Premises You Own, Rent or Occupy:

____

____

CLASSIFICATION	CODE NO.	PREMIUM BASIS	RATE	ADVANCE PREMIUM	
				PR/CO	**ALL OTHER**
				$	**$**
			TOTAL		

Premium shown is payable:$ ____________ **at inception.**

ENDORSEMENTS ATTACHED TO THIS POLICY: IL 00 21 11 85 - Broad Form Nuclear Exclusion

____

____

COUNTERSIGNED ______________________ **BY** ______________________

(Date) **(Authorized Representative)**

NOTE: OFFICERS' FACSIMILE SIGNATURES MAY BE INSERTED HERE, ON THE POLICY COVER OR ELSEWHERE AT THE COMPANY'S OPTION

Notes

COMMERCIAL GENERAL LIABILITY COVERAGE FORM

SECTION I – COVERAGES

1 Our next task is to plug the exposures just discussed into the four coverages of the CGL contract.

COVERAGE A BI and PD	Premises Operations Products Completed Operations Independent Contractors Contractual Fire Legal
COVERAGE B	Personal Injury Advertising Injury
COVERAGE C	Medical Payments
{ **SUPPLEMENTARY PAYMENTS** for Coverages A&B	Supplementary Payments }

2 Before we examine each of these coverages in detail, it is helpful to notice the solid logic behind the coverage arrangement outlined above. Why separate Coverage A and Coverage B? Well, Coverage A is **only** bodily injury and property damage, whereas Coverage B is **never** bodily injury or property damage. Coverage A covers only unintentional acts whereas Coverage B covers specified intentional torts. Why is Coverage C separated from the previous two coverages? Coverages A and B are triggered by your legal obligation to pay but Coverage C (Med Pay) pays regardless of who is at fault. Why do the Supplementary Payments only relate to Coverage A and B? Because Coverage C is not concerned with fault. You do not need a legal defense when it is unimportant whether legal liability is established.

COVERAGE A – Bodily Injury and Property Damage

The basic promises made by Coverage A are contained in the insuring agreement.

3

> We will pay **those sums** that the Insured becomes **legally obligated to pay** as damages because of **"bodily injury"** or **"property damage"** to which this insurance applies. This insurance applies only to **"bodily injury"** and **"property damage" which occurs during the policy period**. The "bodily injury" or "property damage" must be **caused by an "occurrence"**. The "occurrence" must take place in the **"coverage territory"**. We will have the **right and duty to defend any "suit" seeking those damages.**

1 Let's tear the insuring clause apart in order to get a better sense of the true scope of the promise.

"Those Sums" - This promise is very broad. It does not list exposures such as
2 Premises, Operations, Products, etc. Instead, it covers everything except what is excluded.

3 **"Legally Obligated to Pay"** – Settlement or judgment are our two choices here.

4 **"Bodily Injury"** – This includes bodily injury, sickness, disease or death.

5 **"Property Damage"** – Physical injury to tangible property, including loss of use of that property or other property that is not physically injured.

6 **"Policy Period"** – Shown on the Dec Sheet.

"Caused by an Occurrence" – The word *occurrence* includes what most of us would
7 call an accident; however, it is broadened considerably. *Occurrence* also includes the continuous and repeated exposure to substantially the same harmful conditions. Accidents happen at a specific time; occurrences can happen over time. With few exceptions, modern liability policies are written on the broader basis.

8 **"Coverage Territory"** - The U.S., its possessions and territories, Puerto Rico and Canada.

9 **"Defend Any Suit"** – Defense costs.

10 As you can see, the basic promise of Coverage A is very broad. You can really only determine what is covered after seeing what is **not** covered.

Coverage A Exclusions

DICE

- **Intentional Acts**
- **Contractual Liability** assumed **after** an occurrence.
- **Liquor Liability** – is excluded for those in the business of distributing, furnishing or selling alcoholic beverages. If Joe's Restaurant sells liquor, he has no Liquor Liability Coverage under his CGL – he will have to buy a Liquor Liability Policy. On the other hand, his cousin, Moe, who owns a real estate agency has Host Liquor Liability Coverage under his CGL if he provides beer at the company picnic.

"dram shop" or . . . host liquor liability

- **Employees** – Injuries to you and your employees are not covered under your CGL. Remember, the policy only pays for the Other Guy's bodily injury. You and your employees are typically better covered under a Workers Compensation policy.

Worker's Comp

- **Pollution** – The policy absolutely excludes any pollution coverage whatsoever – almost. You do have coverage if **smoke from a hostile fire** at your premises pollutes a neighboring property.

we won't budge for sludge

Notes

- **Aircraft, Autos and Watercraft** – These items are better covered under different policies: Automobile, Aircraft or Watercraft policies. For most businesses, aircraft and watercraft coverages simply are not needed. The most likely problem is the Commercial Auto exposure, which can be covered with the Commercial Auto module of the Commercial Package Policy.

better covered elsewhere

The CGL does, however, **cover mobile equipment**, like a fork lift truck. Therefore, the important issue becomes how to distinguish between commercial autos and mobile equipment. **The basic rule is that if it is designed for use on public roads, it's probably a commercial auto**. This category would include cars, trucks, semi-tractor trailers, snowplows and road maintenance (not construction) equipment.

Mobile equipment is primarily considered to be land vehicles **not designed for use on public roads**, such as farm machinery, fork lifts, bulldozers and other vehicles that travel on crawler treads.

NOT REGISTERED FOR THE ROAD

. . .still

Unfortunately, the distinction between mobile equipment (which is covered under the CGL) and commercial autos (which are not) can become a little blurred based upon usage. For instance, a pick-up truck is considered an auto. But if it is used solely on your premises, it can qualify as mobile equipment. A bulldozer is clearly mobile equipment, but if it is being transported or towed by a commercial auto, it is covered for liability as commercial auto.

The other important border between the CGL and Commercial Auto policies has to do with the loading and unloading of cargo. The CGL provides liability coverage on the goods until they are removed from the loading dock to be loaded into the truck. At that point, Commercial Auto coverage takes over. The Commercial Auto policy provides coverage until the truck is unloaded. When the goods have been placed on the recipient's loading dock, Commercial Auto coverage stops and the CGL's starts.

- **Mobile Equipment Transported by an Auto** – Though normally covered by the CGL, mobile equipment is not covered while being transported by an auto. It is also not covered if it is being used in a racing or demolition contest.

- **War, Rebellion, Civil Commotion, or Revolution**

- **Your Property** – We have made the point that the CGL covers the Other Guy's property – not yours. However, this exclusion may be even broader than it might first appear. Under this exclusion, *your property* is defined as property that you own, occupy, or rent or that is in your care, custody, or control. Whether you own or lease your copier does not matter in insurance. Either way it is considered *your property* and is insured under your Commercial **Property** Policy.

owned, occupied, rented, care, custody, control

- **Your Product** – The CGL is not designed to serve as a product guarantee. If you sell a faulty toaster, the policy does not pay to replace it. However, if your toaster malfunctions and electrocutes the Other Guy (BI) and burns down his house (PD), the policy will pay for that damage. However, it still will not pay for the toaster itself – that's your product, and your problem.

not a guarantee

- **Property in Your Care, Custody, Or Control** – As you saw above, the CGL does not cover your product. It also does not cover your work on the Other Guy's property. Suppose you are a plumber and you are repairing a leaky toilet bowl (real property). If you break the toilet bowl (in your control), water damage to the floor or hallway (PD) is covered. If the Other Guy slips on the water and breaks his leg (BI), that's covered. However, the toilet bowl itself is not covered.

  The same thing is true of the Other Guy's personal property in your control. If you were a TV repairman and caused the Other Guy's TV to explode in his living room, the CGL would cover damage to the Other Guy's body and all of his property **except the television**.

  NOTE: Obviously, the CGL does not provide complete coverage for the plumber or repairman. Theoretically, either could purchase a Bailee's Liability policy to cover items in his care, custody or control.

need a bailee's policy

- **Impaired Property** – The CGL does not cover property that has not sustained physical injury or that cannot be used or is rendered useless by your product or your work. Suppose you install a new furnace in the Other Guy's motel in June. In October when he turns it on, it doesn't work and he cannot rent rooms for a week. Since there was no physical injury to the rooms, there would not be any coverage.

  There is, however, one set of circumstances in which the loss of use of the rooms would be covered. If the loss is the result of **sudden and accidental** physical injury caused by your product or work, there is coverage. If, in the above example, you installed the furnace in November and it exploded and caused the Other Guy to lose room rental, there would be coverage for the loss of use of the guest rooms. This would be true even if the guest rooms were untouched by the explosion.

more

DICE

- **Product Recalls** – Sometimes called the ***Sistership Exclusion***, this eliminates coverage for the cost of product recalls. Suppose that Joe sells homemade salad dressing in his gift shop. Two hundred bottles in one batch were bad and have already triggered a dozen bodily injury claims. If the government orders a recall of all two hundred bottles, the CGL will not pay the recall costs. Remember, the CGL is not designed to insure the fitness or quality of your product or your work; it is designed to pay for bodily injury or property damage that is caused by your product or your work. Coverage for the cost of recalls can be purchased by endorsement.

no recalls

Notes

COVERAGE B – Personal and Advertising Injury Liability

1 The second major coverage of the CGL is Coverage B. Coverage B does for broken reputations what Coverage A did for broken arms. Coverage B never covers bodily injury or property damage. It only covers damage to the Other Guy's good name, his business reputation, the public's image of his product and his good feelings about himself. Words like libel, slander, false arrest, malicious prosecution, wrongful entry and wrongful eviction should spring to mind when you see the words *Personal Injury*.

Not Eligible

2 As we saw with the liquor liability exclusion for liquor stores earlier, again we have the situation where the businesses that need this coverage the most don't get it under the basic CGL. Advertising agencies, publishers, broadcasters and telecasters simply get no Coverage B under the CGL. Their exposure is considered to be so great that a more specialized (and more expensive) coverage must be purchased.

". . .sure, but you could buy it back. . ."

3 The kind of exposure this coverage was designed for is a non-communications business, such as Joe's Restaurant. If Joe loudly accuses the banker of stealing from his salad bar, we have Personal Injury, and we have coverage. If Joe's Restaurant misrepresents a competitor or steals an advertising idea, that is Advertising Injury and there is coverage.

Coverage B Exclusions

4 The exclusions under Coverage B are few, and those that are enumerated in the policy are straight to the point.

- **Lies** – Statements made or published that the Insured knew beforehand were false.

common sense

- **Prior Statements** – Statements made or published before the policy period.
- **Willful Violation** – Statements made or published that were a willful violation of the law.
- **Contractual Liability** – Though the CGL does cover contractual liability under Coverage A (BI and PD), it does not cover liability assumed by contract in the area of Personal Injury.
- **Breach of Contract**
- **Overpromises** – Statements made or published that overpromised the value of the goods or services.
- **Price Errors**

COVERAGE C –
Premises or Operations Medical Payments

As we have discussed, Med Pay covers medical expenses to an injured third party
1 without regard to legal liability. The injury must be a Premises or Operations type of loss, and Med Pay functions like goodwill insurance.

2 The CGL allows for Medical Payments for expenses incurred within **one year** of the date of the accident.

3 As we have already noted, Med Pay does not pay for such things as loss of earnings or pain and suffering. However, the term *medical expenses* is a little broader than most people would think. *Medical expenses* include:

- First aid
- Medical, surgical, x-ray and dental services.
- Necessary ambulance, hospital, and nursing services.
- Funeral expenses

not the same as bodily injury

Medical Payments (Coverage C) Exclusions

- **Insureds** – Remember, this is for the "Other Guy"
- **Employees** – Covered by Workers Compensation – not your CGL
- **Tenants** – If you are a landlord and have a CGL on your apartment building, your Med Pay won't cover a tenant who falls down in his apartment.
- **Athletics** – Anyone injured while taking part in athletics.
- **Products or Completed Operations** types of losses are excluded. Remember, this is **Premises** or **Operations** Med Pay.
- **All Previous Exclusions** – All Coverage A exclusions are also excluded under Coverage C, such as Intentional Acts.
- **War**

Notes

SUPPLEMENTARY PAYMENTS (for Coverages A and B)

1 We have just discussed the first three coverages (A, B, and C) of the CGL. Now we can address the Supplementary Payments section of the CGL, which is one of the most valuable portions of any liability policy.

2 Its benefits include:

- **Defense costs**

other stuff

- All other expenses incurred in investigating or settling the claim.
- Reasonable expenses you incur at the company's request in assisting their defense efforts – including loss of earnings of up to $250 a day.

The Lawyers of America thank you

- The cost of appeal bonds and attachment bonds, but the company is not responsible for actually providing the bonds.
- Any interest awards made to the Other Guy to offset the time between the occurrence or the judgment and the actual payment of damages.

3 Congratulations! You have just finished the biggest chunk of the CGL policy. We didn't tell you up front that the policy is comprised of five sections. Since you've made it this far, we know this additional information won't fry your circuits. So, here it is:

I. Coverages
II. Who Is An Insured?
III. Limits of Insurance
IV. CGL Conditions
V. Definitions

4 Obviously, you can check off Section I from your list – we just covered it. Now, we'll turn our attention to the next four sections.

Notes

SECTION II – WHO IS AN INSURED?

1 In order for you to understand this section of the CGL, you may need a little background in how businesses can be structured. There are essentially three ways to organize a business.

2 **Sole Proprietorship** – Under this arrangement, your business is no different than any other asset you own – your house, car, or bank account. If the business fails, your creditors can attempt to take your non-business assets to pay your debts. From a liability standpoint, you and your spouse are vulnerable . . . even if your spouse has absolutely nothing to do with your business.

spouse too

3 **Partnership** – This is only an extension of the sole proprietorship, but now there are several individuals involved. From the liability standpoint, things are probably even worse. Not only are your personal assets vulnerable if you are sued for your own actions, but now you can be sued for the actions of a partner.

4 **Corporation** – The main advantage of a corporation is the separation of your business assets from your personal assets. If you own a corporation that fails, your personal assets are not fair game for the business creditors. From a liability perspective, the corporation is being sued, not you. Therefore your personal assets (and those of your spouse) are not vulnerable.

5 Since the need for liability insurance varies with the type of business structure, the CGL addresses all three in answering the question, "Who is an Insured?"

- **Sole Proprietorship** – You and your spouse.
- **Partnership, Joint Venture or Limited Liability Company** – You, your partners and your spouses.
- **Corporation** – You, your executive officers, directors and stockholders.

6 NOTE: In all three cases, **employees are also Insureds** for acts within the scope of their employment.

Employees only in the scope of their employment

7 Your CGL would not cover bodily injury to you or your employees, nor would it cover damage done by an employee to your property. Remember, in liability insurance we are talking about damage you or your employees do to the Other Guy's body and the Other Guy's property.

Next Steps

I. Coverages
II. Who Is An Insured?
III. Limits of Insurance
IV. CGL Conditions
V. Definitions

Notes

SECTION III – LIMITS OF INSURANCE

1 Section I told us **what** is covered by the CGL and Section II told us **who** is an Insured. Now, Section III is going to define how far the company will go dollar-wise in covering the damages for which the Insured is legally responsible.

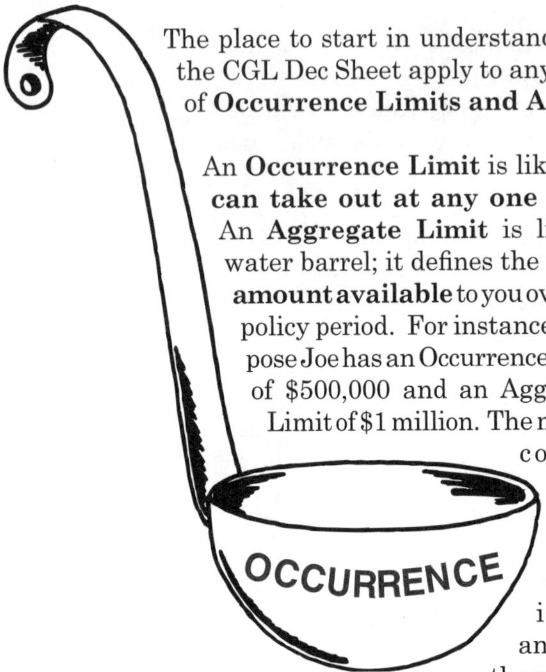

2 The place to start in understanding how the dollar limits shown on the CGL Dec Sheet apply to any particular claim is with the concept of **Occurrence Limits and Aggregate Limits.**

An **Occurrence Limit** is like a water dipper; it is the **most you can take out at any one time**. An **Aggregate Limit** is like a water barrel; it defines the **total amount available** to you over the policy period. For instance, suppose Joe has an Occurrence Limit of $500,000 and an Aggregate Limit of $1 million. The most the company would pay for any one occurrence is $500,000, and the most that could be paid out over the policy period is $1 million.

GENERAL AGGREGATE

OCCURRENCE

Occurrence dipper

Aggregate Bucket

3 As the Agent, you have to raise two questions with Joe:

1) What is the greatest dollar damage that could possibly happen in any one occurrence?

2) How many times during the policy period could this happen?

4 It is with those two answers that adequate limits can be established.

5 NOTE: The Insured may, by endorsement, select separate aggregate limits for individual locations, either owned or rented. Similarly, the Insured could also by endorsement select special aggregate limits for individual projects away from their premises.

6 In the CGL, there is an **Occurrence Limit** which limits the amount that could be paid out for any one incident for the total of:

- **Bodily Injury,**
- **Property Damage,**
- **Medical Payments and**
- **Fire Legal Liability**.

7 There is also a **General Aggregate** which is the maximum to be paid out in any policy period for **all losses**, except Products - Completed Operations claims. (Products - Completed Operations has its own Aggregate Limit as we will see shortly.) Every other kind of loss – Premises, Operations, Med Pay, Fire Legal – counts against the General Aggregate Limit.

not products - completed operations

GENERAL AGGREGATE LIMIT

1 A business with no Products - Completed Operations exposure might have limits of the following:

- General Aggregate – $1 million ($1 M) per policy period
- Personal and Advertising Injury – $500,000 ($500 K) per person or organization
- Occurrence – $500,000 ($500 K) per occurrence
- Fire Legal – $50,000 ($50 K) per fire
- Medical Payments – $5,000 ($5 K) per person

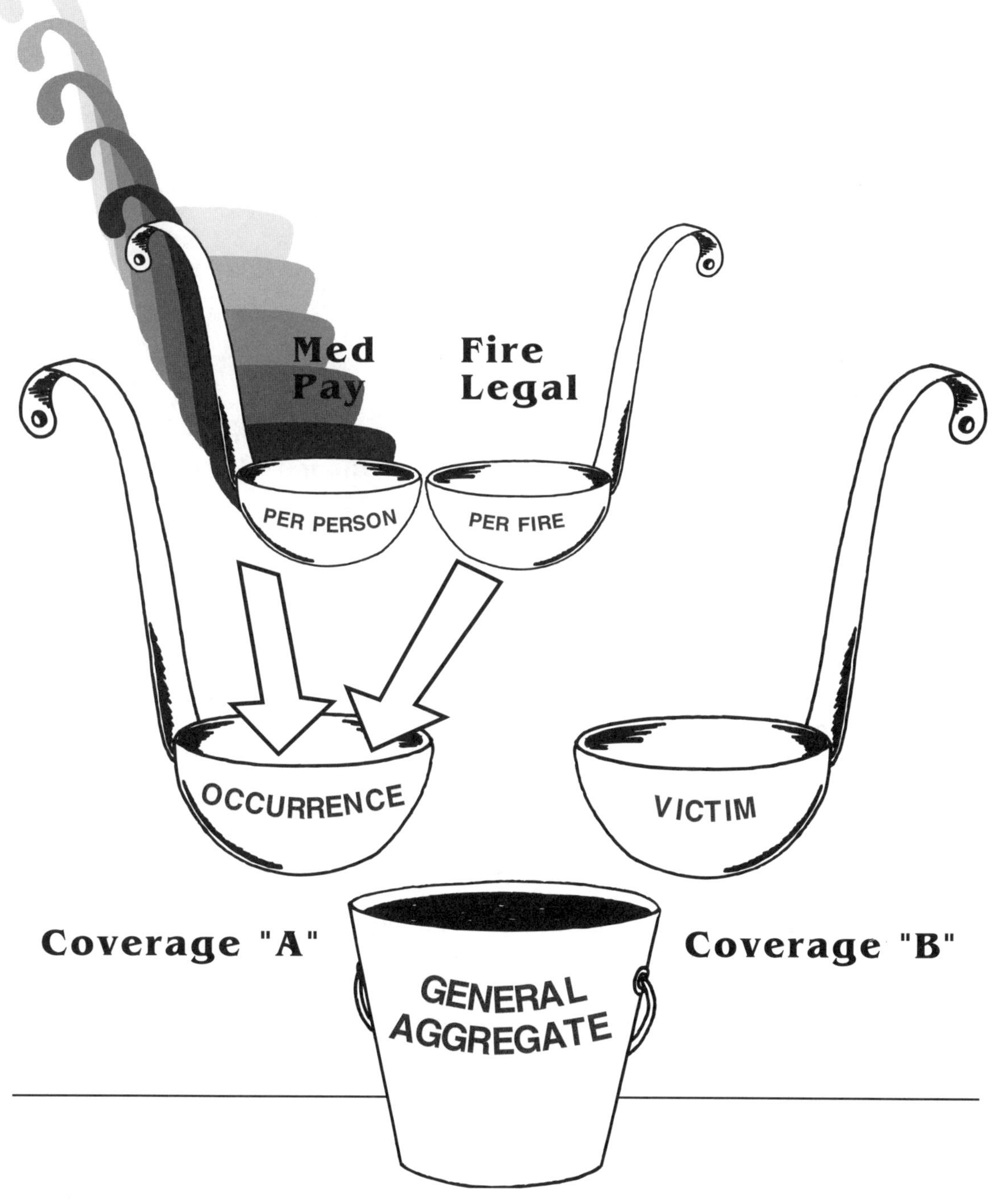

Let's suppose that Joe's sister, Flo, operates a bookstore in a rented building. She
1 negligently starts a fire that does $60,000 worth of damage to the building and injures eight people. Six of those eight people are slightly injured. Five present Med Pay claims in the amount of $4,000 each. The sixth person presents a claim for $7,000. The other two were so severely injured that they by-passed Med Pay, sued Flo and were awarded $100,000 each.

How would the claim be paid? Since Med Pay pays without regard to liability, it
2 always pays first. Therefore, let's start with Med Pay. The five people with $4,000 claims are all under the $5,000 per person limit. The guy with the $7,000 claim exceeds the limit, so he would be paid only to the $5,000 limit. For Med Pay then . . .

5 x $4,000 = $20,000 + $5,000 = $25,000

3 For the two bodily injury claims, the company would pay:

2 x $100,000 = $200,000

4 The fire damage claim is $60,000 but the limit is $50,000, so that is all that would be paid.

5 The total claim paid would be:

$ 25,000	Medical Payments
200,000	Bodily Injury Liability
50,000	Fire Legal
$275,000	Total

The Occurrence limit of $500,000 would easily allow for the payment of the $275,000
6 claim. Since no previous claims have been made against Flo's CGL, at this point, she still has her $1 million General Aggregate intact. After this $275,000 claim, however, her $1 million General Aggregate will be reduced to $725,000 but her Occurrence limit will return to the full $500,000. After all, the next incident would be a new occurrence.

What would have happened if previous claims had reduced her General Aggregate
7 to $200,000? Then only $200,000 would be paid out. The unpaid claimants would have to try to squeeze the money out of Flo. Now, you are probably wondering, "OK, but who gets paid and who gets stiffed for $75,000?" Well, we have already noted that Med Pay always pays first. Beyond that, **he who settles with the insurance company first, gets paid. He who wants to quibble does not.**

NOTE: In the above example, one individual was *shorted* $2,000 on his Medical
8 Payments claim due to the $5,000 limit. Could he sue Flo for his bodily injury damages and collect if she is legally liable? Yes, of course. If he were awarded $7,000, his check would be for $2,000 as he has already collected $5,000 under Med Pay. By the way, does Flo owe her landlord an additional $10,000 for damage to the building? Yes.

Notes

PRODUCTS - COMPLETED OPERATIONS AGGREGATE LIMIT

1 Now that we have seen how a business with no Products - Completed Operations exposure would establish its limits of liability, let's turn our attention to a business that does have this exposure. As a restaurant owner, Joe has a Products - Completed Operations exposure – the food he serves is a product. His limits might look like this:

has its own dipper and bucket

2 Same as before:

- General Aggregate – $1 million ($1 M) per policy period
- Personal and Advertising Injury – $500,000 ($500 K) per person or organization
- Occurrence – $500,000 ($500 K) per occurrence
- Fire Legal – $50,000 ($50 K) per fire
- Medical Payments – $5,000 ($5 K) per person

3 New:

- Products - Completed Operations Aggregate – $1 M per policy period
- Products - Completed Operations Occurrence – $500 K per occurrence

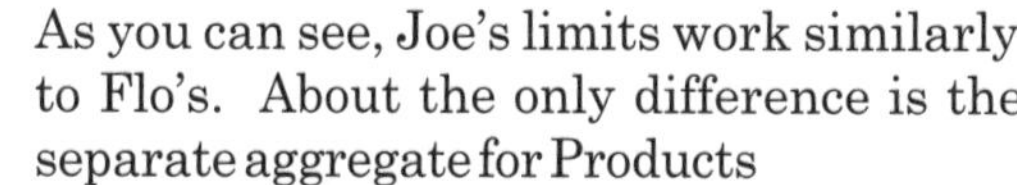

4 As you can see, Joe's limits work similarly to Flo's. About the only difference is the separate aggregate for Products - Completed Operations. If a loss is a Products or Completed Operations type of loss, it is paid out of the Products - Completed Operations Aggregate subject to the Occurrence Limit. A loss under Products - Completed Operations would not deplete the General Aggregate and vice versa. While there is no absolute rule, generally, the two Aggregate limits match.

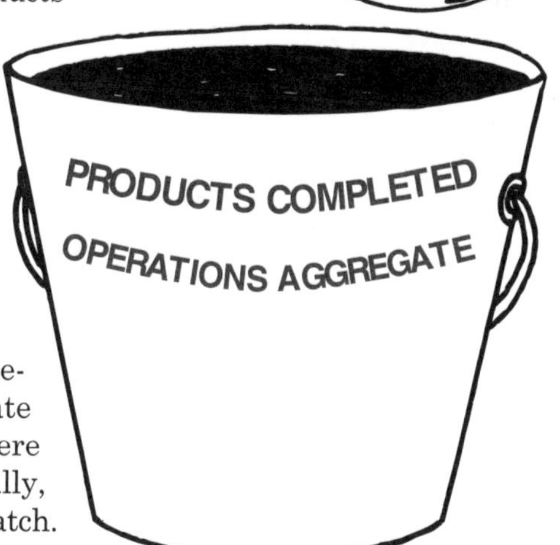

Next Steps

I. Coverages
II. Who Is An Insured?
III. Limits of Insurance
IV. CGL Conditions
V. Definitions

Notes

SECTION IV – CGL CONDITIONS

1 As we pointed out earlier, the Conditions section of the CGL is built right into the coverage form rather than existing as a separate piece of paper as was the case with Commercial Property. These are the *do's and don't's* important to both the company and the CGL policyowner.

ground rules

2 **Premium Audit** – As the premium for a CGL is based upon factors that may change over the policy period (square footage, number of employees, gross revenues, types of products, etc.), the premium paid is considered a **premium deposit**. The company will compute the actual **earned premium** at the end of each audit period (normally annually). Obviously, adjustments could require more premium to be paid or allow for a premium refund. The First Named Insured is obligated to keep appropriate records for premium computation and to submit them to the company upon request.

3 **Bankruptcy** – Bankruptcy of the Insured does not relieve the insurance company of its obligations.

4 **Duties In The Event Of A Loss** – Prompt notification and full cooperation with the company are required. You may not, except at your own cost, voluntarily make any payment, assume any obligation or incur any expense (except first aid) without the company's consent.

pull your own weight

5 **Legal Action Against Us** – The Insured is restricted from suing the company until he or she has complied with all terms of the policy. Also, this section limits an injured party's right to sue the company for damages until after those damages have been established by settlement or judgment.

6 **Other Insurance** – This section applies only to Coverage A (BI and PD) and Coverage B (Personal and Advertising Injury). Coverage C (Med Pay) is not truly part of this discussion due to the nature of Med Pay. Since it pays immediately and without regard to fault, the Med Pay section of the CGL is always considered primary and is not affected by other coverages.

7 With few exceptions, the CGL is considered the **primary** coverage. If that is the case, the CGL pays as if no other insurance exists and any other policy pays as **excess** insurance – it pays for damages that exceed the CGL limits. In the rare cases where the CGL is excess, we reverse the process.

8 If, by chance, there are two **primary** coverages, there are two possibilities for sharing the claim.

> **1st Choice – Equal Shares** – Each company contributes equally to the loss regardless of its proportionate coverage.

50/50

> **2nd Choice – Contribute by Limits (Pro Rata)** – Each company pays its share based upon the ratio of its coverage limits to the total amount of insurance in force.

1 **Representations** – By accepting the policy, the Insured agrees that all statements made in the application are true to the best of his or her knowledge and belief.

Separation of Insureds – Except for the limits of insurance, CGL coverage applies
2 as if each named Insured were the only named Insured and applies separately to
each Insured against whom a claim is made.

3 **Transfer of Rights of Recovery** – The Insured may do nothing to impair the company's rights of subrogation.

Next Steps

I. Coverages
II. Who Is An Insured?
III. Limits of Insurance
IV. CGL Conditions
V. Definitions

SECTION V – DEFINITIONS

The CGL concludes with a Definitions section. To aid in our discussion of the
4 contract, we have already given you those definitions as we encountered the terms
in the policy. In your work as an Agent, however, you may need to know that the
important terms of the CGL are defined in Section V.

CGL OPTIONAL ENDORSEMENTS

There are numerous endorsements that can be added to the CGL. Many are used
5 to eliminate coverages that are not necessary in order to lower the premium, and
others are used to add coverages for exposures excluded under the basic policy.

OCCURRENCE vs. CLAIMS-MADE POLICIES

Historically, general liability policies have been written on an **Occurrence** basis.
6 Put simply, the policy that covered the risk **when the hurt happened** paid the
claim. If a policy covered your business in 1985, it paid for any 1985 "hurt" – even
if a claim was not filed until 1990.

Occurrence - when was the hurt?

From the viewpoint of the insurance company, there were several drawbacks to this
7 approach. Most importantly, ***there was never really an end to the risk***. The
company could not be sure that a claim against a 1985 policy might not show up in 1990. Another drawback under an Occurrence approach is a problem for *Insureds – inflation*. Suppose that you have been a toy manufacturer for 20 years and that you have had Products Liability coverage for the entire period. If you were sued today for injury sustained by a child in 1978, your 1978 policy would be the operable coverage. In 1978 you might have had $100,000 of coverage (adequate at that time) and today you have $5 million. Unfortunately, the applicable limits are the 1978 limits even though that amount might be grossly inadequate in today's legal climate.

Notes
Claims made - when was the claim?

1 For these reasons, the **Claims-Made** approach was developed. The coverage of a Claims-Made policy is **triggered by the claim, not the occurrence**. Suppose you had Policy X in effect in 1987 and Policy Y in 1988.

1987 Policy X
1988 Policy Y

2 Under a Claims-Made policy, if something happens in '87 which provokes a claim first filed in '88, it would be paid by Policy Y because it was in effect when the claim was made. This solves the two problems of the Occurrence approach we have just addressed – no end to the risk and inflation.

3 On the other hand, the Claims-Made approach creates some new problems for Insureds and for Agents. Before we address the unique problems and solutions to those problems for the Claims-Made forms, we should point out that the Occurrence vs. Claims-Made question really only affects two of the three CGL coverages: Coverage A (Bodily Injury and Property Damage) and Coverage B (Advertising and Personal Injury). **However, with either the Occurrence or Claims-Made form, Coverage C (Med Pay) is only written on an Occurrence basis.**

UNIQUE PROBLEMS OF CLAIMS-MADE FORMS

What Is A Claim?

4 Since the coverage of a Claims-Made form is triggered by *a claim first made against any Insured during the policy period*, we must precisely define the actions that constitute a *claim*.

5 A claim is first made when notice of the claim is received by any Insured or by the insurance company, whichever comes first. All claims for bodily injury and/or property damage to the same person are considered *first made* at the time the initial claim is made.

When Does Coverage Start?

6 In a traditional insurance policy, we have a definite start date and termination date, which outline when coverage exists. If a *hurt* happened between those dates, you had coverage. In a Claims-Made policy, however, the focus is not on when the hurt happened, but on when the claim was made. Therefore, it is quite possible for a Claims-Made policy written today to cover occurrences from last year, the year before that, or from the beginning of time for that matter. Obviously, a Claims-Made policy with no limit on how far back in time we would go would be taking on a major exposure. Assume we have a toy manufacturer who has been in business for 10 years with **no Products Liability** coverage. If we sold him a Claims-Made policy today with no time restriction, that policy would be covering a 10 year exposure. While that would be desirable from the Insured's viewpoint and possibly acceptable to the company, it would be a big exposure and rates would be established accordingly.

Notes

Retroactive Date

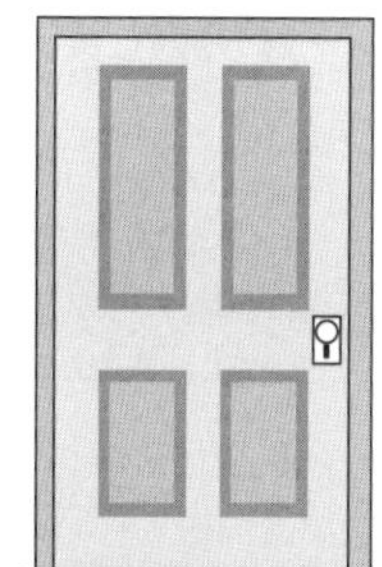

Retroactive date shuts the back door

1 A policy device called the *Retroactive Date* allows the company and the Insured to establish exactly how far back in time the company will go to cover past hurts. **The policy will pay no claims for occurrences prior to the Retroactive Date** – even if the claim is made during the policy period. If it were desirable (as in the above case) to pick up all previous years, you could enter *None* (as the Retroactive Date) in the Declarations.

2 If the policyowner has been adequately covered in the past by an Occurrence policy, then he already has coverage for claims that are reported today for occurrences in the past. In this case, the Retroactive Date should be set as the date of the first Claims-Made policy.

3 If, however, the policyowner had a continuum of Occurrence policies but was worried that the limits might be too low, he could still choose None as the Retroactive Date. The policy would cost more, but the new Claims-Made policy would provide excess insurance over the prior Occurrence policy limits.

4 **Normally, if a Claims-Made policy is replacing an Occurrence policy, the Retroactive Date would be the date of the new policy.** There would be no coverage gap under this arrangement. However, there would be a dangerous coverage gap if, in future years, the Retroactive Date were moved forward as the Claims-Made policy is renewed. Suppose, for example, that your first Claims-Made policy was written for the calendar year 1993 with a Retroactive Date of 1/1/93. Upon renewal, suppose the Retro Date is moved forward to 1/1/94. A claim submitted against you in 1994 for an occurrence in 1993 would not be covered by either your '93 or your '94 policy. The '93 policy won't pay because the claim wasn't made in '93, and the '94 policy won't pay because the Retro Date was moved forward and established that we would not pay for anything before 1/1/94.

5 Because of the danger involved in moving a Retroactive Date forward in Claims-Made policies, it can only be done with the written consent of the Insured and only for one of the following reasons:

- A change from one insurance company to another.
- A substantial change in the Insured's operations that increases the risk.
- The Insured fails to provide material information requested by the company.
- The Insured requests the change.

Don't leave holes in coverage

6 Why would an Agent be tempted to move a Retroactive Date forward? In a word – **price**. There is significantly reduced risk to the company in the first year of a Claims-Made policy and the premium is substantially lower. It is only after about five years that the risk has matured and requires the full premium rate. If an Agent is only concerned with underbidding the competition, he or she could move the Retro Date forward and do the client a major disservice in the process.

Notes

What Covers Me When The Policy Ends?

1 The other significant problem with the Claims-Made policy comes at the end of the policy period. Assume that your business was covered by Claims-Made policies for the last five years that you were in business. Today, you retire and close the business. What about . . .

- A claim that is made against you two days after the policy ended? *put a tail on it*
- An incident that happened on the last day that the policy was in effect, for which you reported the loss two days after the policy expired, and for which the claim was not filed until five years later?
- A claim that comes out of nowhere eight years after the policy expired?

2 With what you know to this point, all you could say is that there is no coverage. Obviously, this omission would just about eliminate Claims-Made coverage as a reasonable insurance product. A device called an **Extended Reporting Period** (ERP) has been created to solve these problems.

Basic ERP

3 The Basic ERP is an extension of the **reporting period**, not the coverage period. The occurrence must have taken place after the Retroactive Date and before the end of the policy period. The Basic ERP is provided **automatically and without additional charge**. It only provides coverage if no other insurance applies to the claim and cannot be used as excess insurance.

4 The Basic ERP offers two benefits:

Mini-Tail – Provides an additional 60 days after the policy period to report any claims. *mini - 60 days*

Midi-Tail – If notice of a claim is received within 60 days of policy termination, then the claimant has up to five years to file the claim. *midi - 5 years*

Supplemental ERP

5 We still have not covered the claim that came out of nowhere eight years after the policy period ended. This is the purpose of the Supplemental ERP. It **extends the reporting period forever**. It is added by endorsement and there is a charge for this coverage that may not exceed 200% of the last annual premium for the policy. It can pay as excess insurance if any other policy provides coverage. Since there is no time limit on this reporting period, it is sometimes known as **Full-Tail** or **Maxi-Tail** coverage.

full. . .
. . .forever

...IF... purchased within 60 days

Notes

OTHER LIABILITY POLICIES

COMMERCIAL UMBRELLA POLICIES

As you recall, Umbrella policies are relatively inexpensive. This is because most
1 claims are still small claims. The Umbrella policy gets hit hard when it does get
hit, but most claims are adequately covered by the basic policies.

2 **There are really only four basic things to remember about Commercial Umbrellas:**

- **Excess amounts**
- **No standard form**
- **Uneven at the top**
- **Broadens as well as deepens**

3 **Excess Amounts** – Umbrellas are written for excessive amounts – $1 million, $5 million, $10 million and more.

Big Bucks

No Standard Form – Though Umbrella coverage is readily available today, almost
4 every company writing Umbrellas has a few unique twists in its contracts. Therefore, everything in this discussion should be taken in the most general of terms.

No Standard

Uneven At The Top – Since the rating of Umbrella policies is dependent upon the
5 underlying coverages absorbing most of the losses, the Umbrella carrier literally dictates which basic coverages you must have if you are to be eligible for the Umbrella.

Add primary to umbrella

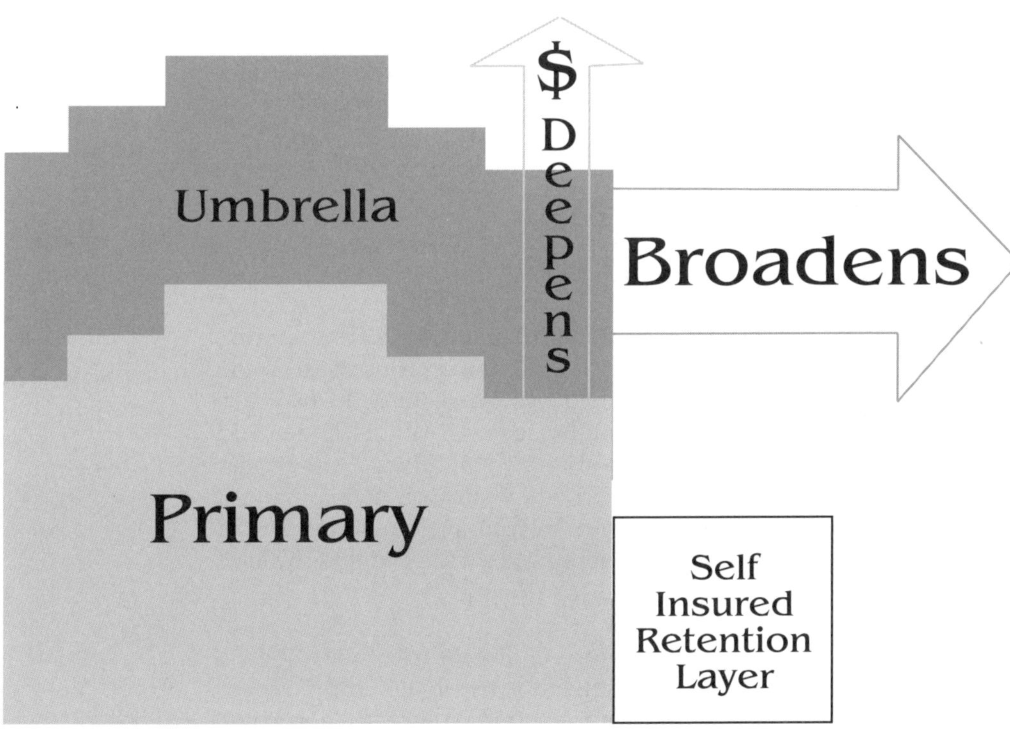

Notes

1 Joe's restaurant might have the following Liability coverages:

- Liquor Liability $1,500,000
- General Aggregate $1,000,000
- Commercial Auto $ 750,000
- Products Aggregate $ 500,000

2 If he also owns a $5 million Commercial Umbrella, then his limits become:

- Liquor Liability $6,500,000
- General Aggregate $6,000,000
- Commercial Auto $5,750,000
- Products Aggregate $5,500,000

3 Coverage is **uneven at the top** because it is **uneven at the bottom**.

4 **Broadens As Well As Deepens** – Without this final characteristic, there are actually two products that would do everything discussed so far:

- Excess Liability policy
- Umbrella liability policy

5 The difference between these two contracts is that the **Excess Liability policy will never pay unless the underlying policy pays first.**

6 Suppose that Joe finds himself doing a local cooking show on television. One Saturday morning he gets carried away and speaks disparagingly of a competitive restaurant. If he is sued by the injured party, his CGL would probably deny coverage on the grounds that Joe is now in the business of telecasting.

7 If the CGL did not pay, the **Excess Liability would not pay**. The Umbrella would, however, **broaden** to cover this advertising injury loss. Joe would be responsible for first paying the **Self -Insured Retention**, which is essentially a large deductible. This could be set at a level of $50,000 or $100,000 for a small business like Joe's and much higher amounts for larger enterprises.

Workers Compensation and Employers Liability Policies

8 In America today, the Workers Compensation system is a compromise. Essentially, workers give up the right to sue their employers for job-related injuries in exchange for quick sure payment of benefits. For covered employees, Workers Comp becomes the **exclusive remedy** for job-related accidents and diseases. All fifty states and the federal government now have some form of Workers Comp plan. Under most of these arrangements, the benefits are funded by private insurance companies or a competitive state fund and sold in a **competitive marketplace**. Five states (North Dakota, Ohio, Washington, West Virginia, and Wyoming) provide benefits through a state operated **monopoly**.

On the job. . . injury and . . . illness. . . "no fault"

9 In all jurisdictions, Workers Comp is **required** for employers with more than a minimum number of employees. Depending upon the laws of the state, owner-employees or partners may be covered. In most jurisdictions, there are also some **exempt employments**. For example, in most states you do not have to cover domestic servants, casual workers, or certain agricultural workers.

Notes

Some more dangerous... premium upped by "Modification Factors"

1 You might wonder if there is anything good about Workers Comp from the employer's viewpoint. Well, yes there is. Since Workers Comp is the exclusive remedy for employment-related injuries and sicknesses, an injured employee or his family may not generally sue the employer for millions of dollars - they must simply accept the benefits of Workers Comp as set (normally) by the legislature in each state.

2 The Workers Comp laws provide for four types of benefits.

- **Medical Expense** benefits - dollars to fix your body. May state inside limits, but overall medical benefits are unlimited in every state. Unlimited dollars, unlimited time.

- **Disability Income** benefits - to replace your income subject to rather low maximums.

- **Death** benefits - pays a small amount to bury you and then pays a specified sum to your survivors.

- **Rehabilitation** benefits - gets you back to work.

Frequency of claims impacts premium more than severity of claims

3 One very real problem for employers is the hiring of handicapped employees. If an employee with two eyes loses sight in one eye, the employees becomes partially disabled. If the same accident happened to an employee with sight in one eye to begin with, the second employee becomes totally disabled. Regrettably, the handicapped employee is a higher risk in Workers Comp.

4 To encourage employers to hire employees with a handicap, all states have established **second injury funds** that are designed to pay all or most of the additional benefits that a second injury would require. Therefore, employers have no disincentive to hire the handicapped.

5 The standard Comp Policy plugs up the hole left by the injuries to employees exclusions found in the CGL. It has three coverage parts:

Part 1 – Workers Compensation
Pays those benefits due under the laws of the states listed in the declarations.

Part 2 – Employers Liability
Pays for liability imposed by law, but not covered under Part 1.

Part 3 – Other States Coverage
Pays those claims that arise under the laws of those states not named under Parts 1 and 2. However, in order to be covered under Part 3, t**he state must have been listed in the Other States section of the policy declarations.**

Notes

WORKERS COMPENSATION (Part 1)

1 The **insuring agreement** of this section simply states that the policy will "pay all sums due the benefits required of you by the workers compensation laws." Coverage is for **bodily injury** caused by either **accident** or **disease**.

on the job -occupational-

2 What is bodily injury? Interestingly, the policy does not define this term. One major source of litigation at the present time is whether or not mental stress is bodily injury. The states are divided at the present time, with the majority holding that bodily injury does not include mental stress.

3 In order to cover injuries arising out of an accident, the accident must have occurred during the policy period. For injuries caused by disease, the disease must be caused by or aggravated by a condition of employment. The employee's last exposure to the condition must have taken place during the policy period.

4 Coverage under this section is only for state workers compensation claims. **Federal claims** are only covered **by endorsement**.

5 Federal Workers Comp plans include:

Federal Employer Liability Act- railroad workers
Longshore & Harbor Workers Act - longshoreman and harbor workers
Jones Act- seamen
Outer Continental Shelf Lands Act- offshore oil rig workers

EMPLOYERS LIABILITY (Part 2)

6 This coverage is for injuries arising out of the course of employment in the states listed in the policy declarations but for some reason are not covered by Workers Compensation. Although Workers Compensation is generally considered to be an exclusive remedy, i.e., employees don't have the choice to sue or take Comp – they must take Comp, there are cases where this coverage is valuable. For instance if an employee were injured due to the willful and wanton behavior of the employer, the courts in some states might allow the employee to waive Comp and sue the employer. If the employee's suit was successful, Part 2 would pay.

Basic Policy Limit

7 The standard limit for Employers Liability Coverage is $100,000 per accident. For disease related claims, the limit is $100,000 per employee, with an aggregate of $500,000. Higher limits are available.

$100,000

Premium based upon payroll

8 Employers Liability exclusions include:

Intentional injuries

Workers Comp claims, both state and federal

Contractual liability

Claims arising from demotion, termination, etc.

Punitive damages, fines, and penalties

Notes

OTHER STATES COVERAGE (Part 3)

1 An employer in State A has employees covered under a Workers Comp contract approved by State A. Infrequently, some of the employees do work in State B and, on one of these occasions, an employee sustains an on-the-job injury. The injury is of such a nature that the State A policy does not cover it. However, State B's laws would require coverage. If, and only if, State B were listed on the Dec Sheet under Other States, Part 3 of the policy, could the claim be paid.

Other Policy Parts

2 While the first three parts of the policy outline the coverages, there are three remaining sections which govern the operation of the contract.

Part 4- Duties of the Insured

Notice of Injury to the Carrier
Cooperation in Claim Investigation and Settlement
Aid in any Third Party Recovery

Part 5- Premium

3 This part set out the methods of premium calculation. Workers are classified according to risk. The classifications are listed as well as the premium for each. This section also advises the Insured that the premium is estimated and that the Insured's records are subject to audit...which may result in a premium adjustment. Premiums may also be adjusted by the claims history of a particular Insured. This is called **Experience rating**.

4 Many states allow companies to **discount** premiums for larger Insureds to reflect the reductions in per capita administration costs. Although regulated by state law, the basic rule is *the bigger the group, the better the deal.*

Part 6- Conditions

5 Nothing new and different here.

Voluntary Compensation Endorsement

6 In most states, there are employments that do not fall under the Workers Comp laws - sole proprietors, domestics, agricultural workers. This endorsement allows the employer to pull those employees into Workers Comp coverage within the limits of that particular state. The affected employees must sign a waiver foregoing their right to sue and accepting Workers Comp as their sole remedy for on the job injury.

Notes

PROFESSIONAL LIABILITY INSURANCE ALSO KNOWN AS ERRORS AND OMISSIONS

1 Despite the breadth of coverage offered under the CGL, there is no Professional Liability coverage. Because of the high standards of performance imposed today by professional codes, regulations and statutes as well as the decisions of the courts, professionals are held more accountable for their mistakes than ever before. Professionals who are concerned about their legal liability resulting from negligence or errors and omissions in their professional service should purchase a **Professional Liability Policy**. There are as many Professional Liability Policies as there are professions. Included are Medical Professional, Lawyers Professional and Agents and Brokers (E&O). **Professional Liability policies have no standard form**.

"E&O"

2 The Professional Liability policy replaces the concept of the Reasonable Person with that of the Reasonable Professional. To establish professional liability, the question that must be answered is "What would the reasonable professional (doctor, lawyer or whatever) do under the same or similar circumstances?"

3 You might be surprised by some of the occupations that need Professional Liability insurance today: accountants, architects, barbers and beauticians, chiropractors, insurance Agents, engineers, lawyers, nurses, optometrists, pharmacists, physicians, surgeons, dentists, real estate Agents, and veterinarians.

4 Professional Liability policies never cover fraudulent, dishonest or criminal acts, and the policies are tailored to the nature of the profession insured. Many professionals (like lawyers or insurance Agents) could only damage their clients financially. Therefore, Bodily Injury and Property Damage are excluded. But an architect or engineer could make an error that does cause Bodily Injury or Property Damage, and therefore, BI and PD are covered in polices sold to professionals in the construction trades.

5 Because the **Claims-Made forms** solve the inflation problem so easily, almost all Professional Liability policies are written on this basis. Because a settlement could damage an Insured's professional reputation, some contracts require the company to get permission to **settle out of court**. These are known as **consent to settle** clauses.

Directors and Officers Liability Insurance

6 Directors and Officers coverage, commonly called D&O, became popular during the consumer revolution of the late 60's and early 70's. Unhappy stockholders began to bring claims against corporate directors and officers when investments did not grow as expected. These claims, referred to as stockholder derivative suits, allege that the corporation did not perform as expected because of mistakes made by directors and officers. D&O coverage protects not only the individuals involved, but also the corporation. **There is no standard D&O Form**

keywords - wrongful acts

Notes

1 Some unique characteristics of D&O coverage:

- D&O policies are claims-made.

claims made

- D&O claims are triggered by **wrongful acts** rather than on an accident or occurrence basis. Wrongful acts include misstatements made by the directors and officers, as well as neglect and breach of duty.

- D&O policies will pay only damages that the corporation would, under the law, be required to reimburse the individual director or officer. D&O policies generally will not pay for fines, penalties, or punitive damages.

no penalties

  NOTE: Punitive damages are designed to punish a wrongdoer and not to compensate an injured party.

- Unlike other liability policies, **D&O policies generally include defense costs within the policy limits**.

dangling slowly in the wind

Fiduciary Liability ‡

The Employee Retirement Income Security Act (ERISA) places rather clear duties
2 on the trustees of Employee Benefit Plans. The Fiduciary liability policy insures the "bad acts" of plan fiduciaries, trustees. There is no standard form; however, most companies construct policies with a $1,000 deductible and a $1,000,000 basic limit. The law requires that if the premiums are paid by the fund, the policy must allow for subrogation against the individual trustees involved in the loss.

Pollution Liability ‡

You will remember that the CGL does not cover Pollution losses. This is a reaction
3 to the astronomical sums which have been imposed under the pollution clean-up laws enacted in the 1980's, such as Superfund, or CERCLA, and similar state statutes.

4 There are three basic approaches an Insured can take to cover pollution risks:

Pollution Liability Coverage Endorsement

5 Added to the CGL it will cover bodily injury and property damage arising out of pollution, **but will still not cover the cost of government ordered clean up.**

Pollution Liability Coverage Form

6 This endorsement is:

Claims made
Has limits separate from the underlying policy
Excludes abandoned and closed dumpsites
Excludes waste disposal and treatment operations
Allows for clean up and prevention actions, with prior approval of the company

Notes

Pollution Liability Limited Coverage Form

1 Offers the same coverages as the above form except that it also only applies to Bodily Injury and Property Damage, and not clean up.

Underground Storage ‡

2 This policy provides BI and PD coverage for designated underground storage tanks. It does not cover the tank itself, the loss of the substance that leaked out, corrective action or fines and penalties. It is purely a Claims-Made Liability policy with a Retroactive Date which almost always coincides with the policy's start date.

Surety Bonds ‡

3 Surety bonds are **not** really insurance. However, because the payments are made to a third party, the Other Guy, we will discuss them in this chapter. There are three parties involved in each surety bond:

Principal- the Insured
Obligee- the Other Guy
Surety- the Bonding Company

4 Here's how Surety Bonds work. Joe (Principal) owes an obligation to Betty (Obligee). This obligation is backed by a bond written by Acme Insurance (Surety). Joe does not live up to his obligation. Betty suffers damages. Betty takes action against Joe. The bond only pays Betty if Joe cannot. **Unlike insurance, Surety Bonds only pay when the Insured's assets have been exhausted.**

Types of Surety Bonds

Judicial Bonds

5 These are bonds ordered by judges during the course of a lawsuit or other type of court action:

Executor and Administrator Bonds
Guardians Bonds
Attachment Bonds
Replenvin Bonds
Injunction Bonds
Appeal Bonds

ERISA... Fiduciary contract

Contract Bonds

6 These bonds are required to ensure that individuals perform their obligations under a contract:

Bid Bonds
Labor and Material Payment Bonds
Supply Bonds
Completion Bonds

License and Permit Bonds

1 This guarantees that the principal will indemnify the governmental agency that granted him a license of permit for any liability arising out of their professional activities.

Conclusion

Q: Can you tell me what **Commercial Liability insurance** does?

A: It protects you if you or your stuff hurts somebody else or their stuff and you are legally obligated to pay.

Q: If I am sued, what is the reason most often cited by the injured party as the reason for the suit?

A: Negligence.

Q: Can you explain?

A: Sure. To establish negligence we must prove you had a **duty** to the injured person or property; that you breached that **duty**; that your actions were the **proximate** cause of the loss and there were **financial damages**.

Q: If someone trips over a chair in my business what would you call that?

A: Clumsy.

Q: But I mean, what sort of liability exposure is that?

A: Oh, sorry. That would be **Premises Liability**.

Q: What if I am installing drywall in someone's house and hit them with a hammer?

A: That is **Operations Liability**.

Q: What if I am all done with the job and a piece of drywall falls down and hits somebody?

A: That is called **Completed Operations Liability**.

Q: Can you explain **Products Liability** to me?

A: Yes, I'm sure I can.

Q: Hello? Could you explain it to me now?

A: You bet. Guess I zoned out for a second. If you manufacture, distribute or sell a product that hurts someone it is **Products Liability**.

Q: Aren't there some interesting twists?

A: Yep. Let's say you're selling a saw.

Q: What kind of saw?

A: It doesn't matter. So someone is looking at it in your hardware store. While they are messing with it they cut off their fingers. Your hardware store's **Premises Liability** would be liable for the claim because the person is still on the premises. If, however, they took the saw home and cut off some fingers that would be **Products Liability**.

Q: What about food?

A: I'm not hungry, thanks.

Notes

Q: I mean, isn't food a little different?

A: Yes. When food is served in a restaurant it's **Products Liability**. Even though the person is consuming it on the premises it is still a **Products Liability** claim.

Q: What if I contract with someone to come into my business and while working in my business that person hurts one of my customers. Where would that liability exposure fall?

A: That is **Independent Contractors Liability**.

Q: What does **Contractual Liability** mean?

A: That means that as a condition of doing business with you, another company or organization insists that you first assume their liability.

Q: If I am leasing space in a building I don't own, what would I buy to protect the actual space I am occupying from fire damage stemming from my own negligence?

A: **Fire Legal Liability**.

Q: What is **Personal Injury Liability**?

A: If you defame someone's character, humiliate, maliciously prosecute, falsely imprison, or wrongfully evict them or if wrongful entry is involved then that is classified as **Personal Injury**. You hurt their person, not their body.

Q: How is that different from **Advertising Injury**?

A: **Advertising Injury** means you hurt the reputation of a business or you steal their trademark or copyright.

Q: How does a **Claims Made policy** differ from an **Occurrence policy**?

A: A **Claims Made policy** requires that the company providing coverage in the year the claim is made pay the claim, even if the actual incident happened several years earlier. An **Occurrence policy** requires that the company on the risk at the time of loss pay the claim, even if the claim is made several years later.

Q: What can you tell me about **Medical Payments**?

A: It was a bad 60's TV show starring Chad Everett.

Q: No, that was **Medical Center**, I'm talking about **Medical Payments**. You know, **Med Pay**?

A: Oh, of course, easy mistake to make. **Med Pay** pays for medical bills for those who are hurt on your **premises** or in connection with your **operations**. It is no fault. You do not need to be found legally liable in order for **Med Pay** to pay.

Notes

1 To this point, you have studied the two contracts which appear most frequently in a Commercial Package policy... Property and Liability. It probably would not surprise you that the third biggie is Commercial Auto for businesses that use autos in their operations. Commercial Auto, like Personal Auto, has both Property and Casualty coverages. Therefore, a possible profile at this point might look like the following:

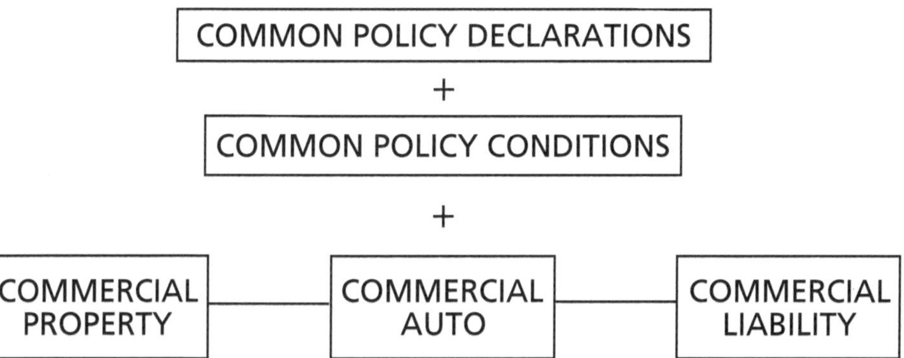

2 As we move through the next several chapters you will see four more contracts that can be part of the Commercial Package. Why are they necessary? Mostly because the three *main* policies are not adequate for some businesses. Commercial Property policies provide no coverage for cash or employee theft. A bank would also need Commercial Crime to cover those exposures. Commercial Property does not cover boiler explosion or mechanical breakdown, therefore, a steam powered factory would need Equipment Breakdown. Commercial Property provides little off-premises coverage... a caterer needs Inland Marine. Neither Commercial Property nor Commercial Casualty fully addresses the needs of a farmer... hence the need for the Farm coverage contract.

3 With these ideas in mind, the profile we will build over the next several chapters will look like this:

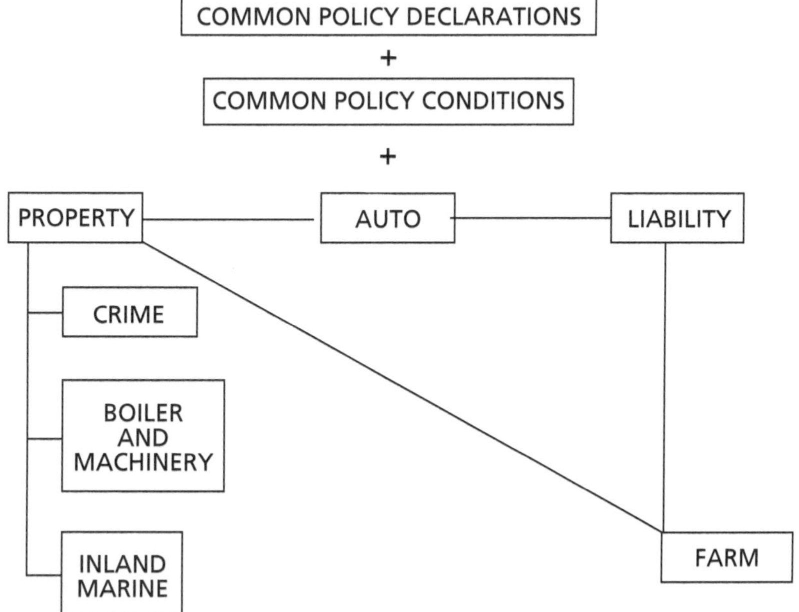

CHAPTER 10
COMMERCIAL GENERAL LIABILITY

Questions 1 - 4 will deal with the following Commercial Liability hazards. You may use a choice once, more than once, or not at all.

(A) Premises liability
(B) Operations liability
(C) Products liability
(D) Completed Operations liability

From the exposures listed above, select the one best exemplified by the circumstances described below.

1. A roofer drops his hammer from the roof of your home onto the windshield of your car and destroys it.

   (A) (B) (C) (D)

2. A customer in your hardware store sniffs some paint thinner to test its strength. He faints, falls, and breaks his arm.

   (A) (B) (C) (D)

3. Two weeks ago, a painter left a bucket on a crossbeam of a warehouse she had finished painting. It falls off the beam and does major damage to some of your business equipment.

   (A) (B) (C) (D)

4. A customer enters your store, trips over a cabbage in the vegetable department, and breaks his arm.

   (A) (B) (C) (D)

5. Which of the following is an example of personal injury as defined in the CGL?

   (A) Food poisoning
   (B) Product recall
   (C) Wrongful entry
   (D) Infringement of copyright

6. A Directors and Officers policy covers which of the following?

(A) Illegal acts
(B) Errors and Omissions
(C) Products Liability
(D) Contractual Liability

7. Which of the following coverages would a radio station have under a CGL?

(A) Advertising Injury
(B) Personal Injury
(C) Neither Advertising Injury nor Personal Injury
(D) Both Advertising Injury and Personal Injury

8. Johnson rents an office/warehouse in an industrial park. He negligently starts a fire that doesn't damage his space but damages the space of three other tenants. Johnson's CGL has a General Occurrence Limit of $500,000 and a Fire Legal Liability Limit $300,000. The damages are as follows:

Damage to the Landlord's Property	$250,000
Landlord's Loss of Rental Income	$150,000

His policy will pay which of the following?

(A) $250,000
(B) $300,000
(C) $400,000
(D) $500,000

9. A small accounting firm is insured under a CGL with an endorsement removing the Advertising Injury and Personal Injury coverages. The firm also has a $1 million Commercial Umbrella. An individual who applied for a job files a complaint for age discrimination in court and is awarded $100,000. The Umbrella company pays $90,000. Why was $10,000 not paid by the Umbrella carrier?

(A) There was a $10,000 deductible.
(B) The CGL paid the first $10,000.
(C) Umbrella policies have a 10% coinsurance requirement.
(D) There was a $10,000 self-insured retention layer.

CHAPTER 10 • COMMERCIAL GENERAL LIABILITY QUIZ

10. You own a standard CGL. For which of the following would Coverage C (Medical Payments) provide coverage?

    (A) Bodily injury to a temporary employee.
    (B) Bodily injury to a nearby resident caused by the discharge of pollutants from your plant.
    (C) Bodily injury to a child caused by a toy you manufactured.
    (D) None of the above.

11. The General Aggregate of the CGL limits the amount to be paid in any policy period for all of the following EXCEPT

    (A) Premises Liability.
    (B) Operations Liability.
    (C) Products Liability.
    (D) Medical Payments.

12. Under CGL coverages, which of the following is defined as mobile equipment?

    (A) Snowplows
    (B) Cherry pickers in transit
    (C) Street sweepers
    (D) Bulldozers on the job site

13. All of the following would be covered by the Products Liability coverage of a CGL EXCEPT

    (A) Pickled beets sold by your store which cause food poisoning.
    (B) A baby blanket manufactured by your company which causes a crib death.
    (C) A machine owned by your vending company which falls on a customer in a service station.
    (D) Aspirin manufactured by your company whose labeling contained no warning to expectant mothers and which caused a miscarriage.

14. Star Bliss Tuna packed a can of tuna in 1987 and sold it to you in 1988. You nearly died of botulism when you ate it in 1989 but you lived to file a lawsuit in 1990. If Star Bliss had an Occurrence policy in each of the four years mentioned, which policy would defend Star Bliss?

    (A) The 1987 policy
    (B) The 1988 policy
    (C) The 1989 policy
    (D) The 1990 policy

15. If in Question #14 Star Bliss had had a series of Claims Made policies with the same company for the years 1987 through 1990 and a retroactive date of January 1, 1987, which policy would defend Star Bliss?

    (A) The 1987 policy
    (B) The 1988 policy
    (C) The 1989 policy
    (D) The 1990 policy

16. In which of the following circumstances would your CGL provide coverage?

    (A) You damage your rented bulldozer.
    (B) Your bulldozer falls from the back of a truck on the highway and squashes a car.
    (C) Your forklift truck runs over a customer in your store.
    (D) The government orders a recall of 10,000 bicycles you've manufactured.

17. A Commercial General Liability policy would cover

    (A) Property in the insured's care, custody or control.
    (B) Personal Injury.
    (C) Bodily injury to the insured.
    (D) Employees injured at work.

CHAPTER 10 • COMMERCIAL GENERAL LIABILITY QUIZ

18. Which of the following would most likely increase the premium of a Workers Comp contract?

    (A) Severity of losses
    (B) Unionization
    (C) Frequency of losses
    (D) A suspected OSHA violation

19. Under Workers Compensation, the employee's obligations include all of the following EXCEPT

    (A) Notify the employer immediately.
    (B) Pay all medical bills.
    (C) Seek medical care.
    (D) Assist in filling out all required forms.

20. Under Workers Compensation, an individual injured on the job who can't work at all now, but is expected to have a complete recovery and return to work would be classified as

    (A) Permanently partially disabled.
    (B) Permanently totally disabled.
    (C) Temporarily totally disabled.
    (D) Temporarily partially disabled.

21. Workers Comp will only cover losses if

    (A) The loss is due to employer's negligence.
    (B) The employee is found to be totally free of fault.
    (C) The employee was not injured by a fellow employee.
    (D) The employee becomes ill or injured as a direct result of their employment.

END

QUIZ ANSWERS & EXPLANATIONS ON NEXT PAGE

CHAPTER 10
COMMERCIAL GENERAL LIABILITY
QUIZ ANSWER KEY

1. B. An operations risk is something the insured is doing away from his premises.

2. A. It cannot be a Products Liability claim, as the product did not leave the premises of the insured.

3. D. Completed Operations coverage is triggered when the insured's job is done.

4. A. A slip and fall is one of the most common Premises Liability claims.

5. C. Personal Injury is damage to an individual's reputation or state of mind. Wrongful entry, trespass, focuses on the state of mind of the property owner rather than any damage to the property.

6. B. The D&O policy provides protection for the officers and directors of a corporation who are sued by stockholders for alleged errors and omissions that have resulted in a loss of investment. The policy specifically excludes criminal acts.

7. C. The CGL provides no Coverage B for a business engaged in advertising, broadcasting or publishing.

8. C. This question focuses on choosing the appropriate limit and the application of the rule of 3 L's. Fire Legal Liability coverage only limits the amount available for the space actually occupied by the insured. In this case, because other tenants occupied the space that was damaged, the General Liability limit is used. The landlord will be compensated for both the direct loss (repair), and indirect loss (lost rental income). As always use the lower of the loss or the limit.

9. D. Deductibles and coinsurance are found in two party and not third party coverage. There was no coverage for this claim under the CGL, however because umbrellas broaden as well as deepen the umbrella will pick up the claim. The part of the claim that is retained by the insured is called the Self Insured Retention Layer.

CHAPTER 10
COMMERCIAL GENERAL LIABILITY
QUIZ ANSWER KEY

10. D. Medical Pay in the CGL doesn't cover products. The Med Pay exclusions mirror the Coverage A exclusions, thus eliminating injuries to employees and pollution losses.

11. C. For rating purposes Products Liability & Completed Operations have their own separate occurrence and aggregate limits.

12. D. Mobile equipment that is being used on the road (street maintenance and repair, snow removal, or in transit,) is treated as an automobile.

13. C. The vending machine is being used as a tool, not being sold, by the vending machine company away from its premises. This is an Operations Risk.

14. C. In an Occurrence based policy look for the hurt...tuna packed, no hurt; tuna bought, no hurt; tuna eaten, here's the hurt.

15. D. In a Claims Made policy look for when the claim was first made. Here it is the filing of the suit. The Retroactive Date is in this case a red herring and has no bearing on the answer.

16. C. The CGL covers damage caused by mobile equipment (the fork lift). The CGL excludes damage to property owned occupied rented or in the care custody or control of the insured; the policy also excludes the cost of recalls, as well as damage caused by mobile equipment in transit.

17. B. The CGL doesn't cover injury to the insured's property, her body, or her employees.

18. C. Frequency rather than severity is the critical factor in rating.

19. B. The employer and not the employee is responsible for medical bills.

20. C. Even though the injury precludes working at all (total), recovery is expected (temporary).

21. D. Workers Compensation provides benefits in the event of on the job illness or injury, without regard to fault.

11 COMMERCIAL CRIME

SOURCE:
ISO Commercial
Crime-2006

1 Another potential coverage available as part of the Commercial Package policy is Crime insurance. As with the other modules, some businesses don't need it at all; others will buy it as part of the Commercial Package; and, still others will purchase it as a separate and distinct monoline policy. As you would guess, different businesses have different concerns about crime. A jewelry store might be most concerned about a burglary or a robbery. A stock brokerage, on the other hand, might be more concerned with embezzlement. Traditionally, Crime insurance has been divided into two piles:

- Employee theft
- Regular theft

2 In years past, employee theft was covered by a Fidelity Bond, and regular theft (like burglary or robbery) was covered by Crime insurance. The modern Commercial Crime policy allows a business concerned with both exposures to cover each under a single policy that combines Fidelity Bond coverage with regular Crime coverage. Obviously, if a business needs only one or the other, each can be purchased separately.

3 For our discussion, we will first examine the Fidelity Bond and then the basic Crime coverages. In each case, you should familiarize yourself with the basic definitions. Finally, we will provide an overview showing how Crime insurance is provided through the modern Commercial Crime contract.

Notes

FIDELITY BONDS

1 As the biggest portion of losses to American business is attributable to employee theft (insiders), we must provide protection from this exposure. This is the purpose of a Fidelity Bond. Fidelity comes from the Latin word for *faithful*, and faithful performance is what is guaranteed by a Fidelity Bond. There are three parties involved in the bond, which are the:

Mr. Inside

Principal – The party who has agreed to fulfill an obligation (the employee). *"P"*

Obligee – The party to whom the obligation is owed, and the one who is paid if the principal defaults (the employer). *"O"*

Surety or Guarantor – The insurance company that issues the bond and agrees to pay if the principal defaults. *"S"*

FIDELITY BOND BASICS

- **Insuring Agreement** – The bond covers losses due to the dishonesty of employees.

- **Bond Period** – Fidelity Bonds are **continuous** in nature. They have no expiration date. They have an inception date and remain in effect until cancelled.

- **Termination of Coverage** – Bonds can be cancelled at any time by either the employer or by the insurance company, with proper notice.

- Coverage on a bonded employee **automatically terminates as soon as the employer becomes aware of a dishonest act** on the part of that employee which is or which **could be** the basis of a claim. There are no second chances.

. . . after they've gone

- **Discovery Period** – Most Fidelity Bonds have a provision called a discovery period. This is a period of time after a bond has been terminated in which to discover a loss. It is generally **12 months**.

- **Prior Coverage** – Generally, Fidelity Bonds will cover acts committed before the inception date and discovered during the coverage period **if** there was a prior bond in effect when the act occurred and the prior bond's discovery period has simply expired.

INSURANCE LITE

Woman:	Someone broke in and stole my television set.
Agent:	Was it a portable television?
Woman:	Evidently!

TYPES OF FIDELITY BONDS

1 **Individual Bond** – Covers one named employee.

2 **Name Schedule Bond** – Covers several named employees for amounts that could vary depending upon the level of exposure.

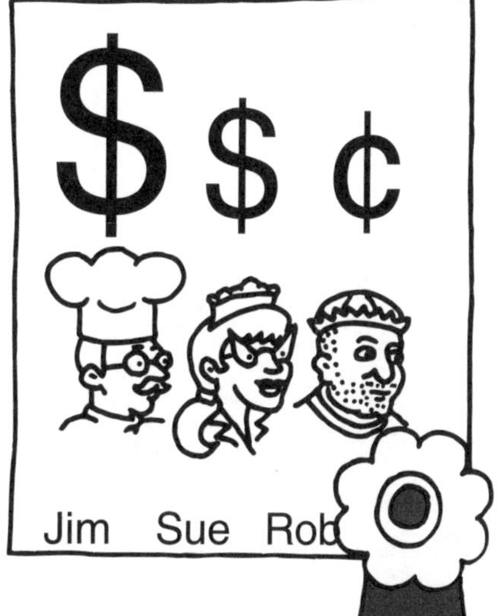

3 **Position Schedule Bond** – Covers multiple employees, but lists them by job title (treasurer, bookkeeper, cashier) rather than by name. As before, different amounts may be applied to different positions.

4 **Commercial Blanket Bond** – Covers all employees and its limits are expressed on a **per loss** basis, i.e., its limit of liability is the face amount of bond, regardless of the number of employees involved in a loss. Coverage will be provided even if a loss is not attributable to any specific employee. The discovery period is **12 months**.

5 **Blanket Position Bond** – Also covers all employees, but its limits are expressed on a **per employee** basis. Its discovery period is **24 months**.

Notes

1 For example, if an employer has a $100,000 Blanket Position Bond and two employees working together steal $200,000, there would be adequate coverage.

$100,000 coverage per employee
x 2 employees involved in the theft
$200,000 coverage

2 Memory Device: The **Blanket Position** Bond leaves the employer in a **better position** in the event of employee conspiracy.

CRIME DEFINITIONS

3 Please note that the following are *insurance* definitions as they relate to crime coverages. They bear little, if any, resemblance to the criminal law definitions.

4 **Robbery** – The taking of property by violence or threat of violence **from a person**.

Robbery. . . Violence/person

5 **Burglary** – The taking of property **from a premises** that is closed and locked tight and leaving marks of forced entry or exit. There must be visible evidence of force at the point of entry or exit.

Burglary. . . Violence/building

6 **Theft** – Any act of stealing. Theft is a broad term and includes robbery and burglary, as well as other forms of stealing, such as shoplifting and embezzlement.

7 **Safe Burglary** – The taking of property from a locked safe or vault, or the taking of the safe itself. As with burglary, there must be visible marks of force. Cash registers, cash drawers and cash boxes are not safes.

8 **Disappearance** – Insured property is simply gone. There is no evidence, or even a probability, of theft. Disappearance is covered only in "All Risk" policies.

It was here. .. . . .now it's gone

9 **Extortion** – Surrender of property as the result of a threat communicated to the Insured to do bodily harm to a named Insured, a relative or an employee who is (or allegedly is) being held captive. You and I would call this kidnapping.

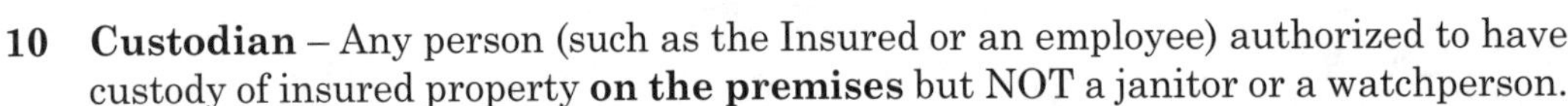

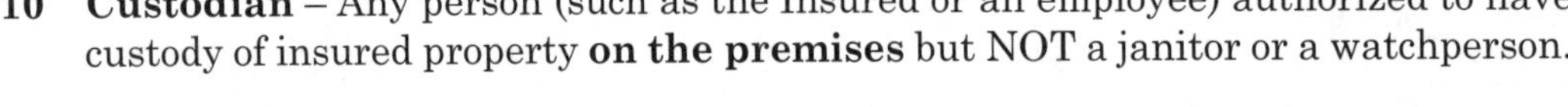

10 **Custodian** – Any person (such as the Insured or an employee) authorized to have custody of insured property **on the premises** but NOT a janitor or a watchperson.

11 **Messenger** – Any person authorized to have custody of insured property **away from the premises**.

12 **Guard** – Anyone, armed or unarmed, between the ages of 17 and 65 who accompanies a messenger (off premises) and is not the driver of a public conveyance.

13 **Watchperson** – Any person the Insured retains to protect insured property **on the premises** and who has no other duties.

14 **Securities** – Instruments representing wealth, such as stocks, bonds, tokens, or tickets, but **not** money.

15 **Money** – Currency, coins, bank notes, traveler's checks, checks, and money orders.

Notes

COMMERCIAL CRIME INSURANCE

A Commercial Crime policy can include coverages for losses due to both outsiders
1 and insiders. It can be written as a monoline policy or as part of the Commercial
Package Policy. As part of the package, it must be accompanied by the **Common
Conditions** and **Common Declarations**. If it is issued as a monoline policy, then
a separate Crime Declarations page must be used. In either case, the crime coverage part consists of:

- Crime Declarations Page
- Crime Provisions Form
- One or more Insuring Agreements
- Applicable Endorsements

There are eight coverages available under the Commercial Crime policy that are
2 designated as Insuring Agreement 1 through Insuring Agreement 8. The policyowner may choose any or all of these.

Insuring Agreement 1 - Employee Theft
Insuring Agreement 2 - Forgery or Alteration
Insuring Agreement 3 - Inside the Premises - Theft of Money and Securities
Insuring Agreement 4 - Inside the Premises - Robbery or Safe Burglary of Other Property
Insuring Agreement 5 - Outside the Premises
Insuring Agreement 6 - Computer Fraud
Insuring Agreement 7 - Funds transfer fraud
Insuring Agreement 8 - Money Orders and Counterfeit Paper Currency

"Exciting, isn't it?"

COMMON CONDITIONS

Though Crime policies generally contain the standard provisions regarding cancel-
3 lation, territory, assignment, appraisal, etc., there are a few unique conditions you
should note:

4 **Records** – Insureds are required to maintain accurate records with regard to the
value of the insured property.

show what's been taken. . .

5 **Notice to Police** – In addition to the usual notice requirements, if a loss occurs,
the Insured must file a crime report with the proper law enforcement agency.

. . .call the doughnut shop

6 **Settlement** – For property other than money or securities, settlement is on the
basis of ACV, with the insurance company's option of repairing or replacing. For
money, settlement is on the basis of the face value of the money. For securities,
settlement is on the basis of the value of the securities on the close of the market
on the day the loss is discovered.

Loss sustained and Discovery Forms - In the area of crime, it is not unusual
7 to discover losses until long after they have occurred. This problem is handled
differently by the two forms of Crime coverage available - The Loss Sustained
Crime Form and the Discovery Form.

Under the Loss Sustained Form, losses that occur during the policy period and dis-
8 covered up to one year after the policy period are covered. Losses discovered after
the one year **discovery period** are covered by subsequent policies as long as there
is no gap in coverage.

Under the Discovery Form losses are covered no matter when they occurred if they
1 are first discovered during the policy period. (Much like the Claims Made form of
the CGL).

COMMON EXCLUSIONS

- Acts by the Named Insured
- War
- Nuclear hazard
- V&MM
- Government action
- Indirect losses
- Legal Expenses

THE CRIME INSURING AGREEMENTS

Insuring Agreement 1 - Employee Theft

Two Types of Employers - There is both a loss sustained and a discovery form for
2 standard business structures (sole proprietorship, partnership, corporation) **and**
for **government entities** that have an employee theft exposure.

Covers - Money, securities and other property from employee theft. There is no
3 coverage for an employee following the discovery of a dishonest act by that employee
. . no second chances.

4 **Exclusions** -Losses which can only be proven by an inventory shortage or profit and loss computations.

Insuring Agreement 2 - Forgery or Alteration

5 **Covers** - The forgery or alteration of **outgoing** checks or drafts. It does **not cover** incoming checks that have been forged.

6 **Exclusions** -Does not cover acts of the Insured or the acts of an employee.

7 **Definitions** -All losses caused by one person constitute a single occurrence - hence only one deductible.

Insuring Agreement 3 - Inside the Premises - Theft of Money and Securities

1 **Covers** - Money or securities inside the premises or inside a bank against **theft, disappearance** and **destruction**.

Exclusions

- Accounting Errors
- Dishonest Acts of Employees
- Trickery
- Fire Damage to the Premises
- Vending Machines
- V&MM
- Voluntary Relinquishment
- Computer Fraud

Insuring Agreement 4 - Inside the Premises - Robbery or Safe Burglary of Other Property

2 **Covers** - Property other than money and securities that might be the subject of a robbery when the business is open and the subject of a safe burglary when the business is closed.

Special Limits - $5,000 limit on gold, silver, jewelry, furs, manuscripts and records.
3 (Though the limits can be raised by endorsement, property of this type should probably be covered by an Inland Marine policy.)

4 **Coverages**

- Robbery of an employee
- Damage to the premises caused by a robbery or safe burglary
- Safe Burglary

Insuring Agreement 5 - Outside the Premises

Covers - Money, securities and other property for theft, disappearance and destruction
5 while outside the premises in the care or custody of a messenger or an armored motor
vehicle company.

6 **Exclusions**

- Dishonest Acts of Employees
- Trickery
- Voluntary Relinquishment
- Unauthorized Transfer as the result of a threat to harm a person or property

Insuring Agreement 6 - Computer Fraud

1 **Covers** - Money, securities and other property which is transferred from the premises or banking premises to a person or location outside those premises.

2 **Perils Insured** - Only one peril - computer fraud.

3 **Exclusions** -Your acts or those of your employees.

4 **Policy Territory** -Worldwide

Insuring Agreement 7 – Funds Transfer Fraud

5 **Covers**-- Covers only money and securities transferred to a person or place off premises due to the fraudulent instructions **transmitted by any means** - computer, fax, telephone, or any other.

Insuring Agreement 8 - Money Orders and Counterfeit Paper Currency

6 **Covers** - Money orders accepted which are not paid upon presentation to any post office, express company or bank as well as counterfeit currency or securities of any country acquired by the Insured during the regular course of business.

ENDORESEMENTS

Extortion - Commerical Entities

7 **Covers** - Property surrendered as the result of a threat to do bodily harm to an Insured, employee or relative who is or is allegedly being held captive.

Lessees of Safe Deposit Boxes

8 **Covers** - Securities in the care of the Insured on the property in a vault or in a safe deposit box due to loss by theft, disappearance, or destruction.

Securities Deposited with Others

9 **Covers** -Securities in the possession of the Insured but not in a safe or safe deposit box. Coverage is for loss due to theft disappearance or destruction

Guests' Property

10 **Covers** - Property of guests inside the premises of a hotel, motel, or nursing home. This endorsement covers an employee's theft of a guest's property.

Safe Depository

11 **Covers** – Provides named Insured for coverage due to theft or destruction of property in their care, custody or control in a safe, vault, or elsewhere on the premises. Also covers damage done to a safe while it is being burglarized.

Conclusion

1 The three parties to a Fidelity Bond are:

- **Principal** (employee)
- **Obligee** (employer)
- **Surety or Guarantor** (insurance company)

An Individual Bond covers one employee. A Schedule Bond can cover several em-
2 ployees by name or by position. The Blanket Bonds cover all employees - The Commercial Blanket on a per loss basis and the Blanket Position on a per employee basis.

Q and A

1. A messeger is held up by a gunman and insured property is taken. What is this?
   A robbery.

2. A window is broken in a business closed for the night allowing insured property to be taken. What is this?
   A burglary.

3. What is shoplifting or pickpocketing?
   Not a burglary, not a robbery, but a **theft**.

4. An employee authorized to have custody of insured property **on premises** is what?
   A custodian.

5. Off Premises?
   A messenger.

6. Accompanying a messenger?
   A **guard**.

7. Which Insuring Agreement covers?

   A. Taking of insured property by an employee.
   Insuring Agreement 1 - Employee Theft

   B. Theft, disappearance or destruction of cash or securities on premises.
   Insuring Agreement 3 - Inside the Premises - Theft of Money and Securities

   C. A messenger is taking a bag of cash to the bank when a hurricane blows the bag out of his hands and cannot be located.
   Insuring Agreement 5 - Outside of Premises

   D. An employee alters his $500 paycheck to make it $5,000. No this is **not Forgery or Alteration**. An employee did it.
   It's Insuring Agreement 1 - Employee Theft

CHAPTER 11
COMMERCIAL CRIME

Questions 1 - 4 refer to the following terms:

(A) Burglary (B) Robbery (C) Theft (D) Extortion

Choose from the terms listed above the one best described by each of the following. A term may be used once, more than once or not at all.

1. A business is closed securely at 6:00 p.m. During the night, the door is smashed open and some business equipment is taken.

   (A) (B) (C) (D)

2. A man enters a drugstore with his hand in his coat pocket. He says he has a gun and demands money.

   (A) (B) (C) (D)

3. An electronics repair business, closed for the night, has a window which was carelessly left open. A man is seen exiting that window carrying a television set.

   (A) (B) (C) (D)

4. An employee is held for ransom by a competitor's marketing department.

   (A) (B) (C) (D)

Questions 5 - 6 refer to the following job titles:

(A) Custodian (B) Messenger (C) Guard (D) Watchperson

Choose from the job titles listed above the one best described by each of the following. A job title may be used once, more than once or not at all.

5. An employee of the named insured authorized to have possession of insured property on company premises, excluding porters and janitors.

   (A) (B) (C) (D)

6. A person authorized by the insured to transport insured property off company premises.

   (A) (B) (C) (D)

CHAPTER 11
COMMERCIAL CRIME QUIZ ANSWER KEY

1. A. Visible signs of forced entry or exit to a business with property stolen = burglary.

2. B. Theft using force or threat of force = Robbery.

3. C. Any act of stealing = Theft.

4. D. Taking an individual or their employee or a family member hostage and demanding valuables in return = Extortion.

5. A. An individual entrusted with valuable property at the workplace = Custodian.

6. B. An individual entrusted with valuable property away from the workplace = Messenger.

EQUIPMENT BREAKDOWN (BOILER AND MACHINERY) 12

SOURCE:
ISO Equipment
Breakdown 2008

1 For many years this coverage form was called Boiler and Machinery. However, changes in the way commercial enterprises do business and their specific coverage needs prompted a change in the name of this coverage to Equipment Breakdown. Equipment Breakdown still covers boilers, but as the name change implies, they are not necessarily the leading piece of equipment that today's business wish to cover. References to Boiler and Machinery are not wrong, they are simply, at this juncture, more of a historical reference than a reflection of the coverage's new name.

2 Like Property, Casualty, and Crime, Equipment Breakdown coverage is available as part of the Commercial Package policy or as a separate, monoline contract. Obviously, many businesses have no need for this coverage, but the businesses who do need it, really need it. Other policies exclude coverage – this is the one that provides it. In fact, the place to start our discussion of Equipment Breakdown coverage is with a review of the applicable exclusions we've seen already and to develop an example that clearly demonstrates the need for this policy.

The Need For EQUIPMENT BREAKDOWN

3 Let's suppose that Joe's restaurant is heated by a boiler. The "pop-off" valve malfunctions and the boiler explodes. Customers are injured, employees are injured, adjacent businesses are damaged, Joe's restaurant is severely damaged, and he has to shut down for 60 days to repair the damage. What's covered, and what's not covered by the policies we've discussed up to this point?

. . .let's let off a little steam. . .

4 From a liability viewpoint, Joe is in pretty good shape; there is no boiler exclusion in the CGL. Therefore, the bodily injury to patrons is covered within the limits of the CGL. The damage to the adjacent buildings (property damage liability) is also covered under the CGL. Even the injury to Joe's own employees is covered because there is no boiler exclusion in a Workers Compensation contract.

Notes

1 Joe's main problem is his Commercial Property policy. As you will recall, there were three major coverage parts in that contract that defined **what** is covered:

a. Building
b. Business Personal Property
c. Property of Others

2 Each of these coverage parts was tied to a Cause of Loss form (Basic, Broad, or Special) that defined **against what** perils coverage was provided. Even if Joe had selected the Special Cause of Loss form across the board, he would still have big problems.

3 In one way or another, all three Cause of Loss forms exclude "explosion of steam boilers owned, leased or operated under your control." Therefore, without Equipment Breakdown coverage, Joe would have no coverage for his building, his own business property or other people's property in his care, custody or control. Furthermore, since Joe's Business Income policy is also tied to one of the Cause of Loss forms, his 60 day loss of revenues would not be covered either.

4 Though our industry has historically classified Equipment Breakdown as a casualty coverage, today it has become a device to fill exclusions in the Commercial Property policy. In the previous example, a Equipment Breakdown policy could cover all of Joe's losses excluded by his Commercial Property policy.

AN OVERVIEW

5 If you had to summarize a Equipment Breakdown contract in three words, they would be that the purpose of this policy is to insure **objects against accidents**. Since most modern policies are written on an *occurrence basis* rather than an *accident basis*, let's begin with the word accident.

objects. . .
. . .accidents

6 The central objective of a Equipment Breakdown policy is to protect the businesowner who meticulously maintains his equipment. If a valve or bearing wears out, it's replaced. The policy is not intended for the guy who allows his equipment to deteriorate to the point that a loss occurs – this is an insurance contract, not a maintenance contract. Therefore, losses that happen *over time* (occurrences) are not covered; sudden and accidental events (accidents) are covered. In the language of the policy, the Equipment Breakdown contract covers the **sudden and accidental breakdown** of the equipment, causing a loss and necessitating the repair or replacement of the equipment. Essentially, the policy covers **mechanical breakdown** and it excludes anything and everything that has to do with wear and tear, deterioration and improper maintenance... accidents, not occurrences. The *One Accident Rule* does state, however, that if one boiler explodes and causes two more to explode, the event is viewed as **one accident**.

broke. . .
not worn out.
. .

. . . and hurt
"all at once"

7 The word *object* obviously can mean Joe's boiler – if it breaks down, terrible losses can occur. But, Joe has other equipment that could cause losses (though probably smaller losses) if a mechanical breakdown occurs. While it is possible for Joe to list only his boiler as an object on the Equipment Breakdown Dec Sheet, it is more common to broaden the coverage to include other equipment subject to breakdown. If mechanical objects are included in the coverage, the Equipment Breakdown contract is again filling an exclusion found in Commercial Property which eliminates coverage for **mechanical breakdown**. If electrical objects are covered, the exclusion concerning **electrical arcing** is filled.

Objects on
the dec sheet

Notes

1 Currently, there are six categories of objects that can be covered under a Boiler and Machinery policy.

1. **Pressure and Refrigerator Objects** – including boilers, refrigeration units, air conditioning units, and vacuum units
2. Mechanical Objects – including engines, pumps, compressors, and fans
3. Electrical Objects – which includes a variety of electrical apparatus
4. Turbine Objects – covers turbines
5. Comprehensive (Excluding Production Machines) – covers everything above, but no production equipment
6. Comprehensive (Including Production Machines) – as before, but including production equipment

6 types of coverage

THE EQUIPMENT BREAKDOWN POLICY

2 Now that we understand the purpose served by the Equipment Breakdown policy and further understand that the contract insures against the damage caused by an accident (mechanical breakdown) of an object, it is time to look at the contract itself.

SECTION A – COVERAGE

damage to . . .

3 The Equipment Breakdown policy covers **direct damage** done to **covered property**. Covered property includes:

. . . your stuff

- *Property You Own* – Joe's building, inventory, business property, and the object (boiler or machine) itself

. . .other's stuff

- *Property In Your Care, Custody, or Control and For Which You Are Legally Responsible* – any property for which Joe has a bailee's responsibility

. . .accident

4 This property is covered for loss due to an accident which is defined as **sudden and accidental breakdown** of the insured object. Any wear and tear type losses are excluded.

5 In addition to the basic coverage provided under Section A, there are four extensions of coverage.

. . .back on line

1. **Expediting Expenses** – Up to $25,000 (a limit that can be raised) to reimburse the Insured for reasonable extra expenses to make temporary repairs to expedite permanent replacement . . . items such as employee overtime or the extra cost of express shipments are good examples.

new/90

2. **Automatic Coverage for Newly Acquired Locations** – 90 day automatic coverage for newly acquired locations. The dollar limits and the deductible amount are the highest amounts shown in the declarations for the same type of object.

wow. . . some liability too

3. **Defense** – If a claim or suit is brought against the Insured for property in his care, custody or control, the company will defend the Insured.
4. **Supplementary Payments** – If the company defends the Insured in a suit, they will pay for the defense costs along with the other benefits typically covered by Supplementary Payments.

Notes

SECTION B – EXCLUSIONS

- Ordinance or law
- Nuclear hazard
- War
- Flood
- Earth movement
- Fire
- Lightning
- Explosion (other than the type covered by this policy)
- Indirect losses

SECTION C – LIMITS

1 The primary limit of the policy is shown on the Dec Sheet and is written on a per accident basis. In addition, the policy has four interior limits that are part of and not in addition to the limits of insurance.

- Expediting expenses limitation – $25,000
- Hazardous substance (clean up) limitation – $25,000
- Ammonia contamination (clean up) limitation – $25,000
- Water damage limitation – $25,000

SECTION D – DEDUCTIBLE

"D-Duck"

2 The deductible is not stated in this portion of the contract but is found on the Dec Sheet. While most companies require a minimum deductible of $250, higher amounts can be used.

3 This section says that if one or more objects is involved in one accident, only one deductible will apply. Furthermore, if one initial accident triggers subsequent accidents, the company will treat it all as one accident.

SECTION E – CONDITIONS

4 This section reads similarly to the Conditions section of the Commercial Property policy as it regards duties in the event of a loss, other insurance and legal action against the company. Only two conditions are so unique that they should be addressed.

1. **Valuation** – The standard Equipment Breakdown policy settles losses on a **Replacement Cost** basis. By endorsement, the contract can be downgraded to Actual Cash Value.

2. **Suspension – Prevention oriented**

   - Company may **inspect without notice**
   - If defects exist, company may **suspend coverage immediately with written notice**
   - Coverage stays suspended until the **defect is corrected**
   - Coverage is returned by **written endorsement**
   - A pro rata refund is made for any period during which coverage is suspended

inspect without notice

suspend with notice

SECTION F – DEFINITIONS

1 Only four words are included in this section: Accident, Object, One Accident, and Suit. All have been specifically defined earlier in this text or in this chapter.

INDIRECT LOSS ENDORSEMENTS

2 Though many endorsements exist for Equipment Breakdown policies, only one is important in our example of Joe's restaurant. Up to this point, we have not yet found coverage for one loss that Joe suffered when his restaurant boiler exploded – he was out of business for 60 days. In fact, throughout our discussion of the contract, the only time we've mentioned indirect losses is to say that they are excluded.

3 **Business Interruption - Actual Loss** - This endorsement provides business interruption coverage during the *period of restoration* for total or partial business interruption caused by an object specified in the declarations. It will cover actual losses and reasonable expenses to shorten the period of interruption up to the policy limits.

4 The deductible can be expressed as either dollars, time (days or hours), or as a multiple of daily value. *Daily value* is what would have been earned had there been no interruption. If we assume a daily value of $10,000, and further assume that a multiple of 10 is shown on the Dec sheet, the deductible is $100,000.

5 The Insured must furnish annual earning reports within three months of policy inception or renewal. If the estimated annual earnings is less than the actual earnings at the time of loss, a coinsurance penalty applies.

6 **Extra Expense** - As we saw in Commercial Property, the purpose of this endorsement is to pay expenses above the normal costs to continue operating a business following a covered loss. Generally, Extra Expense coverage is written with a dollar deductible.

7 **Combined Business Interruption and Extra Expense** - This endorsement simply combines the previous two for businesses that need Business Interruption to replace income **and** Extra Expense to offset extra expenses of continued operations following a covered loss.

8 **Consequential Damage** - This endorsement essentially covers *spoilage* caused by lack of power, light, heat, steam, or refrigeration following a covered loss. Property covered must be specified in the Declarations. This coverage is normally written with a coinsurance requirement and a dollar deductible.

9 With the Equipment Breakdown Business Interruption Endorsement, business income and extra expense losses are covered. Thus, the final hole in Joe's coverage picture is filled.

The Chapter 12 Quiz is combined with the Chapter 13 Quiz, and can be found at the end of Chapter 13 on page 13-17.

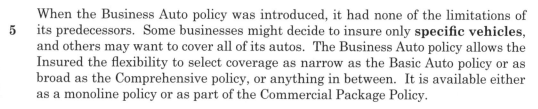

OTHER COMMERCIAL PACKAGE MODULES

13

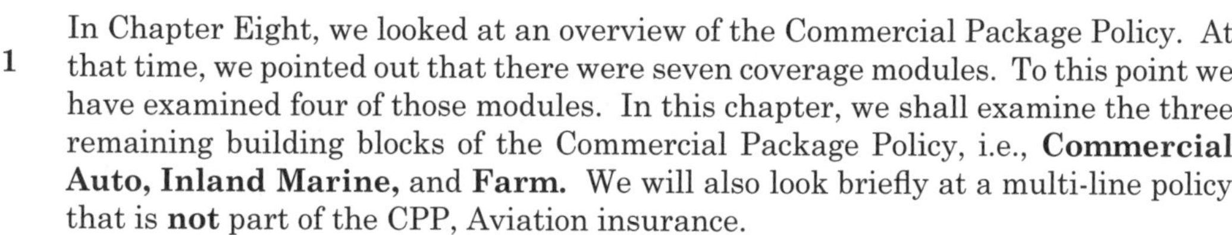

1 In Chapter Eight, we looked at an overview of the Commercial Package Policy. At that time, we pointed out that there were seven coverage modules. To this point we have examined four of those modules. In this chapter, we shall examine the three remaining building blocks of the Commercial Package Policy, i.e., **Commercial Auto, Inland Marine,** and **Farm.** We will also look briefly at a multi-line policy that is **not** part of the CPP, Aviation insurance.

COMMERCIAL AUTO

Commercial Package

Auto | IM | Farm

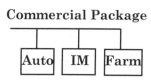

2 **Source: ISO-Commercial Auto 2006**

3 Our discussion of Commercial Automobile coverage will focus on the following coverage forms:

- **Business Auto**
- **Truckers Coverage**
- **Motor Carrier Coverage**
- **Garage Policy**

BUSINESS AUTO

4 Like most individuals, most businesses have many potential automobile risks. For many years, the Basic Auto policy was used to insure these exposures. The principal drawback was that the policy only provided coverage for scheduled automobiles. Hired cars and non-owned autos could be covered only by endorsement. The Comprehensive Auto policy evolved to serve the needs of large businesses with a fleet of autos. To qualify as a fleet, a business had to own **five** or more vehicles, but the policy covered all autos (owned, non-owned, and hired). The broad coverage was nice, but expensive.

5 When the Business Auto policy was introduced, it had none of the limitations of its predecessors. Some businesses might decide to insure only **specific vehicles**, and others may want to cover all of its autos. The Business Auto policy allows the Insured the flexibility to select coverage as narrow as the Basic Auto policy or as broad as the Comprehensive policy, or anything in between. It is available either as a monoline policy or as part of the Commercial Package Policy.

Notes

ELIGIBLE VEHICLES

The Business Auto policy insures vehicles which are owned, leased, hired, or bor-
1 rowed by businesses. It may be used to insure private passenger autos and all types
of trucks, trailers, and commercial vehicles designed for use on public roads.

DECLARATIONS

The Declarations section of the Business Auto policy determines which vehicles are
2 covered and serves the same purposes as the Declarations section of the Personal *coverage by*
Auto Policy. The only unique feature is that the business may choose which vehicles *declaration*
it wishes to insure by selecting one of the following nine symbols used to indicate *. . .not definition*
covered autos:

- #1 Any auto
- #2 Owned autos only
- #3 Owned private passenger autos only
- #4 Owned autos other than private passenger autos
- #5 Owned autos subject to no-fault benefits
- #6 Owned autos subject to compulsory Uninsured Motorists law
- #7 Specifically described autos
- #8 Hired autos only
- #9 Non-owned autos only

3 An Insured may purchase the most narrow coverage (#7, specifically described autos),
the broadest coverage (#1, any auto) or anything in between.

DEFINITIONS

Auto – A land motor vehicle, trailer, or semi-trailer designed for travel on public *on road*
4 roads, but does not include mobile equipment. For liability insurance only, auto does
include mobile equipment but only while it is being carried or towed by a covered auto.

5 **Mobile Equipment** – Any of the following land vehicles, including:

- Most construction equipment.
- Off-road vehicles.
- Vehicles maintained solely to transport permanently attached specialized equipment. *off road*
- Autos maintained solely for use on the Insured's premises and the access roads that adjoin the premises.

COVERED AUTOS

Covered Autos can be identified in the Declarations. A coverage symbol is entered alongside each coverage, and these symbols designate the only vehicles that are subject to that coverage.

Notes

POLICY PERIOD AND TERRITORY

1 The Business Auto policy covers losses occurring during the policy period. The territory is the United States, its possessions, Puerto Rico, or Canada, or while a covered auto is being transported between any of these places.

LIABILITY: AGREEMENTS AND LIMITS

2 The Business Auto policy liability insuring agreement, provisions for the application of limits, and supplementary payments follow the basic pattern of liability coverages. In this policy, the risk arises from the "ownership, maintenance, or use of an automobile."

WHO IS INSURED?

- The Named Insured for any covered auto.
- Anyone **with the permission** of the Named Insured to use a covered auto.

permission

LIABILITY CHOICES

3 Several liability-related coverages are selected by the policyowner on the Dec Sheet. They include:

- **Medical Payments** - This coverage provides approximately the same benefits as the Medical Payments coverage of a Personal Auto policy. It excludes Workers Compensation losses.

- **Uninsured Motorists** - The Uninsured Motorists insurance of the Business Auto policy covers both uninsured and underinsured motorists.

- **Employers Non-Ownership Liability** - This provides coverage for employers whose employees use their own cars on company business.

your people use their cars on your business

LIABILITY EXCLUSIONS

4 The Business Auto policy does not provide liability insurance for:

- pollution
- contractual liability risks
- Workers Compensation claims
- damage to property

looks more like CGL than Auto

Notes

PHYSICAL DAMAGE

1 The Business Auto policy can provide Physical Damage coverage under any of three agreements: **Collision, Comprehensive, or Specified Perils coverage**. The Collision and Comprehensive coverages are similar to the Personal Auto policy. Specified Perils coverage provides only for non-collision losses caused by fire, explosion, theft, windstorm, hail, earthquake, flood, mischief or vandalism, and the sinking, burning, collision, or derailment of any conveyance transporting the covered auto. It can be viewed as comprehensive coverage for the cheapskate.

Specified perils. . . poor man's Comp. . .

2 **TOWING AND LABOR** – Provides a small amount of money to get a stranded vehicle out of harm's way. Simple logic, really. If we pay for the tow truck, we won't have to buy the Insured new tires, battery, radio, etc.

3 **LIMIT OF LIABILITY** – ACV or the amount to repair or replace.

4 **CONDITIONS** –The Business Auto policy conditions are nearly identical to those of the Personal Auto policy.

BUSINESS AUTO POLICY ENDORSEMENTS

5 **Drive Other Car Coverage** - This option provides coverage for employees driving another car for personal use. Suppose Joe owns his own business and has a company car provided for his regular use, both business and personal. Because of this, he has no car of his own and no Personal Auto policy. If he borrows his neighbor's car, the Drive Other Car option would provide coverage. This endorsement can extend both liability and physical damage coverage.

6 **Additional Insured - Lessor** - This endorsement simply adds the car owner who is leasing the auto to the business as an additional Insured on the policy. The lessor has both liability and physical damage coverage.

7 **Individual Named Insured** - This allows a family-owned business to specifically include family members as named Insureds for company vehicles, even if the family member does not normally work within the business. If the policy provides both liability and physical damage coverage then those coverages extend to the family members as well.

8 **Mobile Equipment** - This endorsement transforms mobile equipment into an auto and provides auto liability and physical damage coverage for designated vehicles.

TRUCKER'S COVERAGE ‡

9 There are several variations of the Business Auto policy that are tweaked and tuned for specific needs. One such is the **Trucker's policy**. Section I of the policy allows the choice of any of 10 coverage symbols to designate what vehicles are covered. Section II provides liability coverage identical to the Business Auto policy. And, Section IV does the same for Physical Damage coverage. The only unique feature is **Section III - Trailer Interchange coverage**. Because Insureds in the trucking business often exchange trailers, this section provides the same coverage for a borrowed trailer as for an owned trailer - liability and physical damage.

Notes

MOTOR CARRIER COVERAGE ‡

1 This is another variation of the Business Auto policy and is almost identical to the Truckers form. The difference is that a motor carrier can transport **property or passengers** - so this coverage would pick up taxis, jitneys, vans, busses, and other vehicles transporting people and/or cargo.

LIABILITY INSURANCE REQUIREMENTS ‡

2 The Federal Government, through the **Motor Carrier Act of 1980**, has implemented minimum liability insurance requirements for commercial vehicles that carry cargo. Therefore, this law could impact Insured's under a Business Auto, Trucker's, or Motor Carrier policy. These standards apply to both private and *for hire* vehicles. The requirements vary dependent upon the type of cargo being carried.

Third Party for "Haulers"

3 Minimum Liability Limits

General Cargo	$ 750,000.
Hazardous Materials	$5,000,000.
Oil	$1,000,000.

Public Liability (MCS-90)

4 Policies must be endorsed to show compliance with the Act. Stacking of policies to reach the minimum limits is permitted; however each endorsement used must show whether the coverage provided is **primary or excess**.

5 A **Certificate of Insurance** must be filed with the Interstate Commerce Commission. Should coverage be cancelled, the ICC must be given a **30 day** notice.

GARAGE POLICY

6 The Garage policy is designed to cover people in the auto business: dealers, repair shops, service stations, parking garages, etc. The Business Auto policy does not provide adequate coverage for these businesses because it excludes coverage for property in the Insured's care, custody or control, and it does not cover general liability exposures. The Garage policy combines Automobile liability with General Liability coverages to construct **two possible coverage parts**.

GARAGE LIABILITY COVERAGE

7 This coverage can provide full liability coverage for automobile businesses except for damage to customers' cars. It provides:

- Premises and Operations Liability
- Products and Completed Operations Liability
- Automobile Liability

but not customers' cars. . .

GARAGEKEEPERS LIABILITY COVERAGE

8 This policy **only covers** losses to the autos of customers. It is bailee coverage and, when coupled with Garage Liability, can provide broad liability coverage for automobile businesses which **do handle** their customers' cars.

Notes

OCEAN AND INLAND MARINE

1976 NATIONWIDE MARINE DEFINITION

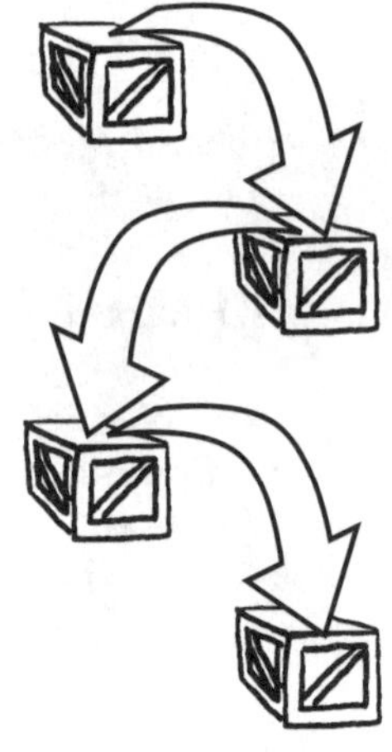

1 The purpose of this definition is to restrict the areas in which marine underwriters can write coverages. Today marine underwriters are limited to six categories:

- Imports
- Exports
- Domestic Shipments
- Bridges, Tunnels, Docks, and other Instruments of Transportation and Communication
- Personal Property Floaters
- Commercial Property Floaters

2 **IMPORTS** – Property being shipped from another country for delivery in the United States. When the import reaches its destination, it ceases to be a proper subject for marine insurance.

coming. . .

3 **EXPORTS** – Property being shipped from the U.S. for delivery in another country. An export becomes a proper subject for marine insurance once it is designated as an export or is being prepared for export.

. . .going. . .

4 **DOMESTIC SHIPMENTS** – Property being shipped from one location to another within the U.S. Trip Transit, Motor Truck Cargo and Parcel Post are typical policies. After a limited period of time specified in the contract, the domestic shipment is no longer considered "in course of transportation" and therefore is no longer a proper subject for marine insurance.

. . .moving

5 **BRIDGES, TUNNELS, DOCKS, and other INSTRUMENTS OF TRANSPORTATION and COMMUNICATION** – Includes piers, marine railways, pipelines and pumping equipment, power transmission lines, telephone lines, radio and TV broadcasts (the theory being that they "transport" words and messages), and outdoor cranes/loading bridges used to load and unload ships. These are classified as marine insurance in recognition of a long standing practice in the business. Such coverages had been written by marine underwriters for years, mainly since fire underwriters did not want to give broad protection on this type of property.

things that help movement

6 Excluded are buildings used in connection with bridges and other instruments of transportation or communication. **Neither ships nor boats are mentioned specifically in the definition since tradition made it obvious that they are eligible for marine coverage.**

7 **PERSONAL PROPERTY FLOATER RISKS** – Mobile property that is excluded, limited or inadequately covered under a Homeowners or Dwelling policy can be covered with a Personal Property Inland Marine Floater.

8 **COMMERCIAL PROPERTY FLOATER RISKS** – *All Risk* policies covering mobile property pertaining to a business, profession, or occupation.

Notes

TWO BRANCHES OF MARINE INSURANCE: OCEAN AND INLAND

1 At one time, it was easy to classify imports and exports as Ocean Marine and the remaining four categories as Inland Marine. But as transportation has become more complex, such classifications have lost their clarity. For example, Toyota automobiles shipped from Japan to the port of Cincinnati (warehouse to warehouse) will travel across both ocean and land and, therefore, must be insured under an Ocean Marine policy. On the other hand, an art collection you take to Europe for exhibit may travel by air over the ocean and can be covered by an Inland Marine Floater policy. How about ships and/or cargo on inland waterways, such as the Great Lakes or the Mississippi River? An Ocean Marine policy must be used because these are waterborne risks.

2 Today the distinction is made in the following manner: if the cargo will be placed on a ship (and thus exposed to the water perils of sinking, etc.), the Ocean Marine policy form must be used. If the cargo is transported over land or in the air (thus not being exposed to the water perils), the Inland Marine coverage form can be used. As you can see, the title *Inland Marine* is somewhat of a misnomer. **Wet** transportation and **dry** transportation would be a more accurate description of the two branches of marine insurance.

one more time - Inland - dry Ocean - wet

INLAND MARINE - "DRY"

3 **Commercial Inland Marine Property Floaters** - These policies are written on an all risk, direct loss basis. The following are a representative sampling of the ISO Commercial Inland Marine contracts. These are available as part of the Commercial Package or as separate monoline coverages.

- **Accounts Receivable** - This coverage is in reality a consequential loss coverage. The risk that is being covered is the Insured's inability to collect amounts due because of the loss of records. Acts involving employee dishonesty are excluded. There are significant rating credits for implementation of loss control measures, such as duplicate copies and the use of safes and vaults.

- **Bailees** - This coverage is for the property of others being held by the Insured for business reasons. NOTE: The CGL will not cover such losses because of the *care, custody and control* exclusion.

- **Commercial Articles Floaters** - This coverage is designed to provide coverage for items used commercially. Eligible types of property include cameras and musical instruments.

- **Contractors Equipment Floaters** - Our friend the Bulldozer. . . on, or off premises.

our friend the bulldozer

- **Valuable Papers and Records** - Coverage is available on either a scheduled or blanket basis. Eligible items include: documents, manuscripts, books, deeds, drawings, films, maps, and mortgages. **The coverage does not include losses to electronically stored data.**

- **Electronic Data Processing** - Fills up the hole in the Valuable Papers and Records coverage.

- **Equipment Dealers** - Coverage for the inventory of farm implement and construction equipment dealers. **The policy will not cover automobiles.** Also covers the property in the care and custody of the Insured.

- **Installation Floater** - The Insured is a contractor installing an air conditioning unit in someone's building. The Insured wants coverage for damage to the unit during the installation process. Not Property....no insurable interest. Not Liability...the unit is in the Insured's care and custody...The Installation Floater...*"dis is it!"*

- **Jewelers Block** - Coverage for the Insured's inventory. Only jewelers with average inventories of less than **$250,000** are eligible. Ineligible risks include wholesalers, manufacturers, industrial diamond dealers, antique dealers and watch repair shops. Off premises risks are classified by the mode of transportation, such as registered mail, armored car, delivery services, etc.

- **Signs** - Coverage for neon, fluorescent, automatic, mechanical and electric signs. **Billboards and ordinary signs are ineligible.**

Commercial Inland Marine Transportation Coverages ‡

Common Carriers and Liability - As a general rule anyone who is in the busi-
1 ness of hauling other people's goods for a fee is a **common carrier**. While common
carriers must accept all customers, they do not have to accept all shipments. For example, cargo such as petroleum products, perishables, and hazardous materials might not be a good fit for the equipment of a specific carrier, and that carrier could refuse services. *In the business* should not be interpreted to mean in the sole business. An orchard owner who carries his neighbor's produce to market is a common carrier if he is compensated.

2 **Common carriers are bailees**. They are liable for the safe delivery of their cargoes in all but a very few situations. The only exceptions are:

- **Acts of God**...earthquake, storm, locusts, etc.

- **War**

- **Acts of Public Authority**...government seizes the cargo

- **Acts of the Shipper**...poor packing job

- **Inherent Vice**...the bacon was improperly cured causing it to mold in transit.

While the liability of a carrier itself cannot be contracted away, carriers can limit
3 the maximum dollar amount of their responsibility. These agreements must be in
writing and appear on the **bill of lading**. The bill of lading is the contract between the shipper and the carrier. It lists the good being shipped, acknowledges their receipt, and promises to deliver the goods to the person named.

Motor Truck Cargo Forms - While there are no official standard policy forms,
1 competition has caused some standards to evolve. There are three primary types of
Motor Truck Cargo insurance:

- **Truckers** - This coverage is for the carriers. It provides coverage for any damage to the cargo for which they are responsible.
- **Shippers** - This is also coverage for the items being shipped, the difference being that the Insured is now the owner of the goods and not the carrier.
- **Owners** - This coverage is for those Insureds who ship cargo on their own trucks

2 **Perils** - Again while there are no standard forms, there are several perils that are generally covered:

- Fire
- Lightning
- Explosion
- Collision
- Upset
- Sinking (while the cargo is in transit on a ferryboat)

3 **Typical Exclusions:**

- Wetness or dampness
- Delay
- Neglect of the Insured to use reasonable means to protect
- Strikes
- Dishonest acts by the Insured's Employees

Transit Coverage Forms-The Policy Period - Transit Coverage Forms are written
4 in two ways. Insureds who make regular shipments would find it most efficient to
purchase their coverage on an **annual** basis. Insureds who rarely make shipments
can purchase coverage for specific shipments through a **Trip Transit Policy**.

OCEAN MARINE - "WET" ‡

While not a part of the Commercial Package Policy, it is appropriate to discuss Ocean
5 Marine coverage at this point due to its similarity to the Inland Marine coverages
that can be a part of the Commercial Package.

Types of Ocean Marine Coverages

includes parts of the ship – like "davits"

6 **Hull Coverage** - This insurance protects the shipowner for damage to the vessel.

7 **Cargo Coverage** - This coverage protects the owner of the cargo for losses to the items being shipped.

Freight Coverage - This coverage also protects the owner of the cargo; however, it
8 does not cover the items being shipped, but rather indemnifies the cargo owner who
prepays shipping charges. The policy pays when a prepaid voyage is not completed.

9 NOTE: **Cargo and Freight coverages are not the same thing**. The owner of the items being shipped may need both Cargo and Freight Coverages to be fully protected.

Notes

1 **Perils** - While Ocean Marine underwriters can tailor coverage to fit a variety of situations, the perils that are generally covered include:

- **Perils of the Sea**...sinking, running aground, collision, storms, in other words all of those things that make sailors so dern salty.
- **Fire**
- **Assailing Thieves**...similar to robbery on dry land, i.e., violence is required.
- **Jettison**...purposefully tossing cargo overboard to preserve the vessel.
- **Barratry of a Master**...in short, embezzlement by the captain.
- **Explosion**
- **Latent Defects**...in the hull, engines, navigational equipment, etc. Sometimes referred to as the *Inchmaree Clause* after a court case involving a ship of that name.
- **All Other Perils**...this **does not** make Ocean Marine Policies all risk. The *Other Perils* must be similar in nature to those already named.

...even war
...but not mutiny

Implied Warranties - Ocean Marine policies come with several implied warran-
2 ties. The most important of these is the implied warranty of Seaworthiness of the Vessel. This simply requires that the vessel be properly constructed, maintained, manned, and provisioned for the voyage. This means different requirements for different situations, delivering sausages down the Ohio river by barge has very different requirements than shipping liquefied natural gas around Cape Horn.

Averages - When dangerous conditions arise at sea, it is often necessary to sacrifice
3 part of the cargo or the vessel itself. It might be necessary in a storm to jettison part of the cargo to keep the ship from sinking, or if the ship were on fire, the captain may have to order part of a cargo hold flooded in order to save the ship.

In either of these, the losses would be born under what is referred to as the **General**
4 **Average**. The effect of the general average is that the costs of the lost property would not be born only by the owners of the property and their insurers, but rather apportioned among all who had an interest in the voyage...the other cargo owners and the shipowner. In order to invoke the General Average three conditions must be met:

- The action must be necessary to save the ship
- The action be reasonable and voluntary
- It must work...the ship must be saved

5 Other marine losses are settled under the rule known as **Particular Average**. In other words, each party is responsible for their own losses.

FARM ‡

Source: ISO Farm-2003

1 The final module available under the Commercial Package concept is Farm. The Farm module contains both two party (property) and third party (casualty) coverages. The definition of farming includes the growing of almost any kind of crops, e.g., vegetables, fruits, nuts, sod; the raising of almost any kind of animal, e.g., livestock, poultry, bees, and aquaculture. The farm, however, must be operated as a business. Homeowners who have some excess acreage upon which they raise food for their own consumption would not qualify for coverage under this module.

Farmer Joe

Farm Property Coverages

Coverage A- Dwellings
Coverage B- Other Private Structures
Coverage C- Household Personal Property
Coverage D- Loss of Use
Coverage E- Scheduled Farm Personal Property
Coverage F- Unscheduled Farm Personal Property
Coverage G- Other Farm Structures

2 You will note that even though the Farm module is considered to a Commercial Lines policy, because of the peculiar nature of the farming business, coverage is included for **both the business and the non-business related property** of the Insured. Coverages A, B, C, and D essentially replicate the Property coverages of Homeowners that were discussed at length earlier in this text. The cause of loss forms available are **Basic**, **Broad**, and **Special**, which means that the Homeowners type coverages duplicate the Property coverages of an HO-1 (Basic), an HO-2 (Broad), or an HO-3 (Special) policy.

3

Coverage E- Scheduled Farm Personal Property is an ACV coverage for categories of farm property for the limits listed on the Dec sheet. These include harvested crops, poultry, and miscellaneous equipment. **Coverage F- Unscheduled Farm Personal Property** is an ACV coverage for all other farm business equipment that does not appear under Coverage E. **Coverage G - Other Farm Structures** provides coverage for buildings and structures like barns, silos, fences and radio towers.

Other Farm Property Coverages

4

Some items can be insured under a more specialized form than the Farm Property coverage parts (Coverage E and F). Two of these are the Mobile Agricultural Machinery and Equipment coverage form and the Livestock coverage form.

5

Mobile Agricultural Machinery and Equipment - This coverage is designed to protect the farmers *mobile equipment* . This coverage is for farmers only, not dealers, repair shops or those in the business of renting equipment.

6

The coverage is written on a direct loss and all risk basis. The exclusions look like a cross between those found in the Commercial Property Special Form and those found in the Comprehensive Coverage in an automobile policy.

Notes

1 **Livestock Coverage -** This coverage is for animals not covered under Coverages E and F of the Farm Policy. Animals that would be covered include, among others:

- horses used exclusively for racing and show
- cattle and sheep on ranges
- livestock of others

2 Animals that are **not** covered include:

- those in transit by common or contract carrier
- those at a stockyard, sales barn or sales yard
- those at a slaughter or packing house

Coverage is written on a named peril basis; the cause of loss form is the Basic, with
3 the addition of Collision. Additional coverages that may be purchased include:
accidental shooting, drowning, electrocution, attack by dogs or wild animals and
loading and unloading accidents.

Farm Casualty Coverages

Coverage H - Bodily Injury and Property Damage
Coverage I - Personal Injury and Advertising Injury
Coverage J - Medical Payments

4 NOTE: Even a quick glance will yield the parallels between H, I, and J of the Farm Policy and A, B, and C of the CGL.

As with the Property Coverages, the Casualty coverages of the Farm policy are a
5 unique blend of personal and Commercial lines. The Exclusions, for instance, take
their inspiration from not only the CGL but also from those found in Section II, of
the Homeowners Policy. The definitions and conditions are not unlike those that
we have already examined, albeit with a *down home* twist.

No separate limit for products

CROP INSURANCE ‡

Crop Insurance is a specialized area of insurance important to those who have an
1 insurable interest in growing crops. Though not part of the Farm coverage available through the Commercial Package, it obviously is an important coverage for farmers. Over 200 different U.S. crops can be covered under these policies - large grain crops like corn, maize and soybean; small grain (cereal grain); cotton; tobacco; fruits and vegetables. Typically, only the marketable portion of the crop is insured. The trees, vines, bushes and blossoms that produce the useful part are excluded.

2 Crop policies are normally written to cover the **reduced yield** following a loss, not the percentage of plants destroyed. For example, a hail storm could destroy 50% of the corn stalks in a farmed field. But, that *thinning* process might allow the surviving stalks to overproduce to a level that the ultimate yield is 80% of normal.

3

The original crop peril was hail, and for many years the term **crop hail insurance** was used to describe the crop insurance contracts available. Even then, crop policies typically covered fire, lightning, and wind. And, in the citrus belt, they tended to cover frost and freezing.

4

Today most crop insurance is **multi-peril**. These contracts cover the crop hail perils as well as hurricane, tornado, flood, earthquake, volcano, drought, excessive moisture, insect infestation, plant disease, wildlife damage and failure of irrigation equipment.

Dual Marketing Systems

5

Today, farmers can purchase crop coverage through the **Federal Crop Insurance Corporation (FCIC)**, which is an agency of the federal government, or through private companies utilizing the **Multi-Peril Crop Insurance (MPCI)** program. The policies are nearly identical and the rates are comparable. The federal government subsidizes and reinsures the MPCI program to make it a more attractive proposition to private carriers. The *expense element* of the MPCI premium is subsidized 100% by the federal government, and *risk element* can be subsidized up to 30%. The current reinsurance program limits the profit or loss of a private carrier to a range
6 between an 11 1/3% loss to an 11 1/3% gain.

Since 1980, more and more farmers are buying multi-peril crop coverage, and most buy it through private companies. This is due in large part to three factors:

- The aforementioned subsidies and reinsurance provided by the feds.
- The requirement that farm loans be protected by crop insurance.
- The reduction of funds available for agricultural disaster relief.

7 Coverage Levels

Under the FCIC or the MPIC program, coverage can be obtained to the levels of 50%, 65%, or 75% of the reduced yield.

Notes

Policy Provisions

1 While there is no standard Multi-Peril Crop policy, most insurers follow the forms developed by the National Crop Insurance Services (NCIS) organization.

These forms provide for coverage on an **annual policy** form, a **three season** form,
2 or a **five season** form. However, even with an annual policy, **coverage is limited**
to the growing season.

The NCIS forms have a **24-hour waiting period**, which states that coverage begins
3 at 12:01 a.m. on the day following the date of application. If a loss occurs during
the waiting period, coverage does not take effect and the Insured has 72 hours to
request the return of premium for the affected acreage.

Coverage starts when the crop is **clearly visible above the ground**, and termi-
4 nates at **harvest or a deadline set in the policy** that corresponds to the latest
harvest date for a particular crop in a particular geographic area.

Coverage Amount

Policy limits are usually stated as a dollar limit per acre. For instance, if the crop
5 is valued at $200 an acre, the insurance amount might be $100 per acre (or 50%).
If the loss is $80 an acre, the policy would pay $40 an acre (50% of $80).

In some regions, crops can be insured under a **farm unit plan** which applies an
6 amount of insurance to the entire farm instead of the percentage payment per acre
arrangements, which are the most common.

Deductibles

Most crop policies are written with some variation of the **excess over deductible**.
7 In other words, the coverage applies as excess insurance and pays nothing until
the loss exceeds a particular threshold of 5%, 10%, or 20%. Once the threshold is
reached, the insurer pays its percentage on the **amount of the loss above the**
deductible percentage.

8 In some states, coverage for **harvested crops** is available for the perils of **fire** and **transit**. Usually these coverages are not subject to a deductible.

AVIATION INSURANCE

1 Though not part of the Commercial Package policy, aviation policies are both property and casualty and, therefore, *package policies.* And, while not all aviation activities are commercially oriented, many are, and those that are totally private still interface with a commercial exposure - the airport at which the plane is kept.

2 While there are no standard policies in aviation, there are major similarities in the policies available.

3 Most aviation policies include:

Bodily Injury Liability
Property Damage Liability
Med Pay
Hull Coverage (Physical Damage)

4 These policies are comparable to a personal Auto policy in terms of coverages available, conditions, and exclusions.

5 The Bodily Injury Liability section is generally divided into two coverages- one for passengers and another for anyone else. Obviously, most aircraft operators need both.

6 **Commercial Aviation -** For the operator of an airport, many companies offer an **airport liability** policy that is somewhat like a CGL for an airport. For the customer's planes, the airport needs **Hangarkeepers**, which is similar to Garagekeepers in that it covers the bailee's liability of the airport for planes belonging to their customers.

Notes

Conclusion

Business Auto can provide coverage for automobiles owned, leased, hired, or even
1 employee's vehicles they use on the job. The **policy declarations section** will spell out which automobiles are covered. **Business Auto** can provide **Physical Damage coverage** for damage done to the cars as well as **Liability coverage**. A company could choose to add **Employer's Non-Ownership Liability** to protect the company against lawsuits if an employee injures someone or damages someone's property while driving their own personal vehicle on company business. **Garage policies** are designed for someone in the automobile business. **Garage Liability** affords a person in the automobile business **liability** protection including, **Premises and Operations, Products and Completed Operations** and **Automobile Liability**. It does not, however, pay for damage done to customer's cars. To cover customer's cars a **Garagekeeper's Liability policy** is required.

Things on the move or associated with transportation are covered by either an **Ocean**
2 **Marine (wet) or Inland Marine (dry) policy. Marine policies** normally provide property-type coverage. Imports, exports, bridges, tunnels, pipelines, communication cables and mobile property can be covered by a **Marine policy**. Ships and barges are also eligible for coverage but not specifically mentioned in the **Marine definition**. **Marine policies** provide **Bailee's Liability coverage** for property in your care, custody or control even if not located at your business.

Like the other coverages available under the Commercial Package, the **Farm** module
3 can be purchased as part of the package or as a monoline policy. The Farm module is designed for a farm that is being operated as a business. It utilizes Coverages A – D of the Homeowners Property coverage and then adds coverage for Scheduled and Unscheduled Farm personal property as well as coverage for Other Farm Structures. Farm Casualty coverages include Coverage H (BI and PD), Coverage I (Personal and advertising Injury), and Coverage J (Med Pay).

CHAPTERS 12 & 13
OTHER COMMERCIAL PACKAGE POLICIES

1. Boiler and Machinery policies accomplish which of the following?

   (A) They provide coverage for Boiler and Machinery exclusions found in the Commercial General Liability Policy.
   (B) They provide Boiler and Machinery coverage for exclusions found in the Commercial Property Policy.
   (C) They provide all risk coverage for business using steam boilers.
   (D) They are designed to provide coverage for bulldozers and other large machines.

2. Under The Commercial Automobile Policy, the minimum number of autos in a fleet is

   (A) 3
   (B) 5
   (C) 10
   (D) There is no minimum number of cars in a fleet.

3. Joan has a Commercial Auto Policy. In order for her to determine what autos shall be afforded coverage under this policy, she should look to

   (A) The Commercial Auto Consumer Manual, published by the NAIC.
   (B) The policy Conditions.
   (C) The policy Declarations.
   (D) The policy Definitions.

4. Which of the following would NOT be an "automobile" under the Commercial Package Policy?

   (A) A twelve wheel Russian army surplus all terrain vehicle used for snow removal under contract with the state highway department
   (B) A steam powered street sweeper
   (C) A mobile well driller in transit
   (D) A backhoe parked at the job site

5. Inland Marine Coverages are

   (A) Commercial lines only
   (B) Able to cover fewer risks than Boiler & Machinery
   (C) Designed to cover cargo moving in water
   (D) Broader than the Special Cause of Loss form

CHAPTERS 12 & 13 • OTHER COMMERCIAL PACKAGE POLICIES QUIZ

6. A restaurant has a large freezer in which it stores its own perishables plus food for a caterer next door. The business has a Commercial Property Policy, a CGL and a Boiler and Machinery Policy. If the freezer suddenly and accidentally breaks down, how will coverage be provided?

   (A) The freezer will be covered by the Boiler and Machinery Policy, and the food inside will be covered by the Commercial Property policy.
   (B) The freezer will be covered by the Boiler and Machinery Policy, and the restaurant's food inside will be covered by the Commercial Property Policy. The caterer's food will be covered by the CGL.
   (C) Both the freezer and all of the food are covered by the Boiler and Machinery Policy.
   (D) Nothing is covered because mechanical breakdown is excluded.

7. The Suspension Provision of the Boiler and Machinery Policy allows for all of the following EXCEPT

   (A) Inspection of the object without notice.
   (B) Suspension of coverage should a dangerous defect exist, with notice to the insured.
   (C) Suspension to remain in effect until the dangerous defect has been corrected.
   (D) Return of coverage when the insured files an Affidavit of Substantial Compliance with the underwriters.

8. Which of the following would be an Inland Marine risk?

   (A) A consignment of television sets being sent to Tokyo by air.
   (B) A shipment of sausage on its way down the Ohio River from Cincinnati to Louisville.
   (C) A forklift truck being used on the insured's premises.
   (D) The compressor for an air conditioning unit of a large office complex.

9. Rose E. Riveter has a small automobile repair shop. She wishes to have coverage for damage to her customers' cars. The best place to find this coverage would be

   (A) A Garage Liability coverage.
   (B) A Garagekeepers coverage.
   (C) Mechanics Non-Owned Automobile coverage.
   (D) Coverage A of her Commercial Automobile Policy.

10. Employers Non-Ownership Liability provides

    (A) Third party coverage for employers whose employees drive their own cars on company business.
    (B) Two party coverage for employers whose cars are driven by employees.
    (C) Coverage for injuries to employees while driving their own cars on company business.
    (D) Third party coverages for rental cars.

11. A company that installs boilers and wants coverage if they damage the boiler in the process would purchase which of the following?

    (A) Boiler & Machinery
    (B) Commercial General Liability
    (C) Inland Marine
    (D) Commercial Property

12. The liability section of a Farm Policy

    (A) Is only available with a single limit.
    (B) Includes Products and Completed Operations in the General Aggregate.
    (C) Covers grain trucks on the highway.
    (D) Covers injuries to employees covered by Workers Comp.

13. The Specified Perils coverage of a Business Auto policy would cover losses due to all of the following EXCEPT

    (A) Vandalism.
    (B) Windstorm.
    (C) Hail.
    (D) Freezing.

END

QUIZ ANSWERS & EXPLANATIONS ON NEXT PAGE

CHAPTERS 12 & 13
OTHER COMMERCIAL PACKAGE POLICIES
QUIZ ANSWER KEY

1. B. Boiler and Machinery Policies plug the holes found in Commercial Property Policies.

2. B. Five cars in a fleet.

3. C. Covered autos will be defined on the dec page.

4. D. A backhoe at the job site would be considered mobile equipment.

5. D. Inland Marine coverage has very few exclusions and thus provides even broader peril coverage than Special Perils.

6. C. Boiler and Machinery policies cover the object, the building, business personal property, and property of others.

7. D. Coverage will only be reinstated after the defect is fixed and coverage is returned by endorsement. There is no "affidavit of substantial compliance."

8. A. Items being moved via air or across terrain are best covered by Inland Marine insurance. Ocean Marine provides coverage for items being moved on the water.

9. B. If a business "keeps" customer's cars, they need Garagekeepers.

10. A. Employers Non-ownership Liability protects a business against liability claims arising from employees driving their own cars on company business.

11. C. Inland Marine is used to cover property of others in the care, custody or control of a business. This is especially true when the property is not located at the business premises.

12. B. In Farm Coverage there is no separate limit for Products and Completed Operations Liability. Both would be included in the General Aggregate limit.

13. D. Even if your car is frozen… it will thaw. Trust us.

BUSINESSOWNERS POLICY 14

SOURCE:
ISO-BOP-2006

1 The Commercial Package Policy which we have studied can be tailored to serve the needs of almost any business – from the neighborhood convenience store to General Motors. Probably the most important element of the Commercial Package Policy is its flexibility. However, flexibility requires that choices be made and decisions be reached. As we noted early on, the Commercial Package Policy does not exist until you and your client build it.

2 There is a large group of small to medium-sized businesses in this country that could literally be overwhelmed by the number of decisions to be reached in constructing a Commercial Package Policy. Imagine explaining aggregate and occurrence liability limits to Pop's Shoe Repair. Think how Pop would respond if you asked him if he needed Business Income or Extra Expense coverages – and at what levels and for how long. A business like Pop's might find that the CPP is just a little overkill. What Pop really wants is the business equivalent of a Homeowners Policy – simple to buy, simple to understand and includes just about everything he could ever need.

3 Well, that policy exists. It is the **Businessowners Policy (BOP)**. The application is short and simple, rating (pricing) is easy for the Agent to do, and there are very few options to consider. In an oversimplified way, the BOP is nothing but a **prepackaged** version of a Commercial Package Policy comprised of **Commercial Property** and a **CGL**. It has far less flexibility, but almost all of the necessary coverages are automatically built into the contract. The BOP is almost like a *Homeowners* for small low risk business.

4 **Good news!** You have already studied every coverage it contains or can be endorsed to contain. **Bad news!** Nearly every company selling a BOP has made some minor modifications to the Insurance Services Office (ISO) form discussed in this text. Therefore, you *will* find minor differences in eligibility requirements and available coverages after you complete this text and begin to familiarize yourself with your own company's product.

Notes

ELIGIBILITY

1 Generally speaking, the BOP is designed for the **small** to medium sized **low risk** businesses. The Insureds have coverage needs that are quite similar and do not include large or complex exposures that need uniquely designed coverage programs.

HOW DO WE KNOW LOW RISK?

2 Carriers limit the types of businesses eligible for BOPs. Businesses typically eligible for a BOP include:

apartments and condominiums
office buildings
stores
service businesses
wholesalers
contractors
convenience stores (even with gas pumps)
fast food restaurants
laundries and dry cleaners
auto parts stores

3 Businesses **not** eligible include

automobile, mobile home, and motorcycle dealers
bars
banks
manufacturing
auto repair
service stations
parking lots and garages
grills
large restaurants
arcades and places of amusement

NO CARS
NO BARS
NO BANKS
NO MANUFACTURING

HOW DO WE KNOW SMALL?

BOPs typically have size limitations, such as

Office buildings: Up to 100,000 square feet, six stories or less.

Retailers: Up to $3 million in volume and up to 25,000 square feet. An additional 25,000 square feet is allowed for storage.

Convenience Stores with gas pumps: Less than seventy-five percent of the total revenues can come from gasoline sales.

Fast Food Restaurants: Up to 7,500 square feet, seating capacity on more than 75, no bar service.

Notes

Wholesalers:	25% or less of gross sales is retail 25% or less of square footage open to the public
Dry Cleaners and Motels	Less than 3 stories tall

POLICY DESIGN

1 The BOP design is similar to the Commercial Package Policy in the sense that there are common policy parts and that the coverages are almost all the same.

2 The Businessowners Policy is comprised of:

- a Declarations Sheet
- a Common Policy Conditions Sheet
- a property coverage form
- a liability coverage form
- any endorsements (limited number available)

3 The big difference is that **the Businessowners Policy must be sold as a package — property and casualty**. It **cannot** be disassembled and sold as a monoline policy. It is a packaged policy, and all of the parts **must** be there. This idea of indivisibility holds true in the individual coverage forms as well. For instance, you generally may not exclude specific liability coverages as you can with the CGL. **On the property side, both the building and the contents must be covered if the Insured owns both**.

4 The Declarations Sheet is very similar to the Declarations under the Commercial Package Policy. There are a number of optional coverages that are available simply by marking the appropriate spots on the Declarations Sheet.

5 The Common Policy Conditions statement is also very similar to the equivalent version in the Commercial Package Policy. The property coverages available are also parallel to the CPP. The major difference is that many of the coverages are automatic rather than optional. The liability side of the BOP is also almost identical to the Commercial General Liability Policy.

PROPERTY FORMS

6 The Insured's Building is defined in much the same way as it was in the Commercial Property policy. Business Personal Property includes property owned by the Insured which is used in the business, property of others in the care, custody or control of the Insured, improvement and betterments made by an Insured tenant and leased personal property for which the Insured has a contractual responsibility.

7 The policy contains an automatic increase in coverage limits, or inflation guard, for the building. There is also an automatic 25% increase in the amount of Business Personal Property coverage to offset any seasonal variations in stock. This would allow a 25% increase in the limit of Business Personal Property for peak seasons, such as Christmas. This mechanism automatically handles a problem that requires a Reporting Form if a business were insured under the more cumbersone Commercial Property policy.

Notes

1 The BOP covers property for losses due to Special Perils. By endorsement, the Insured can purchase Standard (Basic) Perils if desired.

2 The Standard form is a Named Peril policy that almost exactly parallels the Basic form under the Commercial Property Policy. It covers the same original eleven perils plus one new peril called **Transportation**. The peril of Transportation protects your property in transit from losses due to such things as collision and upset. The Special form is an All Risk version almost identical to the Special form in the Commercial Property Policy. With both forms **the standard deductible is $500** but does not apply to fire department service charges, business income or extra expense losses.

3 While the BOP is written with **no coinsurance requirement**, it does give the Insured an incentive to insure to value. If the property is insured to at least 80% of its value, losses are settled on a **replacement cost basis** (with certain exceptions like used or secondhand merchandise, household contents, manuscripts and fine arts). If this level is not maintained, **losses are paid ACV**.

4 Like the Comercial Property policy, the BOP has a lengthy list of **Additional Coverages** which are **automatic**.

- Debris removal
- Preservation of property
- Fire Department service charge
- Collapse
- Water Damage
- Pollutant Clean up
- Acts of Civil Authority
- Money Orders and Counterfeit money
- Forgery and Alteration
- Increased Cost of Construction (ordinance or law)
- Glass Expense (for temporary repairs)
- Fire Extinguisher System Recharge
- Electronic Data
- Interruption of Computer Operations
- Limited Coverage for fungi, wet or dry rot, bacteria
- **Business Income**
- **Extra Expense**
- Business Income from Dependent Properties

Loss of Income--Built-in

5 The **Loss of Income** coverage is exactly the same as the Business Income policy that we have already studied. However, the Loss of Income coverage in a BOP is for a **full 12 months** with no individual monthly limity set. Payroll expenses are limited however to sixty days. The Business Income coverage comes with a **72 hour time based deductible**, which cannot be eliminated or reduced. The Extended Business Income Coverage is limited to 30 days.

Notes

1 Unlike the Commercial Property policy where extensions are earned, under a BOP the **Extensions of Coverage** are **automatic**.

- Personal Business Property on Newly Acquired Premises
- Personal Business Property off premises
- Outdoor Property
- Personal Effects
- Valuable Papers and Records
- Accounts Receivable

2 Optional property coverages are designated on the Dec Sheet and, if selected, require additional premium. Optional property coverages and endorsements include:

- Outdoor Signs
- Employee Dishonesty
- Mechanical Breakdown
- Burglary and Robbery (Standard form)
- Money and Securities (Special form)

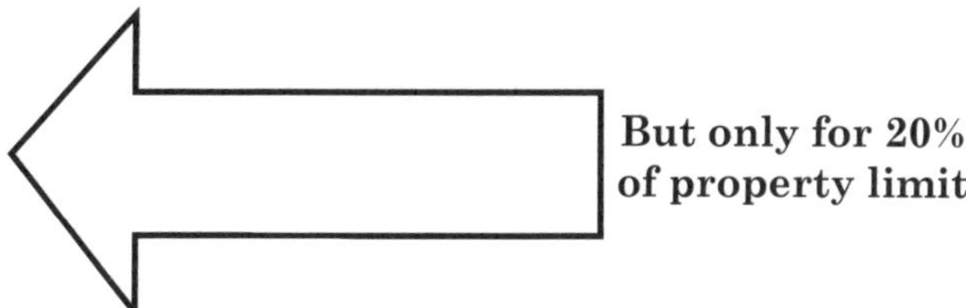

But only for 20% of property limit

LIABILITY COVERAGES

3 The liability coverages under the BOP are almost exactly the same as the Occurrence version of the Commercial General Liability policy. Therefore, the BOP has essentially the same scope of coverages for:

- Premises and Operations
- Products and Completed Operations
- Advertising and Personal Injury and
- Medical Payments

NOTE: Like the CGL, the BOP does **not** cover Workers Comp

4 The major difference between the CGL and the BOP is that the BOP has certain **predetermined fixed limits** rather than the option to pick any limits you wish. The basic occurrence limit is $1 million, with an upgrade to $2 million as an option. The general aggregate is double the occurrence limit and the Products and Completed Operations aggregate equals the occurrence limit. Therefore, if you select a $2 million occurrence limit, your General Aggregate would be $4 million and your Products and Completed Operations Aggregate would be $2 million.

5 The standard Fire Legal liability is $50,000 per fire and can be increased. The Medical Payments limit is $5,000 per person and cannot be increased.

Fire legal has its own limit

6 The liability section of the BOP is written on an **Occurrence** basis only. There is no Claims-Made version.

7 In almost all other respects, the coverages under the liability section of the BOP are the same as those that you have studied under the Commercial General Liability Policy.

Notes

BOP Endorsements ‡

- **Hired Auto and Nonowned Auto Liability - This endorsement adds liability coverage for employees using their personal vehicles on the job.** If the business owns a Business Auto policy, this coverage is an endorsement to the Auto policy. If the business does not own an Auto policy, this endorsement can be added to the BOP.

- **Protective Safeguards** - A premium adjustment giving credit for a local or centralized burglar/fire alarm or sprinklers.

- **Utility Services - Direct Damage** - This endorsement provides coverage for direct damage caused by utility service disruption stemming from a covered peril. Example: The local power company transformer is hit by lightning and Joe's meat locker has no refrigeration for 28 hours. This endorsement would cover the meat.

- **Utility Services - Time Element** - This endorsement would cover Joe's business income or additional expense losses if the incident described caused an interruption of his restaurant business for 10 days.

Conclusion

It could be said that the Businessowners Policy is nothing but a mini prepackaged
1 version of the Commercial Package Policy with certain coverages mandatory and
other coverages not available. It certainly has less flexibility than the Commercial
Package Policy but it is much easier to understand.

The BOP was designed for the low risk, small to medium-sized business, such as a
2 small store, office or apartment complex. High risk businesses, such as manufacturing businesses, are not eligible for coverage under a BOP. Eligibility requirements
limit the size of the building, the type of business, and the overall exposure both in
square feet and in dollar sales volume.

The mandatory coverages under the BOP include the standard property coverages
3 for the building and/or the contents, coverage for Loss of Income and Extra Expense,
protection for the property of others, and an automatic seasonal increase on inventory. Settlement is on Replacement Cost basis if insurance to value is 80% or more.
The liability coverages are almost identical to the Commercial General Liability
coverages with a few minor exceptions and far less flexibility in the dollar amounts
of liability coverages.

For those low risk businesses that qualify, the BOP is normally an excellent alterna-
4 tive to the more complex but more flexible Commercial Package Policy. You should
recognize, however, that it is not a panacea for all qualified businesses. The BOP
offered by most companies does not offer automatic coverage for newly acquired
buildings, and agreed value coverage are normally not available. If you have a client
who truly needs agreed value coverage and want to precisely set his liability limits,
you might do well to recommend the more complex (and probably more expensive)
Commercial Package rather than the BOP.

CHAPTER 14
BOP

1. Which of the following would NOT be qualified for coverage under a BOP?

   (A) A 7500 square foot thirty-seat micro-brewery.
   (B) A 6000 square foot taxidermy shop with a 10,000 square foot separate storeroom.
   (C) A 10,000 square foot shoe repair shop which does 20% of its business through house calls.
   (D) A 50 unit apartment complex.

2. Which of the following is true concerning Property Coverages on an unendorsed BOP?

   (A) BOP has no coinsurance provisions.
   (B) BOP losses are settled on a replacement cost basis if the insurance in force is 70% to value.
   (C) BOP is always all risk.
   (D) BOP covers building losses only.

3. Which of the following is NOT an optional coverage under a BOP?

   (A) Outdoor signs
   (B) Employee Dishonesty
   (C) Extra Expense
   (D) Mechanical Breakdown

4. All of the following are true about a BOP EXCEPT

   (A) Liability limits are fixed at certain levels.
   (B) Premises and Operations liability can be covered.
   (C) The liability section of a BOP is written on a occurrence basis.
   (D) There is no Med Pay coverage.

CHAPTER 14 • BOP QUIZ

5. Which of the following is true concerning a BOP?

   (A) A BOP can be purchased with both Property and Casualty coverages, or just property coverages if the insured has no need for liability coverage.
   (B) By endorsement, a BOP could provide some protection against employee dishonesty and burglaries.
   (C) The property coverage of a BOP can be purchased as a monoline policy.
   (D) A BOP includes Workers Comp.

6. Under a BOP, the Employers Non-owned Liability coverage would pay for

   (A) Losses caused by an employee driving a company car.
   (B) Losses caused by an employee driving their own car on company business.
   (C) Losses to customers' cars.
   (D) Losses to a leased company car.

7. Changes to a BOP may be made by the

   (A) Insured.
   (B) Mortgagee.
   (C) First named insured.
   (D) Anyone listed on the policy.

8. The liability section of a Businessowners Policy would NOT cover

   (A) Animals.
   (B) Motorcycles.
   (C) Golf Carts.
   (D) Products liability.

9. In the property coverage of a BOP, all of the following are common exclusions EXCEPT

   (A) Governmental action.
   (B) Nuclear energy.
   (C) Pollution cleanup.
   (D) Power failure off premises.

10. A BOP with a Protective Safeguard Endorsement would provide what benefit to an insured with a sprinkler system?

    (A) A lower premium
    (B) A higher deductible
    (C) A way to replace loss income in the event of a loss
    (D) All risk coverage on Business Personal Property

11. In the event of a loss of a piece of business property covered by both a BOP and another specialized policy, how would the BOP pay?

    (A) As primary coverage
    (B) As excess coverage
    (C) On a pro rata basis
    (D) The BOP would not provide any coverage

12. All of the following are true about BOPs EXCEPT

    (A) Credit unions are not eligible.
    (B) Loss of Income coverage has a 72-hour deductible.
    (C) Under the Business Protective Safeguard endorsement, the insurance company must be notified within 48 hours if sprinklers are inoperative.
    (D) Any unendorsed BOP covers employee theft.

END

QUIZ ANSWERS & EXPLANATIONS ON NEXT PAGE

CHAPTER 14
BOP QUIZ ANSWER KEY

1. A. A BOP is not available to those in the liquor business.

2. A. A BOP does not have a coinsurance requirement. If the property is insured to 80% of value or more, losses are settled on a Replacement Cost basis. If not, losses are settled ACV.

3. C. Extra Expense is not optional—it's built into the BOP.

4. D. A BOP does have Med Pay coverage.

5. B. A BOP offers some elements of Commercial Crime, but only by endorsement.

6. B. The key here is "Nonownership." The employer doesn't own the car, but could be named in a liability claim arising from the employee using their own car on company business.

7. C. Only First Named Insureds can make changes in any commercial policy.

8. B. A BOP is not available to those in the auto or motorcycle business.

9. C. Just as with Commercial Property a BOP would have coverage additions that would provide for some pollution clean-up and removal.

10. A. The insurance company is glad you have the safeguards and will gladly lower your premium as a result.

11. B. When there are two policies covering a piece of property, the BOP is always excess.

12. D. Must notify the company within 48 hours if sprinklers are non-operational. BOPs do not cover employee theft.

Part IV

EFFECTIVE TEST-TAKING STRATEGIES

EFFECTIVE TEST-TAKING STRATEGIES

We all react a bit differently when taking a test. Some people are excellent test takers, some are good, and others find taking an exam to be a painful experience.

- If you are an **excellent exam-taker**, you may wish to either skim this section or skip it entirely.
- If you consider yourself a **good test-taker**, we suggest that you skim this material and concentrate your attention on any new ideas you may find.
- If taking exams has been **difficult** for you in the past, you may find this section to be as valuable as any contained in the text. You are the person we had in mind when we wrote it.

Your purpose for studying this text is probably to gain the knowledge necessary to pass the exam required to obtain a license as a life and health insurance agent in your state. If this is the case, you have two tasks before you.

- To learn the necessary material.
- To demonstrate on an exam that you have indeed mastered this information.

Most students tend to view the first requirement as a major undertaking and the second as a frightening one. Let's face it, **no one really enjoys taking a test**. Unfortunately, there are times when you have no other choice. To make matters worse, there is usually something quite important riding on your performance – such as your agent's license.

Why are exams so frightening? Well, a major reason is that we have never been taught how to take a test. Driving an automobile for the first time was a bit terrifying for most of us, but once we learned the basic techniques, we found the experience pleasurable. While it is doubtful that this section will make your agent's exam a pleasurable event, we hope to make it a tolerable one.

Since 1977, Pathfinder Insurance Training Institute has prepared thousands of individuals just like you for state insurance exams. The authors of this text are the chief instructors of the Pathfinder classes. We discovered quickly that teaching basic insurance concepts was only half of the battle – the other half was training our students to take the examination in a manner that would trigger **superior test performance**. We have spent at least as much time studying the nuts and bolts of learning theory and test psychology as we have preparing lectures and learning aids. We have observed thousands of students during the test and have carefully noted the problems most often encountered and the errors that were usually made. We have hired educational consultants, communications experts and practicing psychologists to help us develop alternative strategies to improve our students' testing skills. Some ideas worked immediately, some required modification and others were blind alleys. We want to share with you the methods that have been consistently successful for our students.

Before we begin, let's eliminate one very real concern. Will this book give you enough information to pass your state exam? Without exception the answer is yes – the text does contain enough data to get you through the test.

We have taken great pains to include all the information required by any testing organization as well as any individual state-developed test that has published guidelines. Simply, you will find all you need to know for any entry level exam in this book and the appropriate state supplement.

TEST-TAKING – A LEARNED SKILL

There is a tendency on the part of some to dismiss the entire problem of test performance with a shrug of the shoulders and the plaintive cry, "Good test-takers are born that way." Nonsense! Test-taking is nothing more than another form of communication. You were not born knowing how to talk or write or take tests. Someone taught you how to talk and write, but in all probability, no one ever taught you how to take an exam. This is an unfortunate situation, but not necessarily a permanent one. By learning test-taking skills, your abilities can be substantially improved.

A careful reading of this section and some effort in changing behavior patterns will allow you to take advantage of what we have learned from the thousands of students who have preceded you. Please understand that these suggestions should be considered guiding principles, not inviolate rules. These ideas are not carved in granite, and if we propose something that's not comfortable – forget it. Not everything works for everyone. These are simply alternatives to the procedures that may have proven unsatisfactory to you in the past.

STUDYING FOR AN EXAM

It is important to recognize that studying for an exam is more demanding than reading for enjoyment. There are certain actions you can take while reading that will make exam preparation easier. We suggest that you read this section rapidly now and review it carefully when you finish the book.

Note Taking

On each page of the formal text, you will find a column for notes. Use this column. You might use it to rewrite an important sentence in your own words. If something is unclear the first time you read it, put a question mark in the notes column so that you can return to the passage later. If the book refers to a Boatowners policy, and you (or someone you know) just bought one, put that person's name in the column to help you remember Boatowners. You also might find it easier to underline or highlight statements in the book that are particularly important instead of taking notes on separate sheets of paper.

If you are attending a school that uses this book, you may wish to underline the points your instructor indicates as critical with a different color pen. What you consider important might differ from what your instructors think, and knowing that difference could be valuable.

How Do You Learn?

Knowing how you personally store information can be valuable to your study. Consultants tell us that people think and remember in several different ways.

- **SEE (Visual Learners)**

If you are a highly visual person, you function mentally by seeing pictures in your mind. If asked where your car is parked, you would answer after first literally seeing your car in the garage or in its parking space. The numerous illustrations in this book will be very helpful to you in remembering the important information.

- **HEAR (Auditory Learners)**

If you are an auditory person, you probably talk to yourself when no one else is around. (It's only a problem when you start to answer.) If you take an exam following a lecture, you can hear the instructor repeating important points as distinctly as if your mind were a tape recorder. If your thinking processes are highly auditory, you will naturally be able to repeat key phrases and sentences from the book.

- **FEEL (Kinesthetic Learners)**

Kinesthetic students tend to absorb information rather than see it or hear it. If you are a kinesthetic person you typically learn best by doing. You are so in touch with your feelings that you can actually place yourself into the examples in the text and recall the concepts by remembering the feelings triggered in the examples.

The classic illustration of a visual (see) person, auditory (hear) person, and a kinesthetic (feel) person trying to communicate occurs at an art gallery. Looking at a painting, the Visual says, "That would look beautiful in my library." The Auditory responds "That painting tells me that the artist is a joyful person." The Kinesthetic replies, "That painting makes me feel good to be alive."

Now that you have classified yourself as visual, auditory, or kinesthetic, we can tell you that almost no one really operates on only one of these channels. Typically, you have one native language and some fluency in the other two. Some of our instructors are highly auditory (hear), but see pictures when thinking. Others might be extremely visual (see), but process some information both kinesthetically (feeling), and auditorily (hearing). Actually, the more channels you can use while learning, the better. If you think you are primarily visual, try to hear the words of this book as you read them and try to live the examples with the kinesthetics. Whichever is your primary channel will be your basic method of learning, but if you can use the other channels as well, remembering what you have learned will be easier. With a great deal of help from our communications experts, we have written this text to communicate on all three channels. This will enable the visuals to see the big picture, while auditory learners are hearing what we are saying, and kinesthetics are grasping the concepts.

PRACTICING THE ART OF TEST-TAKING

At the end of each chapter in the text, you will find practice quizzes which test your understanding of the information you have read. We urge you to take all of the quizzes and strongly suggest that you follow the method you intend to use on the exam. In doing so, you will not only be testing your knowledge of important information, but you will also be practicing your exam-taking skills.

Before outlining the test procedures we suggest, let's discuss the quality of the test you will be taking. We have conducted licensing schools in a number of states using every conceivable type of examination. For the most part, we have been very impressed with the quality of the exams. Contrary to some opinions, these exams are not designed to test your exam-taking abilities. They test the candidates' understanding of basic insurance concepts and contain very few trivial or trick questions. In almost every state the question structure is multiple-choice. Your task is to pick the correct response from alternatives A, B, C, or D. Though many students complain about "trick questions," we have found that in most cases the question bothering the student was not a "trick question." The student either did not read the question correctly or simply did not know the answer. We have yet to see an insurance exam question that was intended to deceive.

That does not mean that we have never seen a poorly written question – we have. The English language is not an exact science, and question writers are not perfect human beings. However, 95% of the questions you will encounter on your state's exam will be good questions. The only way the 5% can beat you is for you to get so upset by the meaning of one question that you miss 10 others agonizing over the one. Take it easy, and remember that you do not need a perfect score.

Reading Carefully

Now let's get down to specifics. The most important principle of test-taking is to **read carefully**. Read each question and all of the potential answers carefully before responding. Typically, students who do not read the questions properly can be divided into two groups. The first group is composed of the people we call the Speed Demons. Speed Demons seem to think they earn extra points by finishing early. Speed is simply not a factor on most licensing exams. If you are a Speed Demon, practice slowing down. Force yourself to read the entire question and all of the possible answers before responding. If you can develop that habit as you take the practice quizzes in this book, it will be easier for you to slow down when you take the state exam.

The second group is composed of the students we term Agonizers. If you are an Agonizer, you have a strong tendency to read too much into a question. Remember, these exams are written to determine if you have the entry-level knowledge the citizens of your state have a right to expect from an insurance agent. Please use the following guideline when trying to comprehend a question: the question probably means what your first careful reading tells you it means. We always tell our students to "think shallow," and that is what the Agonizer must learn to do. Yes, you should read carefully, but do not allow yourself to start second-guessing.

If you have doubts about the meaning of a question, a good strategy is to ask yourself what the question writer wants to find out if you know – what piece of information is he trying to determine if you remember. Again, the question will most likely mean what your first careful reading tells you it means.

One very common error made by people taking multiple-choice tests is to look at the answers before reading and understanding the question. The sequence works like this. You hurriedly read the question while not really understanding it. Immediately you go to the possible answers and start sorting through them looking for clues to the meaning of the question. The problem with this approach is obvious once you think about it. Three of the four clues are wrong! Three of the choices will take you away from the answer. How can you avoid this problem? Simply cover the answers while you read the question and try to answer in your own mind before you look at the choices. Then carefully study each answer before making your final selection.

As an example, in this book you will learn that the CPP is the Commercial Package Policy. Now for the question.

1. The abbreviation CPP stands for which of the following?

   (A) Comprehensive Property Policy
   (B) Commercial Property Policy
   (C) Comprehensive Package Policy
   (D) Commercial Package Policy

While this question is probably more deceptive than any you will encounter on your licensing exam, you can see that by covering the answers until you have formulated your own answer, you can avoid being misled.

Consider another type of question.

2. All of the following are true concerning HOMEOWNERS insurance EXCEPT

You cannot see the answers yet because we are helping you cover them, but the problem is that you ultimately cannot answer this type of question without the alternatives offered. What can you do? Mentally review the characteristics of HOMEOWNERS insurance and try to anticipate the question writer, thus giving yourself an edge when looking at the possible responses.

A 10-second mental summary could sound like this:

> "Homeowners policies provide property insurance to varying degrees of protection; they all provide theft and liability insurance, and they usually serve the needs of the **average** consumer. They can be endorsed to serve unusual needs."

You might want to remind yourself that this is an **EXCEPT question** so you should expect to see three correct statements about Homeowners insurance. Your task is to identify the one incorrect statement – the exception.

Now you can look at the question and the possible answers.

2. All of the following are true concerning HOMEOWNERS insurance EXCEPT

   (A) It can cover your dwelling.
   (B) It can cover your contents.
   (C) It can cover your personal liability.
   (D) It can cover your factory.

The last choice, (D), is the correct response as it is the exception, or the one incorrect statement about Homewoners insurance. We hope the value of trying to formulate an answer before you read the possible choices is apparent. If you practice these techniques as you take the practice quizzes, they will become second nature by the time you sit for the examination.

Guessing Intelligently

After you have taken several practice quizzes, you will begin to develop another important exam-taking skill – the ability to guess intelligently. There is every possibility that you will encounter questions on our practice quizzes and on the state exam that you cannot answer with 100% certainty. However, if you can eliminate one or two of the options, you have certainly improved your odds. But first, a question: If you really do not know the answer, **should you guess?** Yes, yes, a thousand times, yes. On every state insurance exam we have seen there is no penalty for guessing. Even on tests that do impose a penalty for guessing, it is almost always statistically advantageous to guess. This is not to say that knowledge of the subject matter is in any way unimportant. On the contrary, the more knowledge you have, the better guesser you should be up to the point where you have specific knowledge of the question and guessing becomes unnecessary.

As an example of intelligent guesswork, let's use a question dealing with something other than insurance. We'll use popular music – a subject of which some of you know a great deal while others know very little.

3. The British rock group, the Beatles, were known for their songwriting abilities as well as their performing talents. Which of the famous four wrote the classic ballad Yesterday?

    (A) John Lennon
    (B) Elvis Presley
    (C) Paul McCartney
    (D) Ringo Starr

If you know absolutely nothing about music or think that the Beatles were McCartney's start-up band before Wings, the best you can do is make a random guess. This gives you a 25% (one out of four) chance of identifying the correct response.

If you know a little about pop music, you could eliminate item (B) as a possibility because Elvis Presley was an American and was never a member of a British group. Your odds are thereby improved to 1 out of 3 or 33 1/3%.

If your knowledge is a little more extensive, you could also disregard item (D). Almost every Beatles song was written by John Lennon or Paul McCartney, and the few numbers penned by Ringo Starr were novelty songs, not soulful ballads like Yesterday. With items (A) and (C) the remaining possibilities, your odds are now 50%. This is the point where knowledge of rock music ends for most people, but notice how your odds have improved. For the remaining few who know that John Lennon was the rock-and-roller of the Beatles and that Paul McCartney was more the balladeer, Paul McCartney would be the logical guess. It would also be the correct guess, for item (C) is indeed the right answer.

Of course, a few of you knew the answer as soon as you read the question. Your depth of information made guessing totally unnecessary. However, if you can imagine a question that requires specific knowledge that you do not have, the above procedure will allow you to guess intelligently when circumstances require.

A final word on guessing: use the information provided by other questions on the examination. We have observed that on any test that contains 100 to 150 questions, there will be 10 to 15 questions answered, directly or indirectly, by others on the exam. This provides you with an opportunity to **improve your score** 10% by simply reading carefully.

Perhaps you remember seeing question #2 early in the exam.

2. All of the following are true concerning HOMEOWNERS insurance EXCEPT

   (A) It can cover your dwelling.
   (B) It can cover your contents.
   (C) It can cover your personal liability.
   (D) It can cover your factory.

Suppose that later on your exam, question #23 appeared as below.

23. Though a HOMEOWNERS policy is not intended to cover businesses, it will allow some coverage for a business operated out of your home under all of the following circumstances EXCEPT

    (A) It is a low-risk business.
    (B) You have a proper endorsement.
    (C) The structure is still used primarily as a residence.
    (D) Your business is manufacturing dynamite.

Certainly the stem of question #23 should give you a clue to the answer to #2 or at the very least it could confirm an uncertain answer.

As with the other suggestions made in this chapter, you will be given ample opportunity to practice guessing as you take the multiple-choice review quizzes at the end of each chapter. Rest assured that for the most part, our questions are more detailed and more difficult than those you will find on your state exam. If you are correctly answering 70% to 75% of our questions, you will be in good shape for your licensing test.

Will You Have Time To Finish?

As you take the quizzes in this book, you might wonder how much time you should allow yourself to complete them. As pointed out earlier, time is not normally a factor on state licensing exams. You generally have considerably more time than you need. To check your pace, simply time yourself as you take the first three or four multiple-choice tests. Do not attempt to go faster than normal, just work at a comfortable speed and keep track of the time.

If you average between 30 seconds and 45 seconds per question, you will have no time problems. If you are spending much over 60 seconds per question, you are probably moving a little too slowly, and we would advise trying to work a bit faster. Even at 60 seconds to 90 seconds per question, you would still finish the exam in most states; however, you are probably an Agonizer, and are giving yourself too much time to read too much into the questions.

Planning Your Study Time

How much time should be spent reading this book? The answer to that question is obviously somewhat dependent on your reading and studying skills. If this text is all you use for preparation, as a rule-of-thumb, we suggest a total of 60 hours to study prior to your final review. Even if you attend a licensing school, most people find some pre-study an absolute necessity. We have always recommended 20 hours of advance preparation for the students coming to our schools. We are aware that many arrive with almost no preparation and still pass, but the people who can succeed without pre-study are normally excellent students who work extraordinarily hard during the school.

It is also important that your preparation take place over a reasonable period of time. If you are studying in your spare time, try to allocate at least two to three weeks to your study. If you are able to devote full-time to this task, we recommend that you do not study more than five hours a day. Allow yourself enough time to reach your objective on a five-hour-a-day routine, and you will retain significantly more information.

REVIEWING FOR AN EXAM

Hopefully, you will schedule your time so that you will have finished reading the material and taking the practice quizzes two or three days before your licensing exam. What do you do for a final review? We have several specific suggestions.

First, let's mention a couple of things we would not recommend. We strongly urge that you not reread the book. If you only have a couple of days prior to the exam, you simply do not have the time. This exercise would be exhausting, confusing and counter-productive. If there are several short sections of the book you feel you need to review, fine, but do not get carried away. We also suggest you avoid taking endless numbers of multiple-choice tests, or even worse, taking the same one over and over. We have seen some students memorize 200 or 300 questions and then fail a licensing exam. Why? They did not know the information; they had simply memorized questions and answers. Since most states take their questions from a large question bank, these students saw questions that looked similar to those they had pored over, but the answers they had memorized did not match the slightly altered question on the exam. A good practice quiz is an excellent beginning, but it should not be your total preparation.

When you are ready, tackle the **Practice Final Exams** contained in Appendix I of this text. These questions address the basic subject matter that you will see on your state exam and are of about the same difficulty level. If you are successful on this final examination, you are ready for anything. As much as possible, take this final exam under real test conditions. Allow yourself two hours without interruption to complete it. Most of you will finish much earlier, but this would duplicate the pace you would have to meet in order to finish in accordance with the time allowed in most states.

When you finish, use the answer keys which follow to grade your exam. Then, do some analysis. Notice how many you missed because of reading errors – either you did not read carefully enough or you read too much into the question. On those that you missed because you did not know or understand the subject matter, make note of the subject matter. You should then be able to determine if any specific chapters are a major problem.

THE NIGHT BEFORE THE EXAM

The most important thing for you to do the night before the exam is **get a good night's sleep**. If you have finished your review and you feel reasonably confident about the material, relax and go to bed early. Fight the urge to review it all again. It is simply not necessary. If you have one or two problem areas to review, do so, but know when to stop. If you have an overwhelming need to suffer, have a friend stomp on your toe. You can probably pass the exam with a sore toe, but you will not succeed if you have not slept in 48 hours.

If you have not finished your review prior to the night before the state test, we would recommend that you do what we suggested in the Reviewing for an Exam section, but you will have to do it rather hurriedly. Your number one objective must still be to get a good night's sleep.

If you have not read the book, but you have an I.Q. of 160 and know something about insurance, read Chapters 5, 6, 11 and 14, take the final exam, and set both of your alarm clocks. If you have an average I.Q. and know nothing about insurance, reschedule your exam date, party tonight and forget your alarm clocks.

Seriously, the night before the exam is the time for you to start relaxing and building your confidence. It is not the time to start destroying your attitude with confusing bits of insurance trivia. Rest assured that your state exam will not be as difficult as the quizzes you have already mastered in this book.

You will find that about 80% of your exam questions require broad, conceptual knowledge. Only about 20% cover detailed, specific facts. We have seen some students go so berserk over minute details the night before an exam that they destroyed their understanding of the basic concepts. Obviously, they blew the test. If you can remember the concepts, most of the details are self-evident. The few details that do escape your memory will not cost you the exam, but losing the basic concepts most assuredly will.

If you have followed our suggestions, read the text carefully and scored well on the practice quizzes, you have nothing to worry about. If you scored well on the practice final exam, you are prepared. Relax and get a good night's sleep.

THE MORNING OF THE EXAM

Certainly, on the morning of the exam you will want to get up in time to arrive at your test site promptly without rushing. We strongly recommend that you **avoid any last minute studying**. Last minute cramming on the morning of your test almost guarantees panic. Since there is no time for a relaxed, orderly review, just put your books and notes away and stay calm. Only take with you the materials necessary for the exam and leave everything else behind.

Though it is advisable to plan your arrival at the test site a few minutes early (allowing for getting lost en route, flat tires, flood, pestilence, etc.), we recommend that you do not arrive any earlier than necessary. Test sites are full of panicky candidates engaged in last-minute studying, detailed cramming and a variety of other counter-productive activities. Fear is mighty contagious; prolonged exposure will make you as crazy as they are.

When the proctor indicates that it is time to begin, find a place where you will be comfortable. If you are assigned a desk in a location that makes you uncomfortable, ask the proctor for permission to move. There is no reason to take a test with a gum-popper on one side of you and a mumbler on the other. You have the right to modify your environment to give you every possible edge.

TAKING THE EXAM

If you practice our recommended strategies, your new, positive test-taking habits will now direct your actions. There are only a few additional points to remember.

- **Read The Test Instructions Carefully** – Nothing can destroy your score faster than answering the wrong questions or responding in the wrong places. If you fail to understand some part of the instructions, ask the proctor.

- **If Speed Is A Problem, Handle It** – As we have indicated repeatedly, time will not be a problem for most of you. If, in taking the practice quizzes, you have determined that you are moving too slowly, we would suggest that you develop a test schedule. Assume that you are taking two exams of 100 questions each and that you are permitted 3 1/2 hours to finish. If you allow yourself 15 minutes at the end of each exam to review questions that were difficult, your objective would be to finish 100 questions in an hour and a half (50 questions in 45 minutes). If you start at 8:00 A.M., then jot down on a piece of scratch paper that you should be on question #50 by 8:45 A.M. By 9:30 A.M., you should be on #100, and have 15 minutes to review. Then, do the same for the second exam . . . allowing 45 minutes for 50 questions. Now you can forget time until you reach your first checkpoint, and at that time you can speed up if you are behind.

- **Take A Break** – We always urge our students to take a five-minute break about half-way through the test. The mind is not built to concentrate fully for 3 1/2 hours, so don't fight Mother Nature; take a break, even if you do not get out of your chair.

- **Take The Questions One At A Time** – We suggest that you answer the questions in the order they are asked. It is not wise to skip around. Even if you have 200 questions to answer, you do not have to deal with all of them at once. You still only answer them one at a time. If you do not know an answer, put down your best guess and mark that question for review.

- **Take The Exam Only Once** – When you finish the exam, you may be tempted to take it again. Please do not! Go back to the troublesome questions only. Even with those, we would suggest that you change them only if you misread them the first time or if the question was answered by a later question. If you know nothing more than you did before, leave it alone. Since 90% of the time your first inclination is your best, when you start changing answers, you are normally changing right ones to wrong ones.

- **Don't Be Influenced By Others** – Some students will finish before you do – that is a fact of life for most of us. If you are on your schedule and someone leaves when you are only on question #17 – don't commit suicide. This is a test, not a race. The person that left could have simply been taking another exam with fewer questions. On the other hand, when you are finished, do not hesitate to leave. You do not have to sit in the room and suffer – get up and go. There are no points for longevity.

Freezing On Exams

This last subject is a major problem for more people than you might guess. We have had numerous students in our licensing schools who are intelligent, well-prepared and highly motivated but have had a long history of freezing when taking tests. Experts agree that over 25% of the US population has significant **test anxiety**. As a result, Pathfinder has incorporated all of the knowledge that we have learned about test anxiety in our more than 36 years of experience working with tens of thousands of students into a 70 minute CD. The name of the CD is the ***FREAKY TEST TAKER***. Please see the inside front cover of this book for details.

If you have any possibility whatsoever that test anxiety could keep you from performing at your very best on your exam, we strongly suggest that you order a copy of the CD and listen to it at least twice. **It is guaranteed to change your life!**

Let The Anxiety Wear Itself Out

Under this approach, if you feel yourself freeze up, stop answering questions and forget the test for a few moments. Tell yourself that what is happening is physiologically normal. Your brain has told your body that it is crisis time, and your body has reacted by pumping great quantities of adrenalin. Now, adrenalin is great stuff if the crisis is an attacking bear, and your job is to run like mad. But adrenalin is not very helpful in taking tests. Fortunately, after five or ten minutes the adrenalin will stop and things will return to normal. Therefore, you should simply waste ten minutes reading the test directions, establishing your exam time schedule or day-dreaming. **Do not answer any questions while frozen.** When you feel comfortable again, begin (or continue) your exam. If you follow this procedure, you will never miss a question due to freezing because the procedure is to not answer any questions while frozen. Yes, you will be giving other students a ten minute head start, but so what? This is a test – not a race.

Replace The Anxiety With A Feeling Of Relaxation

This second approach requires a little quiet thought prior to walking into the exam. It is based upon the idea that we have many more options available to us than the ones we habitually select. As you are aware, we develop most of our habits (good and bad) as children, and we reinforce them for the rest of our lives. When you were very young, you may have established a response pattern to tests – freezing. At that time you may have had few other options. And freezing may have worked for you in an odd sort of way – your fear of freezing may have provided the motivation for you to study. As an adult, you have many more options available to you. There's nothing inherently wrong with panic – but there are more productive responses. For example, you might choose to respond to a test by thinking of it as:

- A battle of wits between the exam writer and yourself.
- An opportunity to demonstrate the knowledge you have worked so hard to gain.
- A chance to relax and observe the other victims of frostbite seizure chew the erasers off their pencils.

Obviously, there are numerous mental responses to an exam. If none of the three listed above seems appropriate, think of one that helps you feel comfortable. You can certainly discover one that will be more helpful than freezing.

Before starting the exam, place your feet flat on the floor with your hands resting comfortably in your lap. Take three or four deep breaths and think about something particularly pleasant that has recently happened to you. Try to see the experience as clearly as possible, hear the sounds associated with the event, and relive the good feelings. As you begin to relax, concentrate on your new response to exams in a calm, unruffled way. When you feel completely at ease, resume reading the question and move easily into your work.

Intuitively, you will sense which method will work for you. Re-read the paragraphs outlining your procedure several times. This will prepare your mind to accept your new approach to an old problem. Practice your approach on each exam in this book, and it will soon become as comfortable as an old friend.

If you have doubts that these ideas will work for you, we can't blame you. At first, the habits established by a life-long history of panicked exam-taking may seem difficult to break. But if you will try your new approach, we think you'll be surprised at how well it does work. It has already worked for thousands of people who felt just like you.

After The Exam

Relax! You passed!

CONCLUSION

If tests have been a problem for you in the past, we are confident that you have found many ideas in this section that will greatly improve your test-taking skills. We are equally confident that some of you are still skeptical that anything will really help you.

Recall, however, when you were a teenager facing the challenge of learning to drive a car and getting a license. Remember how you felt? For years you had been a passenger and everything appeared relatively simple. Then you were in the driver's seat and all the things you had to learn seemed totally overwhelming. You were probably horrified the first time you lurched down the street and nearly threw yourself through the windshield. You believed your whole future hung in the balance the day you took your driving test. You may have even felt that everyone you knew would laugh in your face if you failed.

But you passed. You earned your license. Yes, at that point you had to totally concentrate on every move, and you were not a very relaxed driver. Since then, however, driving has become second-nature. When you get behind the wheel today, you think about everything except driving.

Your current need for knowledge about insurance and your desire to pass the state exam probably triggers most of the same fears and feelings your driving test did. But if you will stay with it, the end result will be the same. A few months after you pass your insurance exam, the concepts that seem so foreign to you today will be such a part of you that you will wonder how they could have ever seemed difficult at all.

Good luck!

Part V

SAMPLE EXAMINATIONS

SAMPLE EXAMINATIONS

The following practice tests in Personal lines and Commercial Lines are designed to accomplish two objectives: 1) Indicate your state of readiness for your state insurance exam; 2) Identify areas where more study might be helpful.

If you are prepared, you should score about 75% (37 out of 50) on the appropriate tests.

Good Luck!

PERSONAL LINES Practice Test

Directions: Each question is followed by four suggested answers labeled (A), (B), (C), and (D). In each case, select the one that best answers the question.

Note: In some questions the word "basic" or "standard" appears in front of the name of a policy, floater, or other form. In each instance, basic or standard means without endorsements or changes of any kind.

1. One purpose of a deductible is to

   (A) prevent underinsurance
   (B) eliminate small claims
   (C) prevent catastrophic claims
   (D) penalize the insured for physical hazards

2. An insured's Homeowner's Broad Form (HO-2) provides $40,000 coverage on her dwelling and $25,000 coverage on its contents. If vandals cut down a tree on her property valued at $1000, the maximum amount she will receive is which of the following, assuming a $250 deductible?

   (A) $0
   (B) $250
   (C) $400
   (D) $500

3. Which of the following best describes the concept of risk?

   (A) Result of loss
   (B) Amount of loss
   (C) Uncertainty of loss
   (D) Cause of loss

4. Ten years ago an insured purchased a building for $50,000 that would cost $100,000 to rebuild today. If the physical value of the building has depreciated $2,000 each year, the building's present actual cash value is

(A) $100,000
(B) $80,000
(C) $50,000
(D) $30,000

5. Additional Coverages in a Homeowners policy would cover

(A) the dwelling
(B) materials and supplies
(C) other structures
(D) debris removal

6. Which of the following would NOT be covered under the Section 1 of an HO-3 form?

(A) The insured's $2000 collie
(B) Personal property of the insured's daughter who is away at college
(C) The insured's driveway if damaged by a falling object
(D) Losses caused by the sudden and accidental leaking of a water heater

7. An insured carries $25,000 property insurance with 80 percent coinsurance on a building worth $40,000. How much would she collect in the event of a total loss?

(A) $20,000
(B) $25,000
(C) $32,000
(D) $40,000

8. A person may be considered negligent if he

(A) fails to do what a reasonably prudent person would do
(B) commits a deliberate act that injures another
(C) injures another person even though he acted prudently
(D) assists to the best of his ability another person who is in distress

9. In property insurance, a loss would only be paid if insurable interest at the

(A) inception of the policy
(B) time of premium payment
(C) time of application
(D) time of loss

10. Which of the following is NOT true concerning Exclusions?

(A) They exist in part to eliminate coverage for uninsurable perils
(B) They eliminate coverage for certain kind of losses
(C) They are of critical importance in determining what is covered under an All Risk policy
(D) There are no allowable exclusions in an Inland Marine policy

11. A homeowner whose house suffered a $50,000 total loss was insured for $60,000. What principle would be violated if her insurance company paid her $60,000?

(A) Indemnity
(B) Negligence
(C) Liability
(D) Insurable interest

12. Which of the following formulas is used to calculate a claim payment when a policy contains a Coinsurance clause?

(A) $\frac{\text{Insurance Carried}}{\text{Insurance Required}}$ x Loss = Amount Paid

(B) $\frac{\text{Insurance Carried}}{\text{Insurance Required}}$ x Total Value = Amount Paid

(C) $\frac{\text{Insurance Required}}{\text{80\% of Cash Value}}$ x Loss = Amount Paid

(D) $\frac{\text{Insurance Required}}{\text{80\% of Replacement Cost}}$ x Total Value = Amount Paid

13. An application for Homeowners insurance is denied based on a consumer report furnished to the insurance company. Under the provisions of the Fair Credit Reporting Act, the applicant has the right to do which of the following?

(A) Be advised of the name of the credit reporting agency
(B) Sue the insurance company for defamation
(C) Demand the insurance company furnish a copy of the credit report
(D) Be advised of the content of the report, but they have no right to view their credit history

14. Under a Personal Articles Floater, a pair of antique salt and pepper shakers is insured for $1,000. When one of the shakers is broken, the remaining shaker is worth only $200. How much will the insured receive for the loss before the deductible is applied?

(A) $1,000
(B) $800
(C) $500
(D) $200

15. When a Homeowners policy is issued with $75,000 coverage on a dwelling, what is the automatic amount of insurance on personal property?

(A) $7,500
(B) $15,000
(C) $37,500
(D) $45,000

16. The Personal Liability section of a Homeowners policy covers which of the following?

(A) Damage to an insured's property caused by a visitor
(B) Bodily injury to a resident caused by a neighbor's dog
(C) Bodily injury or property damage caused by war
(D) Bodily injury or property damage caused by the non-business activities of an insured

17. Under the terms of a property policy, an insurance company is obligated to

(A) pay covered losses
(B) ensure that the covered property is safe
(C) keep records of the covered property
(D) ensure that the hazard remains the same

18. Z insures his house for $85,000. If he suffered a $50,000 loss to his dwelling structure, he would be able to collect which of the following percentages of loss?

(A) 20%
(B) 80%
(C) 90%
(D) 100%

19. Which of the following should an insurance agent recommend to a prospective insured who owns silverware, jewelry, and furs valued in excess of $50,000?

(A) Homeowners policy
(B) Personal Articles Floater
(C) Personal Effects Floater
(D) Extended Coverage Endorsement

20. Mary Kent has insured her home under a $100,000 HO 3 Form. If she has a fire loss of $15,000 to her unattached garage, her Homeowners policy will reimburse her for which of the following amounts?

(A) $5,000
(B) $7,500
(C) $10,000
(D) $15,000

21. Losses caused by all of the following are covered under a National Flood Insurance Program EXCEPT

(A) overflow of tidal waters
(B) mudslides and mudflows
(C) rapid accumulation or runoff of surface water
(D) sewer backup

22. An HO 2 Form sets special coverage limits on all of the following items EXCEPT

(A) money
(B) television sets
(C) jewelry
(D) boats

23. The plumbing in Mrs. Sander's home suddenly burst and the ceilings were damaged by water. All of the following Homeowners Forms would cover the loss EXCEPT an

(A) HO 1 Form
(B) HO 2 Form
(C) HO 3 Form
(D) HO 5 Form

Directions: The group of questions below consists of four lettered headings followed by a list of numbered sentences. For each numbered sentence, select the one heading that is most closely related to it. One heading may be used once, more than once, or not at all.

Questions 24-25

(A) Coinsurance
(B) Actual cash value
(C) Replacement cost
(D) Excess loss coverage

Select the concept listed above which is best illustrated by each of the following.

24. An insured's loss payment is reduced by depreciation.

25. An insured is reimbursed by his insurance company for the cost of a new chair after a 10-year-old one is destroyed by fire.

26. Which of the following statements is true about the Medical Payments Section of the Personal Automobile Policy?

(A) Coverage is only provided if the insured is in an automobile
(B) Coverage is no fault
(C) Expenses must be incurred within 1 year
(D) Coverage is provided for pain and suffering

27. An automobile that you lease on a three year contract should be insured as a(n)

(A) owned auto.
(B) hired auto.
(C) non-owned auto.
(D) temporary substitute auto.

28. If the state minimum limit for automobile liability insurance is 25/50/10, then a driver with limits of 20/40/5 is a(n)

(A) uninsured motorist.
(B) underinsured motorist.
(C) high risk motorist.
(D) hazard to other drivers.

29. Which of the following statements is true about an insured who wishes to cancel her insurance policy?

(A) She must give the insurance company 5 days written notice.
(B) She must give the insurance company legal notice on a pre-approved form.
(C) She may cancel the policy only after it has been in effect for 10 days.
(D) She may cancel the policy at any time.

30. In automobile insurance, Additional (Supplementary) Payments refer to which of the following?

(A) Payments made by the insured for damages exceeding his policy limits
(B) Payments received by the insured directly form the person or persons who caused a loss
(C) Payments made by the insurance company for the insured's own medical expenses, to supplement any other medical insurance
(D) Payment of defense and other expenses by the insurance company beyond the limits of liability

31. Actual cash value is best defined as

(A) replacement cost minus physical depreciation
(B) replacement cost minus tax depreciation
(C) original cost minus physical depreciation
(D) original cost minus tax depreciation

32. Your automobile dealer loans you a car to drive while your car is in for repair. The "loaner" would be classified under your automobile policy as a

(A) hired auto.
(B) non-owned auto.
(C) temporary substitute auto.
(D) lemon.

33. An insured whose legally parked car is damaged by a mudslide may collect for damages under which of the following coverages?

(A) Property Damage Liability
(B) Medical Payments
(C) Comprehensive (Other Than Collision)
(D) Collision

34. The Chens host a party for close friends. When the guests arrive, they place their coats in the bedroom. Two days later, Mr. Chen discovers that his wristwatch is missing from the dresser. This loss is referred to as a

(A) burglary.
(B) mysterious disappearance.
(C) robbery.
(D) theft.

35. Coverage B Medical Payments of a Personal Auto Policy would NOT pay for

(A) pain and suffering.
(B) hospital bills.
(C) dental bills.
(D) funeral expenses.

36. On an automobile policy application, an applicant states that she has had no accidents in the past 3 years. This statement is known as which of the following, if any?

(A) A representation
(B) A warranty
(C) A concealment
(D) None of the above

37. Jim Johnson has an automobile policy with a combined single limit of $50,000. He has an at-fault accident and incurs the following expenses.

    $30,000 bodily injury judgment
    $30,000 property damage judgment
    $5,000 damage to traffic light
    $6,000 attorney's fees for his defense
    $300 in premiums for appeal bond
    $75 in bail bond premiums for related traffic violations

    Which of the following is the maximum amount his insurance company will pay?

    (A) $50,000
    (B) $56,375
    (C) $65,000
    (D) $71,375

38. Benjamin Knight carries an automobile policy with Company A that has limits of $50,000. He borrows an auto from a neighbor who carries an automobile policy with Company B that has limits of $100,000. While driving the borrowed auto, Mr. Knight is involved in an at-fault accident in which a judgment of $125,000 was rendered against him. The loss will be paid in which of the following ways?

	Company A	Company B
(A)	$25,000	$100,000
(B)	$50,000	$75,000
(C)	$62,500	$62,500
(D)	$75,000	$50,000

39. Which of the following best describes the purpose of Insuring Agreements?

    (A) To name the insured
    (B) To describe the coverage
    (C) To explain the duties of the insured
    (D) To set forth conditions and exclusions

40. Cars driven by Sue Trent and Jim Higgins were involved in an automobile accident. Ms. Trent's $10,000 car was a total loss, and she obtained a settlement of $25,000 for her injuries. Scot Finley, Ms. Trent's passenger, was injured and incurred $6,000 in medical expenses. Mr. Higgins, the responsible party, carries Bodily Injury coverage with limits of $15,000 per person and $30,000 per accident, and Property Damage coverage of $5,000. His policy will pay a maximum of which of the following amounts?

    (A) $26,000
    (B) $29,000
    (C) $35,000
    (D) $39,000

41. A deductible usually applies to which of the following automobile policy coverages?

    (A) Bodily Injury Liability
    (B) Property Damage Liability
    (C) Physical Damage
    (D) Medical Payments

42. The purpose of the Declarations section of an insurance policy is to list the

(A) duties of the insurance company and the insured.
(B) persons or property covered.
(C) perils covered.
(D) perils not covered.

43. The Fair Credit Reporting Act does which of the following?

(A) It requires the insurance companies to notify an applicant in advance that an inspection report may be ordered.
(B) It prevents insurance companies from using information that is disputed by an applicant.
(C) It requires the insurance companies to send all applicants copies of any reports obtained from an inspection company.
(D) It makes the disclosure of the source of information illegal.

44. All of the following are true concerning bodily injury EXCEPT

(A) Bodily injury is an important of Personal Auto Liability coverage.
(B) Bodily injury is another name for Personal Injury.
(C) In Personal Auto, Bodily injury coverage usually comes with specific dollar limits.
(D) Pain and suffering losses can be paid from bodily injury limits.

45. Adele Sullivan's car is hit from the rear by Clarence Brown's car. Mrs. Sullivan's insurance company pays her Physical Damage coverage and makes a claim against Mr. Brown's insurance company for the same amount. This process is called

(A) matriculation.
(B) reciprocity.
(C) subrogation.
(D) arbitration.

46. The Other Than Collision (Comprehensive) coverage of a Personal Automobile policy would include all of the following losses EXCEPT

(A) theft.
(B) glass breakage.
(C) upset of the vehicle.
(D) contact with a bird or animal.

47. Under an automobile policy with Uninsured Motorists coverage, a disagreement between an insurance company and an insured on the amount of a loss can be settled by

(A) subrogation
(B) elimination
(C) arbitration
(D) declaration

Directions: The group of questions below consists of four lettered headings followed by a list of numbered sentences. For each numbered sentence, select the one heading that is most closely related to it. One heading may be used once, more than once, or not at all.

Questions 48-50

(A) Bodily Injury and Property Damage Liability
(B) Comprehensive (Other Than Collision)
(C) Collision
(D) Medical Payments

Jean Tyler has the automobile coverages listed above under a Personal (Family) Auto policy. Select the coverage that would apply in each of the following situations.

48. A baseball is hit through Ms. Tyler's windshield.

49. Ms. Tyler runs over a log and damages her auto.

50. A deer leaps onto Ms. Tyler's car and causes extensive damage.

End of the PERSONAL LINES Test

COMMERCIAL LINES Practice Test

1. The right of a property insurance company to take possession of damaged insurance property on which it has paid a total loss claim is called

   (A) Right of Abandonment.
   (B) Right of Cancellation.
   (C) Right of Salvage.
   (D) Mortgagee Rights.

2. Which of the following losses would best fit the insurance definition of an occurrence?

   (A) rust
   (B) an automobile wreck
   (C) a boiler explosion
   (D) a flood/a fire caused by a short-circuited wire

3. Real property that contains no people nor any personal property would be defined under insurance terminology as

   (A) abandoned.
   (B) uninhabitable.
   (C) vacant.
   (D) unoccupied.

4. Which of the following statements is true about Additional Coverages?

   (A) They are automatically included only if Medical Payments coverage is purchased.
   (B) They are included for a minimum premium.
   (C) They are included at no extra cost.
   (D) They are optional on the part of the insured.

5. An insurance policy's Appraisal clause is used to determine the

   (A) person who is liable for damages
   (B) amount of company liability
   (C) existing coverage
   (D) facts so the case can be heard in court

6. Which of the following would NOT be classified as part of the building under a Commercial Building and Personal Property coverage form?

   (A) personal effects
   (B) fire extinguishing equipment
   (C) a snowblower used in the maintenance of the building
   (D) the microwave oven in the employee's dining room

7. An individual who has responsibility for another person's property is called a(n)

   (A) assignee.
   (B) bailee.
   (C) mortgagee.
   (D) appraiser/custodian.

8. A sudden, unintended, and unexpected event that occurs at a known time and place is called

   (A) negligence
   (B) a warranty
   (C) an accident
   (D) an occurrence

9. The purpose of the Coinsurance clause is to

   (A) require the insurance company to pay all losses in full
   (B) encourage the insured to insure property close to full value
   (C) allow the insured to choose any amount of coverage
   (D) permit other insurance on the same property

10. The standard deductible on a Businessowners policy is which of the following?

    (A) $100
    (B) $250
    (C) $500
    (D) $1000

11. Which of the following conditions of a property policy, if any, describes the procedure for an insured to use in a disagreement with the insurance company about the amount of a loss?

    (A) Pro Rata Liability
    (B) Subrogation
    (C) Audit
    (D) None of the above

12. Which of the following must an insured do after suffering a property loss?

    (A) Have the damaged property appraised.
    (B) Take steps to reduce any further loss.
    (C) Hire an outside claims adjuster.
    (D) Increase his coverage.

13. Which of the following types of property would NOT be included under Coverage A of a Building and Personal Property Coverage Form?

    (A) A central air-conditioning system
    (B) Wall-to-wall carpeting
    (C) A permanently installed intercom system
    (D) Building improvements made by the insured to a space they lease

14. Joe Insured owns a restaurant that is heated by a boiler. The boiler explodes. Joe needs a Boiler and Machinery policy to insure himself against

    (A) lawsuits from injured neighbors.
    (B) bodily injury claims from injured patrons who were in the restaurant.
    (C) bodily injury claims from injured employees.
    (D) the loss of his building and business personal property.

15. The ABC Office Supply Corporation carries $100,000 insurance on a storage building held under a $50,000 mortgage acknowledged in the policy. ABC stores dynamite in the building without informing the insurance company. There is an explosion and the building is destroyed. Which of the following amounts is the maximum that the mortgagee can recover?

    (A) $0
    (B) $25,000
    (C) $50,000
    (D) $100,000

16. Under a basic Building and Personal Property Coverage Form, loss valuation is based on which of the following?

    (A) Market value
    (B) Actual cash value
    (C) Original cost
    (D) Replacement cost

17. The Conditions section of an insurance contract specifies which of the following?

    (A) The property location
    (B) The first named insured
    (C) The insured's responsibilities
    (D) The policy duration

18. A newspaper is interested in protecting against additional costs of continuing to print the newspaper in the event its buildings were destroyed. Which of the following coverages should the newspaper purchase?

(A) Open Perils (All-Risk)
(B) Extra Expense
(C) Loss of Rents
(D) Contingent Gross Earnings

19. Brian Gabriel insures his television repair shop under a Building and Personal Property Coverage Form with limits of $100,000 on the building and $50,000 on the contents. A fire causes $10,000 in damage to the building and $20,000 in losses to the contents. Mr. Gabriel also has to pay $1,000 for debris removal. If the policy has a deductible of $100, Mr. Gabriel will receive a maximum of which of the following amounts from his insurance company?

(A) $29,900
(B) $30,000
(C) $30,900
(D) $31,000

20. Fire Legal Liability coverage is important for which of the following kinds of property?

(A) Real property which is owned
(B) Real property which is leased
(C) Personal property which is owned
(D) Personal property which is leased

21. Subrogation may follow which of the following events?

(A) An insured collects from her insurance company for damage caused by a third party.
(B) An insured causes damage to her own goods.
(C) Forces of nature damage the insured's property.
(D) Firefighters damage the insured's property while putting out a fire.

22. A Businessowners policy would cover which of the following liability expenses?

(A) Professional liability
(B) Employee Injury liability
(C) Products liability
(D) Directors and Officers liability

23. A dead tree beside a home is best described as which of the following types of hazard?

(A) Physical
(B) Proximate
(C) Moral
(D) Morale

24. A Building and Personal Property Coverage Form provides coverage for all of the following types of property EXCEPT

(A) growing crops and lawns
(B) tenants' improvements and betterments
(C) yard fixtures
(D) business personal property

25. All of the following make a property insurance policy an indemnity contract EXCEPT

(A) liberalization
(B) insurable interest
(C) actual cash value
(D) subrogation

26. The premium charged for a standard Workers Compensation policy is based primarily on a company's

(A) gross sales
(B) payroll
(C) federal tax
(D) employee population

27. Worker's Compensation would pay in all of the following cases EXCEPT

(A) The risk of injury was known to the worker.
(B) The injury was due to the carelessness of a fellow worker.
(C) The injured worker was guilty of contributory negligence.
(D) An employee hurts a customer of your store.

28. Michelle Winters seeks coverage for her manufacturing company to include Premises Liability, Products Liability, Insured Contracts, and Completed Operations. Which of the following policies would cover all of these loss exposures?

(A) Premises and Operations Liability
(B) Products and Completed Operations Liability
(C) Commercial General Liability
(D) Personal Injury Liability

29. Sue Green has Crime Insuring Agreement 3 - Inside the Premises - Theft of Money and Securities on her restaurant. If an employee steals some cash by breaking into the premises on a holiday, the policy would

(A) cover the loss
(B) not cover the loss, since acts by employees are excluded
(C) not cover the loss, since daytime burglaries are excluded
(D) not cover the loss, since only loss of merchandise is covered

30. Which of the following policies would be best suited for a prospective insured who wants coverage against liability assumed by him under specific written agreements?

(A) Products and Completed Operations Liability
(B) Contractual Liability
(C) Fidelity Bond
(D) Premises and Operations Liability

31. An employee authorized to have custody of insured property off premises is known as which of the following?

(A) Guard
(B) Watchperson
(C) Custodian
(D) Messenger

32. When switching from a series of Occurrence for CGLs to a Claims Made CGL, a major underwriting consideration is whether to accept coverage for incidents prior to the date of the first Claims Made form. The device which determines the answer is known as the

(A) Policy Date.
(B) Retroactive Date.
(C) Extended Reporting Period.
(D) Period of Restoration.

33. A Commercial General Liability policy **excludes** coverage for which of the following?

(A) Bodily Injury Liability
(B) Property Damage Liability
(C) Personal Injury Liability
(D) Professional Liability

34. Basic benefits available under a typical Workers Compensation policy would include all of the following EXCEPT

(A) Medical expenses.
(B) Loss of income.
(C) Rehabilitation.
(D) College tuition.

35. Which of the following terms is NOT consistent with the concept of negligence?

(A) No fault
(B) Breach of duty
(C) Legal obligation
(D) Proximate cause

36. Joseph Pinelli, who is insured under a Business (Commercial) Auto policy, is involved in an accident. He and the insurance company disagree on the amount to be paid for the damage to his car. Under the terms of the policy, which of the following statements is true?

(A) Mr. Pinelli must accept the insurance company's estimate
(B) Each party engages an appraiser, and the appraisers will decide the amount
(C) Each party engages an appraiser, and the appraisers will select an umpire
(D) The estimates of both parties will be averaged

37. While installing an air-conditioning unit in a building, an ABC Contracting Company employee drops and damages the unit. Which of the following coverages, if any, would protect the company for this loss?

(A) Commercial General Liability
(B) Personal Injury Liability
(C) Products Liability
(D) None of the above

38. Betty Jones claims that the bicycle manufactured last year by Daryl Lanier's firm was the cause of her daughter's accident. Which of the following coverages would have provided protection for Mr. Lanier?

    (A) Commercial General Liability
    (B) Owners and Contractors Protective Liability
    (C) Workers Compensation
    (D) Contractual Liability

39. While inspecting a recently insured building, an insurance company representative notices a loose handrail on a stairway. When writing to the agent, the company would refer to this situation as which of the following?

    (A) A risk
    (B) A hazard
    (C) A liability
    (D) A peril

40. If an insured fails to comply with the immediate Notice of Claim requirement, which of the following may result?

    (A) Her policy may be cancelled.
    (B) Her loss may be only partially paid.
    (C) Her loss may be denied.
    (D) Her premium may be increased.

41. A Commercial General Liability policy provides coverage for exposures to loss arising out of which of the following operations?

    (A) Business and personal
    (B) Away from the insured's premises only
    (C) On the insured's premises only
    (D) On or away from the insured's premises

42. A Pro Rata Liability clause is included in an insurance policy to deal with the problem of

    (A) excessive policies.
    (B) multiple policies.
    (C) inadequate coverages.
    (D) conditional coverages.

43. Products and Completed Operations Liability coverage excludes which of the following?

    (A) Damage caused by a defective product
    (B) Damage occurring after possession of the product has been relinquished
    (C) A vendor's liability for the products of others
    (D) Recall of products

44. The Conditions section of an insurance contract sets forth the

    (A) limits of liability under the contract.
    (B) coverages provided by the contract.
    (C) rules of conduct for the insured and insurance company.
    (D) exclusions of coverage under the contract.

45. Under a CGL policy, to determine the maximum amount that is available for any one slip and fall accident, you should look at which of the following limits?

(A) the General Aggregate Limit
(B) the Occurrence Limit
(C) the Personal and Advertising Injury Limit
(D) the Products and Completed Operations Aggregate Limit

46. In insurance, which of the following terms is defined as "any act of stealing"?

(A) Mysterious disappearance
(B) Burglary
(C) Robbery
(D) Theft

47. Which of the following is NOT an accident?

(A) A pedestrian is killed when struck by a power crane excavating at a street intersection.
(B) An employee is injured when his hand is caught in a power press.
(C) A home is damaged by flying rocks from a dynamite blast.
(D) Paint is damaged by dust from trucks going to and from a construction site.

48. A Workers Comp policy would be required for a business with which of the following groups of employees?

(A) Bank employees
(B) Farm laborers
(C) Household servants
(D) Casual workers

49. An employee injured on the job who cannot work at all but is expected to completely recover is described by which of the following in the Workers Comp contract?

(A) Permanent Partial Disability
(B) Permanent Total Disability
(C) Temporary Total Disability
(D) Temporary Partial Disability

50. Someone breaks down the door to a store and steals merchandise. This loss relates to the peril of

(A) embezzlement.
(B) barratry.
(C) robbery.
(D) burglary.

End of the COMMERCIAL LINES Test

PERSONAL LINES	COMMERCIAL LINES
Question	Question
1. B	1. C
2. D	2. A
3. C	3. C
4. B	4. C
5. D	5. B
6. A	6. A
7. B	7. B
8. A	8. C
9. D	9. B
10. D	10. C
11. A	11. D
12. A	12. B
13. A	13. D
14. B	14. D
15. C	15. C
16. D	16. B
17. A	17. C
18. D	18. B
19. B	19. C
20. C	20. B
21. D	21. A
22. B	22. C
23. A	23. A
24. B	24. A
25. C	25. A
26. B	26. B
27. A	27. D
28. A	28. C
29. D	29. B
30. D	30. B
31. A	31. D
32. C	32. B
33. C	33. D
34. B	34. D
35. A	35. A
36. A	36. C
37. B	37. D
38. A	38. A
39. B	39. B
40. A	40. C
41. C	41. D
42. B	42. B
43. A	43. D
44. B	44. C
45. C	45. B
46. C	46. D
47. C	47. D
48. B	48. A
49. C	49. C
50. B	50. D

Part VI
GLOSSARY & INDEX

GLOSSARY AND INDEX

A

ABANDONMENT In property insurance, an attempt by the named insured to forfeit the damaged property to the insurance company in exchange for payment of the full face value of the insurance contract. Abandonment is not permitted under property insurance policies.

Page 3-14, 9-15

ABSOLUTE LIABILITY A tort liability theory in which duty and breach of duty are not an issue. Used in liability cases which involve, for instance, wild animals, explosives or pollution.

Page 4-6

ACCEPTANCE In contract law, a complete assent to the offer. The acceptance must be a "mirror image" of the offer. An offer and its acceptance comprise the agreement.

Page 2-9

ACCIDENT A sudden, unforeseen and unintended event that happens at a known place and a known time. Also called a fortuitous event. For contrast, see Occurrence.

Page 1-7, 12-2

ACT OF GOD A natural catastrophic disaster that human intervention would not have prevented. Examples are hurricanes, earthquakes and tidal waves. Such acts are harder to predict than more mundane human being-caused losses such as automobile accidents and work-related accidents.*

ACTION OF CIVIL AUTHORITY When access to your property is prohibited by civil authority because of direct loss to a nearby property. This is covered under Business Interruption Insurance in the Commercial Property Form.

Page 9-22

ACTUAL CASH VALUE (ACV) In property insurance, Actual Cash Value is Replacement Cost less Depreciation. ACV is the most basic definition of value in a property policy. Property insured under ACV is depreciated over time. For contrast, see Agreed Value, Fair Market Value and Replacement Cost.

Page 3-10

ACTUARY A mathematician professionally trained in the technical aspects of insurance who calculates premiums, reserves, and other related values and expenses.*

ADDITIONAL COVERAGES In property insurance, coverage for additional expenses, such as fire department service charge and debris removal, some of which may pay benefits in addition to the face amount of the contract.

Page 3-15, 5-15, 9-12

ADDITIONAL INSURED ENDORSEMENT Under Homeowners policies, an endorsement which covers a person or persons not originally protected under the policy. An example would be adding a contract seller under the new owner's Homeowners policy as an additional named insured.

Page 5-6

ADDITIONAL INSURED - LESSOR A Commercial Auto endorsement which makes the lessor of the auto an additional insured.

Page 13-4

ADDITIONAL LIVING EXPENSES Under Dwelling/Homeowners policies, coverage which pays for the additional expenses of living someplace else while your house is being rebuilt. Typically, you move to a motel and eat restaurant food, which is more expensive than being at home. The coverage will pay for the extra costs of living elsewhere during repairs.

Page 5-13

* definition only, term not found in text

ADJUSTER An individual who settles insurance claims.*

ADMITTED COMPANY See authorized company

ADVERSE SELECTION/ANTI-SELECTION The tendency for people who have a high need for a particular coverage to buy, while those who have a lesser need do not buy. For example, people who live on the top of the mountain do not buy flood insurance, while those who live on the riverbank do.
Page 7-1

ADVERTISING INJURY LIABILITY The liability which arises from a business harming another business by misrepresentation or stealing the other business' trademark, copyright, etc... It is, essentially, Personal Injury in a commercial setting. For contrast, see Personal Injury Liability.
Page 4-2, 10-6, 10-14

AGENCY AGREEMENT Contract between the insurance company and the agent that will specifically explain what the agent can and cannot do. It will also spell out how and when the agent will receive compensation.
Page 2-17

AGGREGATE LIMITS As in General Aggregate Limits, or total policy limits. Found typically in liability policies utilized by businesses. The aggregate limit represents the total obligation of the insurance company during the policy period. An aggregate limit of one million dollars means the insurance company would pay only up to that amount during the policy period. Also see General Aggregate.
Page 10-18

AGREED VALUE The insurance company and the insured agree to a specific price for each piece of property before the contract is written. If there is a loss, the company pays the Agreed Value as specified with no regard for depreciation or for the replacement cost of the item. For contrast, see Actual Cash Value and Replacement Cost.
Page 3-11, 9-19

AGREEMENT In contract law, the offer and acceptance together make up the agreement.
Page 2-9

AIRPORT LIABILITY Contracts which provide liability coverage for businesses which are in the airplane business – repair, rental, storage etc.
Page 13-15

ALEATORY CONTRACT An aleatory contract is one in which one party (such as the insurance company) is only obligated to pay if a fortuitous event occurs and in which one party may obtain far greater value under the agreement than the other. There is a possibility that the company will never be obligated to pay. An insurance contract is an aleatory contract as there may be an uneven exchange of values.
Page 2-13

ALIEN COMPANY A company chartered in another country.
Page 2-6

"ALL RISK" (OPEN PERILS) POLICY "All Risk" is the outdated term for what is now called "Open Perils". Property insurance can be written on either a Named Perils basis or an Open Perils basis. An Open Perils policy covers every conceivable peril (even an unusual one) except for those specifically excluded in the policy.
Page 3-9

APPARENT AUTHORITY The authority that the general public could logically assume that the insurance agent could have.
Page 2-18

APPRAISAL A method for determining value if the parties to the contract (the insurance company and the insured) cannot agree on the amount of a claim settlement.
Page 3-14, 9-15

APPURTENANT STRUCTURE See Other Structure.

ARBITRATION A method of settling a dispute without taking the matter to court in which outside parties hear both sides and make a decision which may or may not be binding.
Page 6-18

ARSON The crime of purposely setting fire to property.*

 * definition only, term not found in text

ASSIGNED RISK PLAN In fire, flood, crime, workers compensation, and auto insurance, a state-sponsored program of insurance for high risk individuals who are unable to obtain coverage.*

ASSIGNMENT The legal transfer of ownership of an insurance policy from the current policyowner to a new policyowner. An assignment must be agreed to in writing by the old policyowner, the new policyowner and the insurance company.

Page 3-5

ASSUMPTION OF RISK If you knowingly place yourself in a dangerous position, your ability to collect from a wrongdoer may be eliminated. Also see Comparative Fault/Negligence.

Page 4-5

ATTRACTIVE NUISANCE A dangerous place, condition, vehicle or object that is particularly attractive to young children, such as a swimming pool with no fence around it.*

AUDIT Some types of coverages such as workers compensation have next year's premium estimated based on what is known today. The actual premium to be charged will be determined by an audit at the end of the insuring period and any adjustments required will be made at that time.

Page 10-31

AUTOMOBILE A land motor vehicle, trailer, or semitrailer designed for travel on public roads, but does not usually include mobile equipment.

Page 6-2, 13-2

AUTHORIZED COMPANY A company that has been admitted to do business in a particular state. To become authorized the state will give the company a Certificate of Authority.

Page 2-7

AVIATION INSURANCE Insurance dealing with the ownership, maintenance or use of airplanes.

Page 13-15

B

BAILEE A person or business having property committed in trust by the owner.

Page 9-11, 10-13

BARRATRY OF A MASTER Embezzlement or dishonest acts by a ship's captain. A named peril available in Ocean Marine policies.

Page 13-10

BASIC CAUSES OF LOSS/PERILS Property policies designate which perils are covered. The Basic Cause of Loss form covers 11 listed perils in Commercial Property. In Homeowners and Dwelling policies, the Basic form normally covers the Standard Fire perils, the EC perils and V&MM.

Page 3-19, 5-14

BILL OF LADING The contract between the shipper and the carrier that lists the goods being shipped, acknowledges their receipt, and promises to deliver the goods to the person named.

Page 13-8

BINDER An interim insuring agreement that provides coverage until the actual policy is issued. However, a binder does not guarantee that a policy will, in fact, be issued. A binder may be either oral or written.

Page 2-12

BLANKET COVERAGE Applicable to Commercial Property coverage, Blanket Basis simply means that the insured is covered for losses to property up to the policy limits without specifically listing all property by name.

Page 3-8

BLANKET POSITION BOND A type of Fidelity Bond which covers all employees.

Page 11-3

BOATOWNERS POLICY A multi-line contract covering the boat itself and the liability arising from the use of the boat. Generally written for craft not large enough or valuable enough to merit a Yacht policy.

Page 7-7

BODILY INJURY (BI) The physical injury or death of a human being.

Page 4-2, 10-10

BOILER AND MACHINARY See Equipment Breakdown.

BREACH OF CONTRACT The violation of, or failure to perform, the terms of a contract; the breaking of a legally binding agreement.*

* definition only, term not found in text

BREACH OF DUTY Failure to live up to your duty. Breach of duty is second element of negligence.
Page 4-4

BROAD CAUSES OF LOSS/PERILS A list of named perils that insured property is covered against. In both commercial lines and personal lines, the Broad form covers more perils than the Basic form, but fewer than the Special (All Risk) form.
Page 3-21, 5-14, 9-25

BROKER The legal representative of the insured. Their job is to determine the client's needs and then find the best product on the market to fill that need.
Page 2-18

BUILDING ORDINANCE A building law or ordinance which dictates the construction and safety of a building, and sometimes requires the demolition of a damaged building. Under a Commercial Property policy, losses due to the enforcement of a building ordinance (nowadays called "Ordinance or Law") are not covered.
Page 9-26

BUILDERS RISK A Commercial Property coverage form which covers buildings under construction.
Page 9-28

BURGLARY The taking of property from a premises that is closed or locked tight and leaving marks of forced entry or exit. Burglary is a crime directed against property. Also see Robbery.
Page 3-24, 11-4

BUSINESS INCOME A coverage available under the Commercial Property policy which pays a business for the actual loss of business income (net income plus continuing operating expenses such as payroll) during a period of restoration after a covered direct loss up to the limits of the policy.
Page 9-21

BUSINESS INTERRUPTION INSURANCE Coverages under a Commercial Property policy which are designed to reimburse indirect losses, such as business income and extra expenses during a period of restoration.
Page 9-19, 12-5

BUSINESS PERSONAL PROPERTY Movable property that a business owns, used in the performance of the business, such as desks, chairs, computers, and copy machines. Business Personal Property also includes stock or inventory.
Page 9-10

BUSINESSOWNERS POLICY (BOP) A prepackaged property and casualty policy designed for small to medium-sized low risk businesses.
Page 14-1

BUSINESS PURSUITS ENDORSEMENT An endorsement added to a homeowners policy which provides coverage for an in-home business.
Page 5-35

C

CANCELLATION Termination of a contract of insurance during the policy period by voluntary act of the insurer or insured in accordance with the provisions in the contract or by mutual agreement.
Page 1-6, 8-5

CAPTIVE AGENCY The insurance company contracts with an agency to market insurance exclusively for that company.
Page 2-16

CARGO COVERAGE An Ocean Marine coverage which protects the owner of the cargo for damage to that cargo.
Page 13-9

CASUALTY/LIABILITY INSURANCE Insurance which is designed to cover legal liability imposed upon the insured for injury or damage to others or the property of others.
Page 1-3, 4-1, 10-1

CATASTROPHIC LOSS A loss of unusual size caused by the simultaneous occurrence of a peril to a very large number of insureds and generally excluded from coverage, such as war, nuclear catastrophe, flood and earthquake.
Page 1-5, 2-14

CAUSE OF LOSS FORMS Several levels of peril power from which the insured may choose. In the Commercial Property policy, the Basic Cause of Loss form covers 11 named perils; the Broad form, 14 perils. The Special form is Open Perils (All Risk).
Page 3-19, 9-24

 * definition only, term not found in text

CERTIFICATE OF INSURANCE A statement providing evidence that a policy is in force and outlining the coverages in effect.

Page 1-6

CHARTERED PROPERTY AND CASUALTY UNDERWRITER (CPCU) A professional designation awarded by the American Institute for Property and Liability Underwriters for successful completion of a series of examination and experience requirements in the fields of insurance, plus accounting, financing, economics and law.*

CIVIL COMMOTION A peril consisting of the uprising of a large number of people, usually resulting in damage to property; in property insurance, the peril of "Riot or Civil Commotion" includes acts done by striking employees, and looting which occurs at the time and place of the civil commotion or riot.

Page 3-19

CLAIM Notification to an insurance company that payment of an amount is due under the terms of a policy.

Page 10-23

CLAIMS-MADE POLICY A Commercial General Liability policy may be written on either an Occurrence or a Claims-Made basis. Under the Claims-Made approach, coverage is triggered by the claim, not the occurrence.

Page 10-22

COINSURANCE CLAUSE In property insurance, a clause under which the insured shares in losses to the extent that he is underinsured at the time of the loss according to the formula: Did Carry/Should Have Carried x Loss = Claim Paid.

Page 3-12, 9-18

COLLAPSE A falling to pieces, as when supports or sides fail to hold. Collapse can be caused by a number of perils such as fire or weight of rain or snow. Collapse is an additional coverage under the Commercial Property policy and a Broad form peril in the Dwelling and Homeowners policies.

Page 9-26

COLLISION Physical damage coverage for the insured's own vehicle for damage resulting from a crash with another object (such as a car, tree, or pole) or upset.

Page 6-7, 6-19, 13-4

COMMERCIAL BLANKET BOND Type of Fidelity bond that covers all employees and its limits are expressed on a per loss basis regardless of the number of employees involved in the loss.

Page 11-3

COMMERCIAL LINES Insurance written to meet the needs of businesses, such as the Commercial Package policy and the Businessowners policy.

Page 1-4

COMMERCIAL PACKAGE POLICY A combination of two or more of the following coverage modules: Commercial Property, Commercial General Liability, Commercial Crime, Commercial Automobile, Commercial Inland Marine, Boiler & Machinery and Farm.

Page 8-1

COMMON CARRIER Anyone who is in the business of hauling other people's goods for a fee.

Page 13-8

COMPARATIVE FAULT/NEGLIGENCE If you are injured by the Other Guy, but it is partly your fault, then the damages you collect from the Other Guy will be reduced by the percent of your fault. For example, if it was 20% your fault, then your award will be reduced by 20%. Also see Assumption of Risk.

Page 4-5

COMPENSATORY DAMAGES Arising from a liability claim, these damages are awarded to the injured party to compensate them for their injury and to restore them, as best as possible, to their original condition.

Page 4-5

COMPETENT PARTIES The parties to the insurance policy must be competent, which means that they must be of legal age, sane, sober and under no pressure or duress.

Page 2-9

COMPLETED OPERATIONS LIABILITY Many of the same kinds of businesses which need Operations Liability coverage need Completed Operations Liability coverage. Operations Liability provides protection while the work is being done; Completed Operations offers protection after the work is done. It offers protection for bodily injury or property damage caused by the work itself.

Page 10-3

* definition only, term not found in text

COMPREHENSIVE Physical damage coverage for the insured's own vehicle for damage resulting from perils such as fire, theft, hail, or contact with a bird or animal. Comprehensive coverage excludes collision. Also called Other Than Collision Coverage.
Page 6-7, 13-4

COMPUTER FRAUD (Agreement 6) A crime coverage which protects the insured from electronic theft.
Page 11-7

CONCEALMENT Concealment is the intentional failure of the applicant/insured to disclose to the insurance company a material fact on an application or on a proof of loss. The applicant/insured has the duty to reveal all material information. Failure to do so may void the contract. Also see Warranties and Representations.
Page 2-11

CONCURRENT CAUSATION When two losses occur and one is caused by a covered peril and the other one is caused by an excluded peril. The property policy will only cover the damage attributed to the covered peril.
Page 9-26

CONCURRENT POLICIES Two or more policies covering the same property that are identical in peril coverages. If two property policies cover the same piece of property, they must be concurrent. Also see Nonconcurrent Policies.
Page 3-16, 9-8

CONDITIONAL A contract in which promises will only be honored if the parties do certain things, e.g., the company will pay the loss...if...the insured pays the premium.
Page 2-12

CONDITIONS The Conditions section of the policy spells out the procedures which enable the parties to function effectively under the contract. They establish the rules of conduct between the parties of the contract, such as: how to report a loss, appraisal provisions, time and manner of paying a loss, subrogation, cancellation, assignment rights and definitions of terms. The policy Conditions are the bulk of the policy.
Page 2-13

CONDOMINIUM ASSOCIATION COVERAGE A form of Commercial Property coverage which provides coverage for common property in a condominium complex.
Page 5-3, 9-30

CONDOMINIUM UNIT OWNERS COVERAGE A Commercial Property coverage which functions much like an HO-6 for those who operate their businesses out of a "commercial" condominium.
Page 9-30

CONSEQUENTIAL LOSS An endorsement available for the Boiler and Machinery Policy covering spoilage caused by lack of power, light, heat, steam, or refrigeration following a covered loss.
Page 12-5

CONSIDERATION Something of value; consideration is an essential element of a binding contract; in a P&C contract, the applicant's consideration consists of premium and the statements made in the application for insurance; the insurance company's consideration is the promises contained in the policy.
Page 2-9

CONTRACT An agreement, such as an insurance policy.
Page 2-8

CONTRACT OF ADHESION A "take it or leave it" agreement, such as an insurance policy. A contract of adhesion is drafted by one party (the insurance company) while the other party (the insured) either accepts the terms and conditions of the contract "as is" or rejects them. Any ambiguities in the contract will generally be decided in favor of the non-drafting party (the insured).
Page 2-8

CONTRACTUAL LIABILITY Liability that you voluntarily agree to take on, generally for business purposes.
Page 10-4

CONTRIBUTORY NEGLIGENCE If an injured party is even 1% responsible for their own injury, they will collect nothing under this theory of negligence.
Page 4-5

 * definition only, term not found in text

CORPORATION A legal entity, chartered by a U.S. state or the federal government, which is separate and distinct from the persons who own it (the stockholders). A corporation is a legal "person" that can own property, incur debts, sue, or be sued.
Page 10-16

COUNTERSIGNATURE Many states have laws requiring that newly issued policies sold by a nonresident agent be countersigned (signed a second time) by a licensed resident agent of that state before delivery to the policyowner.
Page 2-12

COVERAGE EXTENSIONS In property insurance, Coverage Extensions provide extra benefits. For an insured to receive these benefits they must earn them by maintaining 80% or more insurance to value on the Declarations Page.
Page 3-14, 9-12

COVERAGE FOR DAMAGE TO YOUR AUTO This optional automobile coverage is also known as Physical Damage, and consists of Collision and Comprehensive.
Page 6-7

CROP INSURANCE A federal government insurance program which provides protection for damage to growing crops.
Page 13-13

CUSTODIAN Any person (such as the insured or an employee) authorized to have custody of insured property on the premises but NOT a janitor or a watchperson. Also see Messenger, Guard and Watchperson.
Page 11-4

D

DAMAGE TO YOUR AUTO See Coverage for Damage to Your Auto.

DAMAGES Injuries translated into dollars, such as medical bills, repair bills, lost wages, and pain and suffering. In order to establish that the Other Guy was negligent, one of the four elements you must show is that he caused you financial damages.
Page 4-4

DAY CARE ENDORSEMENT An endorsement added to an HO policy which primarily provides third party coverage for a child care business operated in the home.
Page 5-35

DEBRIS REMOVAL An additional coverage under the Commercial Property module and under all Homeowners forms which covers the cost of hauling away the debris left by a covered peril. Example: the costs of hauling away the burnt down walls, furniture and carpeting after a fire.
Page 5-15, 9-12

DECLARATIONS ("DEC SHEET") The Declarations Sheet is usually the first page of the policy and contains the following basic information: the Named Insured(s), the covered property, the description of the property, the policy period and the premium.
Page 2-13

DEDUCTIBLE A dollar amount of a claim which the insured must pay before the policy starts paying benefits. The company pays benefits only for the losses in excess of the amount specified in the deductible provision.
Page 3-12

DEFENSE COSTS For any claim or lawsuit filed against you (to which the insurance applies), the insurance company will provide your legal defense. These costs are part of the Supplementary Payments and are paid in addition to the limits of liability of the policy.
Page 10-6

DEPRECIATION The decrease in value of property over time as the result of deterioration, obsolescence or wear and tear. Depreciation is a factor used in calculating Actual Cash Value.
Page 3-10

DIFFERENCE IN CONDITIONS (DIC) FORM A form of Inland Marine insurance usually used in combination with the Basic Form of the Commercial Property policy. It offers coverages usually not found in property policies, e.g., flood and goods in transit. The DIC form has no coinsurance requirement.
Page 9-30

DIRECT LOSS The financial loss caused by the destruction of covered property from a covered peril, such as the cost of rebuilding a house destroyed by fire. Compare Indirect Loss.
Page 1-2

* definition only, term not found in text

DIRECTORS AND OFFICERS LIABILITY POLICY Provides liability coverage for wrongful acts of a board of directors (or similar group) of a corporation or even a not-for-profit organization.
Page 10-32

DISABILITY INCOME BENEFITS A type of benefit typically provided by Workers Compensation insurance which pays a disabled employee an income to replace his or her lost income during a period of total or partial disability. The dollar amount of income and total length of time that benefits will be paid vary greatly from state to state.
Page 10-29

DISCOVERY PERIOD This is a period of time after a fidelity bond has been terminated in which to discover a loss.
Page 11-2

DOCTRINE OF REASONABLE EXPECTATIONS An underlying principal of any contract which holds that contracts inherently offer to all parties a certain reasonable expectation of what the contract will do. If you buy a homeowners insurance policy that covers property damage to your dwelling, you have a reasonable expectation that the insurance company will pay for damage not excluded.
Page 2-8

DOCTRINE OF UTMOST GOOD FAITH An underlying principal of any contract which holds that contract will not work unless all parties involved pledge to make it work.
Page 2-8

DOMESTIC COMPANY A company chartered in your state.
Page 2-6

DOMESTIC SHIPMENTS Property being shipped from one location to another within the United States.
Page 7-13, 13-6

DRAM SHOP See Liquor Liability Insurance.

DUTY The obligation to exercise reasonable care. Duty is one element of Negligence.
Page 4-3

DWELLING A building in which people live. A dwelling includes the building, additions attached to the dwelling such as an attached garage, building materials used to repair the dwelling, permanently installed equipment such as heating and air conditioning units, and equipment used to maintain the dwelling if owned by the insured.
Page 5-8

DWELLING POLICY A property only coverage usually used for residential premises where the owner does not live on the premises. There are four dwelling forms, none of which contain any casualty coverages. Today, for the large part, the dwelling forms have been replaced by the use of the Homeowners Policy.
Page 5-37

E

EARTH MOVEMENT This is an exclusion found in the Basic, Broad and Special cause of loss forms which excludes losses due to earthquake, settlement of earth, creep or slide of soil, or other instability of the earth.
Page 9-27

EARTHQUAKE A shaking or tumbling of the crust of the earth. Earthquake is a typical exclusion. In order to have coverage in Commercial Property for losses due to earthquake, you must have an Earthquake coverage form added to one of the three major cause of loss forms. With Homeowners, you purchase an endorsement.
Page 9-5, 9-27

EARTHQUAKE ENDORSEMENT An endorsement found in a two party policy which adds either the peril of earthquake and volcanic eruption to the causes of loss covered.
Page 5-20, 9-27

EMBEZZLEMENT The stealing of money or property entrusted to you; a type of theft committed by an insider such as an employee. Coverage for a loss due to embezzlement could be obtained through a Fidelity Bond.
Page 11-4

EMPLOYERS LIABILITY Covers common law liability of an employer for accidents to employees, as distinguished from liability imposed by the state workers' compensation law. Typically, Part II of a workers compensation policy.
Page 10-29

 * definition only, term not found in text

EMPLOYERS NON-OWNED AUTOMOBILE LIABILITY COVERAGE In automobile insurance, this coverage protects a businessowner against potential lawsuits as a result of employees driving their own automobiles on company business and doing bodily injury or property damage.
Page 13-3

ENDORSEMENT A change or modification made to a policy to make it fit the needs of the policyowner. An endorsement is not valid unless signed by an executive officer of the company and attached to and made part of the policy.
Page 1-7

EQUIPMENT BREAKDOWN POLICY A contract written to cover boilers and other scheduled equipment against accidental mechanical breakdown.
Page 12-1

ERP See Extended Reporting Period.

ESTOPPEL A legal principle based on fairness which prevents someone from enforcing a legal right he or she would otherwise have.
Page 2-11

EXCLUSIONS Losses which a policy does not cover. Exclusions generally fall into one of the following categories: Catastrophic Losses, Losses That Are Better Covered Elsewhere and Predictable Losses.
Page 1-5, 2-13

EXCLUSIVE REMEDY In Workers Compensation claims the workers give up their right to sue their employer for job related injuries in exchange for quick payment of benefits.
Page 10-28

EXPERIENCE RATING Premium additions and reductions are made to reflect the actual claims history of the risk in previous years.
Page 2-15, 10-30

EXPORTS Property being shipped from the United States for delivery in another country.
Page 7-13, 13-6

EXPLOSION This peril includes internal explosions like gases within a furnace or any fired vessel as well as external explosions. Certain types of explosions like the rupture or bursting of steam boilers are better covered elsewhere (Boiler & Machinery). Also see Inherent Explosion.
Page 3-20

EXPOSURE The state of being subject to a loss. If you own a car or a home or a business you have both property and liability exposures.
Page 1-1

EXPRESSED AUTHORITY The authority specifically granted to the agent in the Agency Contract.
Page 2-18

EXPRESSED WARRANTY Product guarantees in writing.
Page 10-3

EXTENDED BUSINESS INCOME PERIOD A benefit which accompanies the Business Income coverage form of the Commercial Property coverage which is a period of time, generally 30 days, after a period of restoration which pays a partial income to a business after re-opening until it gets back up to speed.
Page 9-20

EXTENDED NONOWNER COVERAGE FOR NAMED INSUREDS ENDORSEMENT An endorsement to the PAP which plugs up the "company car exclusion".
Page 6-23

EXTENDED REPORTING PERIOD (ERP) An extension of the reporting period (not the coverage period) beyond the policy period.
Page 10-26

EXTENSIONS OF COVERAGES See Coverage Extensions.

EXTORTION The insurance definition of "extortion" is a surrender of property away from the premises as the result of a threat communicated to the insured to do bodily harm to a named insured, a relative or to an employee who is (or allegedly is) being held captive.
Page 11-4

EXTRA EXPENSE A coverage available under a Commercial Property policy for businesses which cannot stop operating after their building is destroyed. It is designed to pay for extra expenses actually incurred during the period of restoration up to the limits of the policy.
Page 9-23, 12-5

* definition only, term not found in text

F

FAIR CREDIT REPORTING ACT A federal statute which governs the collection, reporting, and use of consumer credit information. This Act was designed to protect consumers against the misuse of such information. In order to obtain a credit report on an applicant for insurance, the insurance company must comply with this law.

Page 2-14

FAIR MARKET VALUE The price a buyer would pay today for property offered by a seller. Fair Market Value is rarely used in determining property insurance limits because it reflects the value of real estate, not the actual cost of rebuilding. In property insurance, policy limits are generally determined by the calculating the Replacement Cost or the Actual Cash Value.

Page 3-12

FALLING OBJECTS This is a peril which is covered on the Broad Cause of Loss Form in both Commercial Property and Dwelling/Homeowners.

Page 3-21, 9-25

FEDERAL EMPLOYER LIABILITY ACT A federal Workers Comp program for Railroad employees.

Page 10-30

FIDELITY BOND A contract involving three parties which is designed to protect an employer against dishonest or fraudulent acts by employees. The obligee (employer) buys the bond from the surety (insurance company), who guarantees against losses due to dishonest acts by the principal (employee).

Page 11-2

FIDUCIARY An individual who has a responsibility for the financial affairs of another. As an insurance agent, you have a fiduciary responsibility to your clients for the safekeeping of their premiums and a limited responsibility for their financial affairs. It would be a breach of your fiduciary responsibility, for example, to use your policyowners' money for your own purposes.

Page 2-11

FIDUCIARY LIABILITY A Commercial Liability policy which covers the risk imposed under ERISA.

Page 10-33

FIELD UNDERWRITING Those activities by an agent to help in determining acceptable risks, to assist applicants with filling out the application and perhaps even doing initial drive-by inspections of property being considered for coverage by the company.

Page 2-15

FIRE Fire always has been and still is the greatest risk in property insurance. It is a peril covered under the Basic Cause of Loss form. Fire coverage includes payment for damages due not only to the flames, but also due to smoke, firefighters, and water used to fight the fire.

Page 3-20

FIRE DEPARTMENT SERVICE CHARGE This is an additional coverage automatically built into a property policy which pays up to a specified dollar limit to cover a fee charged by the fire department for making a call.

Page 5-15, 9-12

FIRE LEGAL LIABILITY This is the financial responsibility you have for having burned down your landlord's building. For example, if you have your own business but you rent your office space and you cause a fire which burns up the office, then you would need fire legal liability coverage to pay for the damage to your landlord's building. Fire Legal Liability is also found in Section II of all Homeowners forms.

Page 4-9, 5-33

FIRST AID TO OTHERS In most liability policies, first aid is covered under Med Pay. In Homeowners, it falls under Supplementary Payments.

Page 5-34

FIRST NAMED INSURED The First Named Insured is the first individual listed on the Declarations under the Named Insured category. There may be several Named Insureds, but only one First Named Insured. The First Named Insured is the individual who has the right to cancel or change the policy and the duty to pay the premium and should be the one notified should the insurance company wish to cancel the policy.

Page 1-7, 8-5

 * definition only, term not found in text

FLOATER A coverage for mobile commercial or personal property, such as furs, cameras, jewelry, sports equipment, musical instruments, sales equipment, etc. A floater can be written as a separate Inland Marine policy, or as an endorsement to a policy, such as a Homeowners or Commercial Property policy.
Page 5-12, 13-6

FLOOD A peril generally excluded from property policies which is defined as a general and temporary condition of partial or complete inundation by water of what is normally dry land. "Free-flowing or liquid" mudslides caused by flooding are also considered to be "floods". Flood insurance is available through the National Flood Insurance Program.
Page 7-1

FOREIGN COMPANY A company chartered in another state, territorial possession or Washington D.C..
Page 2-6

FORGERY ALTERATION (Agreement 2) A crime coverage which protects the insured from losses due to alteration of outgoing checks.
Page 11-5

FORTUITOUS Unforeseen and unexpected; accidental. One of the principles of insurance is that the insurance company will only pay for fortuitous losses, i.e., they will not pay for predictable, foreseeable losses.
Page 1-5

FRAUD Intentional and material misrepresentation or concealment for the purpose of deception or cheating to the detriment of someone else.
Page 2-11

FREIGHT COVERAGE An Ocean Marine coverage which covers the owner of the cargo, not for the cargo itself but rather for prepaid freight charges.
Page 13-9

"FRIENDLY FIRE" A fire started intentionally which is under control and is in its intended area (like a fire in a fireplace, on a stove, or in a water heater). Damage done by a "friendly fire" is not covered.
Page 3-20

FULL VALUE REPORTING FORM Under the Commercial Property policy, a form of the Reporting Form endorsement.
Page 9-18

FUNCTIONAL REPLACEMENT COST A method of calculating the cost to replace irreplaceable materials with functionally equivalent materials. Also known as repair cost.
Page 3-11

G

GARAGE POLICIES Contracts which provide liability coverage for businesses which are in the auto business – repair, sales, rental, storage, or parking.
Page 13-5

GENERAL AGGREGATE LIMITS Under a Commercial General Liability policy (CGL), the maximum to be paid out in any policy period for all losses, except Products-Completed Operations claims which have their own limit.
Page 10-18

GOVERNMENTAL ACTION The seizure or destruction of covered property as an act of governmental authority. Under a Commercial Property policy, losses due to governmental action are not covered, except for destruction of property ordered to prevent the more general spread of fire when the fire itself would be a covered cause of loss.
Page 9-26

GUARANTOR One of the three parties involved in a bond. The guarantor, or surety, is the insurance company which sells and issues the bond, and the one who must pay to the obligee if the principal does not fulfill his or her obligation.
Page 11-2

GUARANTY ASSOCIATION Most states by law require all insurance companies writing business in that state to contribute to a fund to provide for the payment of claims to resident policyowners of insolvent insurers. Membership in the state's Guaranty Association is mandatory. To collect money to pay the claims, insurance companies are generally assessed according to the amount and type of insurance they sell in the state.*

GUARD In Crime insurance, anyone, armed or unarmed, between the ages of 17 and 65 who accompanies a messenger (off premises) and is not the driver of a public conveyance.
Page 11-4

* definition only, term not found in text

H

HAZARD Any factor or situation that increases or contributes to the probability that a peril will occur. There are three types of hazards: a Physical Hazard is a physical object or situation, such as oily rags or faulty wiring which increase the likelihood of Fire; a Moral Hazard is a circumstance in which the insured knowingly and intentionally increases the risk, such as an insured who misrepresents a loss or hires an arsonist; a Morale Hazard is a situation which increases the likelihood of loss occurring due to the insured's carelessness, laziness, or indifference, such as an insured who smokes in bed.

Page 3-10

HIRED AUTO AND NONOWNED AUTO LIABILITY ENDORSEMENT A Commercial Auto endorsement which protects the employer from vicarious liability exposures.

Page 14-16

HOSTILE FIRE A fire which was started unintentionally, or which was started intentionally but then got out of control.

Page 3-20

HULL COVERAGE An Ocean Marine coverage which protects the shipowner for damage to the vessel.

Page 13-9

I

IMPLIED AUTHORITY The authority that includes the powers not specifically listed in the Agency Contract, but that the agent can assume they must have in order to do their job.

Page 2-18

IMPLIED WARRANTY The unwritten promise that a product will not be unreasonably dangerous.

Page 10-3

IMPORTS Property being shipped from another country for delivery in the United States.

Page 7-13, 13-6

INCHMAREE CLAUSE A named peril, i.e., latent defects, available in Ocean Marine policies.

Page 13-10

INCIDENTAL OCCUPANCIES ENDORSEMENT A homeowners endorsement which provides coverage for an in-home business.

Page 5-35

INDEMNIFY To repay an insured for what has been damaged, lost, or destroyed; to compensate an insured but not to make him better off (profit) from the loss.

Page 1-4

INDEPENDENT CONTRACTORS LIABILITY This is one of the nine General Liability exposures covered under a Commercial General Liability policy. It provides liability coverage for the insured due to the negligence of an independent contractor hired by the insured. For example, Joe, a restaurant owner, hires a carpenter who negligently injures a restaurant patron, who then sues Joe. Joe's Independent Contractors Liability coverage under his CGL would provide coverage.

Page 10-4

INDIRECT LOSS A form of financial damage that occurs as the result of a direct loss, such as the cost of renting a motel room to live in after a fire, or the lost profits of a business after a business fire.

Page 1-2

INDIVIDUAL BOND A type of fidelity bond that covers only one named employee.

Page 11-3

INDIVIDUAL NAMED INSURED A Commercial Auto endorsement which makes family members named insureds when operating company cars.

Page 13-4

INFLATION GUARD An optional coverage or endorsement on a property policy in which the insured selects a percentage which will automatically cause the policy limits to increase by that percentage over the year.

Page 9-7, 14-3

INHERENT VICE A latent defect or natural deterioration which is a characteristic of the property itself and is commonly excluded by property contracts.

Page 1-5

 * definition only, term not found in text

INLAND MARINE INSURANCE Insurance, generally written on an open perils basis, which covers mobile property, such as property in transit over land or in the air, and instruments of transportation and communication, such as bridges, tunnels, and docks, against risks of direct physical loss. Inland Marine insurance has nothing to do with water. There are both personal lines and commercial lines Inland Marine coverages, generally referred to as "floaters".

Page 7-8, 13-7

INSURABLE INTEREST In property insurance, an insurable interest is any financial interest you have in a piece of property. An insurable interest exists when damage or destruction to the property would result in a direct financial loss to you. In property insurance, you will only collect benefits under a policy if you have an insurable interest in that property at the time of the loss.

Page 1-4

INSURANCE Insurance is the transfer of risk of financial loss from an individual to a company, which, for consideration (premium and statements on the application), assumes that risk for a stated period of time against a stated peril(s), up to a stated amount.

Page 1-2

INSURANCE AGENT The legal representative of the insurance company.

Page 2-17

INSURANCE SERVICES OFFICE (ISO) A not-for-profit organization which provides a variety of services to the property and casualty insurance industry, such as development of policy forms, rating, actuarial, and statistical services, and advisory services.*

INSURED A person covered by an insurance policy (but not necessarily named in the policy).

Page 1-7

INSURED CONTRACT A specific type of agreement whereby one party voluntarily assumes the liability of another party. If A assumes B's liability, it is usually possible for A to purchase insurance to cover that risk which would pay for any subsequent resulting liability.

Page 10-4

INSURING AGREEMENT/CLAUSE The provision of an insurance policy containing the insurance company's promises. It establishes the obligation of the company to provide the insurance coverages as stated in the policy.

Page 2-13

INTENTIONAL WATER Water that the insured brings into a building on purpose e.g. plumbing. This peril is covered under the Broad Cause of Loss Form.

Page 3-21, 9-4

INTERVENING CAUSE A factor outside the control of the defendant, e.g., an illegal act, which results in injury to a third party.

Page 4-5

J

JETTISON A named peril, i.e., purposefully tossing cargo overboard in order to save a ship, available in Ocean Marine policies.

Page 13-10

JEWELERS BLOCK A type of Inland Marine insurance used to cover a retail jeweler's stock in trade, i.e., jewelry, precious and semiprecious stones, watches, and precious metals, and other stock such as porcelains and crystal.

Page 13-8

JOINT OWNERSHIP ENDORSEMENT An endorsement to the PAP which allows unrelated persons to purchase coverage together.

Page 6-23

JONES ACT A federal Workers Comp program for seaman.

Page 10-30

JUDGMENT A legal decision; order, decree, or sentence given by a court; a debt or other obligation resulting from a court order. If a court finds a party liable for negligence, the usual consequence is a judgment against the party with an order to pay money (damages).

Page 4-2

* definition only, term not found in text

L

LASER BEAM ENDORSEMENT A type of endorsement added to a Commercial General Liability policy written on a Claims-Made basis which excludes coverage for specific accidents, products, work, or locations.*

LAW OF LARGE NUMBERS The "law" that states that the probability of loss for a large group of insured with similar situations is very predictable. This law is the heart of all insurance underwriting.
Page 2-13

LEASEHOLD INTEREST A Commercial Property coverage form which protects the tenant if a favorable lease is cancelled as a result of damage to the property.
Page 9-29

LEGAL LIABILITY COVERAGE A coverage form under the Commercial Property policy which offers similar, yet broader coverage to the CGL's Fire Legal Liability coverage.
Page 9-29

LEGAL PURPOSE The objective of a contract must not be against the law. That is, the end cannot be illegal or against public policy.
Page 2-9

LIABILITY In insurance, a legal obligation to pay, such as being required by law to make good a loss or damage for which you are responsible; a potential damage which you may be required to pay. Also referred to as Casualty.
Pagc 4-1, 10-1

LIBERALIZATION CLAUSE A clause which states that if the insurance company, during your policy period, improves the terms or benefits of new policies of the same form to new insureds for the same price, then your policy will automatically have the same improved rights and benefits as the improved policies.
Page 1-5

LIMIT OF INDEMNITY/LIABILITY The maximum amount an insurance company will pay under a policy.
Page 1-4, 9-14

LIQUOR LIABILITY The legal obligation to pay for any loss or damage that occurs due to having served, distributed, or furnished alcoholic beverages to a minor or an intoxicated person. Depending upon your business, your liquor (dram shop) liability may or may not be covered.
Page 10-11

LLOYD'S OF LONDON An association of insurance underwriters, formed in the early 1700's in a coffeehouse in London, well-known for insuring huge, unusual, and sometimes bizarre risks. Lloyd's is not an insurance company.
Page 2-2

LONGSHORE & HARBOR WORKERS ACT A federal Workers Comp Program for harbor workers.
Page 10-30

LOSS A financial damage; the basis for a claim under an insurance policy; the amount for which the insurance company becomes obligated to pay the insured in the event of the insured's financial harm. Losses are either Direct or Indirect.
Page 1-2

LOSS RATIO The loss ratio is the relationship between the dollars collected in premium and the dollars paid out in claims.
Page 2-16

LOSS OF USE A form of indirect loss resulting from the inability to use a piece of property, such as a house, a commercial building or an automobile. For example, if your car is wrecked, in addition to having to pay the repair bill, you will suffer a financial loss if you have to go rent a car while yours is being repaired.
Page 1-2

LOSS PAYABLE CLAUSE A variation on the Mortgagors Protection Clause, with reservations.
Page 9-18

LOSS PAYMENT The method of paying a loss under a policy, such as Actual Cash Value, Replacement Cost, etc., stated in the Conditions section of the policy.
Page 3-10

M

MALICIOUS MISCHIEF See Vandalism and Malicious Mischief.

 * definition only, term not found in text

MARINE INSURANCE Insurance written primarily for property in transit; transportation insurance. Marine insurance is comprised of two branches: Ocean Marine & Inland Marine Insurance.
Page 7-8, 13-6

MATERIAL FACT A significant statement of fact given to an insurance company by an applicant. A fact is material if the company would have rejected the risk or charged the applicant a different premium if it had known the truth about the statement.
Page 2-10

MEDICAL EXPENSE BENEFITS In Workers Compensation insurance, these benefits cover hospital, surgical, doctor, nursing and drug types of expenses associated with a job related injury or illness.
Page 10-29

MEDICAL MALPRACTICE INSURANCE See Professional Liability Insurance.

MEDICAL PAYMENTS In a policy with liability coverage such as a Commercial General Liability, Homeowners or Automobile policy, the Medical Payments section pays for medical costs following an accident without regard to fault. Normally, the purpose of the coverage is to avoid lawsuits.
Page 4-7, 5-34, 6-6, 10-6

MESSENGER In Crime insurance, any person authorized to have custody of insured property away from the premises.
Page 11-4

MISCELLANEOUS TYPE VEHICLES ENDORSEMENT An endorsement to an auto policy. The endorsement covers such vehicles as snowmobiles, ATV's, etc.
Page 6-23

MISREPRESENTATION A false statement; a lie. If a misrepresentation on an insurance application is material (important) to the risk, then the policy could be voided by the insurance company within a specified period of time. It is a violation of insurance law for an agent to misrepresent the terms, benefits, etc. of a policy.
Page 2-10

MOBILE EQUIPMENT Land vehicles or machinery such as those used in the construction industry or on a farm and not designed for use on public roads. Examples of mobile equipment: fork lifts, bulldozers, cranes, steam rollers. Some types of vehicles ordinarily considered to be "autos" can be classified as "mobile equipment", and vice versa, depending upon how and where they are being used.
Page 9-12, 10-11, 13-2

MODULE A coverage unit of the Commercial Package Policy, such as Commercial Property, General Liability, Crime, Automobile, Inland Marine, etc.
Page 8-1

MONEY Any type of currency including: coins, bank notes, traveler's checks, checks and money orders. Money is not a security.
Page 11-4

MONOLINE POLICY A commercial policy consisting of only one coverage module.
Page 8-2

MORAL HAZARD A circumstance in which the insured attempts to defraud the insurance company through intentional and deliberate destruction of the insured property. The company determines the Moral Hazard by reviewing the proposed insured's reputation, financial record and past tendency to take advantage of others in business. Also see Hazard.
Page 3-10

MORALE HAZARD A situation which increases the likelihood of loss occurring due to the insured's indifference, carelessness, laziness, disorderliness or lack of concern for the insured property. Examples of Morale Hazards are leaving keys in a car, smoking in bed or exceeding the posted speed limit. Also see Hazard.
Page 3-10

MORTGAGE HOLDERS This clause states the rights and duties of the mortgagee (the mortgage holder, such as the bank) under the policy.
Page 9-18

MORTGAGE HOLDERS ERRORS AND OMISSIONS COVERAGE A form of the CPP designed to protect mortgage holders.
Page 9-30

* definition only, term not found in text

MOTOR CARRIER ACT OF 1980 A federal statute which sets minimum liability insurance limits for cargo haulers.

Page 13-5

MOTOR CARRIER COVERAGE A variation of the Business Auto policy for businesses carrying property or passengers.

Page 13-5

MUTUAL INSURANCE COMPANY An insurance company which has no capital stock or stockholders. It is managed by a board of directors chosen by the policyowners. Any earnings in addition to those necessary for the operation of the company are returned to the policyowners in the form of policy dividends (return of unneeded premium). For contrast, see Stock Insurance Company.

Page 2-3

MYSTERIOUS DISAPPEARANCE Property which disappears from a known location as a result of misplacing or losing; **not theft**. Modern policies just call it disappearance.

Page 11-4

N

NAIC (National Association of Insurance Commissioners) An association of the 50 state insurance commissioners that meets on a regular basis to discuss regulatory problems and to propose model legislation designed to achieve uniformity in insurance law among all states in the country.*

NAME SCHEDULE BOND A type of fidelity bond which literally names the individual employees that are covered by the bond on a list for amounts which could vary depending upon the level of exposure.

Page 11-3

NAMED INSURED As the policyowner(s), the Named Insured(s) have most of the rights and duties under the policy. Every person owning part of the property should be listed as a Named Insured. Also see First Named Insured.

Page 1-7

NAMED NON-OWNER COVERAGE This Personal Automobile Policy Endorsement allows an individual who does not own an automobile to purchase a personal automobile policy. The policy would provide you with coverage for borrowed automobiles and for rented automobiles. City dwellers frequently do not own automobiles but borrow or rent automobiles on a fairly regular basis.

Page 6-23

NAMED PERIL POLICY A policy in which the covered perils are literally named in the policy, such as the Standard Fire Policy which covers the perils of Fire, Lightning, and Removal. Perils not named are excluded from coverage. For contrast, see "All Risk" (Open Perils) Policy.

Page 3-9

NATIONAL FLOOD INSURANCE PROGRAM The federal government's program to make flood insurance available at reasonable (subsidized) rates to the general public. Coverages are marketed by private insurance companies, but the risk is borne by the federal government.

Page 7-2

NATIONWIDE MARINE DEFINITION In an attempt to restrict the area of business that marine insurers could underwrite, Congress defined "marine" as limited to goods in transit, such as imports, exports, domestic shipments, personal or commercial property in transit (floater policies) or instrumentalities of transportation, such as bridges, tunnels, docks and communication equipment such as broadcast towers and satellite dishes.

Page 7-9, 13-6

NEGLIGENCE A tort theory that essentially is a failure to do, or not to do, what a reasonably prudent person would do, or would not have done, in the same or similar circumstances. Negligence results from carelessness, ignorance, thoughtlessness or inaction. It is never an intentional act. If you are found negligent, you may be liable to pay for the damages you caused.

Page 4-3

* definition only, term not found in text

NO-FAULT INSURANCE In automobile liability insurance, bodily injury and property damage done to you by a guilty third party requires you and/or your insurance company to proceed against them to collect damages. The process is both expensive and time consuming. The concept of "No Fault" simply states that, in this situation, your insurance company will take care of you even though the damage was caused by a guilty third party. In other words, you do not try to prove "fault" against the guilty third party in order to collect. You simply collect from your own insurance carrier. In theory, it simplifies the procedures and should cost less.
Page 6-24

NON-ADMITTED COMPANY A company not admitted to do business in your state.
Page 2-7

NON PARTICIPATING COMPANY See Stock Company

NONCONCURRENT POLICIES When two or more property policies are used to insure a single piece of property, the "peril power" of the two or more policies should be exactly the same. If they are not, you have a situation called "nonconcurrency." A peril covered under one policy is not covered under another policy, and the latter will not pay on the claim. As a result, the insured suffers financial loss. The agent is responsible for maintaining concurrency. Also see Concurrent Policies.
Page 3-16, 9-8

NONRENEWAL Termination of the policy at the end of the policy period.
Page 1-6

NUCLEAR HAZARD Any losses due to a nuclear reaction, radiation, or radioactive contamination regardless of the cause are excluded from basic policies, but may be bought back for a substantial increase in premium.
Page 9-28

OBJECTS Under a Boiler and Machinery policy, the designated property which is insured is called an "object," such as a boiler or a specific piece of machinery. In order to have coverage, the object(s) you want covered must be listed on the declaration sheet.
Page 12-2

OBLIGEE In fidelity bonds and surety bonds, the party to whom the obligation is owed, and who is paid if the principal defaults, i.e., the party protected from loss under the bond. Also see Principal and Surety.
Page 11-2

OCCUPANCY In automobile insurance, "occupy" has to do with the use of the automobile and is defined as being in the car, being on the car, getting into or out of the car, getting onto or off of a car. In other words, just about every activity concerning being around a car is "occupying" the car. In property insurance, "occupying" means that somebody is living in or using a building. Unoccupied . . . nobody is home. Also see Vacancy.
Page 6-4

OCCUPATIONAL Work related; an occupational accident is an accident that occurs at work, such as a piece of factory equipment that falls on and injures a worker; an occupational hazard is a condition that increases the risk of loss at work, such as oil on the factory floor or contaminated air that a worker breathes; an occupational disease is a sickness contracted primarily at work, such as asbestosis from working around asbestos.
Page 10-30

OCCURRENCE This is a very broad definition of "accident," which includes the continuous or repeated exposure to substantially the same general harmful conditions that occur over time. Whereas an "accident" is a sudden event, an "occurrence" is a condition caused by continuous and repeated exposure to the same peril over a long period of time.
Page 1-7

OCCURRENCE LIMIT Under a liability policy, the limit that can be paid for any one claim.
Page 10-18

OCCURRENCE POLICY With a liability policy written on an Occurrence basis, you determine if a claim is covered by first determining if the "hurt" happened during the policy period. For contrast, see Claims-Made Policy.
Page 10-25, 14-4

OCEAN MARINE INSURANCE One of the two main branches of marine insurance, which is divided into "wet" and "dry". Ocean Marine insurance is "wet" and has to do with transportation exposures on any form of water such as rivers, lakes or oceans. Examples are ships and/or cargo that sail any body of water. "Dry" transportation insurance is called Inland Marine Insurance.

Page 7-12, 13-9

OFFER One of the necessary elements to the formation of a contract; an offer is a proposal which is firm enough to be accepted by another party. If the offer is accepted, an agreement is formed.

Page 2-9

OPEN PERILS ("ALL RISK") POLICY In property insurance, the highest form of peril coverage available. An Open Perils property policy covers all risks not specifically excluded in the contract. They are more frequently referred to as "All Risk" policies. However, this term can be misinterpreted by the insuring public; hence, the new term, "Open Perils." For contrast, see Named Peril Policy.

Page 3-9

OPERATIONS LIABILITY In commercial liability, the exposure that you as the businessowner have while conducting operations away from your normal business premises. For example, if you are a restaurant owner, catering a wedding at a church would expose your business to an Operations liability; Off-premises operations. Also see Completed Operations Liability.

Page 10-2

OTHER INSURANCE CLAUSE In property insurance, a clause in the contract that states how claims will be settled if the policyowner owns two or more policies that cover a given loss.

Page 3-16, 9-8

OTHER STRUCTURE In property insurance, a secondary structure not attached to the primary insured building, such as a detached garage, tool shed, outhouse, swimming pool, barn or satellite dish. Also called Appurtenant Structure.

Page 5-9

OTHER THAN COLLISION COVERAGE In the Personal Automobile Policy, the new name for Comprehensive coverage; in other words, coverage for almost all perils other than collision, including fire, theft, contact with bird or animal, breakage of glass, windstorm, hail, and V&MM.

Page 6-20

OUTBOARD/INBOARD BOATS Boats generally in the range from 14 feet to 26 feet. Boats in this range are bigger than car-top boats (which might be insured under a Homeowners policy) and are smaller than yachts. Outboard/inboard boats, which include sailboats, are generally "trailerable," can be towed behind the family automobile, and do not have living accommodations. Outboard/inboard boats are normally insured by a Boatowners policy.

Page 7-7

OUTER CONTINENTAL SHELF LANDS ACT A federal Workers Comp program for workers on offshore oil and natural gas drilling rigs.

Page 10-30

OWNERS, LANDLORDS & TENANTS POLICY (OL&T) The old name for what is now called Premises Liability. See Premises Liability.*

P

PACKAGE POLICY Simply, the combination of two or more coverage parts into one contract with one premium. Homeowners, Personal Auto and the Commercial Package Policy are examples.

Page 8-3

PAIR & SET CLAUSE In property insurance, certain collections of items have more value as a total set than the separate value of each of its pieces. For example, one rare dueling pistol may be worth $1,000 but a matched set could be worth $5,000. Such disparities create problems in settling such property claims. The Pair & Set Clause solves the problem by stating that the settlement will be equal to the value of the total set less the value of what is remaining after the loss occurs, or, at the company's option, the cost of repairing or replacing with like kind and quality.

Page 5-18

 * definition only, term not found in text

PARTIAL LOSS A loss for less than either (a) the value of the property, or (b) the value of the insurance covering the property. When there is a partial loss of property and the owner has not insured to value, Coinsurance applies.

Page 3-12

PARTICIPATING COMPANY See Mutual Company

PEAK SEASON ENDORSEMENT An endorsement to the CPP designed to fill the needs of businesses who operate with seasonally fluctuating inventory values, e.g. a toy store.

Page 9-19

PERCENTAGE DEDUCTIBLE In property insurance, the deductible expressed as a percentage of the face amount of the contract rather than in a flat dollar amount. Used for commercial earthquake coverage.

Page 9-28

PERIL The cause of loss. Examples of perils are fire, lightning, windstorm, hail, earthquake, collision, sprinkler damage, robbery, etc. In property insurance, covered perils are either listed (Named Peril Policy) or are covered on an "All Risk" (Open Perils) basis, which covers all perils not specifically excluded.

Page 3-9

PERIOD OF INDEMNITY The time period during which losses are covered; also called the Policy Period.*

PERIOD OF RESTORATION In the Business Income property coverage form, the period of time elapsed from the date of a loss until the property is or should be repaired for continued usage. For example, suppose that your building burns down on January 1 and it takes until July 1 (which is a reasonable period of time) for it to be ready to be moved back into. The interim period would be referred to as the Period of Restoration.

Page 9-22

PERSONAL & ADVERTISING INJURY LIABILITY Under Commercial General Liability, a coverage for non-communications businesses that covers (a) Personal Injury and (b) Advertising Injury. See Personal Injury and Advertising Injury.

Page 10-14

PERSONAL ARTICLES FLOATER An Inland Marine floater policy designed for specific categories of personal property such as furs, jewelry, musical instruments, cameras, silverware, or coin collections. The Personal Articles Floater specifies a category of personal property that is covered.

Page 5-12

PERSONAL AUTOMOBILE POLICY In personal lines, the name for the automobile policy designed for individuals or family units. It used to be called the Family Automobile Policy. The Personal Auto Policy is a package policy combining both property and casualty with coverage both on your automobile and the contents of the automobile plus the liabilities associated with operating your automobile. Medical Payments and Uninsured Motorist coverages are also available.

Page 6-1

PERSONAL CONTRACT Property and casualty insurance policies are for people, i.e., the agreement is between persons and insurance companies. A Personal Contract covers a person's insurable interest in the property, not the property.

Page 2-12

PERSONAL EFFECTS In Commercial Property insurance, employees' personal belongings that happen to be at the office, such as golf clubs, purses, pictures, etc., but not property of the business itself. Also see Extensions of Coverage.

Page 9-13

PERSONAL INJURY Damage to a person's reputation or mental state; examples of personal injury include libel, slander, defamation of character, false arrest, detention, or imprisonment, etc. Personal injury has nothing to do with physical injury to a person's body (bodily injury). Personal Injury Liability is a coverage under the Commercial General Liability policy.

Page 4-2

PERSONAL INJURY ENDORSEMENT An endorsement added to an HO policy which adds certain personal injury coverages to Section II.

Page 5-36

PERSONAL LIABILITY ENDORSEMENT An endorsement to add liability to a Dwelling Policy.

Page 5-38

* definition only, term not found in text

PERSONAL LIABILITY POLICY Section II of the Homeowners Policy. Can buy this section alone if homeowner's property coverage is not needed.
Page 5-30

PERSONAL LINES Insurance written to meet the needs of individuals and families, such as Homeowners or the Personal Automobile Policy.
Page 1-4

PERSONAL PROPERTY The movable contents of your house such as furniture, clothing, stereo equipment, wall hangings, dishes, etc. Under a Dwelling Policy or Homeowners, Personal Property coverage excludes animals, birds, fish, automobiles, and aircraft.
Page 5-10

PERSONAL PROPERTY OF OTHERS Property of someone else which you are responsible for and which is in your care, custody or control. Businesses like TV repair and dry cleaners purchase this coverage. This coverage is automatic and primarily intended to cover the belongings of guests in your home.
Page 5-7, 9-13

PERSONAL UMBRELLA POLICY See Umbrella Insurance.

PHYSICAL HAZARD See Hazard.

PHYSICAL DAMAGE See Coverage for Damage to Your Auto.

POLLUTION LIABILITY A third party coverage which is used to plug up the holes in a CGL left by the pollution exclusion.
Page 10-33

POSITION SCHEDULE BOND A fidelity bond which covers multiple employees by job title (treasurer, cashier, etc.) rather than by name. Different amounts of coverage may be applied to different positions. Also see Fidelity Bonds.
Page 11-3

POWER FAILURE OFF PREMISES An exclusion under the Commercial Property policy which consists of a failure of power or other utility service which causes consequential property damage on the premises. This peril can be covered by an endorsement to the Commercial Property policy.
Page 9-26

PREDICTABLE LOSSES Foreseeable or expected losses such as deterioration, wear and tear and mechanical breakdown. Insurance is not designed to cover predictable losses. Predictable losses are, therefore, excluded.
Page 1-5

PREMISES LIABILITY The liability which arises out of owning or occupying a business premises; the condition of the premises which causes bodily injury or property damage to the Other Guy, such as a slippery floor in the supermarket or a rickety chair in a restaurant. Premises Liability is one of the coverages under the Commercial General Liability policy and under a Businessowners Policy.
Page 10-2

PREMIUM The money a policyowner pays the insurance company for insurance coverage; the amount of money the insurance company charges for insurance coverage. Premium is a portion of a policyowner's consideration in an insurance contract.
Page 2-9

PRINCIPAL One of the three parties involved in a fidelity or surety bond; the principal is the person who is obligated to do something for someone else.
Page 11-2

PRO RATA In proportion; share; ratio. The term "pro rata" is used frequently in property insurance such as in "Pro Rata Refund", "Pro Rata Coverage" and "Pro Rata Liability" clauses.
Page 1-5

PRODUCTS-COMPLETED OPERATIONS AGGREGATE A total limit of liability available over the policy period for a Products-Completed Operations exposure under a Commercial General Liability policy.
Page 10-20

PRODUCTS LIABILITY The liability that arises from the manufacturing, distributing, or selling of a product. Products Liability, generally, is strict liability - it is based upon a theory of warranties. A higher standard of care is imposed in Products Liability than in other forms of liability, so a manufacturer, for example, has a greater risk of loss in the Products Liability area than, say, in Premises Liability.
Page 10-2

 * definition only, term not found in text

PROFESSIONAL LIABILITY Liability which a person or organization that renders professional services has that results from a failure to use due care and the degree of skill expected of a person in that particular profession; the liability which arises from negligence or errors and omissions which result from performing one's professional services; also called malpractice or errors and omissions liability.
Page 10-32

PROOF OF LOSS A sworn statement concerning a loss under a property policy. Insurance companies often settle claims without requiring a Proof of Loss.
Page 3-14

PROPERTY Anything tangible that you can see, feel, own, touch or possess (except people) is property, such as your house, your car, your business, your computer, your furniture, your dog, and your money. There is also intangible property, such as a copyright. Property insurance protects an insured against loss of specific property against specific perils.
Page 1-3

PROPERTY DAMAGE The physical destruction or damage to property. If it is your property that is damaged, then a Property policy can provide coverage. If it is another person's property that is damaged due to your negligence, then a Liability policy is necessary.
Page 4-2

PROPERTY DAMAGE LIABILITY Liability which causes physical damage to tangible property.*

PROTECTIVE SAFEGUARDS ENDORSEMENT A BOP endorsement which provides a premium reduction for certain alarm systems.
Page 14-6

PROXIMATE CAUSE Legal cause; the specific event or peril that caused a foreseeable harm to a foreseeable person. Proximate cause is one of the essential elements in establishing Negligence.
Page 4-4

PUNITIVE DAMAGES Arising from a liability claim, these damages are awarded to the injured party to punish the offending party and perhaps prevent future similar bad acts.
Page 4-5

PURE RISK There is only the chance of lose on the risk. The risk is inherent e.g. if you own a car, it could be stolen.
Page 1-1

R

RATE The amount of premium charged for a coverage.
Page 2-15

"REASONABLE PERSON" RULE A legal concept that uses a fictitious person, "the Reasonable Man" (the Reasonable Person), to review the behavior of an insured to decide if he or she acted in a logical and prudent manner or if the insured acted in a careless, imprudent, neglectful manner.
Page 4-3

RECIPROCAL INSURANCE EXCHANGE A not-for-profit organization designed to offer homeowners and auto insurance to the public. Operating much like a Mutual Company a Reciprocal Insurance Exchange sells policies to subscribers who agree to share in each others losses.
Page 2-4

REHABILITATION BENEFITS In Workers Compensation insurance, rehabilitation benefits pay part of the costs to provide an injured employee physical and vocational rehabilitation following an accident that results in the employee's disability. Rehabilitation benefits are not required, however, in many states.
Page 10-29

REINSURANCE The transfer of an insurance company's risk to another insurer which, for consideration, will indemnify losses suffered by the insurance company to a predetermined limit. State risk pools, risk retention groups and Lloyd's of London are examples of reinsurers. The two types of reinsurance are: Facultative, which means reinsurance is negotiated on a policy by policy basis, and Treaty, which is a blanket agreement under which one company automatically reinsures a percentage of policies of another company.
Page 2-2

RELATIVE (OR FAMILY MEMBER) A person living with the Named Insured and related to the Named Insured by blood, marriage or adoption, including a foster child. A student away at school is still considered to be a family member.
Page 6-4

* definition only, term not found in text

REMOVAL A peril under the old Standard Fire Policy, now called "Preservation of Property" in modern policies and considered an additional coverage. If the moving of insured property from the insured location to another location in order to save it from being damaged by a covered peril results in damage to that property, it is covered.

Page 3-5

RENTAL VALUE An indirect loss coverage under a Dwelling Policy which pays the insured up to 10% of the face amount of the contract to cover the loss of rental income. An option under Homeowners.

Page 5-13

REPAIR COST A method of settlement often used with older buildings having a very high replacement cost but a much lower market value. The company agrees to replace, for instance, your roof with functionally equivalent materials. In other words, if your slate roof is destroyed by a covered peril, the company may replace it with asphalt shingle. Also known as functional replacement cost.

Page 3-11

REPLACEMENT COST A form of settlement under which the insurance company, after a covered loss, will pay the insured enough to replace the destroyed property with new property of a like kind and quality without deducting depreciation. Also see Actual Cash Value and Fair Market Value.

Page 3-11

REPRESENTATION A statement made by an applicant or an insured which is true to the best of his or her knowledge and belief. A representation which is not the absolute literal truth is allowable, as long as it is the truth to the best knowledge or belief of the person making the statement. For contrast, see Warranty.

Page 2-10

RESIDENCE PREMISES Under a Homeowners policy, the "residence premises" includes the dwelling, other structures and grounds or that part of any building where the Named Insured lives which is identified as the "residence premises" on the Declarations Sheet.

Page 5-7

RESIDENT AGENT A person authorized and licensed as a Resident Agent by the State's Department of Insurance to sell policies of insurance. Each state has its own requirements for Resident and Nonresident licenses. A person may only be licensed as a Resident Agent in one state, but may hold any number of Nonresident licenses.

Page 2-12

RETROACTIVE DATE Under a Commercial General Liability policy, a provision on a claims-made coverage form which defines how far back in time the insurance company will go to cover claims which occurred prior to the inception of the policy.

Page 10-25

RIDER See Endorsement.

RIGHT OF SALVAGE One of the conditions of a property insurance policy is that the insurance company has the option to take all or any part of the damaged property at its agreed to or appraised value as salvage, or to repair damaged property or replace it with similar property rather than paying the actual cash value of the property.

Page 3-14

RIOT A wild, violent public disturbance of the peace; in property insurance, the peril of "Riot or Civil Commotion" includes acts done by striking employees, and looting which occurs at the time and place of the civil commotion.

Page 3-19

RISK Chance of loss; uncertainty of loss.

Page 1-1

ROBBERY In Crime insurance, the forcible taking of property from an individual through the use of violence, fear or the threat of violence. Robbery is a crime committed against a person. Also see Burglary and Theft.

Page 3-25, 11-4

SAFE BURGLARY The taking of property from a locked safe or vault, or the taking of the safe itself. As with burglary, there must be visible marks of force. Cash registers, cash drawers and cash boxes are not safes.

Page 3-26, 11-4

SECOND INJURY FUNDS A part of Workers Comp programs designed to cover "knocking out the eye of a one-eyed man".

Page 10-29

SECURITIES Instruments representing wealth, such as stocks, bonds, tokens, or tickets — but NOT money.

Page 11-4

SELF INSURED RETENTION LAYER A liability under may cover losses not covered by the underlying liability contracts. In this event the umbrella pays, however the insured must pay self insured retention layer first.

Page 10-28

SETTLEMENT A legal obligation to pay which is agreed upon by the parties out of court by means of a contract, as opposed to a Judgment, which is a legal obligation incurred in court.

Page 4-2

SHORT RATE REFUND A refund of premium which is less than a Pro Rata Refund because all of the company expenses are loaded up front. If a policyowner cancels a Commercial policy before the end of the coverage period, the insurance company will give the policyowner a short rate refund.

Page 1-6

SINGLE LIMITS An automobile insurance limit of liability for all bodily injury and property damage stemming from any one accident. Also see Split Limits.

Page 6-9

SINKHOLE COLLAPSE A peril consisting of the sinking or collapse of land into underground spaces created by the action of water, limestone or dolomite, but NOT due to a man-made underground cavity, like a coal mine.

Page 3-20

SMALL BUSINESS BOILER AND MACHINERY Provides Boiler and Machinery coverage for small business. See Boiler and Machinery.

Page 12-3

SMALL BUSINESS BROAD FORM BOILER AND MACHINERY Again, Boiler and Machinery for the small business, but with a broader definition of insured object.

Page 12-3

SMOKE A peril which consists of sudden and accidental smoke other than from a hostile fire.

Page 3-20

SOLICITOR In some states an individual who contracts with an agent to represent that agent's product line to the public.

Page 2-17

SPECIAL CAUSE OF LOSS FORM A Cause of Loss form which is on an Open Perils ("All Risk") basis, which means that all perils are covered except for those specifically excluded.

Page 3-23, 5-14, 9-26

SPECIFIC COVERAGE Coverage for only that property specifically listed on the Declarations Page of the policy.

Page 3-8

SPECULATIVE RISK Can either win or lose on the risk. The risk is created e.g. placing a bet.

Page 1-1

SPLIT LIMITS In automobile insurance, internal limits of liability for each of three types of liability losses: (1) bodily injury per person, (2) bodily injury per accident, and (3) property damage per accident, e.g. 25/50/10.

Page 6-9

SPOILAGE A coverage which can be purchased to cover the destruction of perishable stock.

Page 9-19

SPRINKLER LEAKAGE A peril consisting of leakage or discharge from an automatic sprinkler system, including the collapse of the system's tank if there is one.

Page 3-20

STANDARD FIRE POLICY A property policy form used widely in the United States from 1943 until the mid-1980's when the Commercial Package Policy was developed.

Page 3-3

STANDARD PROPERTY COVERAGE A no options version of the Commercial Property policy.

Page 9-30

STANDARD PROPERTY FORM Under a Businessowners Policy, one of the choices available for property coverage and which is written on a Named Peril basis.

Page 14-3

STATED VALUE Most Property and Casualty policies are written on a Stated Value basis. The insured tells the company the value of the item and insurance is written for that amount. Following a loss, the company can challenge value. If the item can be repaired or replaced for a lesser amount, the company can settle the loss for less than the amount of insurance.

Page 3-11

STATUTE OF LIMITATIONS The length of time that an injured party, a plaintiff, has to bring a civil lawsuit.

Page 4-6

STOCK INSURANCE COMPANY An insurance company that is owned and controlled by a group of stockholders whose investment in the company provides the capital necessary to start the business. The stockholders share in the profits (and losses) of the company; typically, the policyowners do not. A stock insurance company is one which generally issues non-participating policies to its policyowners. For contrast, see Mutual Insurance Company.

Page 2-3

STRICT LIABILITY A tort liability theory in which duty is not an issue. Used as an alternative to negligence in areas such as products liability.

Page 4-6

SUBROGATION The legal process by which an insurance company, once it reimburses someone for a loss caused by someone else, assumes the legal right to sue the "guilty" third party. In commercial policies, subrogation is also called Transfer of Rights of Recovery Against Others to the Insurer.

Page 3-17

SUPPLEMENTARY PAYMENTS Extra coverages provided by a liability policy consisting of benefits such as defense costs. Supplementary Payments are is not triggered by your legal obligation to pay and are paid in addition to the limits of liability of the policy in most cases.

Page 4-7, 6-13, 10-6

SURETY One of the three parties involved in a bond. The surety, or guarantor, is the insurance company which sells and issues the bond, and the one who must pay to the obligee if the principal does not fulfill his or her obligation.

Page 11-2

SURETY BONDS Bonds which ensure that obligations imposed by operation of law or contract will be met. Surety bonds are truly not insurance as the term is normally used, as the benefits available are a "last resort".

Page 10-33

SURPLUS LINES TRANSACTION A transaction that makes it possible to buy an insurance policy from an unauthorized company.

Page 2-7

SURVIVORS' BENEFITS Under Workers Compensation insurance, a type of benefit which pays a benefit to the surviving spouse and/or dependent children of an employee killed on the job.

Page 10-29

SUSPENSION PROVISION Under a Boiler and Machinery policy, a provision which allows the insurance company to immediately suspend coverage on a specific object which is in a dangerous condition once notice is delivered to the insured. The provision also allows for unannounced inspections.

Page 12-4

T

TAIL COVERAGES (Extended Reporting Periods) A reporting period extending beyond the coverage period for liability claims. This is not additional coverage, it is just an additional period of time to report claims.

Page 10-25

TEMPORARY SUBSTITUTE A non owned vehicle being used by the insured due to the unavailability of a covered vehicle due to breakdown, servicing, repair, loss or destruction.

Page 6-4

THEFT Any wrongful act of taking the property of another. Theft is a broad term and includes robbery, burglary, shoplifting, and embezzlement.

Page 3-25, 11-4

 * definition only, term not found in text

THIRD PARTY CONTRACT A contract of insurance involving three parties: the insurance company, the insured and an unknown third party. All casualty (liability) contracts are Three Party Contracts. They are designed to protect the insured(s) against negligence claims by an injured third party.
Page 1-3

TOBACCO SALES WAREHOUSE COVERAGE A two party coverage, a form of CPP, for tobacco auction houses.
Page 9-30

TORT A tort is any wrongful act (or failure to act) on the part of one person which gives another person a right to sue for damages. Negligence, an unintentional tort, is what is covered by liability (casualty) insurance.
Page 4-2, 4-6

TOTAL LOSS A loss of all of the insured property or totaling the policy limit. Most property losses are not total, but rather partial losses.
Page 3-12

TOWING AND LABOR ENDORSEMENT An endorsement found in automobile policies designed to get a covered auto to a safe harbor.
Page 6-23

TRAILER A vehicle designed to be pulled by a private passenger vehicle.
Page 6-4

TRANSFER OF RIGHTS OF RECOVERY AGAINST OTHERS TO THE INSURER See Subrogation.

TRANSPORTATION A covered peril under the Businessowners policy.
Page 14-4

TRUCKER'S POLICY A variation of the Business Auto policy designed for businesses transporting property.
Page 13-4

TWO PARTY CONTRACT A contract in which there are only two parties or persons involved: the insured and the insurance company. All property contracts are Two Party Contracts.
Page 1-3

U

UMBRELLA POLICIES A personal or commercial liability coverage which is designed to increase the limits of a primary liability policy. If you are found negligent, your basic liability policy (such as a CGL or Homeowners) would pay first; your umbrella would provide coverage for an amount over the limits of your basic policy.
Page 10-27

UNAUTHORIZED COMPANY See Non-Admitted Company.

UNDERINSURED MOTORIST COVERAGE A driver who meets the state's financial responsibility requirements but who causes more damage than what he has coverage for is an underinsured motorist.
Page 6-15, 6-17

UNDERWRITE In insurance, to assume risk in exchange for premium; to assume liability in the event of specified loss or damage; to insure.
Page 2-14

UNILATERAL CONTRACT A contract, such as an insurance policy, in which only one party makes a promise. The insurance company makes a promise contained in the policy. The policyowner can continue the coverage in force by paying premium (no promise is required on the policyowner's part to forever pay premium).
Page 2-12

UNINSURED MOTORIST COVERAGE An uninsured motorist is someone who (1) has no insurance, (2) has less than the state's minimum limits, (3) is insured by a company that denies coverage or becomes insolvent, or (4) for bodily injury claims only, a hit and run driver. This coverage pays you if the negligent third party is uninsured.
Page 6-15

UNOCCUPANCY People gone, but contents remaining in a building.
Page 3-15

UTILITY SERVICES - DIRECT DAMAGE ENDORSEMENT A BOP endorsement which provides direct loss coverage for utility service disruption.
Page 14-5

UTILITY SERVICES - TIME ELEMENT ENDORSEMENT A BOP endorsement which provides indirect loss coverage for utility service disruption.
Page 14-5

V

VACANCY Containing no people or property; devoid of contents and occupants; empty. Vacancy is a hazard; therefore, the insurance company may cancel the insurance, exclude coverage, or limit payment of claims if a loss occurs while covered property is vacant. Under a Commercial Property Policy, a building is "vacant" if it does not contain enough business property to conduct customary operations, i.e., under this policy, it does not have to be literally empty to be considered "vacant."
Page 3-15, 9-17

VALUATION The basis on which a loss is paid, such as Actual Cash Value, Agreed Value, or Replacement Cost.
Page 3-10, 9-17

VALUED CONTRACT See Agreed Value

VANDALISM AND MALICIOUS MISCHIEF (V&MM) A peril consisting of willful and malicious damage to or destruction of property. V&MM is not theft.
Page 3-20

VEHICLES OR AIRCRAFT, THE PERILS OF If it flies through the air or falls from the sky, it is an aircraft, e.g., airplanes, meteors, spacecraft, self-propelled missiles, or a Skylab falling to earth. If it runs along the ground, it is a vehicle. This includes automobiles, trucks, motorcycles, road repair equipment, bulldozers, cherry pickers, and so on.
Page 3-20

VICARIOUS LIABILITY Legal responsibility for another's action e.g. an employer for an employee.
Page 4-6

VOLCANIC ACTION A peril consisting of damage done above ground by a volcano, such as damage from the blast or shock waves, ash, dust or lava flow.
Page 3-20

VOLCANIC ERUPTION The peril consisting of damage done below ground by a volcano. This peril is covered under the Earthquake Cause of Loss Form in Commercial Property and by endorsement in Homeowners.
Page 5-18, 9-27

W

WAIVER The intentional relinquishment (giving up) of a right or privilege.
Page 2-11

WARRANTY (A) A statement made by the insured which is taken to be the absolute literal truth; a breach of warranty is sufficient to render the policy void. Warranties are used in Ocean Marine and Jewelers Block policies and in the case of fraud; in most other situations, the insured's statements are taken to be Representations. (B) Promises from a manufacturer or seller of a product to a consumer. See Implied Warranty.
Page 2-10, 10-3

WATCHPERSON In Crime insurance, any person the insured retains to protect insured property inside the premises and who has no other duties.
Page 11-4

WATER DAMAGE A Broad form peril due to leaking and freezing of pipes, appliances or systems which contain water.
Page 3-21, 9-24

WINDSTORM A peril which includes hurricanes, tornadoes, high winds, and cyclones.
Page 3-19

WORKERS COMPENSATION Insurance purchased by an employer to pay for medical expenses, lost wages, and/or death benefits for employees who suffer a work-related injury or illness. Workers Compensation is regulated on the state level, so benefits and requirements vary from state to state.
Page 10-28

Y

YACHT Under a yacht policy, a watercraft (either sailboat or motorized) over 26 feet long with cooking and living facilities.
Page 7-7

End!

 * definition only, term not found in text

P&C Toolbox

TABLE OF CONTENTS

Section 1

PROPERTY & CASUALTY SUMMARY NOTES

P&C SUMMARY NOTES

I. GENERAL INSURANCE CONCEPTS

A. CLASSIFYING INSURANCE COMPANIES

Insurance Companies can be classified in 3 ways:

1. **By place of origin / where the Company was started:**

   a. **Domestic**: Started in this State.

   b. **Foreign**: Started in another State of the U.S.A.

   c. **Alien**: Started in another Country.

2. **By how the Insurance Company is structured:**

   a. **Stock**: A **For-Profit** Company that is operated for the benefit of its **stockholders / investors**.

   b. **Mutual: A Not-For-Profit** Company operated for the benefit of its **Policyowners**.

   c. **Fraternal**: A **"club"** that offers insurance to its **members**. Similar to a Mutual, but you must join the Club before you can buy their insurance.

3. **By Authority:**

   a. **Admitted** / **Authorized** to do business in this State.

   b. **Non-Admitted** / **Unauthorized** to do business in this State.

B. CONTRACT LAW

1. THE FIVE ESSENTIAL ELEMENTS OF A CONTRACT ARE:

a. *Offer*

b. *Acceptance*

c. *Consideration (something of value)*

d. *Competent Parties*

e. *Legal Purpose*

2. THE PROCESS

a. **Offer:** You have something to sell for $50.

b. **Acceptance:** I agree to buy it from you for $50.

c. **Consideration:** You give me the item; I give you the money (there must be an exchange of values).

d. **Competent Parties:** We are not under the influence of a mind altering substance, or under age.

e. **Legal Purpose:** We are not doing anything illegal.

3. "LET'S COME TO TERMS": SOME IMPORTANT INSURANCE CONTRACT TERMS TO KNOW

a. **Offer:** Application for insurance **and money** (prepaid APP).

b. **Invitation to Make an Offer:** An application for insurance **without money**.

c. **Counter-Offer:** Making an **alternate proposal** other than the original Offer.

d. **Unilateral**: Only **one party** (the insurance company) makes legally enforceable promises.

e. **Adhesion**: One party (the insurance company) writes the policy, and offers it to the public on a "take it or leave it" basis; There is **no negotiating** for policy terms. Any contract errors will go against the Company.

f. **Aleatory**: The two parties to the contract will probably **not benefit equally** from the policy / contract.

g. **Concealment**: Part of the truth is **hidden**.

h. **Warranty**: Statements that must be **absolutely / literally** true.

i. **Representations:** Statements that are true to the best of your knowledge and belief / **believe** to be true.

j. **Misrepresentations**: Not true / **lying**.

k. **Fraud**: The attempt to **personally benefit** from a lie.

l. **Binder**: Immediate, temporary coverage before the actual policy is issued. Binders can be written, or oral.

4. THREE TYPES OF AGENT'S <u>AUTHORITY</u>

a. **Expressed Authority**: The Authority **specifically granted** in writing to the Agent / Producer by the Insurance Company in the Agency Agreement.

b. **Implied Authority**: The Authority **not specifically granted**, but that is **assumed** or <u>implied</u> as being necessary to fulfill the Agent's duties and obligations.

Example: Even though it is not specifically mentioned in the Agency Agreement, an Agent can assume that they have the authority to have business cards printed, use a cell phone, drive, make appointments, etc.

c. **Apparent Authority**: The authority that customers **can assume** an Agent has, regardless of whether or not the Agent actually has that authority.

*Example: Even though Agents may not have the power to bind coverage on the spot, a customer may **assume** the Agent apparently has **BINDING** authority.*

II. PROPERTY AND CASUALTY BASICS

A. <u>PROPERTY BASICS</u>

1. WHAT IS PROPERTY?

Property insurance covers your **stuff**, i.e. your buildings, your home / dwelling, your personal property, your business property / business equipment, your car, your boat, your airplane, etc.

2. IN WHICH POLICIES IS PROPERTY COVERAGE FOUND?

Property coverage is found in:

a. Homeowners Section I

b. Dwelling Policies

c. *Personal Auto: Coverage D Collision* and *Other Than Collision;* and in Commercial Auto policies

d. Commercial Property (part of the CPP)

e. Ocean and Inland Marine

f. Boiler and Machinery / Equipment Breakdown

g. Farm & Crop

h. Flood

i. Crime

j. Business Owners Policy (BOP)

k. Boat, Yacht & Aircraft

3. **THREE LEVELS OF *PERIL POWER***

a. **Named Peril Coverage:** Only losses caused by the listed / named perils will be covered.

i. **Basic Perils (11):** WR ELF VVV SSS (see Pathfinder P&C text Chapter Three).

ii. **Broad Perils (14):** The 11 Basic Perils, plus **WWF** (*Weight of Ice, Snow & Sleet; Water Damage & **F**alling Objects*), plus adds ***Collapse***.

b. **Open Peril Coverage:** If a loss is caused by a peril **NOT** specifically **excluded** from coverage, then the loss **will be covered**: aka "Special Perils", or **"All Risk**" coverage.

4. **COMING TO *TERMS***

a. **Hazard:** Something that increases the likelihood of a peril occurring. There are three types of Hazards:

i. **Physical Hazards:** An **observable** hazard, such as icy roads, faulty wiring, or oily floors.

ii. **Moral Hazards:** Someone who might **intentionally** cause a loss, such as hiring an arsonist to burn down their building in order to collect the insurance.

iii. **Morale Hazards:** Someone who doesn't care if there is a loss, and may be lazy, **careless** or **indifferent** about risk management, such as smoking in bed.

b. **SIX DEFINITIONS FOR EXPRESSING *VALUE***

i. **Replacement Cost (RC):** Get a new one for an old one / **the cost of a new one TODAY**. Replacement Cost is the method of valuation used for Homeowners Coverage A *Dwelling* and Coverage B *Other Structures.* If a tornado rips off your roof, the insurance company will pay to put a **new roof** on your house.

ii. **Actual Cash Value (ACV) = Replacement Cost today minus depreciation.** **ACV = RC – D**

The concept of ACV is that certain types of property wear out, and are worth less, over time. In other words, these items **depreciate** over time. Example: You purchased a new car three years ago for $24,000. It has depreciated 50% over the last three years. The Replacement Cost **today** of your car is now $26,000. The ACV of your old car today is $13,000 ($26,000 minus 50% of $26,000 = $13,000).

iii. **Fair Market Value (FMV):** The amount of cash someone is willing to pay for the item today. Fair Market Value is usually **not** used in Property insurance for at least two reasons: (1) FMV usually reflects the value of the property's **location,** both good and bad; and (2) property insurance does NOT insure the **land** that buildings are located on, while FMV usually DOES reflect the value of the land. That being said, the Homeowner's **HO 8** DOES use FMV for insuring **older homes** to limit the risks of fraud (see the Pathfinder Text Chap 5).

iv. **Stated Value:** The amount the Insured / Policyowner **states** that a piece of property costs / is worth at the time the policy is written. However, the Insurance Company will determine the value (amount to pay on a claim) at the time of the loss. Frequently used in Property Floater policies.

v. **Agreed Value:** The Insured Policyowner and the Insurance Company **agree up front** to the value of an item, such as an airplane or a fine arts painting, when the policy is written. This is the dollar amount that WILL be paid if a covered loss occurs. Frequently used when insuring antiques, classic cars, vintage airplanes, works of art, rare collectibles, etc. (Situations where the Replacement Cost is not available because the item cannot be replaced).

vi. **Functional Replacement Cost / Repair Cost:** In situations where the insured property is very ornate and exceedingly expensive to replace, such as hand carved mantle pieces in an older building, the Policyowner and the Company agree, in order to keep the premium reasonable, that if a loss occurs, the Company will only pay for **functionally equivalent** replacement items, not the higher cost actual originals. Examples: an asphalt roof instead of a handmade slate roof; a wooden slab mantle instead of the original hand carved mantle.

c. **VACANT = NO PEOPLE or NO STUFF = EMPTY**

A vacant building is one that contains **no people OR no stuff**. Insurance companies will not cover certain perils for vacant buildings (both homes and businesses) that have been vacant for more than a certain amount of time, usually 60 days.

B. CASUALTY (LIABILITY) BASICS

1. THREE PARTY CONTRACTS

All Liability / Casualty insurance policies are **Three Party** contracts. The Parties are the **Policyowner**, the **Insurance Company** and an **Unknown Third Party**, "The Other Guy," who is the injured party.

2. PURPOSE OF LIABILITY COVERAGES

Liability insurance never directly benefits the Policyowner. The primary purpose of liability insurance is to protect the assets of the Policyowner / Insured, should they become legally obligated to pay for damage they did to someone else's body (Bodily Injury / B.I.) or their property (Property Damage / P.D.).

3. NO PROPERTY COVERAGE FOR POLICYOWNER

Your Property is NOT covered under your Liability Policy, because it is "Better Covered Elsewhere" under your Property insurance coverage.

4. **LIABLILTY COVERAGES** are found in:

a. Homeowners Section II
b. Personal Auto Coverage A
c. Commercial General Liability (CGL)
d. Commercial Auto
e. Farm
f. BOP
g. Workers Compensation (WC)
h. Umbrellas
i. Professional Liability (E&O) (D&O)
j. Boat / Watercraft / Yacht
k. Aircraft
l. Pollution
m. Liquor

C. <u>NOT KNOWING THESE CASUALTY DEFINITIONS COULD BE A *LIABILITY*</u>

1. **Negligence:** the failure to do, or not do, what a Reasonable Person would do, or not do, in the same or similar circumstances. Translation: *Just do what the average person would do, and you won't be "negligent".*

2. **Legally Obligated to Pay:** As the result of an in-court judgment or an out-of-court settlement, you have a legal obligation to pay "The Other Guy". Translation: the ruling of the Court was that the accident was your fault, and now you must pay for the damage that you did to "The Other Guy".

3. **Duty:** The obligation for you to use a reasonable standard of care (act prudently). Every right that you have has a corresponding duty to act in a reasonable manner. For example, if you have a ***Right*** to cut down a tree, you have a corresponding ***Duty*** to make certain that the tree doesn't cause damage (BI or PD) when it falls. If the tree DID fall on "The Other Guy", you would have ***BREECHED YOUR DUTY***.

4. **Proximate Cause:** A direct and foreseeable link between your actions, and the resulting Bodily Injury (BI) and / or Property Damage (PD) you caused to "The Other Guy".

5. **Comparative Fault:** A legal defense to a case of *Negligence* under which a judgment could be reduced proportionately if the Claimant "The Other Guy" in a liability case is found to be somewhat responsible for their own injuries. Translation: the Policyowner / Insured cut down the tree, which fell on "The Other Guy". And, yes, our Guy DID chop down the tree, but "The Other Guy" was using his cell phone while driving, and therefore not properly watching what was going on down the road. If he had not been talking on his cell phone, he could have seen the tree falling, stopped in time, and avoided the accident.

6. **Assumption of Risk:** A legal defense to a case of *Negligence* under which it can be argued that a Claimant in a liability case undertook an action or activity that they knew to be dangerous. EXAMPLES: Sky diving, rock climbing, scuba diving, bungee jumping, race car driving, etc.

III. HO HO HO
HOMEOWNERS POLICY

A. HO ELIGIBILITY

1. **HOME MUST BE** **Owner Occupied** **:**

   a. Single Family Dwellings (HO 1,2,3,5)

   b. Multi-Family Dwellings (HO 1,2,3,5)

   c. Mobile Homes (HO 2 or 3)

   d. "Hobby Farm" Dwellings (HO 1,2,3,5)

   e. Condominiums (HO 6)

2. **Tenant Occupied** **:** (HO 4)

   a. Apartments

   b. Rental Houses

B. HO COVERAGES

1. **PROPERTY (SECTION I)**

   a. Coverage A Dwelling

   b. Coverage B Other Structures

   c. Coverage C Personal Property / Contents

   d. Coverage D Loss Of Use

2. **LIABILITY (SECTION II)**

a. Coverage E Personal Liability

b. Coverage F Medical Payments to Other

C. HOMEOWNERS

	Section I Property		Section II Casualty	
HO Form	**Dwelling and Other Structures Coverages A* & B***	**Personal Property Coverage C***	**Liability Coverage E**	**Med Pay Coverage F**
	REPLACEMENT COST	**ACTUAL CASH VALUE**		
HO-1 & HO-8**	Basic & Theft	Basic & Theft	$100,000/ Occurrence	$1,000/Person
HO-2	Broad & Theft	Broad & Theft	↓	↓
HO-3	Special & Theft	Broad & Theft	↓	↓
HO-5	Special & Theft	Special & Theft	↓	↓
HO-4	N/A	Broad & Theft	↓	↓
HO-6	$1000 . . . Broad & Theft	Broad & Theft	↓	↓

* Coverage D Loss Of Use will pay if a covered loss makes the dwelling uninhabitable. Hotel $$$'s.
** HO-8 settlement on buildings can be written one of three ways: Fair Market Value, ACV or Repair Cost, but never on a Replacement Cost basis.

ALL 7 HO FORMS AUTOMATICALLY COVER THE PERIL OF
THEFT

D. FIVE IMPORTANT THINGS TO KNOW ABOUT HOMEOWNERS PROPERTY COVERAGE

1. **CAUSE OF LOSS** Homeowners pays for losses to your property **ONLY** if the loss is caused by a **covered** peril (**Basic**, **Broad**, or **Special**).

2. **80% + RULE** ***Dwellings (Coverage A)*** and ***Other Structures (Coverage B)*** are insured on a **Replacement Cost Basis,** but **ONLY IF** the buildings are insured for **80% or more of their Replacement Cost.** Otherwise (if the insurance in force is LESS THAN 80% of the Replacement Cost), the loss will be paid on an ACV basis. This can be tragic!

3. ***COVERAGE B*** ***Other Structures*** include detached garages, outbuildings, tool sheds, towers, swimming pools, satellite dishes, fences, etc.

4. ***COVERAGE C*** ***Personal Property / Contents*** is covered on an Actual Cost Basis (**ACV**). However, Personal Property / Contents coverage can be upgraded to ***Replacement Cost*** by **endorsement for an increase in premium**.

5. ***WORLD WIDE COVERAGE*** ***Personal Property*** is covered no matter where you take it in the entire world.

E. SIX IMPORTANT THINGS TO KNOW ABOUT HOMEOWNERS LIABILITY COVERAGE

1. **AT FAULT** Homeowners Liability pays when the actions of the Policyowner / Insured lead to injury of another person (BI) or damage to someone else's property (PD) , and the Insured is **legally obligated to pay**. (For more details, check out Property and Casualty Basics in the Pathfinder P&C text).

2. **ON PURPOSE** Liability **never** covers **intentional acts**.

3. **EXCLUSIONS** HO Liability covers most of your personal liability exposures, **except in a car**, **in a boat**, or **in an airplane,** all of which are *Better Covered Elsewhere*. However, your Homowners policy will provide liability coverage if you are operating a small, slow, low risk "toy" boat (canoe, kayak, sailboat, etc.), but NOT a serious (dangerous) boat.

   Remember:

   No Cars

   No Boats HO HO NO NOs

   No Airplanes

   No Business

4. **LOSS OF USE** Homeowners Liability can pay for both **direct** and **indirect losses**.

5. **INSUREDS** Homeowners covers the liability exposure of the Named Insureds and all Insureds (relatives / family members - your kids, for example, while they are living at home).

6. **PROPERTY DAMAGE** Homeowners Liability can pay for the damage an Insured does to "The Other Guy's" property (PD).

F. HOMEOWNERS POLICIES COVER *THE OTHER GUYS'* MEDICAL BILLS (MED PAY)

Don't forget…HO Med Pay pays to "The Other Guy".
AUTO MED PAY pays to US!

G. FIVE IMPORTANT THINGS TO KNOW ABOUT HOMEOWNERS MEDICAL PAYMENTS COVERAGE

1. Medical Payments (Med Pay) pays to **Other People**, NOT to the Policyowner / Insureds / Family Members. Med Pay covers medical bills, dental bills, and funeral expenses.

2. Med Pay does **NOT** cover **Indirect Losses**, such as loss of wages, or pain and suffering.

3. HO Med Pay will only pay losses filed **within 3 years** of the date of the occurrence.

4. Med Pay pays without regard to fault **(No fault).**

5. Medical Payments coverage:

   $1000 Per Person in all unendorsed HO forms. Need more? Buy more. Everyone needs more!

IV. PERSONAL AUTOMOBILE

LET'S GET PERSONAL WITH AUTO

HERE ARE THE FOUR COVERAGES YOU NEED TO KNOW

A. COVERAGE A = LIABILITY (BI & PD)

Liability: Pays for the Bodily Injury (**BI**) **to other people** and for Property Damage (**PD**) damage to **other people's property** caused by the negligence of our Insured / Policyowner.

1. **SPLIT LIMITS** The policy limits are per occurrence (per accident), and are typically expressed as a **split limit** (i.e. **25/50/10**).

   #1 The **first** number (**25** in our example) means the maximum dollar amount the policy will pay for Bodily Injury to **any one person**. In this example, no more than $25,000 BI will be paid to **any one** person.

   #2 The **second** number (**50** in our example) means the maximum dollar amount the policy will pay for Bodily Injury (BI) in **any one occurrence ($50,000),** no matter how many people are injured.

   #3 The **third** number (**10** in our example) is the maximum dollar amount the policy will pay for **Property Damage** in any one occurrence.

   PLEASE KNOW HOW TO APPLY LIABILITY SPLIT LIMITS TO CLAIMS QUESTIONS. SEE THE PATHFINDER TEXT CHAPTER SIX FOR AN EXPLANATION.

2. **SINGLE LIMITS** To determine the equivalent Single Limit of Liability as compared to Split Limits, simply add the Split Limit Total BI # to the Total PD #. For example, to determine the Single Limit equivalent to 25/50/10, just add the total BI of 50 to the total PD of 10, which equals 60.

NOTE: Liability is the only mandatory AUTO coverage necessary to comply with State insurance laws in most states.

B. COVERAGE B = MED PAY TO US

Medical Payments (Med Pay): Pays for medical bills, dental bills and funeral expenses (DIRECT LOSSES ONLY).

1. Unlike all other P&C policies, Med Pay in Auto pays to **US / Our Family**, **not to "The Other Guy"**.

2. Auto Med Pay pays to us / our family / relatives, for medical bills caused by **ANY** motor vehicle accident.

3. Med Pay covers us as the Named Insured and our Family / Relative if any of us are injured by a car when we are a **Pedestrian**.

4. Med Pay also covers our **invited guests** when they are riding as **passengers** in our car.

5. Med Pay coverage ***Limits*** are expressed on a Per Person Per Occurrence basis.

*Med Pay pays without regard to fault (***NO FAULT***).*

Med Pay limits are often as low as $1000 per person per occurrence.

NOTE: Buy / recommend higher limits. You may need them (a Life Line helicopter ride to the hospital is $1000/minute!).

C. <u>COVERAGE C = UN & UNDER INSURED</u>

1. UN/UNDER INSURED MOTORISTS

a. **<u>THE OTHER GUY IS AT FAULT</u>** UN/UNDER provides coverage for the Insured Policyowners and their Family / Relatives if they are injured **by another motorist WHO <u>MUST</u> BE AT FAULT**.

b. **<u>UN/UNDER</u>** Think of Coverage C as the reverse of Coverage A Liability. Under Coverage A *Liability*, the Insured Policyowner causes the accident (is AT FAULT), and inflicts BI or PD on "The Other Guy". So our Guy / Policyowner has to pay "The Other Guy".

c. **<u>UN/UNDER</u>** Coverage C is just the reverse of Coverage A. Under Coverage C UN/UNDER, "The Other Guy" **causes the accident** (is AT FAULT), and inflicts BI and PD on our Policyowner / Insured. However, "The Other Guy" is **UN** Insured, or **UNDER** Insured (*see definitions below*) and cannot pay for the damage they caused. So our Policyowner / Insured collects from his / her **own** policy under Coverage C UN/UNDER.

d. **<u>UMBI</u>** (Uninsured Motorist Bodily Injury) coverage, as explained above, covers BI losses to the Insured / Policyowner and their Family in their car, or as a pedestrian.

e. **<u>UMPD</u>** (Uninsured Motorist Property Damage) covers PD losses to the Insured / Policyowner's property (their car) up to the limits specified in the policy. Buy enough coverage to cover the full value of your car.

2. UN & UNDER DEFINITIONS

a. **"UNINSURED MOTORISTS"** are defined as any one of the four following types of Drivers:

i. **NONE** Drivers who have **NO** car insurance.

ii. **NOT LEGAL** Drivers who are driving with liability limits **lower** than those legally required in the state in which they are driving. For example, driving with Liability Limits of 5/10/5 in a state that mandates 25/50/10.

iii. **BANKRUPT COMPANY** Drivers with legal auto liability insurance, but their insurance **company has denied the claim**; or Drivers who no longer have insurance because their insurance **company went bankrupt**.

iv. **"HIT AND RUN"** Drivers who **leave the scene** of the accident. If you don't know who hit you, it is difficult to get them to pay for your damages!

b. **"UNDER Insured Motorists"** are defined as Drivers who have caused an accident (they are **AT FAULT**), they DO have auto Liability insurance equal to, or greater than the State's minimum limits, but they **DON'T have enough insurance to pay for the damage** (BI or PD) they have inflicted on our Insured / Policyowner.

In the above case, our Policyowner / Insured can collect from their own policy's (Coverage C) ***UNDER*** *INSURED MOTORIST COVERAGE*. The amount collectable is the **DIFFERENCE** between the Policyowner's (Coverage C) limits, and "The Other Guy's" liability limits.

D. COVERAGE D = DAMAGE TO YOUR CAR / PHYSICAL DAMAGE

1. ***Coverage for Damage to Your Auto***: Covers damage to the Insured's car. The policy will pay to repair the Policyowner's car **even if the Insured is at fault**. This is the "Property" insurance part of the policy; covers your **STUFF.**

2. Two coverages are available:

   a. ***Collision*** is defined as crashing your car into virtually **anything other than a bird or animal**. Examples would include running into another vehicle, a house, tree, mailbox, bridge abutment, telephone pole, etc. Also includes rolling the car over (**UPSET / ROLLOVERS)**, or having your car hit by another car, even if your car is parked.

   b. ***Other than Collision* (OTC), or *Comprehensive*** *Collision* is a named peril coverage, while *Other than Collision* is Open Perils / All Risk coverage (obviously, excluding *Colllision*). Perils included are: Falling Objects, Fire, Flood, Windstorm, Hail, Glass Breakage, etc.

   OTC (Other Than Collision / Comprehensive) importantly, includes **hitting a bird or animal** with your car (because OTC usually has a lower deductible). **Bambi is OTC!**

E. A FEW MORE AUTO THINGS TO CONSIDER

1. **UMBI/UMPD:** If another car strikes your car, and the at-fault driver drives away (**Hit & Run**), your bodily injuries will be covered by your UMBI. However, your UMPD will **NOT** pay to fix your car.

   Said again, Insurance companies will **NOT pay UMPD** when a hit-and-run accident occurs.

   However, your *Collision* coverage **will pay** to fix your car **if** you have Collision coverage.

2. **WHO IS AN INSURED DRIVER: Anyone** to whom you **give permission** to drive your car, is considered an "*Insured Driver*". One noteworthy exception is a **garage mechanic**. Their coverage is Better Provided Elsewhere (by a Garage Keepers Liability policy).

3. **WHEN ARE YOU COVERED:** Your Personal Auto Policy covers you while driving your car (even if you are driving it on business). It will also cover you driving **any car** (with permission) that is **not** provided for your regular and frequent use, including a **RENTAL car**.

4. **PRIMARY COVERAGE GOES WITH THE CAR:** If you are driving Mary's car (with her permission), and you are at fault for causing an auto accident, Mary's Coverage A Liability will pay first **(Primary)**. If more coverage is required to pay the damages you caused, then YOUR auto policy will pay **(Secondary)** up to its policy limits. In other words, you can "stack" Coverage A *Liability* limits.

V. COMMERICAL PACKAGE POLICY (CPP)

There are Seven Modules / Coverages that are available in the Commercial Package Policy.

You should recommend the modules that are appropriate for the Insured's business.

1. Property
2. Casualty / Liability (CGL)
3. Crime
4. Auto
5. Mechanical Breakdown (Boiler & Machinery)
6. Inland Marine
7. Farm

A. COMMERCIAL PROPERTY: COVERS YOUR BUSINESS *STUFF*

1. **What Property do you want covered?**

   a. Your Building(s)

   b. Your Business Personal Property

   c. Personal Property of Others in your Care, Custody and Control (CCC)

   d. Indirect Losses / Loss of Use of your building(s)

      i. Business Income

      ii. Extra Expense

2. **From What? = Peril Power**

   a. **Basic** 11 Perils : WR ELF VVV SSS

   b. **Broad** 14 Perils : Basic + WWF + Collapse

   c. **Special** All Perils, ***except*** **Earthquake**

3. **Not Covered / Exclusions** (not a complete list)

   a. Cash (better covered elsewhere in the Crime module)

   b. Animals (unless they are your business / inventory)

   c. Building foundations

   d. Land

   e. Underground pipes, flues and drains

   f. Mechanical breakdown

   g. Lost Information

   h. Cars, trucks, boats and airplanes (Better Covered Elsewhere)

   i. Growing crops

4. **ADDITIONAL (AUTOMATIC) COVERAGES**

   a. Fire Department Service Charge ($1000)

   b. Preservation of Property (30 days at a new location)

   c. Pollutant Clean-up and Removal ($10,000 over policy limits)

   d. Debris Removal (limits plus $10,000)

B. COMMERCIAL GENERAL LIABILITY (CGL): THE BAD THINGS YOU DO TO "THE OTHER GUY"

1. Covers **BI** and **PD** losses **caused by the Insured's negligence** to "The Other Guy". Also known as Casualty, or the CGL (Commercial General Liability policy).

2. **Not Covered / Exclusions**

   a. Property in your Care, Custody or Control (CCC).

   b. Your Property

   c. Automobile, boat and aircraft losses

   d. Injuries sustained by employees (better covered by Workers Compensation)

   e. Government recalls

3. **Seven Liability Exposures Covered by the CGL**

   a. **Premises Liability**: Hurt that happens on your business premises.

   b. **Operations Liability**: Hurt that happens while you are performing work away from your business premises.

   c. **Products Liability**: Hurt caused by a product you manufactured, sold or distributed.

   d. **Completed Operations Liability**: Hurt that happens as a result of work you've completed at a job site, or items you left behind.

   e. **Fire Legal Liability**: Fire damage you cause to real property that you have leased or rented and is in your care, custody and control (CCC).

   f. **Personal Injury**: Hurt feelings. Damage to an individual's reputation. Includes humiliation, malicious prosecution, defamation, wrongful entry and eviction.

   g. **Advertising Injury**: Damaging the reputation of a business, or stealing their trademark, slogan, logo, etc.

C. COMMERCIAL CRIME: SOMEONE STEALS YOUR STUFF

Covers losses due to employee theft, or theft by others. Specific Crime forms designed to cover specific crimes are available. For instance, Form A covers Employee Theft, Form B covers Forgery or Altercation, while Form C is "All Risk" coverage for Cash.

D. COMMERCIAL AUTOMOBILE: YOUR BUSINESS HITS THE ROAD

There are three coverages available:

1. **Business Auto**: Provides coverage for businesses that own, lease, hire, or borrow cars, trucks, trailers, semi-trailers, or commercial vehicles, or ask their employees to drive their own cars on company business. Coverages offered are very similar to Personal Auto.

2. **Garage Liability**: Provides liability coverage for dealerships / companies in the automobile business. Includes Premises Liability and Automobile Liability, but does **NOT** provide coverage for damage to customer's cars.

3. **Garagekeepers Liability**: Provides coverage for **damage to customer's cars**. Primarily for auto dealerships that have customer cars in for service and repair.

E. MECHANICAL BREAKDOWN (BOILER AND MACHINERY): IF IT BLOWS UP OR BREAKS DOWN

Covers objects against accidents, such as a boiler explosion. Also covers machinery against sudden and accidental mechanical breakdown. The coverage also includes coverage for destruction of the Policyowner's buildings due to a boiler explosion, or mechanical breakdown.

F. INLAND MARINE: YOUR STUFF IN MOTION: YOUR STUFF IN MOTION : YOUR STUFF IN MOTION: YOUR STUFF IN MOTION

Covers your property on the move. Example: our friend, the bulldozer on a job site (floater policies).

G. FARM: GROW YOUR OWN

Covers farm Property, including farmhouses and contents, farm buildings, farm equipment, agricultural equipment and livestock, plus farm Liability. Growing crops are NOT covered (Better Covered Elsewhere by Crop insurance).

VI. BOP 'TIL YOU DROP THE BUSINESSOWNERS POLICY (BOP)

A. WHAT IS A BOP?

A BOP is a **prepackaged** Property and Casualty policy designed for small to medium **low risk** businesses. The BOP is the business equivalent of the Homeowners policy... a prepackaged mini version of the Commercial Package Policy which contains both the Property coverages and the Liability coverages that the typical small business needs.

B. WHAT DOES A BOP CONTAIN?

A BOP contains both property and liability coverage. Please remember that all of the characteristics you learned about the Commercial Package Policy (CPP) still apply to the BOP. This includes items like ***Additional Coverages,*** which are **automatic**, such as:

1. Debris Removal
2. Collapse
3. Water Damage
4. Pollution Clean Up
5. Forgery and Alteration
6. Business Income (12 months)
7. Extra Expense

C. BOP RULES

1. **CONTENTS If the Policyowner owns the Business, then the Personal Property (Contents) MUST be insured.**

2. ***SPECIAL* ONLY There is only ONE level of Peril Power in the BOP, which is Special or "All Risk". So both the building and the contents are covered with the same level of peril power, which is the maximum. This eliminated another key decision for the Policyowner.**

3. PACKAGE ONLY BOPs must be sold as a **package**, which means that they must include both Property and Casualty coverages. In other words, BOPs cannot be sold as a monocline policy, and coverages cannot be eliminated.

4. **AS IS, ONLY BOPs are far less flexible that the Commercial Package Policy / CPP, but they are far less complicated to explain because most of the decisions have already been made by the insurance company.**

5. **SMALL, LOW RISK BUS BOPs are great for "Mom & Pops".**

6. **NO CO BOPs do NOT have Coinsurance requirements.**

7. **SAVE $$$ BOPs should save the Policyowner premium / money.**

D. BOP LIABILITY COVERAGES

1. **The Liability Limit options of the BOP are FIXED, as opposed the flexible like they are under the Commercial General Liability (CGL) policy. For example, the BOP Policyowner could select limits, of say $1 million, or $2 million, but not $1.5 million, or $200 million.**

2. **The General Aggregate Limit (maximum that could be paid out in any one policy period) is fixed at two times (2X) the occurrence limit. For example, if the Policyowner selects the $2 million occurrence limit, the General Aggregate Limit will automatically be set at $4 million.**

3. The Liability coverage is written on an **occurrence basis**. There is no Claims Made BOP.

4. BOPs do NOT cover Workers' Compensation.

5. The BOP Liability coverages are just about the same as the CGL.

    a. Premises and Operations

    b. Products and Completed Operations

    c. Advertising and Personal Injury

    d. Fire Legal

    e. Products

SO BOP UNTIL YOU DROP!

VII. WORKER'S COMPENSATION (WC): COVERS YOUR INJURY / SICKNESS OCCURRING ON THE JOB

(Very Important Subject on Thompson Prometric Exams)

A. DEFINITION

Workers Compensation (WC) insurance is insurance purchased by the Employer at their expense to pay for the medical expenses, lost wages, rehabilitation expenses, and / or death benefits for their Employees who suffer a work-related injury or illness. Workers Compensation is regulated on the state level, so benefits and requirements vary from state to state.

B. HERE'S AN EXCLUSIVE REMEDY FOR WHAT AILS YOU

Workers Comp is called an **Exclusive Remedy**, because for the most part, employees **cannot sue** their employer if the employees are injured or become ill as a result of their employment. They must seek compensation from Workers Comp, and, for the most part, **cannot sue** their employers for damages.

C. WHAT'S COVERED?

Occupationally related **injuries or illnesses** (both work related accidents and sicknesses).

D. WHAT'S EXCLUDED?

Very little. Typically the kinds of work related injuries or illnesses that would **not** be covered by WC are those caused by the blatant disregard of safety regulations by the injured employee, or if the employee commits an illegal act, or they intentionally injure themselves.

E. <u>WHO NEEDS TO BE COVERED?</u>

1. Most employees, in most jobs in most states.

2. There are a **few exceptions,** such as:

    a. Farm Laborers

    b. Household / Domestic Employees (Nanny, Cook, etc.)

    c. Casual Workers (Babysitter, Grass Cutter)

    d. Railroad Employees (Better Covered Elsewhere)

    e. Sworn Police and Firefighters (Better Covered Elsewhere)

3. Sole proprietors and actively involved partners do not have to be covered by Workers Comp, but they **can elect** to be covered if they so choose.

F. <u>WHAT KIND OF BENEFITS DOES WORKERS COMP OFFER?</u>

1. Death Benefits

2. Medical Expense Benefits (usually **Unlimited**)

3. Disability Income Benefits

4. Rehabilitation Benefits

While WC benefits vary from state to state, as a general rule, the Disability Income benefits replace a portion of the injured Employee's lost income, and the Medical Expense benefits are unlimited.

G. KNOW YOUR DISABILITY

1. **PERMANENTLY AND TOTALLY DISBALED**

   Can't work at all, and **never** will be able to again.

2. **TEMPORARILY TOTALLY DISABLED**

   Can't work at all now, but will one day be able to return to work full time.

3. **PERMANENTLY PARTIALLY DISABLED**

   Can work part time now, but will **never** be able to return to work full time.

4. **TEMPORARILY PARTIALLY DISABLED**

   Can work part time now, and someday will be able to return to work full time.

H. OTHER STATES COVERAGE

If workers are injured while working in a state other than the one in which the policy was sold, the state must be listed on the Declaration Sheet of the Workers Compensation policy for the second state's Workers Comp laws to apply and the workers to be insured. In other words, the Employer must list every state in which they do work in order to have WC coverage in those states.

I. THE SECOND INJURY FUND

The purpose of the Second Injury Fund is to provide incentive for employers to hire the handicapped.

VIII. HERE ARE SOME ODDS AND ENDS. WHY CALL THEM THAT? BECAUSE THEY ARE ODD, AND THEY'RE AT THE END

Note: The following definitions all deal with Commercial Insurance or specialized coverages, and are of more importance to students who are testing in states where **Thompson Prometric** is the testing authority.

A. DEFINITIONS

1. **Hangarkeeper's Insurance:** Covers damage to customer's airplanes. An airport management company that keeps airplanes for customers would need this coverage. Very similar to a Garagekeepers Liability policy in the auto business.

2. **Hull Coverage:** In Ocean Marine this is coverage for damage to a ship or boat. In Aviation, this is coverage for physical damage to the airplane. If you own or lease a boat or plane, you would need this coverage.

3. **Trucker's Coverage:** A Trucking company needs this coverage to cover damage done to goods being shipped that are in their care, custody or control for which they are liable.

4. **Shipper's Coverage:** Companies that ship their goods in **other people's trucks** need this coverage in case the goods are damaged during shipment.

5. **Owner's Coverage:** Companies that ship their own goods on **their own trucks** need this coverage.

6. **Bill of Lading:** Establishes the limit to which trucking companies are liable for the goods they are hauling.

7. **Jones Act:** Federal Workers Compensation Insurance for Seamen.

8. **Federal Employer Liability Act:** Federal Workers Compensation Insurance for Railroad Workers.

9. **Strict Liability:** A legal principle under which an entity can be found to be legally liable without being negligent.

Section 2

DRILLING DEEPER

CHAPTER 1

Match Selection

1. A chance of loss ___________
2. A direct loss ___________
3. Transfer of risk ___________
4. Casualty ___________
5. Property ___________
6. Financial stake ___________
7. Make whole ___________
8. War, floods, and earthquakes ___________
9. A natural defect ___________
10. Paying a fair share ___________
11. Written modifications ___________
12. Could expand your benefits ___________
13. Happens at a known place and a known time ___________
14. The person with the rights and duties ___________
15. Losses not covered ___________

A. First Named Insured
B. Insurance
C. Accident
D. Pro Rata
E. Short Rate
F. Insurable Interest
G. Two Party Contract
H. Exclusions
I. Exemptions
J. Indirect Loss
K. Destruction of Insured Property
L. Liberalization Clause
M. Third Party Contract
N. Endorsements
O. Inherent Vice
P. Indemnify
Q. Risk
R. Catastrophic Losses

CHAPTER 2

Fill In The Blank

1. Mutual Companies are operated for the benefit of______________.

2. A group that self-insures is known as a ________________.

3. A company formed in Puerto Rico would be a _________________.

4. Insurance companies must adhere to what they have written which means insurance contracts are ___________________.

5. The Doctrine which states that both parties to a contract must want it work is known as ___________________.

6. Consideration is best defined as _________________.

7. A statement that must be true is a__________________.

8. A statement that is believed to be true is a ________________.

9. A lie is considered a _________________________.

10. Hiding a portion of the truth is called __________________.

11. A ___________means relinquishing a legal right.

12. Immediate temporary protection is provided by a ____________.

13. A __________contract is one in which only one party makes legally enforceable promises.

14. ___________authority is authority specifically granted.

15. A company operated for the benefit of shareholders is a _______________.

16. _____________is the process of selecting and classifying risks.

17. In the contract process an _____________typically follows an offer.

18. The authority that customers presume you have is called _____________.

CHAPTER 3

Match selection

1. Where promises are found _______
2. Cause of loss _______
3. Increases the likelihood of a peril _______
4. Peril form in which everything is covered if not excluded _______
5. Replacement cost minus depreciation_______
6. New for old _______
7. Same as repair cost _______
8. Value decided before a loss _______
9. Value decided at the time of the loss _______
10. Value based on what someone is willing to pay _______
11. A way to control overutilization of the policy _______
12. No people and no stuff _______
13. Bailee _______
14. Transferring right of recovery _______
15. Timeframe for notifying the company of a loss _______
16. The peril under which tornado damage would be covered _______
17. Excluded under basic peril of fire _______
18. The peril under which lava damage would be covered _______
19. Collapse is covered with this named peril form _______
20. Taking property from a business that is closed and locked ______

A. 30 days
B. Hazard
C. Peril
D. Broad Perils
E. Someone with control of valuable property
F. Robbery
G. Burglary
H. Promptly
I. Subrogation
J. Unoccupied
K. Deductible
L. Vacant
M. Open Perils
N. Functional Replacement Cost
O. Fair Market Value
P. Actual Cash Value
Q. Stated Value
R. Agreed Value
S. Insuring clause
T. Wind and Hail
U. Volcanic Action
V. Hostile Fire Damage
W. Friendly Fire Damage
X. Replacement Cost

CHAPTER 4

Fill in the blank

1. A Liability policy is designed to pay to a ___________.
2. In order for a Liability policy to pay, an insured must be _____________to pay.
3. ____________and____________are the two ways an insured can be legally obligated.
4. The failure to do or not do what a reasonable person would do or not do defines _________________.
5. _________is the obligation of the insured to use a reasonable standard of care.
6. If failing to use a reasonable standard of care results in injury or damage, the insured has ______________their duty.
7. _______________ is a direct and foreseeable link between the insured's actions and the resulting injury.
8. _______________ are damages meant to punish the wrongdoer.
9. _______________ are damages meant to restore the injured party to their pre-injury status.
10. A legal defense to negligence that could result in a reduced award to the injured party is called _____________.
11. In ________________claims, an insured who owns a wild animal can be found legally liable even though they were not negligent.
12. In _________________claims, an employer can be found liable for the actions of their employees.
13. Medical bills could be paid from Med Pay without regard to ___________.
14. Defense costs are paid in addition to _____________.
15. An ______________ policy provides excess liability coverage.
16. ___________________is a legal defense to negligence in which the injured party knowingly engaged in a dangerous activity.

CHAPTER 5

Choose either COVERED (C) or EXCLUDED (E) for the following HOMEOWNER'S QUESTIONS:

1.	Med Pay for a live-in domestic worker	**C or E**
2.	Med Pay for your child living in your home	**C or E**
3.	Property loss sustained by your child in college	**C or E**
4.	Liability claim arising from the actions of your 15 year old foster child	**C or E**
5.	Collapse under an HO-1	**C or E**
6.	Falling object loss under an HO-1	**C or E**
7.	Theft under an HO-2	**C or E**
8.	Water damage caused by flooding	**C or E**
9.	Water damage caused by a firefighter	**C or E**
10.	Vandalism damage to your home after it has been vacant for 90 days	**C or E**
11.	Fire damage to a fur coat	**C or E**
12.	Theft of your camera while on vacation	**C or E**
13.	Fire loss to your car parked in your garage	**C or E**
14.	Fire damage caused by you to a rented cabin	**C or E**
15.	Earthquake damage under an unendorsed HO-5	**C or E**
16.	Building loss under an HO-4	**C or E**
17.	Power failure off premises	**C or E**
18.	Liability claim arising from the use of your speed boat	**C or E**
19.	Professional Liability	**C or E**
20.	Fire Legal Liability Claims	**C or E**

Match the selection

21. The maximum amount payable for the loss of a tree _______
22. How losses to Personal Property are valued _______
23. The limits for Coverage C: Personal Property with an HO-2 _______
24. The limits for Coverage C: Personal Property with an HO-2 with a Mobile Home Endorsement _______
25. How dwelling losses are valued _______
26. A built-in appliance would be considered _______
27. The peril coverage for a dwelling with a DP-3 _______
28. The peril coverage for Personal Property with an HO-3 _______
29. The limits of an HO-8 are based upon this _______
30. The maximum payable for the theft of a fur coat _______
31. All earthquakes and aftershocks are treated as a single occurrence if they occur within this time frame _______
32. The Loss to a Pair or Set clause formula is Value of the minus the value of the _______

A. Loss
B. Personal Property
C. Actual Cash Value
D. Remainder
E. Broad
F. Special
G. Fair Market Value
H. 72 Hours
I. 168 Hours
J. $2000
K. $1500
L. 50%
M. 40%
N. $500
O. $250
P. 10%
Q. Replacement Cost
R. Dwelling

CHAPTER 6

Pick from these choices

FROM YOUR PERSONAL AUTO POLICY WHICH WOULD PROVIDE COVERAGE:

A: LIABILITY
B: MED PAY
C: COLLISION
D: OTHER THAN COLLISON

1. You hit a deer and damage your car ____________
2. You hit a deer and you are hurt ____________
3. You hit a car and damage your car ____________
4. You hit a car and damage the other car ____________
5. A tree falls on your car and damages your car ____________
6. A friend is hurt while riding in your car ____________
7. You hit your next-door neighbor with your car ____________
8. Your car is unoccupied, when it rolls down a hill and hits a tree ____________
9. You run off the road and your car turns over ____________
10. Someone steals your car and then wrecks it ____________
11. A Third Party contract ____________
12. A named peril coverage ____________
13. An open peril coverage ____________
14. Pays without regard to fault ____________
15. Could pay for loss of earnings ____________

Fill in the blank

16. Primary coverage goes with the _________.

17. Vehicles with less than four wheels are_______.

18. Additional vehicles are covered for _________days.

19. Med Pay pays for ________medical bills.

20. A driver with no insurance who causes an accident is an ____________.

21. A driver with legal liability limits who causes an accident could be an _____________.

22. The maximum BI coverage for one person under a 25/50/10 policy would be __________.

23. Physical Damage losses are settled on an _________basis.

24. A person who is driving your car with your permission is _____________.

25. Med Pay can pay medical bills that were incurred within ________.

26. UMPD fixes the __________car.

CHAPTER 7

Fill in the blank

1. National Flood Insurance Program is underwritten by the _____________.

2. Under the NFIP losses due to sewer backup are _____________.

3. Flood deductibles can be applied to both the ___________and the___________.

4. Flood insurance typically goes into effect _______days after application.

5. A Homeowners policy covers property losses to a watercraft up to ____________.

6. In a Boatowners policy, personal property in a boat is _____________.

7. If a boat owner warrants the boat will only be used in certain inland waterways their premium will be

   _____________.

8. Items being shipped via air would best be covered by _________Marine.

9. Items being shipped by boat would best be covered by

   _________Marine.

CHAPTERS 8 & 9

Select either Building Coverage (B) or Personal Property (PP) Coverage:

1. A business leasing space would not be eligible for: **B or PP**

2. Permanently installed fixtures: **B or PP**

3. Furniture and fixtures: **B or PP**

4. Completed additions: **B or PP**

5. Use interest in improvements made to a non-owned building: **B or PP**

Match the selection on the following page with the correct statement listed below:

6. The standard Commercial Property deductible __________

7. A means to motivate businesses to insure to value __________

8. Two policies covering the same risk with different perils __________

9. The attempt to benefit from a lie __________

10. Property losses to animals __________

11. Bulldozers, forklifts, etc. __________

12. Typical Fire Department service charge __________

13. Property removed from a building damaged by covered perils will be covered for __________

14. Your golf clubs, jogging shoes, etc. __________

15. Coverage for newly acquired property can be provided if the insured is __________

16. Most the company will pay for a tree __________

17. Most the company will pay for a sign __________

18. Losses with an unendorsed Commercial Property Policy are settled on this basis __________

19. There will be no coverage for vandalism if a commercial building has been vacant for more than __________

20. Business Income insurance pays during the __________

21. A 30 day start-up feature of Business Income coverage is called __________

22. Damage by falling objects would be covered under __________

23. Mechanical breakdowns are __________

24. Earthquake coverage covers damage caused by earthquakes and __________

25. The entire Commercial Property claims process should be completed in __________

SELECTIONS

A. $1000

B. Actual Cash Value

C. Basic Perils

D. Broad Perils

E. Period of Restoration

F. Fraud

G. Mobile Equipment

H. 60 Days

I. 90 Days

J. Non-concurrency

K. 30 Days

L. $250

M. $500

N. Volcanic Eruption

O. Volcanic Action

P. Excluded

Q. Personal Effects

R. Business Personal Property

S. Coinsurance

T. 80% insured to value

U. Extended Business Income

CHAPTER 10

Select the correct type of Commercial Liability for the following examples:

1. Someone gets hurt at your business: Premises or Operations
2. You damage property while doing work at someone's home: Premises or Operations
3. Someone cuts off a finger with a saw in your hardware store: Premises or Products
4. A customer buys a saw and cuts off their finger at home: Operations or Products
5. Someone buys a burger at your restaurant and gets sick: Premises or Products
6. Work you've done injures someone: Operations or Completed Operations
7. A hired painter hurts a customer in your office Independent Contractors or Contractual
8. You accidentally burn up your leased office Premises or Fire Legal
9. You injure a person's reputation Personal or Advertising Injury
10. You damage the reputation of a business Personal or Advertising Injury

Fill in the blank

11. A bar would have no coverage for ___________under the CGL

12. A radio station would have no coverage for _____________under the CGL

13. An employee hurt at work would not be covered by a CGL but by _____________

14. Injury caused by a forklift would be covered because a forklift is considered _______________

15. Property in your care, custody, or control is __________under the CGL

16. A CGL under which the company insuring the risk the year a hurt happens will settle or defend the claim is called an___________policy

17. A CGL under which the company insuring the risk the year a claim occurs will settle or defend the claim is called a___________policy

18. A Claims Made policy limits the company's exposure to losses occurring before a certain time by using a _____________

19. Worker's Comp is referred to as the ___________remedy for employees who are hurt at work

20. _____________of claims has more of an impact on premiums than the severity of claims

21. The_______________fund encourages employers to hire handicapped employees

22. The ________________is a Federal Worker's Comp program for seamen

23. _______________insurance is a professional liability policy for insurance producers

24. Med Pay will only pay medical bills for ____________or ____________claims.

25. A business which owns a building would not need ___________liability in their CGL

CHAPTER 11

Match selections

1. The employee in a Fidelity Bond _______
2. The employer in a Fidelity Bond _______
3. The discovery period in a Commercial Blanket Fidelity Bond _______
4. Taking property from a person _______
5. Taking a person hostage and demanding payment _______
6. A person authorized to have control of property at the work place _______
7. A person authorized to have control of property away from the work place _______
8. Covered by Insuring Agreement 1 _______
9. Covered by Insuring Agreement 3 _______
10. Covered by Insuring Agreement 5 _______

A. 12 Months

B. 18 Months

C. Robbery

D. Extortion

E. Burglary

F. Money at the premises

G. Money outside the premises

H. Employee theft

I. Principal

J. Obligee

K. Custodian

L. Messenger

CHAPTER 12

Fill in the blank

1. A Boiler and Machinery/Equipment Breakdown Policy covers Objects against ______________________________.

2. Boiler and Machinery fills holes found in ______________.

3. The policy covers direct damage, indirect losses can be covered by ____________________________.

4. Boiler and Machinery values losses on a ___________________________.

5. The company may ____________________coverage with written notice.

6. A policy that has been suspended can only be reinstated by _____________________________.

CHAPTER 13

Match the selection

1. Cars in a fleet _______
2. Owned, leased, hired, or borrowed cars and trucks _______
3. Coverage territory _______
4. Protects employers _______
5. Coverage for business transporting property or people _______
6. Third Party contract for those in the automobile business _______
7. Covers damage to customer's cars _______
8. Truckers, carriers, and owners would buy this _______
9. Covers damage to a ship _______
10. Crop policies are written to cover _______
11. Covers damage to customer's airplanes _______

A. Eligible Vehicles

B. Motor Truck Cargo Form

C. Reduced Yield

D. Motor Carrier Coverage

E. Garage Liability

F. Garage-keepers

G. Hangar-keepers

H. Hull Damage

I. U.S. and Canada only

J. U.S., Canada, and Puerto Rico

K. 10

L. 5

M. Non-Ownership Liability

CHAPTER 14

CIRCLE THE BUSINESSES THAT WOULD BE ELIGIBLE FOR A BOP

1. Bar
2. Bank
3. Store with 20,000 square feet of space
4. Convenience store with no gas pumps
5. Car dealership
6. Four story office building
7. Fast Food restaurant with seating for 30
8. Factory
9. Automobile repair business
10. Laundry

CIRCLE THE TRUE STATEMENTS

11. A BOP Contains both Property and Casualty coverages
12. The Insured can cover his building or his contents, but not both
13. Losses are always valued on an ACV basis
14. A BOP has no Co-insurance requirement
15. Loss of Income is a built-in coverage in the BOP
16. BOP Liability coverage is Occurrence based
17. A Protective Safeguard endorsement increases premium

DRILL ANSWERS

Chapter 1

1. Q
2. K
3. B
4. M
5. G
6. F
7. P
8. R
9. O
10. D
11. N
12. L
13. C
14. A
15. H

Chapter 2

1. Policyowners
2. Risk Retention Group
3. Foreign
4. Contracts of Adhesion
5. Doctrine of Utmost Good Faith
6. Something of Value
7. Warranty
8. Representation
9. Misrepresentation
10. Concealment
11. Waiver
12. Binder
13. Unilateral
14. Express
15. Stock
16. Underwriting
17. Acceptance
18. Apparent Authority

Chapter 3

1. S
2. C
3. B
4. M
5. P
6. X
7. N
8. R
9. Q
10. O
11. K
12. L
13. E
14. I
15. H
16. T
17. W
18. U
19. D
20. G

Chapter 4

1. Third Party
2. Legally Obligated
3. Judgment and Settlement
4. Negligence
5. Duty
6. Breeched
7. Proximate Cause
8. Punitive
9. Compensatory
10. Comparative
11. Strict
12. Vicarious
13. Fault
14. Policy Limits
15. Umbrella
16. Assumption of Risk

Chapter 5

1. Covered
2. Excluded
3. Covered
4. Covered
5. Excluded
6. Excluded
7. Covered
8. Excluded
9. Covered
10. Excluded
11. Covered
12. Covered
13. Excluded
14. Covered
15. Excluded
16. Excluded
17. Excluded
18. Excluded
19. Excluded
20. Covered
21. N
22. C
23. L
24. M
25. Q
26. R
27. F
28. E
29. G
30. K
31. H
32. D

Chapter 6

1. D
2. B
3. C
4. A
5. D
6. B
7. A
8. C
9. C
10. D
11. A
12. C
13. D
14. B
15. A
16. The Car
17. Excluded
18. Fourteen
19. Your
20. Uninsured Motorist
21. Underinsured Motorist
22. $25,000
23. Actual Cash Value
24. Covered by your Policy
25. Three Years
26. Insured's

Chapter 7

1. The Federal Government
2. Excluded
3. Building , contents
4. 30
5. $1500
6. Excluded
7. Reduced
8. Inland
9. Ocean

Chapters 8 and 9

1 Building
2. Building
3. Business Personal Property
4. Building
5. Business Personal Property
6. M
7. S
8. J
9. F
10. P
11. G
12. A
13. K
14. Q
15. T
16. L
17. A
18. B
19. H
20. E
21. U
22. D
23. P
24. N
25. I

Chapter 10

1. Premises
2. Operations
3. Premises
4. Products
5. Products
6. Competed Operations
7. Independent Contractors
8. Fire Legal
9. Personal Injury
10. Advertising Injury
11. Liquor Liability
12. Personal and Advertising Injury
13. Worker's Comp
14. Mobile Equipment
15. Excluded
16. Occurrence Based
17. Claims Made
18. Retroactive date
19. Exclusive
20. Frequency
21. Second Injury
22. Jones Act
23. E & O
24. Premises or Operations
25. Fire Legal

Chapter 11

1. I
2. J
3. A
4. C
5. D
6. K
7. L
8. H
9. F
10. G

Chapter 12

1. Accidents
2. Commercial Property
3. Endorsement
4. Replacement Cost Basis
5. Suspend
6. Endorsement

Chapter 13

1. L
2. A
3. J
4. M
5. D
6. E
7. F
8. B
9. H
10. C
11. G

Chapter 14

1. Not eligible
2. Not eligible
3. Eligible
4. Eligible
5. Not eligible
6. Eligible
7. Eligible
8. Not eligible
9. Not eligible
10. Eligible
11. True
12. False (Must cover both)
13. False (Replacement cost basis)
14. True
15. True
16. True
17. False (Lowers premiums)

Section 3

SHARPENING TESTING SKILLS

GENERAL CONCEPTS QUIZ

1. Joe tells the insurance company that his car was stolen, when in reality he gave it away. This is an example of a

   (A) Concealment
   (B) Misrepresentation
   (C) Twisting
   (D) Representation

2. An insurance company from Alberta, Canada, formed for the benefit of its shareholders, and authorized to do business in this state would be a

   (A) Stock, Alien, Admitted Company
   (B) Stock, Foreign, Non - Admitted Company
   (C) Mutual, Alien, Admitted Company
   (D) Mutual, Foreign, Admitted Company

3. Hiring a cleaning person to clean the Agency office is an example of an Agent's

   (A) Express authority
   (B) Implied authority
   (C) Apparent authority
   (D) Delegated authority

4. Binders do all of the following EXCEPT:

   (A) Provide immediate coverage
   (B) Provide permanent coverage
   (C) Speed up coverage
   (D) Represent a legal contract

5. An Insured/ Policyowner has no right to modify the wording of a policy / contract because insurance contracts are

   (A) Contracts of Adhesion
   (B) Aleatory Contracts
   (C) Written entirely by the Agent
   (D) Contracts that can never be modified or changed

6. In many states, Solicitors can be licensed. Solicitors work for

(A) The customer
(B) The Agent
(C) The Insurance Company
(D) Tips

7. An Agent who, by contract, represents only one insurance company is referred to as (a) an

(A) Independent Agent
(B) Dependent Agent
(C) Captive Agent
(D) Indentured Agent

8. The section of an insurance policy which lists losses not covered is the

(A) Insuring Agreement
(B) Exempted Section
(C) Declarations Sheet
(D) Exclusions Section

9. An insurance policy / contract could be terminated for all the following reasons EXCEPT:

(A) Non-payment of premium
(B) Material misrepresentations
(C) Material concealments
(D) A request for claim payment

10. A Commercial Insurance Policy can be terminated by either

(A) The Company or the Named Insured
(B) The Agent or the Named Insured
(C) The lender or the Agent
(D) The Company or the First Named Insured

PROPERTY AND CASUALTY BASICS QUIZ

1. Coverage for a customer's clothing located in a Dry Cleaning establishment, which accidentally burns to the ground, would most likely come from the Dry Cleaner's

   (A) Commercial Crime Policy
   (B) Mechanical Breakdown/Boiler and Machinery Policy
   (C) Commercial Liability Policy
   (D) Commercial Property Policy

2. Which of the following is NOT true concerning a theft loss?

   (A) Theft of an auto would be covered as an *Other Than Collision* Loss in Personal Auto.
   (B) Theft of cash from a business could be covered under Commercial Crime.
   (C) An H0-1 has no theft coverage.
   (D) A Commercial Property Policy with Special Perils coverage contains some theft coverage.

3. All of the following are true concerning liability coverage EXCEPT:

   (A) Liability will only pay if there is a legal obligation to do so.
   (B) Unendorsed Homeowner's policies provide liability coverage.
   (C) Umbrella Liability Policies are only available to businesses.
   (D) *Proximate Cause* is a critical element in establishing negligence.

4. Depreciation is a major factor in determining

   (A) Replacement Cost
   (B) ACV
   (C) Agreed Value
   (D) Fair Market Value

5. Which of the following is true concerning property coverage for vacant buildings?

   (A) Vacant buildings have no property coverage.
   (B) A building that has been vacant for a specified period of time could have certain limitations in the perils that are covered.
   (C) Fire losses to a vacant building are excluded from coverage.
   (D) Payment for covered losses to a vacant building are 50% less than they normally would be.

6. In which of the following situations would a Liability policy NOT provide ccoverage?

(A) A homeowner's 10 year old intentionally breaks a neighbor's window.
(B) A sleepy driver runs a red light and hits another car.
(C) A business negligently runs a cord across a floor, and a customer trips and falls.
(D) A man accidentally drives his company car into a ditch and damages the car.

7. All of the following are true concerning property covered by Broad Perils EXCEPT:

(A) The property would be covered if damaged by a falling object.
(B) The property is covered for damage caused by named perils.
(C) The sudden and accidental water damage to a property from a burst pipe would be covered.
(D) Every peril is covered unless specifically excluded.

8. Defense Costs can be covered by all the following policies EXCEPT:

(A) Commercial Property
(B) Homeowners
(C) Personal Auto
(D) Mechanical Breakdown/Boiler and Machinery

9. Damages awarded in a Liability claim to punish the wrongdoer are called

(A) Compensatory Damages
(B) Retribution
(C) Punitive Damages
(D) Judicial Supplements

10. All of the following policies can contain both property and casualty coverages EXCEPT:

(A) Homeowners
(B) Personal Automobile
(C) CGL
(D) BOP

11. Property policies contain deductibles in order to

(A) Punish the property owner.
(B) Control the over utilization of the policy.
(C) Reduce liability exposure.
(D) Pay for the insurance company's claims administrative costs.

12. Liability policies are designed to

(A) Protect the Insured's property against loss.
(B) Replace the Insured's lost income after a direct loss.
(C) Protect the Insured's assets in the event of a covered claim.
(D) Defend the Insured in the event of an intentional act.

HOMEOWNERS QUIZ

1. In which of the following occurrences would the Medical Payments section of an Insured's Homeowners Policy provide coverage?

A) The Insured's wife falls down the steps at home.
B) The Insured's wife falls down the steps at a neighbor's home.
C) The Insured's neighbor falls down the steps at the Insured's home.
D) The Insured runs over a neighbor while driving the neighbor's car.

2. Homeowners Liability would provide coverage in all of the following scenarios EXCEPT:

(A) The Insured's dog bites the mail man.
(B) The Insured's five-year old son bites the mail man.
(C) The Insured hits a golf ball in his backyard. The golf ball flies over the house and hits the mail man.
(D) The Insured punches the mail man.

3. An Insured has Basic Peril coverage on his dwelling and personal property. Which of the following losses would NOT be covered under his Homeowners policy?

(A) A water pipe bursts and damages some furniture.
(B) A grill fire gets out of hand and burns some construction materials he was using to remodel his home.
(C) A tornado levels his detached garage.
(D) A gas water heater explodes and damages his basement.

4. An Insured has B**road Peril** coverage on his dwelling and personal property. Which of the following losses would be covered under his Homeowners policy?

(A) A water pipe bursts,and the leak is not detected for three weeks.
(B) A meteor falls out of the sky and crushes his company car in the driveway.
(C) A fire causes his home to collapse.
(D) A flood sweeps away his tool shed.

5. Under an unendorsed Homeowner's policy, the Insured can expect losses to personal property to be valued

(A) On a Replacement Cost basis.
(B) At Fair Market Value.
(C) On an Agreed Value basis.
(D) Based on the Actual Cash Value (ACV) of the property.

6. A camera is stolen from an Insured's hotel room while she is on vacation. Which of the following is true concerning the theft?

(A) The camera would only be covered by her Homeowner's policy if it had a Personal Property Floater attached.
(B) The camera would not be covered because it was stolen while located away from the residence premises.
(C) The camera would be covered on an ACV basis if the Insured owns an unendorsed Homeowner's policy.
(D) The camera would not be covered because theft is excluded under Homeowners policies.

7. Which of the following peril combinations describes the level of peril coverage for *Dwelling* and *Personal Property* under an HO-3?

(A) Basic - Basic
(B) Broad - Basic
(C) Broad - Broad
(D) Special - Broad

8. Joe owns a Homowners Policy. Which of the following individuals would be considered an *Insured* under Joe's policy?

(A) Joe's 12 year old son while away at summer camp.
(B) A Boarder who rents a room from Joe.
(C) Joe's 18 year old daughter who is in the military.
(D) A 22 year old foreign exchange student living in Joe's home.

9. Homeowners Liability would provide coverage for Joe if he runs over:

(A) Three swimmers with his speed boat.
(B) Three joggers with his car.
(C) A neighbor's foot with his riding lawn mower.
(D) A customer with a forklift vehicle while at work in a home improvement store.

10. An HO - 4 contains

    (A) Only dwelling coverage.
    (B) Only personal property coverage.
    (C) Only liability coverage.
    (D) Both personal property and liability coverage.

PERSONAL AUTOMOBILE QUIZ

1. Which of the following occurrences would NOT be covered under the Liability section of your Personal Auto policy?

    (A) Your 12 year old son backs your car over an elderly lady.
    (B) Your neighbor who borrows your car with your permission runs over an elderly man.
    (C) A thief who steals your car hits an elderly couple.
    (D) Your 18 year-old daughter at college runs over the school mascot.

2. Which of the following coverages in an Insured's Personal Auto policy would not benefit the Insured directly?

    (A) Liability
    (B) Med Pay
    (C) UMBI
    (D) Collision

3. You are at fault for an auto accident. If you have all of the appropriate coverages, your Personal Auto policy will

    (A) Only fix your car.
    (B) Only pay your medical bills.
    (C) Fix your car and pay your medical bills.
    (D) Provide no benefits because you are at fault.

4. The maximum a Personal Auto policy with Liability limits of 100/300/100 would pay for any one occurrence is:

    (A) $100,000
    (B) $500,000
    (C) $200,000
    (D) $400,000

5. A deductible is a normal feature of which Personal Auto coverage?

(A) Liability
(B) Med Pay
(C) Physical Damage coverage
(D) UMBI

6. You are at fault for an accident. Your pain and suffering and lost wages will

(A) Be payable to you from your Liability coverage.
(B) Be payable to you from your Med Pay.
(C) Be payable to you from your Uninsured Motorists coverage.
(D) Not be compensated by your Personal Auto Policy.

7. Which of the following would NOT be a covered loss under *Other Than Collision* auto coverage?

(A) You hit a cow.
(B) You swerve to avoid a cow, and your car turns over.
(C) Your car is swept away by a tornado (that also contains a cow, like in the movie "Twister").
(D) Your car is stolen by a man who is fleeing from a mad cow.

8. A person with 50/100/50 Personal Auto Liability limits is driving in a state where the minimum liability requirements are 25/50/10. If this person negligently causes an accident, they could:

(A) Be considered an Uninsured Motorist.
(B) Depending on the coverage and the injuries caused to the other driver, be considered an Underinsured Motorist.
(C) Be considered both an Uninsured and Underinsured Motorist.
(D) Pay for the losses suffered by the other driver with their Underinsured Motorists Coverage.

9. You cause an accident. Your *Collision* coverage will:

(A) Not pay for any losses because you are at fault.
(B) Will pay to fix the other driver's car and your car.
(C) Will only pay to fix the other driver's car.
(D) Will only pay to fix your car.

10. Your Personal Auto policy will NOT provide coverage if:

(A) You drive a neighbor's car.
(B) You drive a rental car while your car is in the shop for repair.
(C) You are driving a company car provided for your regular and frequent use.
(D) You are driving a relative's car who you later find out has no car insurance.

11. A friend is riding in your car with you when you are involved in an accident. Your friend is hurt. Your Personal Auto Policy will:

(A) Pay for your friend's lost wages even though there is no legal obligation to do so.
(B) Pay for your friend's medical bills even though there is no legal obligation to do so.
(C) Pay for your friend's pain and suffering even though there is no legal obligation to do so.
(D) Not pay any expenses incurred by your friend.

12. In Personal Auto, Med Pay will pay medical bills for what time period?

(A) One year from the date of the occurrence
(B) Three years from the date of the occurrence
(C) Five years from the date of the occurrence
(D) Indefinitely

COMMERICAL PACKAGE QUIZ

1. A theater company has sets worth thousands of dollars that they move from city to city. The most appropriate policy to cover the sets would be which of the following?

   (A) Commercial Property
   (B) Inland Marine
   (C) Commercial Liability
   (D) Commercial Umbrella

2. An auto transmission repair business operating out of an owned building needs to have which of the following coverages?

   (A) Garage Liability
   (B) Garagekeepers Liability
   (C) Commercial Property
   (D) All of the above

3. A pizza restaurant (named Dominics) has a home delivery service. The restaurant does not own any automobiles. Instead, the employees use their own cars to deliver the pizzas. Does the restaurant need to buy Business Auto?

   (A) Yes, because of Vicarious Liability.
   (B) No, not if the employees have Personal Auto policies of their own.
   (C) No, because Contractual Liability is a covered exposure under their CGL.
   (D) No. Workers Compensation is all the restaurant needs.

4. A small retail business with a need for both property and liability coverage would be eligible for

   (A) Commercial Property
   (B) Commercial Liability
   (C) A BOP
   (D) All of the above

5. A medical supply salesperson drives a company car loaded with valuable medical instruments to a city 500 miles away. The car is stolen and the medical supplies burn up in a fire. Coverage would be provided under:

(A) A CGL and Commercial Property.
(B) Commercial Auto and Inland Marine.
(C) Commercial Property and Commercial Crime.
(D) Commercial Auto and Equipment Breakdown.

6. A commercial building has a Commercial Property policy with Basic Peril coverage. All of the following losses to the building would be covered by the Commercial Property policy EXCEPT:

(A) Tornado damage.
(B) Fire damage.
(C) Damage caused by an exploding gas hot water heater.
(D) Damage caused by an exploding boiler.

7. Which of the following would NOT be an Insured under the CGL of a sole proprietor who owns a commercial office building?

(A) The sole proprietor's spouse
(B) The sole proprietor's tenants who rent the building
(C) The sole proprietor's employees
(D) The sole proprietor

8. Theft of cash from a business

(A) Is covered under their Commercial Property policy as long as an employee did not steal the cash.
(B) Is covered under their Inland Marine policy.
(C) Can never be covered.
(D) Is best covered by Commercial Crime Form C.

9. Which of the following is NOT an *Additional Coverage* provided by a Commercial Property Policy?

(A) Debris Removal
(B) Preservation of Property
(C) Coverage for Newly Constructed Property
(D) Fire Department Service Charge

10. Which of the following businesses would be eligible for a BOP?

   (A) Joe's Bar & Grill
   (B) Key Bank & Trust
   (C) Meggie's Bakery
   (D) D&B BMW automobile dealership

11. The first step in resolving a claim dispute between a Claimant and their Commercial Property Insurer is called:

   (A) Arbitration
   (B) Appeasement
   (C) Appraisal
   (D) Apparition

12. A Mechanical Breakdown/Boiler and Machinery Policy could cover all of the following EXCEPT:

   (A) A freezer
   (B) An air conditioning unit
   (C) A bulldozer
   (D) An industrial generator

WORKERS COMPENSATION QUIZ

1. Which of the following individuals would be required by law to be covered by Workers Comp?

   (A) A maid
   (B) A sole proprietor
   (C) A part time employee of a restaurant
   (D) A police officer

2. Joe is injured at Fred's home while working for ABC Roofing Company installing a new roof. Joe's injuries would best be covered by:

   (A) Fred's Homeowners Policy.
   (B) Joe's Medical Expense Policy.
   (C) ABC's Commercial General Liability Policy.
   (D) ABC's Workers Compensation Policy.

3. Motivating employers to hire handicapped individuals is one of the primary purposes of:

   (A) The Second Injury Fund
   (B) Other States Coverage
   (C) Accidental Dismemberment Health Insurance
   (D) The Disability Relief Act

4. A Workers Comp claim would NOT be covered if:

   (A) The employee was in any way responsible for their own injury.
   (B) The injury sustained by the employee happened somewhere other than on the business premises.
   (C) The employee does not notify the employer of the injury within the time frame stipulated by law.
   (D) The employee continues to work.

5. The term "Exclusive Remedy" means in general that:

   (A) Employees have no rights.
   (B) Employees cannot sue employers.
   (C) By law, employers can only compensate employees who are injured at work with benefits from a Workers Comp policy.
   (D) Employees who contract an occupational illness can only be prescribed those medicines specified in the Workers Comp policy.

GENERAL INSURANCE CONCEPTS ANSWERS

1. B
2. A
3. B
4. B
5. A
6. B
7. C
8. D
9, D
10. D

PROPERTY AND CASUALTY BASICS ANSWERS

1. D
2. C
3. C
4. B
5. B
6. D
7. D
8. A
9, C
10. C
11. B
12. C

HOMOWNERS ANSWERS

1. C
2. D
3. A
4. C
5. D
6. C
7. D
8. A
9. C
10. D
11. D
12. B

PERSONAL AUTOMOBILE ANSWERS

1. C
2. A
3. C
4. D
5. C
6. D
7. B
8. B
9. D
10. C
11. B
12. B

COMMERICAL LINES ANSWERS

1. B
2. D
3. A
4. D
5. B
6. D
7. B
8. D
9, C
10. C
11. C
12. C

WORKER'S COMP ANSWERS

1. C
2. D
3. A
4. C
5. B